The Speeches of President Barack Obama

Contents

Chapter 1

President Barack Obama's Addresses to Congress

1.1 Barack Obama's First State of the Union Address

Madame Speaker, Mr. Vice President, Members of Congress, and the First Lady of the United States:

I've come here tonight not only to address the distinguished men and women in this great chamber, but to speak frankly and directly to the men and women who sent us here.

I know that for many Americans watching right now, the state of our economy is a concern that rises above all others. And rightly so. If you haven't been personally affected by this recession, you probably know someone who has - a friend; a neighbor; a member of your family. You don't need to hear another list of statistics to know that our economy is in crisis, because you live it every day. It's the worry you wake up with and the source of sleepless nights. It's the job you thought you'd retire from but now have lost; the business you built your dreams upon that's now hanging by a thread; the college acceptance letter your child had to put back in the envelope. The impact of this recession is real, and it is everywhere.

But while our economy may be weakened and our confidence shaken; though we are living through difficult and uncertain times, tonight I want every American to know this:

We will rebuild, we will recover, and the United States of America will emerge stronger than before.

The weight of this crisis will not determine the destiny of this nation. The answers to our problems don't lie beyond our reach. They exist in our laboratories and universities; in our fields and our factories; in the imaginations of our entrepreneurs and the pride of the hardest-working people on Earth. Those qualities that have made America the greatest force of progress and prosperity in human history we still possess in ample measure. What is required now is for this country to pull together, confront boldly the challenges we face, and take responsibility for our future once more.

Now, if we're honest with ourselves, we'll admit that for too long, we have not always met these responsibilities — as a government or as a people. I say this not to lay blame or look backwards, but because it is only by understanding how we arrived at this moment that we'll be able to lift ourselves out of this predicament.

The fact is, our economy did not fall into decline overnight. Nor did all of our problems begin when the housing market collapsed or the stock market sank. We have known for decades that our survival depends on finding new sources of energy. Yet we import more oil today than ever before. The cost of health care eats up more and more of our savings each year, yet we keep delaying reform. Our children will compete for jobs in a global economy that too many of our schools do not prepare them for. And though all these challenges went unsolved, we still managed to spend more money and pile up more debt, both as individuals and through our government, than ever before.

In other words, we have lived through an era where too often, short-term gains were prized over long-term prosperity; where we failed to look beyond the next payment, the next quarter, or the next election. A surplus became an excuse to transfer wealth to the wealthy instead of an opportunity to invest in our future. Regulations were gutted for the sake of a quick profit at the expense of a healthy market. People bought homes they knew they couldn't afford from banks and lenders who pushed those bad loans anyway. And all the while, critical debates and difficult decisions were put off for some other time on some other day.

Well that day of reckoning has arrived, and the time to take charge of our future is here.

Now is the time to act boldly and wisely — to not only revive this economy, but to build a new foundation for lasting prosperity. Now is the time to jumpstart job creation, re-start lending, and invest in areas like energy, health care, and education that will grow our economy, even as we make hard choices to bring our deficit down. That is what my economic agenda is designed to do, and that's what I'd like to talk to you about tonight.

It's an agenda that begins with jobs.

As soon as I took office, I asked this Congress to send me a recovery plan by President's Day that would put people back to work and put money in their pockets. Not because I believe in bigger government — I don't. Not because I'm not mindful of the massive debt we've inherited — I am. I called for action because the failure to do so would have cost more jobs and caused more hardships. In fact, a failure to act would have worsened our long-term deficit by assuring weak economic growth for years. That's why I pushed for quick action. And tonight, I am grateful that this Congress delivered, and pleased to say that the American Recovery and Reinvestment Act is now law.

Over the next two years, this plan will save or create 3.5 million jobs.More than 90% of these jobs will be in the private sector — jobs rebuilding our roads and bridges; constructing wind turbines and solar panels; laying broadband and expanding mass transit.

Because of this plan, there are teachers who can now keep their jobs and educate our kids. Health care professionals can continue caring for our sick. There are 57 police officers who are still on the streets of Minneapolis tonight because this plan prevented the layoffs their department was about to make.

Because of this plan, 95% of the working households in America will receive a tax cut — a tax cut that you will see in your paychecks beginning on April 1st.

Because of this plan, families who are struggling to pay tuition costs will receive a $2,500 tax credit for all four years of college. And Americans who have lost their jobs in this recession will be able to receive extended unemployment benefits and continued health care coverage to help them weather this storm.

I know there are some in this chamber and watching at home who are skeptical of whether this plan will work. I understand that skepticism. Here in Washington, we've all seen how quickly good intentions can turn into broken promises and wasteful spending. And with a plan of this scale comes enormous responsibility to get it right.

That is why I have asked Vice President Biden to lead a tough, unprecedented oversight effort — because nobody messes with Joe. I have told each member of my Cabinet as well as mayors and governors across the country that they will be held accountable by me and the American people for every dollar they spend. I have appointed a proven and aggressive Inspector General to ferret out any and all cases of waste and fraud. And we have created a new website called recovery.gov so that every American can find out how and where their money is being spent.

So the recovery plan we passed is the first step in getting our economy back on track. But it is just the first step. Because even if we manage this plan flawlessly, there will be no real recovery unless we clean up the credit crisis that has severely weakened our financial system.

I want to speak plainly and candidly about this issue tonight, because every American should know that it directly affects you and your family's well-being. You should also know that the money you've deposited in banks across the country is safe; your insurance is secure; and you can rely on the continued operation of our financial system. That is not the source of concern.

The concern is that if we do not re-start lending in this country, our recovery will be choked off before it even begins.

You see, the flow of credit is the lifeblood of our economy. The ability to get a loan is how you finance the purchase of everything from a home to a car to a college education; how stores stock their shelves, farms buy equipment, and businesses make payroll.

But credit has stopped flowing the way it should. Too many bad loans from the housing crisis have made their way onto the books of too many banks. With so much debt and so little confidence, these banks are now fearful of lending out any more money to households, to businesses, or to each other. When there is no lending, families can't afford to buy homes or cars. So businesses are forced to make layoffs. Our economy suffers even more, and credit dries up even further.

That is why this administration is moving swiftly and aggressively to break this destructive cycle, restore confidence, and re-start lending.

We will do so in several ways. First, we are creating a new lending fund that represents the largest effort ever to help provide auto loans, college loans, and small business loans to the consumers and entrepreneurs who keep this economy running.

Second, we have launched a housing plan that will help responsible families facing the threat of foreclosure lower their monthly payments and re-finance their mortgages. It's a plan that won't help speculators or that neighbor down the street who bought a house he could never hope to afford, but it will help millions of Americans who are struggling with declining home values - Americans who will now be able to take advantage of the lower interest rates that this plan has already helped bring about. In fact, the average family who re-finances today can save nearly $2000 per year on their mortgage.

Third, we will act with the full force of the federal government to ensure that the major banks that Americans depend on have enough confidence and enough money to lend even in more difficult times. And when we learn that a major bank has serious problems, we will hold accountable those responsible, force the necessary adjustments, provide the support to clean up their balance sheets, and assure the continuity of a strong, viable institution that can serve our people and our economy.

I understand that on any given day, Wall Street may be more comforted by an approach that gives banks bailouts with no strings attached, and that holds nobody accountable for their reckless decisions. But such an approach won't solve the problem. And our goal is to quicken the day when we re-start lending to the American people and American business and end this crisis once and for all.

I intend to hold these banks fully accountable for the assistance they receive, and this time, they will have to clearly demonstrate how taxpayer dollars result in more lending for the American taxpayer. This time, CEOs won't be able to use taxpayer money to pad their paychecks or buy fancy drapes or disappear on a private jet. Those days are over.

Still, this plan will require significant resources from the federal government — and yes, probably more than we've already set aside. But while the cost of action will be great, I can assure you that the cost of inaction will be far greater, for it could result in an economy that sputters along for not months or years, but perhaps a decade. That would be worse for our deficit, worse for business, worse for you, and worse for the next generation. And I refuse to let that happen.

I understand that when the last administration asked this Congress to provide assistance for struggling banks, Democrats and Republicans alike were infuriated by the mismanagement and results that followed. So were the American taxpayers. So was I.

So I know how unpopular it is to be seen as helping banks right now, especially when everyone is suffering in part from their bad decisions. I promise you - I get it.

But I also know that in a time of crisis, we cannot afford to govern out of anger, or yield to the politics of the moment. My job — our job — is to solve the problem. Our job is to govern with a sense of responsibility. I will not spend a single penny for the purpose of rewarding a single Wall Street executive, but I will do whatever it takes to help the small business that can't pay its workers or the family that has saved and still can't get a mortgage.

That's what this is about. It's not about helping banks — it's about helping people. Because when credit is available again, that young family can finally buy a new home. And then some company will hire workers to build it. And then those workers will have money to spend, and if they can get a loan too, maybe they'll finally buy that car, or open their own business. Investors will return to the market, and American families will see their retirement secured once more. Slowly, but surely, confidence will return, and our economy will recover.

So I ask this Congress to join me in doing whatever proves necessary. Because we cannot consign our nation to an open-ended recession. And to ensure that a crisis of this magnitude never happens again, I ask Congress to move quickly on legislation that will finally reform our outdated regulatory system. It is time to put in place tough, new common-sense rules of the road so that our financial market rewards drive and innovation, and punishes short-cuts and abuse.

The recovery plan and the financial stability plan are the immediate steps we're taking to revive our economy in the short-term. But the only way to fully restore America's economic strength is to make the long-term investments that will lead to new jobs, new industries, and a renewed ability to compete with the rest of the world. The only way this century will be another American century is if we confront at last the price of our dependence on oil and the high cost of health care; the schools that aren't preparing our children and the mountain of debt they stand to inherit. That is our responsibility.

In the next few days, I will submit a budget to Congress. So often, we have come to view these documents as simply numbers on a page or laundry lists of programs. I see this document differently. I see it as a vision for America — as a blueprint for our future.

My budget does not attempt to solve every problem or address every issue. It reflects the stark reality of what we've inherited — a trillion dollar deficit, a financial crisis, and a costly recession.

Given these realities, everyone in this chamber - Democrats and Republicans — will have to sacrifice some worthy priorities for which there are no dollars. And that includes me.

But that does not mean we can afford to ignore our long-term challenges. I reject the view that says our problems will simply take care of themselves; that says government has no role in laying the foundation for our common prosperity.

For history tells a different story. History reminds us that at every moment of economic upheaval and transformation, this nation has responded with bold action and big ideas. In the midst of civil war, we laid railroad tracks from one coast to another that spurred commerce and industry. From the turmoil of the Industrial Revolution came a system of public high schools that prepared our citizens for a new age. In the wake of war and depression, the GI Bill sent a generation to college and created the largest middle-class in history. And a twilight struggle for freedom led to a nation of highways, an American on the moon, and an explosion of technology that still shapes our world.

In each case, government didn't supplant private enterprise; it catalyzed private enterprise. It created the conditions for thousands of entrepreneurs and new businesses to adapt and to thrive.

We are a nation that has seen promise amid peril, and claimed opportunity from ordeal. Now we must be that nation again. That is why, even as it cuts back on the programs we don't need, the budget I submit will invest in the three areas that are absolutely critical to our economic future: energy, health care, and education.

It begins with energy.

We know the country that harnesses the power of clean, renewable energy will lead the 21st century. And yet, it is China that has launched the largest effort in history to make their economy energy efficient. We invented solar technology, but we've fallen behind countries like Germany and Japan in producing it. New plug-in hybrids roll off our assembly lines, but they will run on batteries made in Korea.

Well I do not accept a future where the jobs and industries of tomorrow take root beyond our borders - and I know you don't either. It is time for America to lead again.

Thanks to our recovery plan, we will double this nation's supply of renewable energy in the next three years. We have also made the largest investment in basic research funding in American history - an investment that will spur not only new discoveries in energy, but breakthroughs in medicine, science, and technology.

We will soon lay down thousands of miles of power lines that can carry new energy to cities and towns across this country. And we will put Americans to work making our homes and buildings more efficient so that we can save billions of dollars on our energy bills.

But to truly transform our economy, protect our security, and save our planet from the ravages of climate change, we need to ultimately make clean, renewable energy the profitable kind of energy. So I ask this Congress to send me legislation that places a market-based cap on carbon pollution and drives the production of more renewable energy in America. And to support that innovation, we will invest fifteen billion dollars a year to develop technologies like wind power and solar power; advanced biofuels, clean coal, and more fuel-efficient cars and trucks built right here in America.

As for our auto industry, everyone recognizes that years of bad decision-making and a global recession have pushed our automakers to the brink. We should not, and will not, protect them from their own bad practices. But we are committed to the goal of a re-tooled, re-imagined auto industry that can compete and win. Millions of jobs depend on it. Scores of communities depend on it. And I believe the nation that invented the automobile cannot walk away from it.

None of this will come without cost, nor will it be easy. But this is America. We don't do what's easy. We do what is necessary to move this country forward.

For that same reason, we must also address the crushing cost of health care.

This is a cost that now causes a bankruptcy in America every thirty seconds. By the end of the year, it could cause 1.5 million Americans to lose their homes. In the last eight years, premiums have grown four times faster than wages. And in each of these years, one million more Americans have lost their health insurance. It is one of the major reasons why small businesses close their doors and corporations ship jobs overseas. And it's one of the largest and fastest-growing parts of our budget.

Given these facts, we can no longer afford to put health care reform on hold.

Already, we have done more to advance the cause of health care reform in the last thirty days than we have in the last decade. When it was days old, this Congress passed a law to provide and protect health insurance for eleven million American children whose parents work full-time. Our recovery plan will invest in electronic health records and new technology that will reduce errors, bring down costs, ensure privacy, and save lives. It will launch a new effort to conquer a disease that has touched the life of nearly every American by seeking a cure for cancer in our time. And it makes the largest investment ever in preventive care, because that is one of the best ways to keep our people healthy and our costs under control.

This budget builds on these reforms. It includes an historic commitment to comprehensive health care reform — a down-payment on the principle that we must have quality, affordable health care for every American. It's a commitment that's paid for in part by efficiencies in our system that are long overdue. And it's a step we must take if we hope to bring down our deficit in the years to come.

Now, there will be many different opinions and ideas about how to achieve reform, and that is why I'm bringing together businesses and workers, doctors and health care providers, Democrats and Republicans to begin work on this issue next week.

I suffer no illusions that this will be an easy process. It will be hard. But I also know that nearly a century after Teddy Roosevelt first called for reform, the cost of our health care has weighed down our economy and the conscience of our nation long enough. So let there be no doubt: health care reform cannot wait, it must not wait, and it will not wait another year.

The third challenge we must address is the urgent need to expand the promise of education in America.

In a global economy where the most valuable skill you can sell is your knowledge, a good education is no longer just a pathway to opportunity — it is a pre-requisite.

Right now, three-quarters of the fastest-growing occupations require more than a high school diploma. And yet, just over half of our citizens have that level of education. We have one of the highest high school dropout rates of any industrialized nation. And half of the students who begin college never finish.

This is a prescription for economic decline, because we know the countries that out-teach us today will out-compete us tomorrow. That is why it will be the goal of this administration to ensure that every child has access to a complete and competitive education — from the day they are born to the day they begin a career.

Already, we have made an historic investment in education through the economic recovery plan. We have dramatically expanded early childhood education and will continue to improve its quality, because we know that the most formative learning comes in those first years of life. We have made college affordable for nearly seven million more students. And we have provided the resources necessary to prevent painful cuts and teacher layoffs that would set back our children's progress.

But we know that our schools don't just need more resources. They need more reform. That is why this budget creates new incentives for teacher performance; pathways for advancement, and rewards for success. We'll invest in innovative programs that are already helping schools meet high standards and close achievement gaps. And we will expand our commitment to charter schools.

It is our responsibility as lawmakers and educators to make this system work. But it is the responsibility of every citizen to participate in it. And so tonight, I ask every American to commit to at least one year or more of higher education or career training. This can be community college or a four-year school; vocational training or an apprenticeship. But whatever the training may be, every American will need to get more than a high school diploma. And dropping out of high school is no longer an option. It's not just quitting on yourself, it's quitting on your country — and this country needs and values the talents of every American. That is why we will provide the support necessary for you to complete college and meet a new goal: by 2020, America will once again have the highest proportion of college graduates in the world.

I know that the price of tuition is higher than ever, which is why if you are willing to volunteer in your neighborhood or give back to your community or serve your country, we will make sure that you can afford a higher education. And to encourage a renewed spirit of national service for this and future generations, I ask this Congress to send me the bipartisan legislation that bears the name of Senator Orrin Hatch as well as an American who has never stopped asking what he can do for his country — Senator Edward Kennedy.

These education policies will open the doors of opportunity for our children. But it is up to us to ensure they walk through them. In the end, there is no program or policy that can substitute for a mother or father who will attend those parent/teacher conferences, or help with homework after dinner, or turn off the TV, put away the video games, and read to their child. I speak to you not just as a President, but as a father when I say that responsibility for our children's education must begin at home.

There is, of course, another responsibility we have to our children. And that is the responsibility to ensure that we do not pass on to them a debt they cannot pay. With the deficit we inherited, the cost of the crisis we face, and the long-term challenges we must meet, it has never been more important to ensure that as our economy recovers, we do what it takes to bring this deficit down.

I'm proud that we passed the recovery plan free of earmarks, and I want to pass a budget next year that ensures that each dollar we spend reflects only our most important national priorities.

Yesterday, I held a fiscal summit where I pledged to cut the deficit in half by the end of my first term in office. My administration has also begun to go line by line through the federal budget in order to eliminate wasteful and ineffective programs. As you can imagine, this is a process that will take some time. But we're starting with the biggest lines. We have already identified two trillion dollars in savings over the next decade.

In this budget, we will end education programs that don't work and end direct payments to large agribusinesses that don't need them. We'll eliminate the no-bid contracts that have wasted billions in Iraq, and reform our defense budget so that we're not paying for Cold War-era weapons systems we don't use. We will root out the waste, fraud, and abuse in our Medicare program that doesn't make our seniors any healthier, and we will restore a sense of fairness and balance to our tax code by finally ending the tax breaks for corporations that ship our jobs overseas.

In order to save our children from a future of debt, we will also end the tax breaks for the wealthiest 2% of Americans. But let me perfectly clear, because I know you'll hear the same old claims that rolling back these tax breaks means a massive tax increase on the American people: if your family earns less than $250,000 a year, you will not see your taxes increased a single dime. I repeat: not one single dime. In fact, the recovery plan provides a tax cut — that's right, a tax cut — for 95% of working families. And these checks are on the way.

To preserve our long-term fiscal health, we must also address the growing costs in Medicare and Social Security. Comprehensive health care reform is the best way to strengthen Medicare for years to come. And we must also begin a conversation on how to do the same for Social Security, while creating tax-free universal savings accounts for all Americans.

Finally, because we're also suffering from a deficit of trust, I am committed to restoring a sense of honesty and accountability to our budget. That is why this budget looks ahead ten years and accounts for spending that was left out under the old rules - and for the first time, that includes the full cost of fighting in Iraq and Afghanistan. For seven years, we have been a nation at war. No longer will we hide its price.

We are now carefully reviewing our policies in both wars, and I will soon announce a way forward in Iraq that leaves Iraq to its people and responsibly ends this war.

And with our friends and allies, we will forge a new and comprehensive strategy for Afghanistan and Pakistan to defeat al Qaeda and combat extremism. Because I will not allow terrorists to plot against the American people from safe havens half a world away.

As we meet here tonight, our men and women in uniform stand watch abroad and more are readying to deploy. To each and every one of them, and to the families who bear the quiet burden of their absence, Americans are united in sending one message: we honor your service, we are inspired by your sacrifice, and you have our unyielding support. To relieve the strain on our forces, my budget increases the number of our soldiers and Marines. And to keep our sacred trust with those who serve, we will raise their pay, and give our veterans the expanded health care and benefits that they have earned.

To overcome extremism, we must also be vigilant in upholding the values our troops defend — because there is no force in the world more powerful than the example of America. That is why I have ordered the closing of the detention center at Guantanamo Bay, and will seek swift and certain justice for captured terrorists - because living our values doesn't make us weaker, it makes us safer and it makes us stronger. And that is why I can stand here tonight and say without exception or equivocation that the United States of America does not torture.

In words and deeds, we are showing the world that a new era of engagement has begun. For we know that America cannot meet the threats of this century alone, but the world cannot meet them without America. We cannot shun the negotiating table, nor ignore the foes or forces that could do us harm. We are instead called to move forward with the sense of confidence and candor that serious times demand.

To seek progress toward a secure and lasting peace between Israel and her neighbors, we have appointed an envoy to sustain our effort. To meet the challenges of the 21st century - from terrorism to nuclear proliferation; from pandemic disease to cyber threats to crushing poverty — we will strengthen old alliances, forge new ones, and use all elements of our national power.

And to respond to an economic crisis that is global in scope, we are working with the nations of the G-20 to restore confidence in our financial system, avoid the possibility of escalating protectionism, and spur demand for American goods in markets across the globe. For the world depends on us to have a strong economy, just as our economy depends on the strength of the world's.

As we stand at this crossroads of history, the eyes of all people in all nations are once again upon us - watching to see what we do with this moment; waiting for us to lead.

Those of us gathered here tonight have been called to govern in extraordinary times. It is a tremendous burden, but also a great privilege - one that has been entrusted to few generations of Americans. For in our hands lies the ability to shape our world for good or for ill.

I know that it is easy to lose sight of this truth — to become cynical and doubtful; consumed with the petty and the trivial.

But in my life, I have also learned that hope is found in unlikely places; that inspiration often comes not from those with the most power or celebrity, but from the dreams and aspirations of Americans who are anything but ordinary.

I think about Leonard Abess, the bank president from Miami who reportedly cashed out of his company, took a $60 million bonus, and gave it out to all 399 people who worked for him, plus another 72 who used to work for him. He didn't tell anyone, but when the local newspaper found out, he simply said, *I knew some of these people since I was 7 years old. I didn't feel right getting the money myself."*

I think about Greensburg, Kansas, a town that was completely destroyed by a tornado, but is being rebuilt by its residents as a global example of how clean energy can power an entire community - how it can bring jobs and businesses to a place where piles of bricks and rubble once lay. "The tragedy was terrible," said one of the men who helped them rebuild. "But the folks here know that it also provided an incredible opportunity."

And I think about Ty'Sheoma Bethea, the young girl from that school I visited in Dillon, South Carolina — a place where the ceilings leak, the paint peels off the walls, and they have to stop teaching six times a day because the train barrels by their classroom. She has been told that her school is hopeless, but the other day after class she went to the public library and typed up a letter to the people sitting in this room. She even asked her principal for the money to buy a stamp. The letter asks us for help, and says, "We are just students trying to become lawyers, doctors, congressmen like yourself and one day president, so we can make a change to not just the state of South Carolina but also the world. We are not quitters."

We are not quitters.

These words and these stories tell us something about the spirit of the people who sent us here. They tell us that even in the most trying times, amid the most difficult circumstances, there is a generosity, a resilience, a decency, and a determination that perseveres; a willingness to take responsibility for our future and for posterity.

Their resolve must be our inspiration. Their concerns must be our cause. And we must show them and all our people that we are equal to the task before us.

I know that we haven't agreed on every issue thus far, and there are surely times in the future when we will part ways. But I also know that every American who is sitting here tonight loves this country and wants it to succeed. That must be the starting point for every debate we have in the coming months, and where we return after those debates are done. That is the foundation on which the American people expect us to build common ground.

And if we do — if we come together and lift this nation from the depths of this crisis; if we put our people back to work and restart the engine of our prosperity; if we confront without fear the challenges of our time and summon that enduring spirit of an America that does not quit, then someday years from now our children can tell their children that this was the time when we performed, in the words that are carved into this very chamber, "something worthy to be remembered."

Thank you, God Bless you, and may God Bless the United States of America.

1.2   Barack Obama speech to joint session of Congress, September 2009

President Obama delivering his speech on health care to the United States Congress

Madame Speaker, Vice President Biden, members of Congress, and the American people:

When I spoke here last winter, this nation was facing the worst economic crisis since the Great Depression. We were losing an average of 700,000 jobs per month. Credit was frozen. And our financial system was on the verge of collapse.

As any American who is still looking for work or a way to pay their bills will tell you, we are by no means out of the woods. A full and vibrant recovery is many months away. And I will not let up until those Americans who seek jobs can find them; until those businesses that seek capital and credit can thrive; until all responsible homeowners can stay in their homes. That is our ultimate goal. But thanks to the bold and decisive action we have taken since January, I can stand here with confidence and say that we have pulled this economy back from the brink.

I want to thank the members of this body for your efforts and your support in these last several months, and especially those who have taken the difficult votes that have put us on a path to recovery. I also want to thank the American people for their patience and resolve during this trying time for our nation.

But we did not come here just to clean up crises. We came to build a future. So tonight, I return to speak to all of you about an issue that is central to that future — and that is the issue of health care.

I am not the first President to take up this cause, but I am determined to be the last. It has now been nearly a century since Theodore Roosevelt first called for health care reform. And ever since, nearly every President and Congress, whether Democrat or Republican, has attempted to meet this challenge in some way. A bill for comprehensive health reform was first introduced by John Dingell Sr. in 1943. Sixty-five years later, his son continues to introduce that same bill at the beginning of each session.

Our collective failure to meet this challenge — year after year, decade after decade — has led us to a breaking point. Everyone understands the extraordinary hardships that are placed on the uninsured, who live every day just one accident or illness away from bankruptcy. These are not primarily people on welfare. These are middle-class Americans. Some can't get insurance on the job. Others are self-employed, and can't afford it, since buying insurance on your own costs you three times as much as the coverage you get from your employer. Many other Americans who are willing and able to pay are still denied insurance due to previous illnesses or conditions that insurance companies decide are too risky or expensive to cover.

We are the only advanced democracy on Earth — the only wealthy nation — that allows such hardships for millions of its people. There are now more than 30 million American citizens who cannot get coverage. In just a two-year period, one in every three Americans goes without health care coverage at some point. And every day, 14,000 Americans lose their coverage. In other words, it can happen to anyone.

But the problem that plagues the health care system is not just a problem of the uninsured. Those who do have insurance have never had less security and stability than they do today. More and more Americans worry that if you move, lose your job, or change your job, you'll lose your health insurance too. More and more Americans pay their premiums, only to discover that their insurance company has dropped their coverage when they get sick, or won't pay the full cost of care. It happens every day.

One man from Illinois lost his coverage in the middle of chemotherapy because his insurer found that he hadn't reported gallstones that he didn't even know about. They delayed his treatment, and he died because of it. Another woman from Texas was about to get a double mastectomy when her insurance company canceled her policy because she forgot to declare a case of acne. By the time she had her insurance reinstated, her breast cancer more than doubled in size. That is heartbreaking, it is wrong, and no one should be treated that way in the United States of America.

Then there's the problem of rising costs. We spend one-and-a-half times more per person on health care than any other country, but we aren't any healthier for it. This is one of the reasons that insurance premiums have gone up three times faster than wages. It's why so many employers — especially small businesses — are forcing their employees to pay more for insurance, or are dropping their coverage entirely. It's why so many aspiring entrepreneurs cannot afford to open a business in the first place, and why American businesses that compete internationally — like our automakers — are at a huge disadvantage. And it's why those of us with health insurance are also paying a hidden and growing tax for those without it — about $1,000 per year that pays for somebody else's emergency room and charitable care.

Finally, our health care system is placing an unsustainable burden on taxpayers. When health care costs grow at the rate they have, it puts greater pressure on programs like Medicare and Medicaid. If we do nothing to slow these skyrocketing costs, we will eventually be spending more on Medicare and Medicaid than every other government program combined. Put simply, our health care problem is our deficit problem. Nothing else even comes close.

These are the facts. Nobody disputes them. We know we must reform this system. The question is how.

There are those on the left who believe that the only way to fix the system is through a single-payer system like Canada's, where we would severely restrict the private insurance market and have the government provide coverage for everyone.

On the right, there are those who argue that we should end the employer-based system and leave individuals to buy health insurance on their own.

I have to say that there are arguments to be made for both approaches. But either one would represent a radical shift that would disrupt the health care most people currently have. Since health care represents one-sixth of our economy, I believe it makes more sense to build on what works and fix what doesn't, rather than try to build an entirely new system from scratch. And that is precisely what those of you in Congress have tried to do over the past several months.

During that time, we have seen Washington at its best and its worst.

We have seen many in this chamber work tirelessly for the better part of this year to offer thoughtful ideas about how to achieve reform. Of the five committees asked to develop bills, four have completed their work, and the Senate Finance Committee announced today that it will move forward next week. That has never happened before.

Our overall efforts have been supported by an unprecedented coalition of doctors and nurses; hospitals, seniors' groups and even drug companies — many of whom opposed reform in the past. And there is agreement in this chamber on about 80 percent of what needs to be done, putting us closer to the goal of reform than we have ever been.

But what we have also seen in these last months is the same partisan spectacle that only hardens the disdain many Americans have toward their own government. Instead of honest debate, we have seen scare tactics. Some have dug into unyielding ideological camps that offer no hope of compromise. Too many have used this as an opportunity to score short-term political points, even if it robs the country of our opportunity to solve a long-term challenge. And out of this blizzard of charges and countercharges, confusion has reigned.

Well the time for bickering is over. The time for games has passed. Now is the season for action. Now is when we must bring the best ideas of both parties together, and show the American people that we can still do what we were sent here to do. Now is the time to deliver on health care.

The plan I'm announcing tonight would meet three basic goals:

It will provide more security and stability to those who have health insurance. It will provide insurance to those who don't. And it will slow the growth of health care costs for our families, our businesses, and our government. It's a plan that asks everyone to take responsibility for meeting this challenge — not just government and insurance companies, but employers and individuals. And it's a plan that incorporates ideas from Senators and Congressmen; from Democrats and Republicans — and yes, from some of my opponents in both the primary and general election.

Here are the details that every American needs to know about this plan:

First, if you are among the hundreds of millions of Americans who already have health insurance through your job, Medicare, Medicaid, or the VA, nothing in this plan will require you or your employer to change the coverage or the doctor you have. Let me repeat this: nothing in our plan requires you to change what you have.

What this plan will do is to make the insurance you have work better for you. Under this plan, it will be against the law for insurance companies to deny you coverage because of a pre-existing condition. As soon as I sign this bill, it will be against the law for insurance companies to drop your coverage when you get sick or water it down when you need it most. They will no longer be able to place some arbitrary cap on the amount of coverage you can receive in a given year or a lifetime. We will place a limit on how much you can be charged for out-of-pocket expenses, because in the United States of America, no one should go broke because they get sick. And insurance companies will be required to cover, with no extra charge, routine checkups and preventive care, like mammograms and colonoscopies — because there's no reason we shouldn't be catching diseases like breast cancer and colon cancer before they get worse. That makes sense, it saves money, and it saves lives.

That's what Americans who have health insurance can expect from this plan — more security and stability.

Now, if you're one of the tens of millions of Americans who don't currently have health insurance, the second part of this plan will finally offer you quality, affordable choices. If you lose your job or change your job, you will be able to get coverage. If you strike out on your own and start a small business, you will be able to get coverage. We will do this by creating a new insurance exchange — a marketplace where individuals and small businesses will be able to shop for health insurance at competitive prices. Insurance companies will have an incentive to participate in this exchange because it lets them compete for millions of new customers. As one big group, these customers will have greater leverage to bargain with the insurance companies for better prices and quality coverage. This is how large companies and government employees get affordable insurance. It's how everyone in this Congress gets affordable insurance. And it's time to give every American the same opportunity that we've given ourselves.

For those individuals and small businesses who still cannot afford the lower-priced insurance available in the exchange, we will provide tax credits, the size of which will be based on your need. And all insurance companies that want access to this new marketplace will have to abide by the consumer protections I already mentioned. This exchange will take effect in four years, which will give us time to do it right. In the meantime, for those Americans who can't get insurance today because they have pre-existing medical conditions, we will immediately offer low-cost coverage that will protect you against financial ruin if you become seriously ill. This was a good idea when Senator John McCain proposed it in the campaign, it's a good idea now, and we should embrace it.

Now, even if we provide these affordable options, there may be those — particularly the young and healthy — who still want to take the risk and go without coverage. There may still be companies that refuse to do right by their workers. The problem is, such irresponsible behavior costs all the rest of us money. If there are affordable options and people still don't sign up for health insurance, it means we pay for those people's expensive emergency room visits. If some businesses don't provide workers health care, it forces the rest of us to pick up the tab when their workers get sick, and gives those businesses an unfair advantage over their competitors. And unless everybody does their part, many of the insurance reforms we seek — especially requiring insurance companies to cover pre-existing conditions — just can't be achieved.

That's why under my plan, individuals will be required to carry basic health insurance — just as most states require you to carry auto insurance. Likewise, businesses will be required to either offer their workers health care, or chip in to help cover the cost of their workers. There will be a hardship waiver for those individuals who still cannot afford coverage, and 95 percent of all small businesses, because of their size and narrow profit margin, would be exempt from these requirements. But we cannot have large businesses and individuals who can afford coverage game the system by avoiding responsibility to themselves or their employees. Improving our health care system only works if everybody does their part.

While there remain some significant details to be ironed out, I believe a broad consensus exists for the aspects of the plan I just outlined: consumer protections for those with insurance, an exchange that allows individuals and small businesses to purchase affordable coverage, and a requirement that people who can afford insurance get insurance.

And I have no doubt that these reforms would greatly benefit Americans from all walks of life, as well as the economy as a whole. Still, given all the misinformation that's been spread over the past few months, I realize that many Americans have grown nervous about reform. So tonight I'd like to address some of the key controversies that are still out there.

Some of people's concerns have grown out of bogus claims spread by those whose only agenda is to kill reform at any cost. The best example is the claim, made not just by radio and cable talk show hosts, but prominent politicians, that we plan to set up panels of bureaucrats with the power to kill off senior citizens. Such a charge would be laughable if it weren't so cynical and irresponsible. It is a lie, plain and simple.

There are also those who claim that our reform effort will insure illegal immigrants. This, too, is false — the reforms I'm proposing would not apply to those who are here illegally.

At this point in the speech, Representative Joe Wilson pointed at Obama and shouted, **"You lie!"**
Obama reiterated in response, "Not true."

And one more misunderstanding I want to clear up — under our plan, no federal dollars will be used to fund abortions, and federal conscience laws will remain in place.

My health care proposal has also been attacked by some who oppose reform as a "government takeover" of the entire health care system. As proof, critics point to a provision in our plan that allows the uninsured and small businesses to choose a publicly sponsored insurance option, administered by the government just like Medicaid or Medicare.

So let me set the record straight. My guiding principle is, and always has been, that consumers do better when there is choice and competition. Unfortunately, in 34 states, 75 percent of the insurance market is controlled by five or fewer companies. In Alabama, almost 90 percent is controlled by just one company. Without competition, the price of insurance goes up and the quality goes down. And it makes it easier for insurance companies to treat their customers badly — by cherry-picking the healthiest individuals and trying to drop the sickest; by overcharging small businesses who have no leverage; and by jacking up rates.

Insurance executives don't do this because they are bad people. They do it because it's profitable. As one former insurance

The interruption by Congressman Joe Wilson. (September 9, 2009).

executive testified before Congress, insurance companies are not only encouraged to find reasons to drop the seriously ill; they are rewarded for it. All of this is in service of meeting what this former executive called "Wall Street's relentless profit expectations."

Now, I have no interest in putting insurance companies out of business. They provide a legitimate service, and employ a lot of our friends and neighbors. I just want to hold them accountable. The insurance reforms that I've already mentioned would do just that. But an additional step we can take to keep insurance companies honest is by making a not-for-profit public option available in the insurance exchange. Let me be clear — it would only be an option for those who don't have insurance. No one would be forced to choose it, and it would not impact those of you who already have insurance. In fact, based on Congressional Budget Office estimates, we believe that less than 5 percent of Americans would sign up.

Despite all this, the insurance companies and their allies don't like this idea. They argue that these private companies can't fairly compete with the government. And they'd be right if taxpayers were subsidizing this public insurance option. But they won't be. I have insisted that like any private insurance company, the public insurance option would have to be self-sufficient and rely on the premiums it collects. But by avoiding some of the overhead that gets eaten up at private companies by profits, excessive administrative costs and executive salaries, it could provide a good deal for consumers. It would also keep pressure on private insurers to keep their policies affordable and treat their customers better, the same way public colleges and universities provide additional choice and competition to students without in any way inhibiting a vibrant system of private colleges and universities.

It's worth noting that a strong majority of Americans still favor a public insurance option of the sort I've proposed tonight. But its impact shouldn't be exaggerated — by the left, the right, or the media. It is only one part of my plan, and should not be used as a handy excuse for the usual Washington ideological battles. To my progressive friends, I would remind you that for decades, the driving idea behind reform has been to end insurance company abuses and make coverage affordable for those without it. The public option is only a means to that end — and we should remain open to other ideas that accomplish our ultimate goal. And to my Republican friends, I say that rather than making wild claims about a government takeover of health care, we should work together to address any legitimate concerns you may have.

For example, some have suggested that that the public option go into effect only in those markets where insurance companies are not providing affordable policies. Others propose a co-op or another nonprofit entity to administer the plan. These are all constructive ideas worth exploring. But I will not back down on the basic principle that if Americans can't find affordable coverage, we will provide you with a choice. And I will make sure that no government bureaucrat or insurance company bureaucrat gets between you and the care that you need.

Finally, let me discuss an issue that is a great concern to me, to members of this chamber, and to the public — and that is how we pay for this plan.

Here's what you need to know. First, I will not sign a plan that adds one dime to our deficits — either now or in the future. Period. And to prove that I'm serious, there will be a provision in this plan that requires us to come forward with more spending cuts if the savings we promised don't materialize. Part of the reason I faced a trillion dollar deficit when I walked in the door of the White House is because too many initiatives over the last decade were not paid for — from the Iraq War to tax breaks for the wealthy. I will not make that same mistake with health care.

Second, we've estimated that most of this plan can be paid for by finding savings within the existing health care system — a system that is currently full of waste and abuse. Right now, too much of the hard-earned savings and tax dollars we spend on health care doesn't make us healthier. That's not my judgment — it's the judgment of medical professionals across this country. And this is also true when it comes to Medicare and Medicaid.

In fact, I want to speak directly to America's seniors for a moment, because Medicare is another issue that's been subjected to demagoguery and distortion during the course of this debate.

More than four decades ago, this nation stood up for the principle that after a lifetime of hard work, our seniors should not be left to struggle with a pile of medical bills in their later years. That is how Medicare was born. And it remains a sacred trust that must be passed down from one generation to the next. That is why not a dollar of the Medicare trust fund will be used to pay for this plan.

The only thing this plan would eliminate is the hundreds of billions of dollars in waste and fraud, as well as unwarranted subsidies in Medicare that go to insurance companies — subsidies that do everything to pad their profits and nothing to improve your care. And we will also create an independent commission of doctors and medical experts charged with identifying more waste in the years ahead.

These steps will ensure that you — America's seniors — get the benefits you've been promised. They will ensure that Medicare is there for future generations. And we can use some of the savings to fill the gap in coverage that forces too many seniors to pay thousands of dollars a year out of their own pocket for prescription drugs. That's what this plan will do for you. So don't pay attention to those scary stories about how your benefits will be cut — especially since some of the same folks who are spreading these tall tales have fought against Medicare in the past, and just this year supported a budget that would have essentially turned Medicare into a privatized voucher program. That will never happen on my watch. I will protect Medicare.

Now, because Medicare is such a big part of the health care system, making the program more efficient can help usher in changes in the way we deliver health care that can reduce costs for everybody. We have long known that some places, like the Intermountain Healthcare in Utah or the Geisinger Health System in rural Pennsylvania, offer high-quality care at costs below average. The commission can help encourage the adoption of these common sense best practices by doctors and medical professionals throughout the system — everything from reducing hospital infection rates to encouraging better coordination between teams of doctors.

Reducing the waste and inefficiency in Medicare and Medicaid will pay for most of this plan. Much of the rest would be paid for with revenues from the very same drug and insurance companies that stand to benefit from tens of millions of new customers. This reform will charge insurance companies a fee for their most expensive policies, which will encourage them to provide greater value for the money — an idea which has the support of Democratic and Republican experts. And according to these same experts, this modest change could help hold down the cost of health care for all of us in the long run.

Finally, many in this chamber — particularly on the Republican side of the aisle — have long insisted that reforming our medical malpractice laws can help bring down the cost of health care. I don't believe malpractice reform is a silver bullet, but I have talked to enough doctors to know that defensive medicine may be contributing to unnecessary costs. So I am proposing that we move forward on a range of ideas about how to put patient safety first and let doctors focus on practicing medicine. I know that the Bush Administration considered authorizing demonstration projects in individual states to test these issues. It's a good idea, and I am directing my Secretary of Health and Human Services to move forward on this initiative today.

Add it all up, and the plan I'm proposing will cost around $900 billion over ten years — less than we have spent on the Iraq and Afghanistan wars, and less than the tax cuts for the wealthiest few Americans that Congress passed at the beginning of the previous administration. Most of these costs will be paid for with money already being spent — but spent badly — in the existing health care system. The plan will not add to our deficit. The middle-class will realize greater security, not higher taxes. And if we are able to slow the growth of health care costs by just one-tenth of one percent each year, it will actually reduce the deficit by $4 trillion over the long term.

This is the plan I'm proposing. It's a plan that incorporates ideas from many of the people in this room tonight — Democrats and Republicans. And I will continue to seek common ground in the weeks ahead. If you come to me with a serious set of proposals, I will be there to listen. My door is always open.

But know this: I will not waste time with those who have made the calculation that it's better politics to kill this plan than improve it. I will not stand by while the special interests use the same old tactics to keep things exactly the way they are. If you misrepresent what's in the plan, we will call you out. And I will not accept the status quo as a solution. Not this time. Not now.

Everyone in this room knows what will happen if we do nothing. Our deficit will grow. More families will go bankrupt. More businesses will close. More Americans will lose their coverage when they are sick and need it most. And more will die as a result. We know these things to be true.

That is why we cannot fail. Because there are too many Americans counting on us to succeed — the ones who suffer silently, and the ones who shared their stories with us at town hall meetings, in e-mails, and in letters.

I received one of those letters a few days ago. It was from our beloved friend and colleague, Ted Kennedy. He had written it back in May, shortly after he was told that his illness was terminal. He asked that it be delivered upon his death.

In it, he spoke about what a happy time his last months were, thanks to the love and support of family and friends, his wife, Vicki, and his children, who are here tonight. And he expressed confidence that this would be the year that health care reform — "that great unfinished business of our society," he called it — would finally pass. He repeated the truth that health care is decisive for our future prosperity, but he also reminded me that "it concerns more than material things." "What we face," he wrote, "is above all a moral issue; at stake are not just the details of policy, but fundamental principles of social justice and the character of our country."

I've thought about that phrase quite a bit in recent days — the character of our country. One of the unique and wonderful things about America has always been our self-reliance, our rugged individualism, our fierce defense of freedom and our healthy skepticism of government. And figuring out the appropriate size and role of government has always been a source of rigorous and sometimes angry debate.

For some of Ted Kennedy's critics, his brand of liberalism represented an affront to American liberty. In their mind, his passion for universal health care was nothing more than a passion for big government.

But those of us who knew Teddy and worked with him here — people of both parties — know that what drove him was something more. His friend, Orrin Hatch, knows that. They worked together to provide children with health insurance. His friend John McCain knows that. They worked together on a Patient's Bill of Rights. His friend Chuck Grassley knows that. They worked together to provide health care to children with disabilities.

On issues like these, Ted Kennedy's passion was born not of some rigid ideology, but of his own experience. It was the experience of having two children stricken with cancer. He never forgot the sheer terror and helplessness that any parent feels when a child is badly sick; and he was able to imagine what it must be like for those without insurance; what it would be like to have to say to a wife or a child or an aging parent — there is something that could make you better, but I just can't afford it.

That large heartedness — that concern and regard for the plight of others — is not a partisan feeling. It is not a Republican or a Democratic feeling. It, too, is part of the American character. Our ability to stand in other people's shoes. A recognition that we are all in this together; that when fortune turns against one of us, others are there to lend a helping hand. A belief that in this country, hard work and responsibility should be rewarded by some measure of security and fair play; and an acknowledgement that sometimes government has to step in to help deliver on that promise.

This has always been the history of our progress. In 1933, when over half of our seniors could not support themselves and millions had seen their savings wiped away, there were those who argued that Social Security would lead to socialism. But the men and women of Congress stood fast, and we are all the better for it. In 1965, when some argued that Medicare represented a government takeover of health care, members of Congress, Democrats and Republicans, did not back down.

They joined together so that all of us could enter our golden years with some basic peace of mind.

You see, our predecessors understood that government could not, and should not, solve every problem. They understood that there are instances when the gains in security from government action are not worth the added constraints on our freedom. But they also understood that the danger of too much government is matched by the perils of too little; that without the leavening hand of wise policy, markets can crash, monopolies can stifle competition, and the vulnerable can be exploited. And they knew that when any government measure, no matter how carefully crafted or beneficial, is subject to scorn; when any efforts to help people in need are attacked as un-American; when facts and reason are thrown overboard and only timidity passes for wisdom; and we can no longer even engage in a civil conversation with each other over the things that truly matter — that at that point we don't merely lose our capacity to solve big challenges. We lose something essential about ourselves.

What was true then remains true today. I understand how difficult this health care debate has been. I know that many in this country are deeply skeptical that government is looking out for them. I understand that the politically safe move would be to kick the can further down the road — to defer reform one more year, or one more election, or one more term.

But that's not what the moment calls for. That's not what we came here to do. We did not come here to fear the future. We came here to shape it. I still believe we can act even when it's hard. I still believe we can replace acrimony with civility, and gridlock with progress. I still believe we can do great things, and that here and now we will meet history's test.

Because that is who we are. That is our calling. That is our character. Thank you, God bless you, and may God bless the United States of America.

1.3 Barack Obama's Second State of the Union Address

Madam Speaker, Vice President Biden, members of Congress, distinguished guests, and fellow Americans:

Our Constitution declares that from time to time, the President shall give to Congress information about the state of our union. For 220 years, our leaders have fulfilled this duty. They've done so during periods of prosperity and tranquility. And they've done so in the midst of war and depression; at moments of great strife and great struggle.

It's tempting to look back on these moments and assume that our progress was inevitable -- that America was always destined to succeed. But when the Union was turned back at Bull Run, and the Allies first landed at Omaha Beach, victory was very much in doubt. When the market crashed on Black Tuesday, and civil rights marchers were beaten on Bloody Sunday, the future was anything but certain. These were the times that tested the courage of our convictions, and the strength of our union. And despite all our divisions and disagreements, our hesitations and our fears, America prevailed because we chose to move forward as one nation, as one people.

Again, we are tested. And again, we must answer history's call.

One year ago, I took office amid two wars, an economy rocked by a severe recession, a financial system on the verge of collapse, and a government deeply in debt. Experts from across the political spectrum warned that if we did not act, we might face a second depression. So we acted -- immediately and aggressively. And one year later, the worst of the storm has passed.

But the devastation remains. One in 10 Americans still cannot find work. Many businesses have shuttered. Home values have declined. Small towns and rural communities have been hit especially hard. And for those who'd already known poverty, life has become that much harder.

This recession has also compounded the burdens that America's families have been dealing with for decades -- the burden of working harder and longer for less; of being unable to save enough to retire or help kids with college.

So I know the anxieties that are out there right now. They're not new. These struggles are the reason I ran for President. These struggles are what I've witnessed for years in places like Elkhart, Indiana; Galesburg, Illinois. I hear about them in the letters that I read each night. The toughest to read are those written by children -- asking why they have to move from their home, asking when their mom or dad will be able to go back to work.

For these Americans and so many others, change has not come fast enough. Some are frustrated; some are angry. They don't understand why it seems like bad behavior on Wall Street is rewarded, but hard work on Main Street isn't; or why Washington has been unable or unwilling to solve any of our problems. They're tired of the partisanship and the shouting and the pettiness. They know we can't afford it. Not now.

So we face big and difficult challenges. And what the American people hope -- what they deserve -- is for all of us, Democrats and Republicans, to work through our differences; to overcome the numbing weight of our politics. For while the people who sent us here have different backgrounds, different stories, different beliefs, the anxieties they face are the same. The aspirations they hold are shared: a job that pays the bills; a chance to get ahead; most of all, the ability to give their children a better life.

You know what else they share? They share a stubborn resilience in the face of adversity. After one of the most difficult years in our history, they remain busy building cars and teaching kids, starting businesses and going back to school. They're coaching Little League and helping their neighbors. One woman wrote to me and said, "We are strained but hopeful, struggling but encouraged."

It's because of this spirit -- this great decency and great strength -- that I have never been more hopeful about America's future than I am tonight. (Applause.) Despite our hardships, our union is strong. We do not give up. We do not quit. We do not allow fear or division to break our spirit. In this new decade, it's time the American people get a government that matches their decency; that embodies their strength. (Applause.) And tonight, tonight I'd like to talk about how together we can deliver on that promise.

It begins with our economy.

Our most urgent task upon taking office was to shore up the same banks that helped cause this crisis. It was not easy to do. And if there's one thing that has unified Democrats and Republicans, and everybody in between, it's that we all hated the bank bailout. I hated it -- (applause.) I hated it. You hated it. It was about as popular as a root canal. (Laughter.)

But when I ran for President, I promised I wouldn't just do what was popular -- I would do what was necessary. And if we had allowed the meltdown of the financial system, unemployment might be double what it is today. More businesses would certainly have closed. More homes would have surely been lost.

So I supported the last administration's efforts to create the financial rescue program. And when we took that program over, we made it more transparent and more accountable. And as a result, the markets are now stabilized, and we've recovered most of the money we spent on the banks. (Applause.) Most but not all.

To recover the rest, I've proposed a fee on the biggest banks. (Applause.) Now, I know Wall Street isn't keen on this idea. But if these firms can afford to hand out big bonuses again, they can afford a modest fee to pay back the taxpayers who rescued them in their time of need. (Applause.)

Now, as we stabilized the financial system, we also took steps to get our economy growing again, save as many jobs as possible, and help Americans who had become unemployed.

That's why we extended or increased unemployment benefits for more than 18 million Americans; made health insurance 65 percent cheaper for families who get their coverage through COBRA; and passed 25 different tax cuts.

Now, let me repeat: We cut taxes. We cut taxes for 95 percent of working families. (Applause.) We cut taxes for small businesses. We cut taxes for first-time homebuyers. We cut taxes for parents trying to care for their children. We cut taxes for 8 million Americans paying for college. (Applause.)

I thought I'd get some applause on that one. (Laughter and applause.)

As a result, millions of Americans had more to spend on gas and food and other necessities, all of which helped businesses keep more workers. And we haven't raised income taxes by a single dime on a single person. Not a single dime. (Applause.)

Because of the steps we took, there are about two million Americans working right now who would otherwise be unemployed. (Applause.) Two hundred thousand work in construction and clean energy; 300,000 are teachers and other education workers. Tens of thousands are cops, firefighters, correctional officers, first responders. (Applause.) And we're on track to add another one and a half million jobs to this total by the end of the year.

The plan that has made all of this possible, from the tax cuts to the jobs, is the Recovery Act. (Applause.) That's right -- the Recovery Act, also known as the stimulus bill. (Applause.) Economists on the left and the right say this bill has helped save jobs and avert disaster. But you don't have to take their word for it. Talk to the small business in Phoenix that will triple its workforce because of the Recovery Act. Talk to the window manufacturer in Philadelphia who said he used to be skeptical about the Recovery Act, until he had to add two more work shifts just because of the business it created. Talk to the single teacher raising two kids who was told by her principal in the last week of school that because of the Recovery Act, she wouldn't be laid off after all.

There are stories like this all across America. And after two years of recession, the economy is growing again. Retirement funds have started to gain back some of their value. Businesses are beginning to invest again, and slowly some are starting to hire again.

But I realize that for every success story, there are other stories, of men and women who wake up with the anguish of not knowing where their next paycheck will come from; who send out resumes week after week and hear nothing in response. That is why jobs must be our number-one focus in 2010, and that's why I'm calling for a new jobs bill tonight. (Applause.)

Now, the true engine of job creation in this country will always be America's businesses. (Applause.) But government can create the conditions necessary for businesses to expand and hire more workers.

We should start where most new jobs do -- in small businesses, companies that begin when -- (applause) -- companies that begin when an entrepreneur -- when an entrepreneur takes a chance on a dream, or a worker decides it's time she became her own boss. Through sheer grit and determination, these companies have weathered the recession and they're ready to grow. But when you talk to small businessowners in places like Allentown, Pennsylvania, or Elyria, Ohio, you find out that even though banks on Wall Street are lending again, they're mostly lending to bigger companies. Financing remains difficult for small businessowners across the country, even those that are making a profit.

So tonight, I'm proposing that we take $30 billion of the money Wall Street banks have repaid and use it to help community banks give small businesses the credit they need to stay afloat. (Applause.) I'm also proposing a new small business tax credit -- one that will go to over one million small businesses who hire new workers or raise wages. (Applause.) While we're at it, let's also eliminate all capital gains taxes on small business investment, and provide a tax incentive for all large businesses and all small businesses to invest in new plants and equipment. (Applause.)

Next, we can put Americans to work today building the infrastructure of tomorrow. (Applause.) From the first railroads to the Interstate Highway System, our nation has always been built to compete. There's no reason Europe or China should have the fastest trains, or the new factories that manufacture clean energy products.

Tomorrow, I'll visit Tampa, Florida, where workers will soon break ground on a new high-speed railroad funded by the Recovery Act. (Applause.) There are projects like that all across this country that will create jobs and help move our nation's goods, services, and information. (Applause.)

We should put more Americans to work building clean energy facilities -- (applause) -- and give rebates to Americans who make their homes more energy-efficient, which supports clean energy jobs. (Applause.) And to encourage these and other businesses to stay within our borders, it is time to finally slash the tax breaks for companies that ship our jobs overseas, and give those tax breaks to companies that create jobs right here in the United States of America. (Applause.)

Now, the House has passed a jobs bill that includes some of these steps. (Applause.) As the first order of business this year, I urge the Senate to do the same, and I know they will. (Applause.) They will. (Applause.) People are out of work. They're hurting. They need our help. And I want a jobs bill on my desk without delay. (Applause.)

But the truth is, these steps won't make up for the seven million jobs that we've lost over the last two years. The only way to move to full employment is to lay a new foundation for long-term economic growth, and finally address the problems that America's families have confronted for years.

We can't afford another so-called economic "expansion" like the one from the last decade — what some call the "lost decade" -— where jobs grew more slowly than during any prior expansion; where the income of the average American household declined while the cost of health care and tuition reached record highs; where prosperity was built on a housing bubble and financial speculation.

From the day I took office, I've been told that addressing our larger challenges is too ambitious; such an effort would be too contentious. I've been told that our political system is too gridlocked, and that we should just put things on hold for a while.

For those who make these claims, I have one simple question: How long should we wait? How long should America put its future on hold? (Applause.)

You see, Washington has been telling us to wait for decades, even as the problems have grown worse. Meanwhile, China is not waiting to revamp its economy. Germany is not waiting. India is not waiting. These nations -- they're not standing still. These nations aren't playing for second place. They're putting more emphasis on math and science. They're rebuilding their infrastructure. They're making serious investments in clean energy because they want those jobs. Well, I do not accept second place for the United States of America. (Applause.)

As hard as it may be, as uncomfortable and contentious as the debates may become, it's time to get serious about fixing the problems that are hampering our growth.

Now, one place to start is serious financial reform. Look, I am not interested in punishing banks. I'm interested in protecting our economy. A strong, healthy financial market makes it possible for businesses to access credit and create new jobs. It channels the savings of families into investments that raise incomes. But that can only happen if we guard against the same recklessness that nearly brought down our entire economy.

We need to make sure consumers and middle-class families have the information they need to make financial decisions. (Applause.) We can't allow financial institutions, including those that take your deposits, to take risks that threaten the whole economy.

Now, the House has already passed financial reform with many of these changes. (Applause.) And the lobbyists are trying to kill it. But we cannot let them win this fight. (Applause.) And if the bill that ends up on my desk does not meet the test of real reform, I will send it back until we get it right. We've got to get it right. (Applause.)

Next, we need to encourage American innovation. Last year, we made the largest investment in basic research funding in history -— (applause) -- an investment that could lead to the world's cheapest solar cells or treatment that kills cancer cells but leaves healthy ones untouched. And no area is more ripe for such innovation than energy. You can see the results of last year's investments in clean energy -— in the North Carolina company that will create 1,200 jobs nationwide helping to make advanced batteries; or in the California business that will put a thousand people to work making solar panels.

But to create more of these clean energy jobs, we need more production, more efficiency, more incentives. And that means building a new generation of safe, clean nuclear power plants in this country. (Applause.) It means making tough decisions about opening new offshore areas for oil and gas development. (Applause.) It means continued investment in advanced biofuels and clean coal technologies. (Applause.) And, yes, it means passing a comprehensive energy and climate bill with incentives that will finally make clean energy the profitable kind of energy in America. (Applause.)

I am grateful to the House for passing such a bill last year. (Applause.) And this year I'm eager to help advance the bipartisan effort in the Senate. (Applause.)

I know there have been questions about whether we can afford such changes in a tough economy. I know that there are those who disagree with the overwhelming scientific evidence on climate change. But here's the thing -- even if you doubt the evidence, providing incentives for energy-efficiency and clean energy are the right thing to do for our future -— because the nation that leads the clean energy economy will be the nation that leads the global economy. And America must be that nation. (Applause.)

Third, we need to export more of our goods. (Applause.) Because the more products we make and sell to other countries, the more jobs we support right here in America. (Applause.) So tonight, we set a new goal: We will double our exports over the next five years, an increase that will support two million jobs in America. (Applause.) To help meet this goal, we're launching a National Export Initiative that will help farmers and small businesses increase their exports, and reform export controls consistent with national security. (Applause.)

We have to seek new markets aggressively, just as our competitors are. If America sits on the sidelines while other nations sign trade deals, we will lose the chance to create jobs on our shores. (Applause.) But realizing those benefits also means enforcing those agreements so our trading partners play by the rules. (Applause.) And that's why we'll continue to shape a Doha trade agreement that opens global markets, and why we will strengthen our trade relations in Asia and with key partners like South Korea and Panama and Colombia. (Applause.)

Fourth, we need to invest in the skills and education of our people. (Applause.)

Now, this year, we've broken through the stalemate between left and right by launching a national competition to improve our schools. And the idea here is simple: Instead of rewarding failure, we only reward success. Instead of funding the status quo, we only invest in reform -- reform that raises student achievement; inspires students to excel in math and science; and turns around failing schools that steal the future of too many young Americans, from rural communities to the inner city. In the 21st century, the best anti-poverty program around is a world-class education. (Applause.) And in this country, the success of our children cannot depend more on where they live than on their potential.

When we renew the Elementary and Secondary Education Act, we will work with Congress to expand these reforms to all 50 states. Still, in this economy, a high school diploma no longer guarantees a good job. That's why I urge the Senate to follow the House and pass a bill that will revitalize our community colleges, which are a career pathway to the children of so many working families. (Applause.)

To make college more affordable, this bill will finally end the unwarranted taxpayer subsidies that go to banks for student loans. (Applause.) Instead, let's take that money and give families a $10,000 tax credit for four years of college and increase Pell Grants. (Applause.) And let's tell another one million students that when they graduate, they will be required to pay only 10 percent of their income on student loans, and all of their debt will be forgiven after 20 years -- and forgiven after 10 years if they choose a career in public service, because in the United States of America, no one should go broke because they chose to go to college. (Applause.)

And by the way, it's time for colleges and universities to get serious about cutting their own costs -- (applause) -- because they, too, have a responsibility to help solve this problem.

Now, the price of college tuition is just one of the burdens facing the middle class. That's why last year I asked Vice President Biden to chair a task force on middle-class families. That's why we're nearly doubling the child care tax credit, and making it easier to save for retirement by giving access to every worker a retirement account and expanding the tax credit for those who start a nest egg. That's why we're working to lift the value of a family's single largest investment -- their home. The steps we took last year to shore up the housing market have allowed millions of Americans to take out new loans and save an average of $1,500 on mortgage payments.

This year, we will step up refinancing so that homeowners can move into more affordable mortgages. (Applause.) And it is precisely to relieve the burden on middle-class families that we still need health insurance reform. (Applause.) Yes, we do. (Applause.)

Now, let's clear a few things up. (Laughter.) I didn't choose to tackle this issue to get some legislative victory under my belt. And by now it should be fairly obvious that I didn't take on health care because it was good politics. (Laughter.) I took on health care because of the stories I've heard from Americans with preexisting conditions whose lives depend on getting coverage; patients who've been denied coverage; families -- even those with insurance -- who are just one illness away from financial ruin.

After nearly a century of trying -- Democratic administrations, Republican administrations -- we are closer than ever to bringing more security to the lives of so many Americans. The approach we've taken would protect every American from the worst practices of the insurance industry. It would give small businesses and uninsured Americans a chance to choose an affordable health care plan in a competitive market. It would require every insurance plan to cover preventive care.

And by the way, I want to acknowledge our First Lady, Michelle Obama, who this year is creating a national movement to tackle the epidemic of childhood obesity and make kids healthier. (Applause.) Thank you. She gets embarrassed. (Laughter.)

Our approach would preserve the right of Americans who have insurance to keep their doctor and their plan. It would reduce costs and premiums for millions of families and businesses. And according to the Congressional Budget Office -- the independent organization that both parties have cited as the official scorekeeper for Congress -- our approach would bring down the deficit by as much as $1 trillion over the next two decades. (Applause.)

Still, this is a complex issue, and the longer it was debated, the more skeptical people became. I take my share of the blame for not explaining it more clearly to the American people. And I know that with all the lobbying and horse-trading, the process left most Americans wondering, "What's in it for me?"

But I also know this problem is not going away. By the time I'm finished speaking tonight, more Americans will have lost their health insurance. Millions will lose it this year. Our deficit will grow. Premiums will go up. Patients will be denied the care they need. Small business owners will continue to drop coverage altogether. I will not walk away from these Americans, and neither should the people in this chamber. (Applause.)

So, as temperatures cool, I want everyone to take another look at the plan we've proposed. There's a reason why many doctors, nurses, and health care experts who know our system best consider this approach a vast improvement over the status quo. But if anyone from either party has a better approach that will bring down premiums, bring down the deficit, cover the uninsured, strengthen Medicare for seniors, and stop insurance company abuses, let me know. (Applause.) Let me know. Let me know. (Applause.) I'm eager to see it.

Here's what I ask Congress, though: Don't walk away from reform. Not now. Not when we are so close. Let us find a way to come together and finish the job for the American people. (Applause.) Let's get it done. Let's get it done. (Applause.)

Now, even as health care reform would reduce our deficit, it's not enough to dig us out of a massive fiscal hole in which we find ourselves. It's a challenge that makes all others that much harder to solve, and one that's been subject to a lot of political posturing. So let me start the discussion of government spending by setting the record straight.

At the beginning of the last decade, the year 2000, America had a budget surplus of over $200 billion. (Applause.) By the time I took office, we had a one-year deficit of over $1 trillion and projected deficits of $8 trillion over the next decade. Most of this was the result of not paying for two wars, two tax cuts, and an expensive prescription drug program. On top of that, the effects of the recession put a $3 trillion hole in our budget. All this was before I walked in the door. (Laughter and applause.)

Now -- just stating the facts. Now, if we had taken office in ordinary times, I would have liked nothing more than to start bringing down the deficit. But we took office amid a crisis. And our efforts to prevent a second depression have added another $1 trillion to our national debt. That, too, is a fact.

I'm absolutely convinced that was the right thing to do. But families across the country are tightening their belts and making tough decisions. The federal government should do the same. (Applause.) So tonight, I'm proposing specific steps to pay for the trillion dollars that it took to rescue the economy last year.

Starting in 2011, we are prepared to freeze government spending for three years. (Applause.) Spending related to our national security, Medicare, Medicaid, and Social Security will not be affected. But all other discretionary government programs will. Like any cash-strapped family, we will work within a budget to invest in what we need and sacrifice what we don't. And if I have to enforce this discipline by veto, I will. (Applause.)

We will continue to go through the budget, line by line, page by page, to eliminate programs that we can't afford and don't work. We've already identified $20 billion in savings for next year. To help working families, we'll extend our middle-class tax cuts. But at a time of record deficits, we will not continue tax cuts for oil companies, for investment fund managers, and for those making over $250,000 a year. We just can't afford it. (Applause.)

Now, even after paying for what we spent on my watch, we'll still face the massive deficit we had when I took office. More importantly, the cost of Medicare, Medicaid, and Social Security will continue to skyrocket. That's why I've called for a bipartisan fiscal commission, modeled on a proposal by Republican Judd Gregg and Democrat Kent Conrad. (Applause.) This can't be one of those Washington gimmicks that lets us pretend we solved a problem. The commission will have to provide a specific set of solutions by a certain deadline.

Now, yesterday, the Senate blocked a bill that would have created this commission. So I'll issue an executive order that will allow us to go forward, because I refuse to pass this problem on to another generation of Americans. (Applause.) And when the vote comes tomorrow, the Senate should restore the pay-as-you-go law that was a big reason for why we had record surpluses in the 1990s. (Applause.)

Now, I know that some in my own party will argue that we can't address the deficit or freeze government spending when so many are still hurting. And I agree -- which is why this freeze won't take effect until next year -- (laughter) -- when the economy is stronger. That's how budgeting works. (Laughter and applause.) But understand -- understand if we don't take meaningful steps to rein in our debt, it could damage our markets, increase the cost of borrowing, and jeopardize our recovery -- all of which would have an even worse effect on our job growth and family incomes.

From some on the right, I expect we'll hear a different argument -- that if we just make fewer investments in our people, extend tax cuts including those for the wealthier Americans, eliminate more regulations, maintain the status quo on health care, our deficits will go away. The problem is that's what we did for eight years. (Applause.) That's what helped us into this crisis. It's what helped lead to these deficits. We can't do it again.

Rather than fight the same tired battles that have dominated Washington for decades, it's time to try something new. Let's invest in our people without leaving them a mountain of debt. Let's meet our responsibility to the citizens who sent us here. Let's try common sense. (Laughter.) A novel concept.

To do that, we have to recognize that we face more than a deficit of dollars right now. We face a deficit of trust -- deep and corrosive doubts about how Washington works that have been growing for years. To close that credibility gap we have to take action on both ends of Pennsylvania Avenue -- to end the outsized influence of lobbyists; to do our work openly; to give our people the government they deserve. (Applause.)

That's what I came to Washington to do. That's why -- for the first time in history -- my administration posts on our White House visitors online. That's why we've excluded lobbyists from policymaking jobs, or seats on federal boards and commissions.

But we can't stop there. It's time to require lobbyists to disclose each contact they make on behalf of a client with my administration or with Congress. It's time to put strict limits on the contributions that lobbyists give to candidates for federal office.

With all due deference to separation of powers, last week the Supreme Court reversed a century of law that I believe will open the floodgates for special interests -- including foreign corporations -- to spend without limit in our elections. (Applause.) I don't think American elections should be bankrolled by America's most powerful interests, or worse, by foreign entities. (Applause.) They should be decided by the American people. And I'd urge Democrats and Republicans to pass a bill that helps to correct some of these problems.

I'm also calling on Congress to continue down the path of earmark reform. (Applause.) Democrats and Republicans. (Applause.) Democrats and Republicans. You've trimmed some of this spending, you've embraced some meaningful change. But restoring the public trust demands more. For example, some members of Congress post some earmark requests online. (Applause.) Tonight, I'm calling on Congress to publish all earmark requests on a single Web site before there's a vote, so that the American people can see how their money is being spent. (Applause.)

Of course, none of these reforms will even happen if we don't also reform how we work with one another. Now, I'm not naïve. I never thought that the mere fact of my election would usher in peace and harmony -- (laughter) -- and some post-partisan era. I knew that both parties have fed divisions that are deeply entrenched. And on some issues, there are simply philosophical differences that will always cause us to part ways. These disagreements, about the role of government in our lives, about our national priorities and our national security, they've been taking place for over 200 years. They're the very essence of our democracy.

But what frustrates the American people is a Washington where every day is Election Day. We can't wage a perpetual campaign where the only goal is to see who can get the most embarrassing headlines about the other side -- a belief that if you lose, I win. Neither party should delay or obstruct every single bill just because they can. The confirmation of -- (applause) -- I'm speaking to both parties now. The confirmation of well-qualified public servants shouldn't be held hostage to the pet projects or grudges of a few individual senators. (Applause.)

Washington may think that saying anything about the other side, no matter how false, no matter how malicious, is just part of the game. But it's precisely such politics that has stopped either party from helping the American people. Worse yet, it's sowing further division among our citizens, further distrust in our government.

So, no, I will not give up on trying to change the tone of our politics. I know it's an election year. And after last week, it's clear that campaign fever has come even earlier than usual. But we still need to govern.

To Democrats, I would remind you that we still have the largest majority in decades, and the people expect us to solve problems, not run for the hills. (Applause.) And if the Republican leadership is going to insist that 60 votes in the Senate are required to do any business at all in this town -- a supermajority -- then the responsibility to govern is now yours as well. (Applause.) Just saying no to everything may be good short-term politics, but it's not leadership. We were sent here to serve our citizens, not our ambitions. (Applause.) So let's show the American people that we can do it together.

(Applause.)

This week, I'll be addressing a meeting of the House Republicans. I'd like to begin monthly meetings with both Democratic and Republican leadership. I know you can't wait. (Laughter.)

Throughout our history, no issue has united this country more than our security. Sadly, some of the unity we felt after 9/11 has dissipated. We can argue all we want about who's to blame for this, but I'm not interested in re-litigating the past. I know that all of us love this country. All of us are committed to its defense. So let's put aside the schoolyard taunts about who's tough. Let's reject the false choice between protecting our people and upholding our values. Let's leave behind the fear and division, and do what it takes to defend our nation and forge a more hopeful future -- for America and for the world. (Applause.)

That's the work we began last year. Since the day I took office, we've renewed our focus on the terrorists who threaten our nation. We've made substantial investments in our homeland security and disrupted plots that threatened to take American lives. We are filling unacceptable gaps revealed by the failed Christmas attack, with better airline security and swifter action on our intelligence. We've prohibited torture and strengthened partnerships from the Pacific to South Asia to the Arabian Peninsula. And in the last year, hundreds of al Qaeda's fighters and affiliates, including many senior leaders, have been captured or killed -- far more than in 2008.

And in Afghanistan, we're increasing our troops and training Afghan security forces so they can begin to take the lead in July of 2011, and our troops can begin to come home. (Applause.) We will reward good governance, work to reduce corruption, and support the rights of all Afghans -- men and women alike. (Applause.) We're joined by allies and partners who have increased their own commitments, and who will come together tomorrow in London to reaffirm our common purpose. There will be difficult days ahead. But I am absolutely confident we will succeed.

As we take the fight to al Qaeda, we are responsibly leaving Iraq to its people. As a candidate, I promised that I would end this war, and that is what I am doing as President. We will have all of our combat troops out of Iraq by the end of this August. (Applause.) We will support the Iraqi government -- we will support the Iraqi government as they hold elections, and we will continue to partner with the Iraqi people to promote regional peace and prosperity. But make no mistake: This war is ending, and all of our troops are coming home. (Applause.)

Tonight, all of our men and women in uniform -- in Iraq, in Afghanistan, and around the world — they have to know that we -- that they have our respect, our gratitude, our full support. And just as they must have the resources they need in war, we all have a responsibility to support them when they come home. (Applause.) That's why we made the largest increase in investments for veterans in decades -- last year. (Applause.) That's why we're building a 21st century VA. And that's why Michelle has joined with Jill Biden to forge a national commitment to support military families. (Applause.)

Now, even as we prosecute two wars, we're also confronting perhaps the greatest danger to the American people -- the threat of nuclear weapons. I've embraced the vision of John F. Kennedy and Ronald Reagan through a strategy that reverses the spread of these weapons and seeks a world without them. To reduce our stockpiles and launchers, while ensuring our deterrent, the United States and Russia are completing negotiations on the farthest-reaching arms control treaty in nearly two decades. (Applause.) And at April's Nuclear Security Summit, we will bring 44 nations together here in Washington, D.C. behind a clear goal: securing all vulnerable nuclear materials around the world in four years, so that they never fall into the hands of terrorists. (Applause.)

Now, these diplomatic efforts have also strengthened our hand in dealing with those nations that insist on violating international agreements in pursuit of nuclear weapons. That's why North Korea now faces increased isolation, and stronger sanctions -- sanctions that are being vigorously enforced. That's why the international community is more united, and the Islamic Republic of Iran is more isolated. And as Iran's leaders continue to ignore their obligations, there should be no doubt: They, too, will face growing consequences. That is a promise. (Applause.)

That's the leadership that we are providing — engagement that advances the common security and prosperity of all people. We're working through the G20 to sustain a lasting global recovery. We're working with Muslim communities around the world to promote science and education and innovation. We have gone from a bystander to a leader in the fight against climate change. We're helping developing countries to feed themselves, and continuing the fight against HIV/AIDS. And we are launching a new initiative that will give us the capacity to respond faster and more effectively to bioterrorism or an infectious disease -- a plan that will counter threats at home and strengthen public health abroad.

As we have for over 60 years, America takes these actions because our destiny is connected to those beyond our shores. But we also do it because it is right. That's why, as we meet here tonight, over 10,000 Americans are working with many nations to help the people of Haiti recover and rebuild. (Applause.) That's why we stand with the girl who yearns to go to school in Afghanistan; why we support the human rights of the women marching through the streets of Iran; why we advocate for the young man denied a job by corruption in Guinea. For America must always stand on the side of freedom and human dignity. (Applause.) Always. (Applause.)

Abroad, America's greatest source of strength has always been our ideals. The same is true at home. We find unity in our incredible diversity, drawing on the promise enshrined in our Constitution: the notion that we're all created equal; that no matter who you are or what you look like, if you abide by the law you should be protected by it; if you adhere to our common values you should be treated no different than anyone else.

We must continually renew this promise. My administration has a Civil Rights Division that is once again prosecuting civil rights violations and employment discrimination. (Applause.) We finally strengthened our laws to protect against crimes driven by hate. (Applause.) This year, I will work with Congress and our military to finally repeal the law that denies gay Americans the right to serve the country they love because of who they are. (Applause.) It's the right thing to do. (Applause.)

We're going to crack down on violations of equal pay laws -- so that women get equal pay for an equal day's work. (Applause.) And we should continue the work of fixing our broken immigration system -- to secure our borders and enforce our laws, and ensure that everyone who plays by the rules can contribute to our economy and enrich our nation. (Applause.)

In the end, it's our ideals, our values that built America -- values that allowed us to forge a nation made up of immigrants from every corner of the globe; values that drive our citizens still. Every day, Americans meet their responsibilities to their families and their employers. Time and again, they lend a hand to their neighbors and give back to their country. They take pride in their labor, and are generous in spirit. These aren't Republican values or Democratic values that they're living by; business values or labor values. They're American values.

Unfortunately, too many of our citizens have lost faith that our biggest institutions -- our corporations, our media, and, yes, our government — still reflect these same values. Each of these institutions are full of honorable men and women doing important work that helps our country prosper. But each time a CEO rewards himself for failure, or a banker puts the rest of us at risk for his own selfish gain, people's doubts grow. Each time lobbyists game the system or politicians tear each other down instead of lifting this country up, we lose faith. The more that TV pundits reduce serious debates to silly arguments, big issues into sound bites, our citizens turn away.

No wonder there's so much cynicism out there. No wonder there's so much disappointment.

I campaigned on the promise of change -- change we can believe in, the slogan went. And right now, I know there are many Americans who aren't sure if they still believe we can change -- or that I can deliver it.

But remember this — I never suggested that change would be easy, or that I could do it alone. Democracy in a nation of 300 million people can be noisy and messy and complicated. And when you try to do big things and make big changes, it stirs passions and controversy. That's just how it is.

Those of us in public office can respond to this reality by playing it safe and avoid telling hard truths and pointing fingers. We can do what's necessary to keep our poll numbers high, and get through the next election instead of doing what's best for the next generation.

But I also know this: If people had made that decision 50 years ago, or 100 years ago, or 200 years ago, we wouldn't be here tonight. The only reason we are here is because generations of Americans were unafraid to do what was hard; to do what was needed even when success was uncertain; to do what it took to keep the dream of this nation alive for their children and their grandchildren.

Our administration has had some political setbacks this year, and some of them were deserved. But I wake up every day knowing that they are nothing compared to the setbacks that families all across this country have faced this year. And what keeps me going -- what keeps me fighting -- is that despite all these setbacks, that spirit of determination and optimism, that fundamental decency that has always been at the core of the American people, that lives on.

It lives on in the struggling small business owner who wrote to me of his company, "None of us," he said, "...are willing to consider, even slightly, that we might fail."

It lives on in the woman who said that even though she and her neighbors have felt the pain of recession, "We are strong.

We are resilient. We are American."

It lives on in the 8-year-old boy in Louisiana, who just sent me his allowance and asked if I would give it to the people of Haiti.

And it lives on in all the Americans who've dropped everything to go someplace they've never been and pull people they've never known from the rubble, prompting chants of "U.S.A.! U.S.A.! U.S.A!" when another life was saved.

The spirit that has sustained this nation for more than two centuries lives on in you, its people. We have finished a difficult year. We have come through a difficult decade. But a new year has come. A new decade stretches before us. We don't quit. I don't quit. (Applause.) Let's seize this moment -- to start anew, to carry the dream forward, and to strengthen our union once more. (Applause.)

Thank you. God bless you. And God bless the United States of America. (Applause.)

1.4   Barack Obama's Third State of the Union Address

Tonight I want to begin by congratulating the men and women of the 112th Congress, as well as your new Speaker, John Boehner. And as we mark this occasion, we are also mindful of the empty chair in this Chamber, and pray for the health of our colleague – and our friend – Gabby Giffords.

It's no secret that those of us here tonight have had our differences over the last two years. The debates have been contentious; we have fought fiercely for our beliefs. And that's a good thing. That's what a robust democracy demands. That's what helps set us apart as a nation.

But there's a reason the tragedy in Tucson gave us pause. Amid all the noise and passions and rancor of our public debate, Tucson reminded us that no matter who we are or where we come from, each of us is a part of something greater – something more consequential than party or political preference.

We are part of the American family. We believe that in a country where every race and faith and point of view can be found, we are still bound together as one people; that we share common hopes and a common creed; that the dreams of a little girl in Tucson are not so different than those of our own children, and that they all deserve the chance to be fulfilled.

That, too, is what sets us apart as a nation.

Now, by itself, this simple recognition won't usher in a new era of cooperation. What comes of this moment is up to us. What comes of this moment will be determined not by whether we can sit together tonight, but whether we can work together tomorrow.

I believe we can. I believe we must. That's what the people who sent us here expect of us. With their votes, they've determined that governing will now be a shared responsibility between parties. New laws will only pass with support from Democrats and Republicans. We will move forward together, or not at all – for the challenges we face are bigger than party, and bigger than politics.

At stake right now is not who wins the next election – after all, we just had an election. At stake is whether new jobs and industries take root in this country, or somewhere else. It's whether the hard work and industry of our people is rewarded. It's whether we sustain the leadership that has made America not just a place on a map, but a light to the world.

We are poised for progress. Two years after the worst recession most of us have ever known, the stock market has come roaring back. Corporate profits are up. The economy is growing again.

But we have never measured progress by these yardsticks alone. We measure progress by the success of our people. By the jobs they can find and the quality of life those jobs offer. By the prospects of a small business owner who dreams of turning a good idea into a thriving enterprise. By the opportunities for a better life that we pass on to our children.

That's the project the American people want us to work on. Together.

We did that in December. Thanks to the tax cuts we passed, Americans' paychecks are a little bigger today. Every business can write off the full cost of the new investments they make this year. These steps, taken by Democrats and Republicans, will grow the economy and add to the more than one million private sector jobs created last year.

But we have more work to do. The steps we've taken over the last two years may have broken the back of this recession – but to win the future, we'll need to take on challenges that have been decades in the making.

Many people watching tonight can probably remember a time when finding a good job meant showing up at a nearby factory or a business downtown. You didn't always need a degree, and your competition was pretty much limited to your neighbors. If you worked hard, chances are you'd have a job for life, with a decent paycheck, good benefits, and the occasional promotion. Maybe you'd even have the pride of seeing your kids work at the same company.

That world has changed. And for many, the change has been painful. I've seen it in the shuttered windows of once booming factories, and the vacant storefronts of once busy Main Streets. I've heard it in the frustrations of Americans who've seen their paychecks dwindle or their jobs disappear – proud men and women who feel like the rules have been changed in the middle of the game.

They're right. The rules have changed. In a single generation, revolutions in technology have transformed the way we live, work and do business. Steel mills that once needed 1,000 workers can now do the same work with 100. Today, just about any company can set up shop, hire workers, and sell their products wherever there's an internet connection.

Meanwhile, nations like China and India realized that with some changes of their own, they could compete in this new world. And so they started educating their children earlier and longer, with greater emphasis on math and science. They're investing in research and new technologies. Just recently, China became home to the world's largest private solar research facility, and the world's fastest computer.

So yes, the world has changed. The competition for jobs is real. But this shouldn't discourage us. It should challenge us. Remember – for all the hits we've taken these last few years, for all the naysayers predicting our decline, America still has the largest, most prosperous economy in the world. No workers are more productive than ours. No country has more successful companies, or grants more patents to inventors and entrepreneurs. We are home to the world's best colleges and universities, where more students come to study than any other place on Earth.

What's more, we are the first nation to be founded for the sake of an idea – the idea that each of us deserves the chance to shape our own destiny. That is why centuries of pioneers and immigrants have risked everything to come here. It's why our students don't just memorize equations, but answer questions like "What do you think of that idea? What would you change about the world? What do you want to be when you grow up?"

The future is ours to win. But to get there, we can't just stand still. As Robert Kennedy told us, "The future is not a gift. It is an achievement." Sustaining the American Dream has never been about standing pat. It has required each generation to sacrifice, and struggle, and meet the demands of a new age.

Now it's our turn. We know what it takes to compete for the jobs and industries of our time. We need to out-innovate, out-educate, and out-build the rest of the world. We have to make America the best place on Earth to do business. We need to take responsibility for our deficit, and reform our government. That's how our people will prosper. That's how we'll win the future. And tonight, I'd like to talk about how we get there.

The first step in winning the future is encouraging American innovation.

None of us can predict with certainty what the next big industry will be, or where the new jobs will come from. Thirty years ago, we couldn't know that something called the Internet would lead to an economic revolution. What we can do – what America does better than anyone – is spark the creativity and imagination of our people. We are the nation that put cars in driveways and computers in offices; the nation of Edison and the Wright brothers; of Google and Facebook. In America, innovation doesn't just change our lives. It's how we make a living.

Our free enterprise system is what drives innovation. But because it's not always profitable for companies to invest in basic research, throughout history our government has provided cutting-edge scientists and inventors with the support that they need. That's what planted the seeds for the Internet. That's what helped make possible things like computer chips and GPS.

Just think of all the good jobs – from manufacturing to retail – that have come from those breakthroughs.

Half a century ago, when the Soviets beat us into space with the launch of a satellite called Sputnik, we had no idea how we'd beat them to the moon. The science wasn't there yet. NASA didn't even exist. But after investing in better research and education, we didn't just surpass the Soviets; we unleashed a wave of innovation that created new industries and millions of new jobs.

This is our generation's Sputnik moment. Two years ago, I said that we needed to reach a level of research and development we haven't seen since the height of the Space Race. In a few weeks, I will be sending a budget to Congress that helps us meet that goal. We'll invest in biomedical research, information technology, and especially clean energy technology – an investment that will strengthen our security, protect our planet, and create countless new jobs for our people.

Already, we are seeing the promise of renewable energy. Robert and Gary Allen are brothers who run a small Michigan roofing company. After September 11th, they volunteered their best roofers to help repair the Pentagon. But half of their factory went unused, and the recession hit them hard.

Today, with the help of a government loan, that empty space is being used to manufacture solar shingles that are being sold all across the country. In Robert's words, "We reinvented ourselves."

That's what Americans have done for over two hundred years: reinvented ourselves. And to spur on more success stories like the Allen Brothers, we've begun to reinvent our energy policy. We're not just handing out money. We're issuing a challenge. We're telling America's scientists and engineers that if they assemble teams of the best minds in their fields, and focus on the hardest problems in clean energy, we'll fund the Apollo Projects of our time.

At the California Institute of Technology, they're developing a way to turn sunlight and water into fuel for our cars. At Oak Ridge National Laboratory, they're using supercomputers to get a lot more power out of our nuclear facilities. With more research and incentives, we can break our dependence on oil with biofuels, and become the first country to have 1 million electric vehicles on the road by 2015.

We need to get behind this innovation. And to help pay for it, I'm asking Congress to eliminate the billions in taxpayer dollars we currently give to oil companies. I don't know if you've noticed, but they're doing just fine on their own. So instead of subsidizing yesterday's energy, let's invest in tomorrow's.

Now, clean energy breakthroughs will only translate into clean energy jobs if businesses know there will be a market for what they're selling. So tonight, I challenge you to join me in setting a new goal: by 2035, 80% of America's electricity will come from clean energy sources. Some folks want wind and solar. Others want nuclear, clean coal, and natural gas. To meet this goal, we will need them all – and I urge Democrats and Republicans to work together to make it happen.

Maintaining our leadership in research and technology is crucial to America's success. But if we want to win the future – if we want innovation to produce jobs in America and not overseas – then we also have to win the race to educate our kids.

Think about it. Over the next ten years, nearly half of all new jobs will require education that goes beyond a high school degree. And yet, as many as a quarter of our students aren't even finishing high school. The quality of our math and science education lags behind many other nations. America has fallen to 9th in the proportion of young people with a college degree. And so the question is whether all of us – as citizens, and as parents – are willing to do what's necessary to give every child a chance to succeed.

That responsibility begins not in our classrooms, but in our homes and communities. It's family that first instills the love of learning in a child. Only parents can make sure the TV is turned off and homework gets done. We need to teach our kids that it's not just the winner of the Super Bowl who deserves to be celebrated, but the winner of the science fair; that success is not a function of fame or PR, but of hard work and discipline.

Our schools share this responsibility. When a child walks into a classroom, it should be a place of high expectations and high performance. But too many schools don't meet this test. That's why instead of just pouring money into a system that's not working, we launched a competition called Race to the Top. To all fifty states, we said, "If you show us the most innovative plans to improve teacher quality and student achievement, we'll show you the money."

Race to the Top is the most meaningful reform of our public schools in a generation. For less than one percent of what we spend on education each year, it has led over 40 states to raise their standards for teaching and learning. These standards were developed, not by Washington, but by Republican and Democratic governors throughout the country. And Race to the Top should be the approach we follow this year as we replace No Child Left Behind with a law that is more flexible and focused on what's best for our kids.

You see, we know what's possible for our children when reform isn't just a top-down mandate, but the work of local teachers and principals; school boards and communities.

Take a school like Bruce Randolph in Denver. Three years ago, it was rated one of the worst schools in Colorado; located on turf between two rival gangs. But last May, 97% of the seniors received their diploma. Most will be the first in their family to go to college. And after the first year of the school's transformation, the principal who made it possible wiped away tears when a student said "Thank you, Mrs. Waters, for showing... that we are smart and we can make it."

Let's also remember that after parents, the biggest impact on a child's success comes from the man or woman at the front of the classroom. In South Korea, teachers are known as "nation builders." Here in America, it's time we treated the people who educate our children with the same level of respect. We want to reward good teachers and stop making excuses for bad ones. And over the next ten years, with so many Baby Boomers retiring from our classrooms, we want to prepare 100,000 new teachers in the fields of science, technology, engineering, and math.

In fact, to every young person listening tonight who's contemplating their career choice: If you want to make a difference in the life of our nation; if you want to make a difference in the life of a child – become a teacher. Your country needs you.

Of course, the education race doesn't end with a high school diploma. To compete, higher education must be within reach of every American. That's why we've ended the unwarranted taxpayer subsidies that went to banks, and used the savings to make college affordable for millions of students. And this year, I ask Congress to go further, and make permanent our tuition tax credit – worth $10,000 for four years of college.

Because people need to be able to train for new jobs and careers in today's fast-changing economy, we are also revitalizing America's community colleges. Last month, I saw the promise of these schools at Forsyth Tech in North Carolina. Many of the students there used to work in the surrounding factories that have since left town. One mother of two, a woman named Kathy Proctor, had worked in the furniture industry since she was 18 years old. And she told me she's earning her degree in biotechnology now, at 55 years old, not just because the furniture jobs are gone, but because she wants to inspire her children to pursue their dreams too. As Kathy said, "I hope it tells them to never give up."

If we take these steps – if we raise expectations for every child, and give them the best possible chance at an education, from the day they're born until the last job they take – we will reach the goal I set two years ago: by the end of the decade, America will once again have the highest proportion of college graduates in the world.

One last point about education. Today, there are hundreds of thousands of students excelling in our schools who are not American citizens. Some are the children of undocumented workers, who had nothing to do with the actions of their parents. They grew up as Americans and pledge allegiance to our flag, and yet live every day with the threat of deportation. Others come here from abroad to study in our colleges and universities. But as soon as they obtain advanced degrees, we send them back home to compete against us. It makes no sense.

Now, I strongly believe that we should take on, once and for all, the issue of illegal immigration. I am prepared to work with Republicans and Democrats to protect our borders, enforce our laws and address the millions of undocumented workers who are now living in the shadows. I know that debate will be difficult and take time. But tonight, let's agree to make that effort. And let's stop expelling talented, responsible young people who can staff our research labs, start new businesses, and further enrich this nation.

The third step in winning the future is rebuilding America. To attract new businesses to our shores, we need the fastest, most reliable ways to move people, goods, and information – from high-speed rail to high-speed internet.

Our infrastructure used to be the best – but our lead has slipped. South Korean homes now have greater internet access than we do. Countries in Europe and Russia invest more in their roads and railways than we do. China is building faster trains and newer airports. Meanwhile, when our own engineers graded our nation's infrastructure, they gave us a "D."

We have to do better. America is the nation that built the transcontinental railroad, brought electricity to rural communities, and constructed the interstate highway system. The jobs created by these projects didn't just come from laying down tracks or pavement. They came from businesses that opened near a town's new train station or the new off-ramp.

Over the last two years, we have begun rebuilding for the 21st century, a project that has meant thousands of good jobs for the hard-hit construction industry. Tonight, I'm proposing that we redouble these efforts.

We will put more Americans to work repairing crumbling roads and bridges. We will make sure this is fully paid for, attract private investment, and pick projects based on what's best for the economy, not politicians.

Within 25 years, our goal is to give 80% of Americans access to high-speed rail, which could allow you go places in half the time it takes to travel by car. For some trips, it will be faster than flying – without the pat-down. As we speak, routes in California and the Midwest are already underway.

Within the next five years, we will make it possible for business to deploy the next generation of high-speed wireless coverage to 98% of all Americans. This isn't just about a faster internet and fewer dropped calls. It's about connecting every part of America to the digital age. It's about a rural community in Iowa or Alabama where farmers and small business owners will be able to sell their products all over the world. It's about a firefighter who can download the design of a burning building onto a handheld device; a student who can take classes with a digital textbook; or a patient who can have face-to-face video chats with her doctor.

All these investments – in innovation, education, and infrastructure – will make America a better place to do business and create jobs. But to help our companies compete, we also have to knock down barriers that stand in the way of their success.

Over the years, a parade of lobbyists has rigged the tax code to benefit particular companies and industries. Those with accountants or lawyers to work the system can end up paying no taxes at all. But all the rest are hit with one of the highest corporate tax rates in the world. It makes no sense, and it has to change.

So tonight, I'm asking Democrats and Republicans to simplify the system. Get rid of the loopholes. Level the playing field. And use the savings to lower the corporate tax rate for the first time in 25 years – without adding to our deficit.

To help businesses sell more products abroad, we set a goal of doubling our exports by 2014 – because the more we export, the more jobs we create at home. Already, our exports are up. Recently, we signed agreements with India and China that will support more than 250,000 jobs in the United States. And last month, we finalized a trade agreement with South Korea that will support at least 70,000 American jobs. This agreement has unprecedented support from business and labor; Democrats and Republicans, and I ask this Congress to pass it as soon as possible.

Before I took office, I made it clear that we would enforce our trade agreements, and that I would only sign deals that keep faith with American workers, and promote American jobs. That's what we did with Korea, and that's what I intend to do as we pursue agreements with Panama and Colombia, and continue our Asia Pacific and global trade talks.

To reduce barriers to growth and investment, I've ordered a review of government regulations. When we find rules that put an unnecessary burden on businesses, we will fix them. But I will not hesitate to create or enforce commonsense safeguards to protect the American people. That's what we've done in this country for more than a century. It's why our food is safe to eat, our water is safe to drink, and our air is safe to breathe. It's why we have speed limits and child labor laws. It's why last year, we put in place consumer protections against hidden fees and penalties by credit card companies, and new rules to prevent another financial crisis. And it's why we passed reform that finally prevents the health insurance industry from exploiting patients.

Now, I've heard rumors that a few of you have some concerns about the new health care law. So let me be the first to say that anything can be improved. If you have ideas about how to improve this law by making care better or more affordable, I am eager to work with you. We can start right now by correcting a flaw in the legislation that has placed an unnecessary bookkeeping burden on small businesses.

What I'm not willing to do is go back to the days when insurance companies could deny someone coverage because of a pre-existing condition. I'm not willing to tell James Howard, a brain cancer patient from Texas, that his treatment might not be covered. I'm not willing to tell Jim Houser, a small business owner from Oregon, that he has to go back to paying $5,000 more to cover his employees. As we speak, this law is making prescription drugs cheaper for seniors and giving uninsured students a chance to stay on their parents' coverage. So instead of re-fighting the battles of the last two years, let's fix what needs fixing and move forward.

Now, the final step – a critical step – in winning the future is to make sure we aren't buried under a mountain of debt.

We are living with a legacy of deficit-spending that began almost a decade ago. And in the wake of the financial crisis, some of that was necessary to keep credit flowing, save jobs, and put money in people's pockets.

But now that the worst of the recession is over, we have to confront the fact that our government spends more than it takes in. That is not sustainable. Every day, families sacrifice to live within their means. They deserve a government that does the same.

So tonight, I am proposing that starting this year, we freeze annual domestic spending for the next five years. This would reduce the deficit by more than $400 billion over the next decade, and will bring discretionary spending to the lowest share of our economy since Dwight Eisenhower was president.

This freeze will require painful cuts. Already, we have frozen the salaries of hardworking federal employees for the next two years. I've proposed cuts to things I care deeply about, like community action programs. The Secretary of Defense has also agreed to cut tens of billions of dollars in spending that he and his generals believe our military can do without.

I recognize that some in this Chamber have already proposed deeper cuts, and I'm willing to eliminate whatever we can honestly afford to do without. But let's make sure that we're not doing it on the backs of our most vulnerable citizens. And let's make sure what we're cutting is really excess weight. Cutting the deficit by gutting our investments in innovation and education is like lightening an overloaded airplane by removing its engine. It may feel like you're flying high at first, but it won't take long before you'll feel the impact.

Now, most of the cuts and savings I've proposed only address annual domestic spending, which represents a little more than 12% of our budget. To make further progress, we have to stop pretending that cutting this kind of spending alone will be enough. It won't.

The bipartisan Fiscal Commission I created last year made this crystal clear. I don't agree with all their proposals, but they made important progress. And their conclusion is that the only way to tackle our deficit is to cut excessive spending wherever we find it – in domestic spending, defense spending, health care spending, and spending through tax breaks and loopholes.

This means further reducing health care costs, including programs like Medicare and Medicaid, which are the single biggest contributor to our long-term deficit. Health insurance reform will slow these rising costs, which is part of why nonpartisan economists have said that repealing the health care law would add a quarter of a trillion dollars to our deficit. Still, I'm willing to look at other ideas to bring down costs, including one that Republicans suggested last year: medical malpractice reform to rein in frivolous lawsuits.

To put us on solid ground, we should also find a bipartisan solution to strengthen Social Security for future generations. And we must do it without putting at risk current retirees, the most vulnerable, or people with disabilities; without slashing benefits for future generations; and without subjecting Americans' guaranteed retirement income to the whims of the stock market.

And if we truly care about our deficit, we simply cannot afford a permanent extension of the tax cuts for the wealthiest 2% of Americans. Before we take money away from our schools, or scholarships away from our students, we should ask millionaires to give up their tax break.

It's not a matter of punishing their success. It's about promoting America's success.

In fact, the best thing we could do on taxes for all Americans is to simplify the individual tax code. This will be a tough job, but members of both parties have expressed interest in doing this, and I am prepared to join them.

So now is the time to act. Now is the time for both sides and both houses of Congress – Democrats and Republicans – to forge a principled compromise that gets the job done. If we make the hard choices now to rein in our deficits, we can make the investments we need to win the future.

Let me take this one step further. We shouldn't just give our people a government that's more affordable. We should give them a government that's more competent and efficient. We cannot win the future with a government of the past.

We live and do business in the information age, but the last major reorganization of the government happened in the age of black and white TV. There are twelve different agencies that deal with exports. There are at least five different entities that deal with housing policy. Then there's my favorite example: the Interior Department is in charge of salmon while they're in fresh water, but the Commerce Department handles them in when they're in saltwater. And I hear it gets even more complicated once they're smoked.

Now, we have made great strides over the last two years in using technology and getting rid of waste. Veterans can now download their electronic medical records with a click of the mouse. We're selling acres of federal office space that hasn't been used in years, and we will cut through red tape to get rid of more. But we need to think bigger. In the coming months, my administration will develop a proposal to merge, consolidate, and reorganize the federal government in a way that best serves the goal of a more competitive America. I will submit that proposal to Congress for a vote – and we will push to get it passed.

In the coming year, we will also work to rebuild people's faith in the institution of government. Because you deserve to know exactly how and where your tax dollars are being spent, you will be able to go to a website and get that information for the very first time in history. Because you deserve to know when your elected officials are meeting with lobbyists, I ask Congress to do what the White House has already done: put that information online. And because the American people deserve to know that special interests aren't larding up legislation with pet projects, both parties in Congress should know this: if a bill comes to my desk with earmarks inside, I will veto it.

A 21st century government that's open and competent. A government that lives within its means. An economy that's driven by new skills and ideas. Our success in this new and changing world will require reform, responsibility, and innovation. It will also require us to approach that world with a new level of engagement in our foreign affairs.

Just as jobs and businesses can now race across borders, so can new threats and new challenges. No single wall separates East and West; no one rival superpower is aligned against us.

And so we must defeat determined enemies wherever they are, and build coalitions that cut across lines of region and race and religion. America's moral example must always shine for all who yearn for freedom, justice, and dignity. And because we have begun this work, tonight we can say that American leadership has been renewed and America's standing has been restored.

Look to Iraq, where nearly 100,000 of our brave men and women have left with their heads held high; where American combat patrols have ended; violence has come down; and a new government has been formed. This year, our civilians will forge a lasting partnership with the Iraqi people, while we finish the job of bringing our troops out of Iraq. America's commitment has been kept; the Iraq War is coming to an end.

Of course, as we speak, al Qaeda and their affiliates continue to plan attacks against us. Thanks to our intelligence and law enforcement professionals, we are disrupting plots and securing our cities and skies. And as extremists try to inspire acts of violence within our borders, we are responding with the strength of our communities, with respect for the rule of law, and with the conviction that American Muslims are a part of our American family.

We have also taken the fight to al Qaeda and their allies abroad. In Afghanistan, our troops have taken Taliban strongholds and trained Afghan Security Forces. Our purpose is clear – by preventing the Taliban from reestablishing a stranglehold over the Afghan people, we will deny al Qaeda the safe-haven that served as a launching pad for 9/11.

Thanks to our heroic troops and civilians, fewer Afghans are under the control of the insurgency. There will be tough fighting ahead, and the Afghan government will need to deliver better governance. But we are strengthening the capacity of the Afghan people and building an enduring partnership with them. This year, we will work with nearly 50 countries to begin a transition to an Afghan lead. And this July, we will begin to bring our troops home.

In Pakistan, al Qaeda's leadership is under more pressure than at any point since 2001. Their leaders and operatives are being removed from the battlefield. Their safe-havens are shrinking. And we have sent a message from the Afghan border to the Arabian Peninsula to all parts of the globe: we will not relent, we will not waver, and we will defeat you.

American leadership can also be seen in the effort to secure the worst weapons of war. Because Republicans and Democrats approved the New START Treaty, far fewer nuclear weapons and launchers will be deployed. Because we rallied the world, nuclear materials are being locked down on every continent so they never fall into the hands of terrorists.

Because of a diplomatic effort to insist that Iran meet its obligations, the Iranian government now faces tougher and tighter sanctions than ever before. And on the Korean peninsula, we stand with our ally South Korea, and insist that North Korea keeps its commitment to abandon nuclear weapons.

This is just a part of how we are shaping a world that favors peace and prosperity. With our European allies, we revitalized NATO, and increased our cooperation on everything from counter-terrorism to missile defense. We have reset our relationship with Russia, strengthened Asian alliances, and built new partnerships with nations like India. This March, I will travel to Brazil, Chile, and El Salvador to forge new alliances for progress in the Americas. Around the globe, we are standing with those who take responsibility – helping farmers grow more food; supporting doctors who care for the sick; and combating the corruption that can rot a society and rob people of opportunity.

Recent events have shown us that what sets us apart must not just be our power – it must be the purpose behind it. In South Sudan – with our assistance – the people were finally able to vote for independence after years of war. Thousands lined up before dawn. People danced in the streets. One man who lost four of his brothers at war summed up the scene around him: "This was a battlefield for most of my life. Now we want to be free."

We saw that same desire to be free in Tunisia, where the will of the people proved more powerful than the writ of a dictator. And tonight, let us be clear: the United States of America stands with the people of Tunisia, and supports the democratic aspirations of all people.

We must never forget that the things we've struggled for, and fought for, live in the hearts of people everywhere. And we must always remember that the Americans who have borne the greatest burden in this struggle are the men and women who serve our country.

Tonight, let us speak with one voice in reaffirming that our nation is united in support of our troops and their families. Let us serve them as well as they have served us – by giving them the equipment they need; by providing them with the care and benefits they have earned; and by enlisting our veterans in the great task of building our own nation.

Our troops come from every corner of this country – they are black, white, Latino, Asian and Native American. They are Christian and Hindu, Jewish and Muslim. And, yes, we know that some of them are gay. Starting this year, no American will be forbidden from serving the country they love because of who they love. And with that change, I call on all of our college campuses to open their doors to our military recruiters and the ROTC. It is time to leave behind the divisive battles of the past. It is time to move forward as one nation.

We should have no illusions about the work ahead of us. Reforming our schools; changing the way we use energy; reducing our deficit – none of this is easy. All of it will take time. And it will be harder because we will argue about everything. The cost. The details. The letter of every law.

Of course, some countries don't have this problem. If the central government wants a railroad, they get a railroad – no matter how many homes are bulldozed. If they don't want a bad story in the newspaper, it doesn't get written.

And yet, as contentious and frustrating and messy as our democracy can sometimes be, I know there isn't a person here who would trade places with any other nation on Earth.

We may have differences in policy, but we all believe in the rights enshrined in our Constitution. We may have different opinions, but we believe in the same promise that says this is a place where you can make it if you try. We may have different backgrounds, but we believe in the same dream that says this is a country where anything's possible. No matter who you are. No matter where you come from.

That dream is why I can stand here before you tonight. That dream is why a working class kid from Scranton can stand behind me. That dream is why someone who began by sweeping the floors of his father's Cincinnati bar can preside as Speaker of the House in the greatest nation on Earth.

That dream – that American Dream – is what drove the Allen Brothers to reinvent their roofing company for a new era. It's what drove those students at Forsyth Tech to learn a new skill and work towards the future. And that dream is the story of a small business owner named Brandon Fisher.

Brandon started a company in Berlin, Pennsylvania that specializes in a new kind of drilling technology. One day last summer, he saw the news that halfway across the world, 33 men were trapped in a Chilean mine, and no one knew how to save them.

But Brandon thought his company could help. And so he designed a rescue that would come to be known as Plan B. His employees worked around the clock to manufacture the necessary drilling equipment. And Brandon left for Chile.

Along with others, he began drilling a 2,000 foot hole into the ground, working three or four days at a time with no sleep. Thirty-seven days later, Plan B succeeded, and the miners were rescued. But because he didn't want all of the attention, Brandon wasn't there when the miners emerged. He had already gone home, back to work on his next project.

Later, one of his employees said of the rescue, "We proved that Center Rock is a little company, but we do big things."

We do big things.

From the earliest days of our founding, America has been the story of ordinary people who dare to dream. That's how we win the future.

We are a nation that says, "I might not have a lot of money, but I have this great idea for a new company. I might not come from a family of college graduates, but I will be the first to get my degree. I might not know those people in trouble, but I think I can help them, and I need to try. I'm not sure how we'll reach that better place beyond the horizon, but I know we'll get there. I know we will."

We do big things.

The idea of America endures. Our destiny remains our choice. And tonight, more than two centuries later, it is because of our people that our future is hopeful, our journey goes forward, and the state of our union is strong.

Thank you, God Bless You, and may God Bless the United States of America.

1.5   Barack Obama's Fourth State of the Union Address

Thank you, thank you. Everybody, please be seated. Mr. Speaker, Mr. Vice President, members of Congress, distinguished guests, and fellow Americans:

Last month, I went to Andrews Air Force Base and welcomed home some of our last troops to serve in Iraq. Together, we offered a final, proud salute to the colors under which more than a million of our fellow citizens fought, and several thousand gave their lives. We gather tonight knowing that this generation of heroes has made the United States safer and more respected around the world.

For the first time in nine years, there are no Americans fighting in Iraq. For the first time in two decades, Osama bin Laden is not a threat to this country. Most of al-Qaeda's top lieutenants have been defeated. The Taliban's momentum has been broken, and some troops in Afghanistan have begun to come home. These achievements are a testament to the courage, selflessness, and teamwork of America's Armed Forces. At a time when too many of our institutions have let us down, they exceed all expectations. They're not consumed with personal ambition. They don't obsess over their differences. They focus on the mission at hand. They work together. Imagine what we could accomplish if we followed their example.

Think about the America within our reach: a country that leads the world in educating its people. An America that attracts a new generation of high-tech manufacturing and high-paying jobs. A future where we're in control of our own energy, and our security and prosperity aren't so tied to unstable parts of the world. An economy built to last, where hard work pays off, and responsibility is rewarded. We can do this. I know we can, because we've done it before. At the end of World War II, when another generation of heroes returned home from combat, they built the strongest economy and middle class the world has ever known.

My grandfather, a veteran of Patton's Army, got the chance to go to college on the G.I. Bill. My grandmother, who worked on a bomber assembly line, was part of a workforce that turned out the best products on Earth. The two of them shared the optimism of a nation that had triumphed over a depression and fascism. They understood they were part of something larger; that they were contributing to a story of success that every American had a chance to share – the basic

American promise that if you worked hard, you could do well enough to raise a family, own a home, send your kids to college, and put a little away for retirement.

The defining issue of our time is how to keep that promise alive. No challenge is more urgent. No debate is more important. We can either settle for a country where a shrinking number of people do really well, while a growing number of Americans barely get by, or we can restore an economy where everyone gets a fair shot, and everyone does their fair share, and everyone plays by the same set of rules.

What's at stake aren't Democratic values or Republican values, but American values. And we have to reclaim them. Let's remember how we got here. Long before the recession, jobs and manufacturing began leaving our shores. Technology made businesses more efficient, but also made some jobs obsolete. Folks at the top saw their incomes rise like never before, but most hardworking Americans struggled with costs that were growing, paychecks that weren't, and personal debt that kept piling up.

In 2008, the house of cards collapsed. We learned that mortgages had been sold to people who couldn't afford or understand them. Banks had made huge bets and bonuses with other people's money. Regulators had looked the other way, or didn't have the authority to stop the bad behavior. It was wrong. It was irresponsible. And it plunged our economy into a crisis that put millions out of work, saddled us with more debt, and left innocent, hard-working Americans holding the bag. In the six months before I took office, we lost nearly four million jobs, and we lost another four million before our policies were in full effect. Those are the facts. But so are these. In the last 22 months, businesses have created more than three million jobs.

Last year, they created the most jobs since 2005. American manufacturers are hiring again, creating jobs for the first time since the late-1990s. Together, we've agreed to cut the deficit by more than two-trillion dollars. And we've put in place new rules to hold Wall Street accountable, so a crisis like this never happens again.

The state of our Union is getting stronger, and we've come too far to turn back now. As long as I'm President, I will work with anyone in this chamber to build on this momentum. But I intend to fight obstruction with action, and I will oppose any effort to return to the very same policies that brought on this economic crisis in the first place.

No. We will not go back to an economy weakened by outsourcing, bad debt, and phony financial profits. Tonight, I want to speak about how we move forward, and lay out a blueprint for an economy that's built to last. An economy built on American manufacturing, American energy, skills for American workers, and a renewal of American values.

Now, this blueprint begins with American manufacturing. On the day I took office, our auto industry was on the verge of collapse. Some even said we should let it die. With a million jobs at stake, I refused to let that happen. In exchange for help, we demanded responsibility. We got workers and automakers to settle their differences. We got the industry to retool and restructure. Today, General Motors is back on top as the world's number one automaker.

Chrysler has grown faster in the U.S. than any major car company. Ford is investing billions in U.S. plants and factories. And together, the entire industry added nearly 160,000 jobs. We bet on American workers. We bet on American ingenuity. And tonight, the American auto industry is back.

What's happening in Detroit can happen in other industries. It can happen in Cleveland and Pittsburgh and Raleigh. We can't bring back every job that's left our shores. But right now, it's getting more expensive to do business in places like China. Meanwhile, America is more productive. A few weeks ago, the CEO of Master Lock told me that it now makes business sense for him to bring jobs back home. Today, for the first time in fifteen years, Master Lock's unionized plant in Milwaukee is running at full capacity.

So we have a huge opportunity, at this moment, to bring manufacturing back. But we have to seize it. Tonight, my message to business leaders is simple: ask yourselves what you can do to bring jobs back to your country, and your country will do everything we can to help you succeed.

We should start with our tax code. Right now, companies get tax breaks for moving jobs and profits overseas. Meanwhile, companies that choose to stay in America get hit with one of the highest tax rates in the world. It makes no sense, and everyone knows it.

So let's change it. First, if you're a business that wants to outsource jobs, you shouldn't get a tax deduction for doing it. That money should be used to cover moving expenses for companies like Master Lock that decide to bring jobs home.

Second, no American company should be able to avoid paying its fair share of taxes by moving jobs and profits overseas.

From now on, every multinational company should have to pay a basic minimum tax. And every penny should go towards lowering taxes for companies that choose to stay here and hire here.

Third, if you're an American manufacturer, you should get a bigger tax cut. If you're a high-tech manufacturer, we should double the tax deduction you get for making products here. And if you want to relocate in a community that was hit hard when a factory left town, you should get help financing a new plant, equipment, or training for new workers.

My message is simple. It's time to stop rewarding businesses that ship jobs overseas, and start rewarding companies that create jobs right here in America. Send me these tax reforms, and I'll sign them right away.

We're also making it easier for American businesses to sell products all over the world. Two years ago, I set a goal of doubling U.S. exports over five years. With the bipartisan trade agreements I signed into law, we are on track to meet that goal ahead of schedule. Soon, there will be millions of new customers for American goods in Panama, Colombia, and South Korea. Soon, there will be new cars on the streets of Seoul imported from Detroit, and Toledo, and Chicago.

I will go anywhere in the world to open new markets for American products. And I will not stand by when our competitors don't play by the rules. We've brought trade cases against China at nearly twice the rate as the last administration, and it's made a difference. Over a thousand Americans are working today because we stopped a surge in Chinese tires. But we need to do more. It's not right when another country lets our movies, music, and software be pirated. It's not fair when foreign manufacturers have a leg up on ours only because they're heavily subsidized.

Tonight, I'm announcing the creation of a Trade Enforcement Unit that will be charged with investigating unfair trade practices in countries like China. There will be more inspections to prevent counterfeit or unsafe goods from crossing our borders. And this Congress should make sure that no foreign company has an advantage over American manufacturing when it comes to accessing finance or new markets like Russia. Our workers are the most productive on Earth, and if the playing field is level, I promise you: America will always win.

I also hear from many business leaders who want to hire in the United States but can't find workers with the right skills. Growing industries in science and technology have twice as many openings as we have workers who can do the job. Think about that: openings at a time when millions of Americans are looking for work.

That's inexcusable. And we know how to fix it.

Jackie Bray is a single mom from North Carolina who was laid off from her job as a mechanic. Then Siemens opened a gas turbine factory in Charlotte, and formed a partnership with Central Piedmont Community College. The company helped the college design courses in laser and robotics training. It paid Jackie's tuition, then hired her to help operate their plant.[1]

I want every American looking for work to have the same opportunity as Jackie did. Join me in a national commitment to train two million Americans with skills that will lead directly to a job. My Administration has already lined up more companies that want to help. Model partnerships between businesses like Siemens and community colleges in places like Charlotte, Orlando, and Louisville are up and running. Now you need to give more community colleges the resources they need to become community career centers: places that teach people skills that local businesses are looking for right now, from data management to high-tech manufacturing.

And I want to cut through the maze of confusing training programs, so that from now on, people like Jackie have one program, one website, and one place to go for all the information and help they need. It's time to turn our unemployment system into a reemployment system that puts people to work.

These reforms will help people get jobs that are open today. But to prepare for the jobs of tomorrow, our commitment to skills and education has to start earlier. For less than one-percent of what our Nation spends on education each year, we've convinced nearly every State in the country to raise their standards for teaching and learning – the first time that's happened in a generation. But challenges remain. And we know how to solve them.

At a time when other countries are doubling down on education, tight budgets have forced States to lay off thousands of teachers. We know a good teacher can increase the lifetime income of a classroom by over $250,000. A great teacher can offer an escape from poverty to the child who dreams beyond his circumstance. Every person in this chamber can point to a teacher who changed the trajectory of their lives. Most teachers work tirelessly, with modest pay, sometimes digging into their own pocket for school supplies, just to make a difference.

Teachers matter. So instead of bashing them, or defending the *status quo*, let's offer schools a deal. Give them the resources to keep good teachers on the job, and reward the best ones. In return, grant schools flexibility: to teach with creativity and passion; to stop teaching to the test; and to replace teachers who just aren't helping kids learn. That's a bargain worth making.

We also know that when students aren't allowed to walk away from their education, more of them walk the stage to get their diploma. When students are not allowed to drop out, they do better. So tonight, I call on every State to require that all students stay in high school until they graduate or turn eighteen.

When kids do graduate, the most daunting challenge can be the cost of college. At a time when Americans owe more in tuition debt than credit card debt, this Congress needs to stop the interest rates on student loans from doubling in July. Extend the tuition tax credit we started that saves middle-class families thousands of dollars. And give more young people the chance to earn their way through college by doubling the number of work-study jobs in the next five years.

Of course, it's not enough for us to increase student aid. We can't just keep subsidizing skyrocketing tuition; we'll run out of money. States also need to do their part, by making higher education a higher priority in their budgets. And colleges and universities have to do their part by working to keep costs down. Recently, I spoke with a group of college presidents who've done just that. Some schools re-design courses to help students finish more quickly. Some use better technology. The point is, it's possible. So let me put colleges and universities on notice: if you can't stop tuition from going up, the funding you get from taxpayers will go down. Higher education can't be a luxury. It's an economic imperative that every family in America should be able to afford.

Let's also remember that hundreds of thousands of talented, hardworking students in this country face another challenge: the fact that they aren't yet American citizens. Many were brought here as small children, are American through and through, yet they live every day with the threat of deportation. Others came more recently, to study business and science and engineering, but as soon as they get their degree, we send them home to invent new products and create new jobs somewhere else.

That doesn't make sense.

I believe as strongly as ever that we should take on illegal immigration. That's why my Administration has put more boots on the border than ever before. That's why there are fewer illegal crossings than when I took office.

The opponents of action are out of excuses. We should be working on comprehensive immigration reform right now. But if election-year politics keeps Congress from acting on a comprehensive plan, let's at least agree to stop expelling responsible young people who want to staff our labs, start new businesses, and defend this country. Send me a law that gives them the chance to earn their citizenship. I will sign it right away.

You see, an economy built to last is one where we encourage the talent and ingenuity of every person in this country. That means women should earn equal pay for equal work. It means we should support everyone who's willing to work; and every risk-taker and entrepreneur who aspires to become the next Steve Jobs.

After all, innovation is what America has always been about. Most new jobs are created in start-ups and small businesses. So let's pass an agenda that helps them succeed. Tear down regulations that prevent aspiring entrepreneurs from getting the financing to grow. Expand tax relief to small businesses that are raising wages and creating good jobs. Both parties agree on these ideas. So put them in a bill, and get it on my desk this year.

Innovation also demands basic research. Today, the discoveries taking place in our federally-financed labs and universities could lead to new treatments that kill cancer cells but leave healthy ones untouched. New lightweight vests for cops and soldiers that can stop any bullet. Don't gut these investments in our budget. Don't let other countries win the race for the future. Support the same kind of research and innovation that led to the computer chip and the Internet; to new American jobs and new American industries.

Nowhere is the promise of innovation greater than in American-made energy. Over the last three years, we've opened millions of new acres for oil and gas exploration, and tonight, I'm directing my Administration to open more than 75% of our potential offshore oil and gas resources. Right now, American oil production is the highest that it's been in eight years. That's right: eight years. Not only that: last year, we relied less on foreign oil than in any of the past sixteen years.

But with only two-percent of the world's oil reserves, oil isn't enough. This country needs an all-out, all-of-the-above strategy that develops every available source of American energy, a strategy that's cleaner, cheaper, and full of new jobs.

We have a supply of natural gas that can last America nearly one hundred years, and my Administration will take every possible action to safely develop this energy. Experts believe this will support more than 600,000 jobs by the end of the decade. And I'm requiring all companies that drill for gas on public lands to disclose the chemicals they use. America will develop this resource without putting the health and safety of our citizens at risk.

The development of natural gas will create jobs and power trucks and factories that are cleaner and cheaper, proving that we don't have to choose between our environment and our economy. And by the way, it was public research dollars, over the course of thirty years, that helped develop the technologies to extract all this natural gas out of shale rock, reminding us that Government support is critical in helping businesses get new energy ideas off the ground.

What's true for natural gas is true for clean energy. In three years, our partnership with the private sector has already positioned America to be the world's leading manufacturer of high-tech batteries. Because of federal investments, renewable energy use has nearly doubled. And thousands of Americans have jobs because of it.

When Bryan Ritterby was laid off from his job making furniture, he said he worried that at 55, no one would give him a second chance. But he found work at Energetx, a wind turbine manufacturer in Michigan. Before the recession, the factory only made luxury yachts. Today, it's hiring workers like Bryan, who said, "I'm proud to be working in the industry of the future."[2]

Our experience with shale gas shows us that the payoffs on these public investments don't always come right away. Some technologies don't pan out; some companies fail. But I will not walk away from the promise of clean energy. I will not walk away from workers like Bryan. I will not cede the wind or solar or battery industry to China or Germany because we refuse to make the same commitment here. We have subsidized oil companies for a century. That's long enough. It's time to end the taxpayer giveaways to an industry that's rarely been more profitable, and double-down on a clean energy industry that's never been more promising. Pass clean energy tax credits and create these jobs.

We can also spur energy innovation with new incentives. The differences in this chamber may be too deep right now to pass a comprehensive plan to fight climate change. But there's no reason why Congress shouldn't at least set a clean energy standard that creates a market for innovation. So far, you haven't acted. Well tonight, I will. I'm directing my Administration to allow the development of clean energy on enough public land to power three million homes. And I'm proud to announce that the Department of Defense, the world's largest consumer of energy, will make one of the largest commitments to clean energy in history, with the Navy purchasing enough capacity to power a quarter of a million homes a year.

Of course, the easiest way to save money is to waste less energy. So here's another proposal: help manufacturers eliminate energy waste in their factories and give businesses incentives to upgrade their buildings. Their energy bills will be $100 billion lower over the next decade, and America will have less pollution, more manufacturing, and more jobs for construction workers who need them. Send me a bill that creates these jobs.

Building this new energy future should be just one part of a broader agenda to repair America's infrastructure. So much of America needs to be rebuilt. We've got crumbling roads and bridges. A power grid that wastes too much energy. An incomplete high-speed broadband network that prevents a small business owner in rural America from selling her products all over the world.

During the Great Depression, America built the Hoover Dam and the Golden Gate Bridge. After World War II, we connected our States with a system of highways. Democratic and Republican administrations invested in great projects that benefited everybody, from the workers who built them to the businesses that still use them today.

In the next few weeks, I will sign an executive order clearing away the red tape that slows down too many construction projects. But you need to fund these projects. Take the money we're no longer spending at war, use half of it to pay down our debt, and use the rest to do some nation-building right here at home.

There's never been a better time to build, especially since the construction industry was one of the hardest-hit when the housing bubble burst. Of course, construction workers weren't the only ones hurt. So were millions of innocent Americans who've seen their home values decline. And while Government can't fix the problem on its own, responsible homeowners shouldn't have to sit and wait for the housing market to hit bottom to get some relief.

That's why I'm sending this Congress a plan that gives every responsible homeowner the chance to save about $3,000 a year on their mortgage, by refinancing at historically low interest rates. No more red tape. No more runaround from the banks. A small fee on the largest financial institutions will ensure that it won't add to the deficit, and will give banks that were rescued by taxpayers a chance to repay a deficit of trust.

Let's never forget: millions of Americans who work hard and play by the rules every day deserve a Government and a financial system that do the same. It's time to apply the same rules from top to bottom: no bailouts, no handouts, and no copouts. An America built to last insists on responsibility from everybody.

We've all paid the price for lenders who sold mortgages to people who couldn't afford them, and buyers who knew they couldn't afford them. That's why we need smart regulations to prevent irresponsible behavior. Rules to prevent financial fraud or toxic dumping or faulty medical devices don't destroy the free market. They make the free market work better.

There is no question that some regulations are outdated, unnecessary, or too costly. In fact, I've approved fewer regulations in the first three years of my presidency than my Republican predecessor did in his. I've ordered every federal agency to eliminate rules that don't make sense. We've already announced over 500 reforms, and just a fraction of them will save business and citizens more than ten-billion dollars over the next five years. We got rid of one rule from forty years ago that could have forced some dairy farmers to spend $10,000 a year proving that they could contain a spill, because milk was somehow classified as an oil. With a rule like that, I guess it was worth crying over spilled milk.

I'm confident a farmer can contain a milk spill without a federal agency looking over his shoulder. But I will not back down from making sure an oil company can contain the kind of oil spill we saw in the Gulf two years ago. I will not back down from protecting our kids from mercury pollution, or making sure that our food is safe and our water is clean. I will not go back to the days when health insurance companies had unchecked power to cancel your policy, deny you coverage, or charge women differently from men.

And I will not go back to the days when Wall Street was allowed to play by its own set of rules. The new rules we passed restore what should be any financial system's core purpose: getting funding to entrepreneurs with the best ideas, and getting loans to responsible families who want to buy a home, start a business, or send a kid to college.

So if you're a big bank or financial institution, you are no longer allowed to make risky bets with your customers' deposits. You're required to write out a "living will" that details exactly how you'll pay the bills if you fail, because the rest of us aren't bailing you out ever again. And if you're a mortgage lender or a payday lender or a credit card company, the days of signing people up for products they can't afford with confusing forms and deceptive practices are over. Today, American consumers finally have a watchdog in Richard Cordray with one job: to look out for them.

We will also establish a Financial Crimes Unit of highly trained investigators to crack down on large-scale fraud and protect people's investments. Some financial firms violate major anti-fraud laws because there's no real penalty for being a repeat offender. That's bad for consumers, and it's bad for the vast majority of bankers and financial service professionals who do the right thing. So pass legislation that makes the penalties for fraud count.

And tonight, I am asking my Attorney General to create a special unit of federal prosecutors and leading state attorneys general to expand our investigations into the abusive lending and packaging of risky mortgages that led to the housing crisis. This new unit will hold accountable those who broke the law, speed assistance to homeowners, and help turn the page on an era of recklessness that hurt so many Americans.

A return to the American values of fair play and shared responsibility will help us protect our people and our economy. But it should also guide us as we look to pay down our debt and invest in our future. Right now, our most immediate priority is stopping a tax hike on 160-million working Americans while the recovery is still fragile. People cannot afford losing $40 out of each paycheck this year. There are plenty of ways to get this done. So let's agree right here, right now: no side issues. No drama. Pass the payroll tax cut without delay.

When it comes to the deficit, we've already agreed to more than two-trillion dollars in cuts and savings. But we need to do more, and that means making choices. Right now, we're poised to spend nearly a trillion dollars more on what was supposed to be a temporary tax break for the wealthiest two-percent of Americans. Right now, because of loopholes and shelters in the tax code, a quarter of all millionaires pay lower tax rates than millions of middle-class households. Right now, Warren Buffett pays a lower tax rate than his secretary.

Do we want to keep these tax cuts for the wealthiest Americans? Or do we want to keep our investments in everything else, like education and medical research, a strong military, and care for our veterans? Because if we're serious about paying down our debt, we can't do both.

The American people know what the right choice is. So do I. As I told the Speaker this summer, I'm prepared to make more reforms that rein in the long term costs of Medicare and Medicaid, and strengthen Social Security, so long as those programs remain a guarantee of security for seniors.

But in return, we need to change our tax code so that people like me, and an awful lot of Members of Congress, pay our fair share of taxes. Tax reform should follow the Buffett rule: if you make more than a million dollars a year, you should not pay less than 30% in taxes. And my Republican friend Tom Coburn is right: Washington should stop subsidizing millionaires. In fact, if you're earning a million dollars a year, you shouldn't get special tax subsidies or deductions. On the other hand, if you make under $250,000 a year, like 98% of American families, your taxes shouldn't go up. You're the ones struggling with rising costs and stagnant wages. You're the ones who need relief.

Now, you can call this class warfare all you want. But asking a billionaire to pay at least as much as his secretary in taxes? Most Americans would call that common sense.

We don't begrudge financial success in this country. We admire it. When Americans talk about folks like me paying my fair share of taxes, it's not because they envy the rich. It's because they understand that when I get tax breaks I don't need and the country can't afford, it either adds to the deficit, or somebody else has to make up the difference – like a senior on a fixed income; or a student trying to get through school; or a family trying to make ends meet. That's not right. Americans know it's not right. They know that this generation's success is only possible because past generations felt a responsibility to each other, and to their country's future, and they know our way of life will only endure if we feel that same sense of shared responsibility. That's how we'll reduce our deficit. That's an America built to last.

I recognize that people watching tonight have differing views about taxes and debt; energy and health care. But no matter what party they belong to, I bet most Americans are thinking the same thing right now: nothing will get done this year, or next year, or maybe even the year after that, because Washington is broken. Can you blame them for feeling a little cynical?

The greatest blow to confidence in our economy last year didn't come from events beyond our control. It came from a debate in Washington over whether the United States would pay its bills or not. Who benefited from that fiasco?

I've talked tonight about the deficit of trust between Main Street and Wall Street. But the divide between this city and the rest of the country is at least as bad, and it seems to get worse every year.

Some of this has to do with the corrosive influence of money in politics. So together, let's take some steps to fix that. Send me a bill that bans insider trading by Members of Congress, and I will sign it tomorrow. Let's limit any elected official from owning stocks in industries they impact. Let's make sure people who bundle campaign contributions for Congress can't lobby Congress, and vice versa, an idea that has bipartisan support, at least outside of Washington.

Some of what's broken has to do with the way Congress does its business these days. A simple majority is no longer enough to get anything, even routine business, passed through the Senate. Neither party has been blameless in these tactics. Now both parties should put an end to it. For starters, I ask the Senate to pass a rule that all judicial and public service nominations receive a simple up or down vote within 90 days.

The executive branch also needs to change. Too often, it's inefficient, outdated and remote. That's why I've asked this Congress to grant me the authority to consolidate the federal bureaucracy so that our Government is leaner, quicker, and more responsive to the needs of the American people.

Finally, none of these reforms can happen unless we also lower the temperature in this town. We need to end the notion that the two parties must be locked in a perpetual campaign of mutual destruction; that politics is about clinging to rigid ideologies instead of building consensus around common sense ideas.

I'm a Democrat. But I believe what Republican Abraham Lincoln believed: that Government should do for people only what they cannot do better by themselves, and no more. That's why my education reform offers more competition, and more control for schools and States. That's why we're getting rid of regulations that don't work. That's why our health care law relies on a reformed private market, not a Government program.

On the other hand, even my Republican friends who complain the most about Government spending have supported federally-financed roads, and clean energy projects, and federal offices for the folks back home.

The point is, we should all want a smarter, more effective Government. And while we may not be able to bridge our biggest philosophical differences this year, we can make real progress. With or without this Congress, I will keep taking actions that help the economy grow. But I can do a whole lot more with your help. Because when we act together, there is nothing the United States of America can't achieve.

That is the lesson we've learned from our actions abroad over the last few years. Ending the Iraq War has allowed us to strike decisive blows against our enemies. From Pakistan to Yemen, the al-Qaeda operatives who remain are scrambling, knowing that they can't escape the reach of the United States of America.

From this position of strength, we've begun to wind down the War in Afghanistan. Ten thousand of our troops have come home. Twenty-three thousand more will leave by the end of this summer. This transition to Afghan lead will continue, and we will build an enduring partnership with Afghanistan, so that it is never again a source of attacks against America.

As the tide of war recedes, a wave of change has washed across the Middle East and North Africa, from Tunis to Cairo; from Sana'a to Tripoli. A year ago, Gaddafi was one of the world's longest-serving dictators, a murderer with American blood on his hands. Today, he is gone. And in Syria, I have no doubt that the Assad regime will soon discover that the forces of change can't be reversed, and that human dignity can't be denied.

How this incredible transformation will end remains uncertain. But we have a huge stake in the outcome. And while it is ultimately up to the people of the region to decide their fate, we will advocate for those values that have served our own country so well. We will stand against violence and intimidation. We will stand for the rights and dignity of all human beings; men and women; Christians, Muslims, and Jews. We will support policies that lead to strong and stable democracies and open markets, because tyranny is no match for liberty.

And we will safeguard America's own security against those who threaten our citizens, our friends, and our interests. Look at Iran. Through the power of our diplomacy, a world that was once divided about how to deal with Iran's nuclear program now stands as one. The regime is more isolated than ever before; its leaders are faced with crippling sanctions, and as long as they shirk their responsibilities, this pressure will not relent. Let there be no doubt: America is determined to prevent Iran from getting a nuclear weapon, and I will take no options off the table to achieve that goal. But a peaceful resolution to this issue is still possible, and far better, and if Iran changes course and meets its obligations, it can rejoin the community of nations.

The renewal of American leadership can be felt across the globe. Our oldest alliances in Europe and Asia are stronger than ever. Our ties to the Americas are deeper. Our iron-clad commitment — and I mean ironclad — to Israel's security has meant the closest military cooperation between our two countries in history. We've made it clear that America is a Pacific power, and a new beginning in Burma has lit a new hope. From the coalitions we've built to secure nuclear materials, to the missions we've led against hunger and disease; from the blows we've dealt to our enemies, to the enduring power of our moral example: America is back.

Anyone who tells you otherwise, anyone who tells you that America is in decline or that our influence has waned, doesn't know what they're talking about. That's not the message we get from leaders around the world, all of whom are eager to work with us. That's not how people feel from Tokyo to Berlin; from Cape Town to Rio; where opinions of America are higher than they've been in years. Yes, the world is changing; no, we can't control every event. But America remains the one indispensable nation in world affairs, and as long as I'm President, I intend to keep it that way.

That's why, working with our military leaders, I have proposed a new defense strategy that ensures we maintain the finest military in the world, while saving nearly half a trillion dollars in our budget. To stay one step ahead of our adversaries, I have already sent this Congress legislation that will secure our country from the growing danger of cyber-threats.

Above all, our freedom endures because of the men and women in uniform who defend it. As they come home, we must serve them as well as they served us. That includes giving them the care and benefits they have earned, which is why we've increased annual VA spending every year I've been President. And it means enlisting our veterans in the work of rebuilding our Nation.

With the bipartisan support of this Congress, we are providing new tax credits to companies that hire vets. Michelle and Jill Biden have worked with American businesses to secure a pledge of 135,000 jobs for veterans and their families. And tonight, I'm proposing a Veterans Job Corps that will help our communities hire veterans as cops and firefighters, so that America is as strong as those who defend her.

Which brings me back to where I began. Those of us who've been sent here to serve can learn from the service of our troops. When you put on that uniform, it doesn't matter if you're black or white; Asian or Latino; conservative or liberal; rich or poor; gay or straight. When you're marching into battle, you look out for the person next to you, or the mission fails. When you're in the thick of the fight, you rise or fall as one unit, serving one Nation, leaving no one behind.

One of my proudest possessions is the flag that the SEAL Team took with them on the mission to get bin Laden. On it are each of their names. Some may be Democrats. Some may be Republicans. But that doesn't matter. Just like it didn't matter that day in the Situation Room, when I sat next to Bob Gates, a man who was George Bush's defense secretary; and Hillary Clinton, a woman who ran against me for president.

All that mattered that day was the mission. No one thought about politics. No one thought about themselves. One of the young men involved in the raid later told me that he didn't deserve credit for the mission. It only succeeded, he said, because every single member of that unit did their job: the pilot who landed the helicopter that spun out of control; the translator who kept others from entering the compound; the troops who separated the women and children from the fight; the SEALs who charged up the stairs. More than that, the mission only succeeded because every member of that unit trusted each other. Because you can't charge up those stairs, into darkness and danger, unless you know that there's someone behind you, watching your back.

So it is with America. Each time I look at that flag, I'm reminded that our destiny is stitched together like those fifty stars and those thirteen stripes. No one built this country on their own. This Nation is great because we built it together. This Nation is great because we worked as a team. This Nation is great because we get each other's backs. And if we hold fast to that truth, in this moment of trial, there is no challenge too great, no mission too hard. As long as we're joined in common purpose, as long as we maintain our common resolve, our journey moves forward, our future is hopeful, and the state of our Union will always be strong.

Thank you, God bless you, and may God bless the United States of America.

1.5.1   Notes

[1] "Speech featured an N.C. success story," Celeste Smith, *The News & Observer*, 25 Jan 2012

[2] "Obama recognizes Holland resident Bryan Ritterby in State of the Union Address," Megan Schmidt, *Holland Sentinel*, 24 Jan 2012

1.6   Barack Obama's Fifth State of the Union Address

Mr. Speaker, Mr. Vice President, Members of Congress, fellow citizens: fifty-one years ago, John F. Kennedy declared to this Chamber that "the Constitution makes us not rivals for power but partners for progress.... It is my task," he said, "to report the State of the Union – to improve it is the task of us all."

Tonight, thanks to the grit and determination of the American people, there is much progress to report. After a decade of grinding war, our brave men and women in uniform are coming home. After years of grueling recession, our businesses have created over six million new jobs. We buy more American cars than we have in five years, and less foreign oil than we have in twenty. Our housing market is healing, our stock market is rebounding, and consumers, patients, and homeowners enjoy stronger protections than ever before.

Together, we have cleared away the rubble of crisis, and can say with renewed confidence that the state of our union is stronger. But we gather here knowing that there are millions of Americans whose hard work and dedication have not yet been rewarded. Our economy is adding jobs – but too many people still can't find full-time employment. Corporate profits have rocketed to all-time highs – but for more than a decade, wages and incomes have barely budged.

It is our generation's task, then, to reignite the true engine of America's economic growth – a rising, thriving middle class. It is our unfinished task to restore the basic bargain that built this country – the idea that if you work hard and meet your responsibilities, you can get ahead, no matter where you come from, what you look like, or who you love. It is our unfinished task to make sure that this government works on behalf of the many, and not just the few; that it encourages free enterprise, rewards individual initiative, and opens the doors of opportunity to every child across this great nation.

The American people don't expect government to solve every problem. They don't expect those of us in this chamber to agree on every issue. But they do expect us to put the nation's interests before party. They do expect us to forge reasonable compromise where we can. For they know that America moves forward only when we do so together; and that the responsibility of improving this union remains the task of us all.

Our work must begin by making some basic decisions about our budget – decisions that will have a huge impact on the strength of our recovery. Over the last few years, both parties have worked together to reduce the deficit by more than $2.5 trillion – mostly through spending cuts, but also by raising tax rates on the wealthiest 1% of Americans. As a result, we are more than halfway towards the goal of $4-trillion in deficit reduction that economists say we need to stabilize our finances. Now we need to finish the job. And the question is: how?

In 2011, Congress passed a law saying that if both parties couldn't agree on a plan to reach our deficit goal, about a trillion dollars' worth of budget cuts would automatically go into effect this year. These sudden, harsh, arbitrary cuts would jeopardize our military readiness. They'd devastate priorities like education, energy, and medical research. They would certainly slow our recovery, and cost us hundreds of thousands of jobs. That's why Democrats, Republicans, business leaders, and economists have already said that these cuts, known here in Washington as "the sequester," are a really bad idea.

Now, some in this Congress have proposed preventing only the defense cuts by making even bigger cuts to things like education and job training, Medicare and Social Security benefits. That idea is even worse. Yes, the biggest driver of our long-term debt is the rising cost of health care for an aging population. And those of us who care deeply about programs like Medicare must embrace the need for modest reforms – otherwise, our retirement programs will crowd out the investments we need for our children, and jeopardize the promise of a secure retirement for future generations.

But we can't ask senior citizens and working families to shoulder the entire burden of deficit reduction while asking nothing more from the wealthiest and most powerful. We won't grow the middle class simply by shifting the cost of health care or college onto families that are already struggling, or by forcing communities to lay off more teachers, cops, and firefighters. Most Americans – Democrats, Republicans, and Independents – understand that we can't just cut our way to prosperity. They know that broad-based economic growth requires a balanced approach to deficit reduction, with spending cuts and revenue, and with everybody doing their fair share. And that's the approach I offer tonight.

On Medicare, I'm prepared to enact reforms that will achieve the same amount of health care savings by the beginning of the next decade as the reforms proposed by the bipartisan Simpson-Bowles commission. Already, the Affordable Care Act is helping to slow the growth of health care costs. The reforms I'm proposing go even further. We'll reduce taxpayer subsidies to prescription drug companies and ask more from the wealthiest seniors. We'll bring down costs by changing the way our government pays for Medicare, because our medical bills shouldn't be based on the number of tests ordered or days spent in the hospital – they should be based on the quality of care that our seniors receive. And I am open to additional reforms from both parties, so long as they don't violate the guarantee of a secure retirement. Our government shouldn't make promises we cannot keep – but we must keep the promises we've already made.

To hit the rest of our deficit reduction target, we should do what leaders in both parties have already suggested, and save hundreds of billions of dollars by getting rid of tax loopholes and deductions for the well-off and well-connected. After all, why would we choose to make deeper cuts to education and Medicare just to protect special interest tax breaks? How is that fair? How does that promote growth?

Now is our best chance for bipartisan, comprehensive tax reform that encourages job creation and helps bring down the deficit. The American people deserve a tax code that helps small businesses spend less time filling out complicated forms, and more time expanding and hiring; a tax code that ensures billionaires with high-powered accountants can't pay a lower rate than their hard-working secretaries; a tax code that lowers incentives to move jobs overseas, and lowers tax rates for businesses and manufacturers that create jobs right here in America. That's what tax reform can deliver. That's what we can do together.

I realize that tax reform and entitlement reform won't be easy. The politics will be hard for both sides. None of us will get 100% of what we want. But the alternative will cost us jobs, hurt our economy, and visit hardship on millions of hardworking Americans. So let's set party interests aside, and work to pass a budget that replaces reckless cuts with smart savings and wise investments in our future. And let's do it without the brinksmanship that stresses consumers and scares off investors. The greatest nation on Earth cannot keep conducting its business by drifting from one manufactured crisis to the next. Let's agree, right here, right now, to keep the people's government open, pay our bills on time, and always uphold the full faith and credit of the United States of America. The American people have worked too hard, for too long, rebuilding from one crisis to see their elected officials cause another.

Now, most of us agree that a plan to reduce the deficit must be part of our agenda. But let's be clear: deficit reduction alone is not an economic plan. A growing economy that creates good, middle-class jobs – that must be the North Star that guides our efforts. Every day, we should ask ourselves three questions as a nation: How do we attract more jobs to our shores? How do we equip our people with the skills needed to do those jobs? And how do we make sure that hard work leads to a decent living?

A year and a half ago, I put forward an American Jobs Act that independent economists said would create more than one million new jobs. I thank the last Congress for passing some of that agenda, and I urge this Congress to pass the rest. Tonight, I'll lay out additional proposals that are fully paid for and fully consistent with the budget framework both parties agreed to just eighteen months ago. Let me repeat – nothing I'm proposing tonight should increase our deficit by a single dime. It's not a bigger government we need, but a smarter government that sets priorities and invests in broad-based growth.

Our first priority is making America a magnet for new jobs and manufacturing. After shedding jobs for more than ten years, our manufacturers have added about 500,000 jobs over the past three. Caterpillar is bringing jobs back from Japan. Ford is bringing jobs back from Mexico. After locating plants in other countries like China, Intel is opening its most advanced plant right here at home. And this year, Apple will start making Macs in America again.

There are things we can do, right now, to accelerate this trend. Last year, we created our first manufacturing innovation institute in Youngstown, Ohio. A once-shuttered warehouse is now a state-of-the art lab where new workers are mastering the 3D printing that has the potential to revolutionize the way we make almost everything. There's no reason this can't happen in other towns. So tonight, I'm announcing the launch of three more of these manufacturing hubs, where businesses will partner with the Departments of Defense and Energy to turn regions left behind by globalization into global centers of high-tech jobs. And I ask this Congress to help create a network of fifteen of these hubs and guarantee that the next revolution in manufacturing is Made in America.

If we want to make the best products, we also have to invest in the best ideas. Every dollar we invested to map the human genome returned $140 to our economy. Today, our scientists are mapping the human brain to unlock the answers to Alzheimer's; developing drugs to regenerate damaged organs; devising new material to make batteries ten times more powerful. Now is not the time to gut these job-creating investments in science and innovation. Now is the time to reach a level of research and development not seen since the height of the Space Race. And today, no area holds more promise than our investments in American energy.

After years of talking about it, we are finally poised to control our own energy future. We produce more oil at home than we have in fifteen years. We have doubled the distance our cars will go on a gallon of gas, and the amount of renewable energy we generate from sources like wind and solar – with tens of thousands of good, American jobs to show for it. We produce more natural gas than ever before – and nearly everyone's energy bill is lower because of it. And over the last four years, our emissions of the dangerous carbon pollution that threatens our planet have actually fallen.

But for the sake of our children and our future, we must do more to combat climate change. Yes, it's true that no single event makes a trend. But the fact is, the twelve hottest years on record have all come in the last fifteen. Heat waves, droughts, wildfires, and floods – all are now more frequent and intense. We can choose to believe that Superstorm Sandy, and the most severe drought in decades, and the worst wildfires some states have ever seen, were all just a freak coincidence. Or we can choose to believe in the overwhelming judgment of science, and act before it's too late.

The good news is: we can make meaningful progress on this issue while driving strong economic growth. I urge this Congress to pursue a bipartisan, market-based solution to climate change, like the one John McCain and Joe Lieberman worked on together a few years ago. But if Congress won't act soon to protect future generations, I will. I will direct my Cabinet to come up with executive actions we can take, now and in the future, to reduce pollution, prepare our communities for the consequences of climate change, and speed the transition to more sustainable sources of energy.

Four years ago, other countries dominated the clean energy market and the jobs that came with it. We've begun to change that. Last year, wind energy added nearly half of all new power capacity in America. So let's generate even more. Solar energy gets cheaper by the year – so let's drive costs down even further. As long as countries like China keep going all-in on clean energy, so must we. In the meantime, the natural gas boom has led to cleaner power and greater energy independence. That's why my Administration will keep cutting red tape and speeding up new oil and gas permits. But I also want to work with this Congress to encourage the research and technology that helps natural gas burn even cleaner and protects our air and water.

Indeed, much of our new-found energy is drawn from lands and waters that we, the public, own together. So tonight, I propose we use some of our oil and gas revenues to fund an Energy Security Trust that will drive new research and technology to shift our cars and trucks off oil for good. If a non-partisan coalition of CEOs and retired generals and admirals can get behind this idea, then so can we. Let's take their advice and free our families and businesses from the painful spikes in gas prices we've put up with for far too long. I'm also issuing a new goal for America: let's cut in half the energy wasted by our homes and businesses over the next twenty years. The states with the best ideas to create jobs and lower energy bills by constructing more efficient buildings will receive federal support to help make it happen.

America's energy sector is just one part of an aging infrastructure badly in need of repair. Ask any CEO where they'd rather locate and hire: a country with deteriorating roads and bridges, or one with high-speed rail and internet; high-tech schools and self-healing power grids. The CEO of Siemens America – a company that brought hundreds of new jobs to North Carolina – has said that if we upgrade our infrastructure, they'll bring even more jobs. And I know that you want these job-creating projects in your districts. I've seen you all at the ribbon-cuttings.

Tonight, I propose a "Fix-It-First" program to put people to work as soon as possible on our most urgent repairs, like the nearly 70,000 structurally deficient bridges across the country. And to make sure taxpayers don't shoulder the whole burden, I'm also proposing a Partnership to Rebuild America that attracts private capital to upgrade what our businesses need most: modern ports to move our goods; modern pipelines to withstand a storm; modern schools worthy of our children. Let's prove that there is no better place to do business than the United States of America. And let's start right away.

Part of our rebuilding effort must also involve our housing sector. Today, our housing market is finally healing from the collapse of 2007. Home prices are rising at the fastest pace in six years, home purchases are up nearly 50%, and construction is expanding again. But even with mortgage rates near a 50-year low, too many families with solid credit who want to buy a home are being rejected. Too many families who have never missed a payment and want to refinance are being told *no*. That's holding our entire economy back, and we need to fix it. Right now, there's a bill in this Congress that would give every responsible homeowner in America the chance to save $3,000 a year by refinancing at today's rates. Democrats and Republicans have supported it before. What are we waiting for? Take a vote, and send me that bill. Right now, overlapping regulations keep responsible young families from buying their first home. What's holding us back? Let's streamline the process, and help our economy grow.

These initiatives in manufacturing, energy, infrastructure, and housing will help entrepreneurs and small business owners expand and create new jobs. But none of it will matter unless we also equip our citizens with the skills and training to fill those jobs. And that has to start at the earliest possible age. Study after study shows that the sooner a child begins learning, the better he or she does down the road. But today, fewer than three in ten four year-olds are enrolled in a high-quality preschool program. Most middle-class parents can't afford a few hundred bucks a week for private preschool. And for poor kids who need help the most, this lack of access to preschool education can shadow them for the rest of their lives.

Tonight, I propose working with states to make high-quality preschool available to every child in America. Every dollar we invest in high-quality early education can save more than seven dollars later on – by boosting graduation rates, reducing teen pregnancy, even reducing violent crime. In states that make it a priority to educate our youngest children, like Georgia or Oklahoma, studies show students grow up more likely to read and do math at grade level, graduate high school, hold a job, and form more stable families of their own. So let's do what works, and make sure none of our children start the race of life already behind. Let's give our kids that chance.

Let's also make sure that a high school diploma puts our kids on a path to a good job. Right now, countries like Germany focus on graduating their high school students with the equivalent of a technical degree from one of our community colleges, so that they're ready for a job. At schools like P-Tech in Brooklyn, a collaboration between New York Public Schools, the City University of New York, and IBM, students will graduate with a high school diploma and an associate degree in computers or engineering.

We need to give every American student opportunities like this. Four years ago, we started Race to the Top – a competition that convinced almost every state to develop smarter curricula and higher standards, for about 1% of what we spend on education each year. Tonight, I'm announcing a new challenge to redesign America's high schools so they better equip graduates for the demands of a high-tech economy. We'll reward schools that develop new partnerships with colleges and employers, and create classes that focus on science, technology, engineering, and math – the skills today's employers are looking for to fill jobs right now and in the future.

Now, even with better high schools, most young people will need some higher education. It's a simple fact: the more education you have, the more likely you are to have a job and work your way into the middle class. But today, skyrocketing costs price way too many young people out of a higher education, or saddle them with unsustainable debt.

Through tax credits, grants, and better loans, we have made college more affordable for millions of students and families over the last few years. But taxpayers cannot continue to subsidize the soaring cost of higher education. Colleges must do their part to keep costs down, and it's our job to make sure they do. Tonight, I ask Congress to change the Higher Education Act, so that affordability and value are included in determining which colleges receive certain types of federal aid. And tomorrow, my Administration will release a new College Scorecard that parents and students can use to compare schools based on a simple criteria: where you can get the most bang for your educational buck.

To grow our middle class, our citizens must have access to the education and training that today's jobs require. But we also have to make sure that America remains a place where everyone who's willing to work hard has the chance to get ahead. Our economy is stronger when we harness the talents and ingenuity of striving, hopeful immigrants. And right now, leaders from the business, labor, law enforcement, and faith communities all agree that the time has come to pass comprehensive immigration reform. Real reform means strong border security, and we can build on the progress my Administration has already made – putting more boots on the southern border than at any time in our history, and reducing illegal crossings to their lowest levels in 40 years.

Real reform means establishing a responsible pathway to earned citizenship – a path that includes passing a background check, paying taxes and a meaningful penalty, learning English, and going to the back of the line behind the folks trying to come here legally. And real reform means fixing the legal immigration system to cut waiting periods, reduce bureaucracy, and attract the highly-skilled entrepreneurs and engineers that will help create jobs and grow our economy. In other words, we know what needs to be done. As we speak, bipartisan groups in both chambers are working diligently to draft a bill, and I applaud their efforts. Now let's get this done. Send me a comprehensive immigration reform bill in the next few months, and I will sign it right away.

But we can't stop there. We know our economy is stronger when our wives, mothers, and daughters can live their lives free from discrimination in the workplace, and free from the fear of domestic violence. Today, the Senate passed the Violence Against Women Act that Joe Biden originally wrote almost 20 years ago. I urge the House to do the same. And I ask this Congress to declare that women should earn a living equal to their efforts, and finally pass the Paycheck Fairness Act this year.

We know our economy is stronger when we reward an honest day's work with honest wages. But today, a full-time worker making the minimum wage earns $14,500 a year. Even with the tax relief we've put in place, a family with two kids that earns the minimum wage still lives below the poverty line. That's wrong. That's why, since the last time this Congress raised the minimum wage, nineteen states have chosen to bump theirs even higher.

Tonight, let's declare that in the wealthiest nation on Earth, no one who works full-time should have to live in poverty, and raise the federal minimum wage to nine dollars an hour. This single step would raise the incomes of millions of working families. It could mean the difference between groceries or the food bank; rent or eviction; scraping by or finally getting ahead. For businesses across the country, it would mean customers with more money in their pockets. In fact, working folks shouldn't have to wait year after year for the minimum wage to go up while CEO pay has never been higher. So here's an idea that Governor Romney and I actually agreed on last year: let's tie the minimum wage to the cost of living, so that it finally becomes a wage you can live on.

Tonight, let's also recognize that there are communities in this country where no matter how hard you work, it's virtually impossible to get ahead. Factory towns decimated from years of plants packing up. Inescapable pockets of poverty, urban and rural, where young adults are still fighting for their first job. America is not a place where chance of birth or circumstance should decide our destiny. And that is why we need to build new ladders of opportunity into the middle class for all who are willing to climb them.

Let's offer incentives to companies that hire Americans who've got what it takes to fill that job opening, but have been out of work so long that no one will give them a chance. Let's put people back to work rebuilding vacant homes in run-down neighborhoods. And this year, my Administration will begin to partner with 20 of the hardest-hit towns in America to get these communities back on their feet. We'll work with local leaders to target resources at public safety, education, and housing. We'll give new tax credits to businesses that hire and invest. And we'll work to strengthen families by removing the financial deterrents to marriage for low-income couples, and doing more to encourage fatherhood – because what makes you a man isn't the ability to conceive a child; it's having the courage to raise one.

Stronger families. Stronger communities. A stronger America. It is this kind of prosperity – broad, shared, and built on a thriving middle class – that has always been the source of our progress at home. It is also the foundation of our power and influence throughout the world.

Tonight, we stand united in saluting the troops and civilians who sacrifice every day to protect us. Because of them, we can say with confidence that America will complete its mission in Afghanistan, and achieve our objective of defeating the core of al Qaeda. Already, we have brought home 33,000 of our brave servicemen and women. This spring, our forces will move into a support role, while Afghan security forces take the lead. Tonight, I can announce that over the next year, another 34,000 American troops will come home from Afghanistan. This drawdown will continue. And by the end of next year, our war in Afghanistan will be over.

Beyond 2014, America's commitment to a unified and sovereign Afghanistan will endure, but the nature of our commitment will change. We are negotiating an agreement with the Afghan government that focuses on two missions: training and equipping Afghan forces so that the country does not again slip into chaos, and counter-terrorism efforts that allow us to pursue the remnants of al Qaeda and their affiliates.

Today, the organization that attacked us on 9/11 is a shadow of its former self. Different al Qaeda affiliates and extremist groups have emerged – from the Arabian Peninsula to Africa. The threat these groups pose is evolving. But to meet this threat, we don't need to send tens of thousands of our sons and daughters abroad, or occupy other nations. Instead, we will need to help countries like Yemen, Libya, and Somalia provide for their own security, and help allies who take the fight to terrorists, as we have in Mali. And, where necessary, through a range of capabilities, we will continue to take direct action against those terrorists who pose the gravest threat to Americans.

As we do, we must enlist our values in the fight. That is why my Administration has worked tirelessly to forge a durable legal and policy framework to guide our counterterrorism operations. Throughout, we have kept Congress fully informed of our efforts. I recognize that in our democracy, no one should just take my word that we're doing things the right way. So, in the months ahead, I will continue to engage with Congress to ensure not only that our targeting, detention, and prosecution of terrorists remains consistent with our laws and system of checks and balances, but that our efforts are even more transparent to the American people and to the world.

Of course, our challenges don't end with al Qaeda. America will continue to lead the effort to prevent the spread of the world's most dangerous weapons. The regime in North Korea must know that they will only achieve security and prosperity by meeting their international obligations. Provocations of the sort we saw last night will only isolate them further, as we stand by our allies, strengthen our own missile defense, and lead the world in taking firm action in response to these threats.

Likewise, the leaders of Iran must recognize that now is the time for a diplomatic solution, because a coalition stands united in demanding that they meet their obligations, and we will do what is necessary to prevent them from getting a nuclear weapon. At the same time, we will engage Russia to seek further reductions in our nuclear arsenals, and continue leading the global effort to secure nuclear materials that could fall into the wrong hands – because our ability to influence others depends on our willingness to lead.

America must also face the rapidly growing threat from cyber-attacks. We know hackers steal people's identities and infiltrate private e-mail. We know foreign countries and companies swipe our corporate secrets. Now our enemies are also seeking the ability to sabotage our power grid, our financial institutions, and our air traffic control systems. We cannot look back years from now and wonder why we did nothing in the face of real threats to our security and our economy.

That's why, earlier today, I signed a new executive order that will strengthen our cyber defenses by increasing information sharing, and developing standards to protect our national security, our jobs, and our privacy. Now, Congress must act as well, by passing legislation to give our government a greater capacity to secure our networks and deter attacks.

Even as we protect our people, we should remember that today's world presents not only dangers, but opportunities. To boost American exports, support American jobs, and level the playing field in the growing markets of Asia, we intend to complete negotiations on a Trans-Pacific Partnership. And tonight, I am announcing that we will launch talks on a comprehensive Transatlantic Trade and Investment Partnership with the European Union – because trade that is free and fair across the Atlantic supports millions of good-paying American jobs.

We also know that progress in the most impoverished parts of our world enriches us all. In many places, people live on little more than a dollar a day. So the United States will join with our allies to eradicate such extreme poverty in the next two decades: by connecting more people to the global economy and empowering women; by giving our young and brightest minds new opportunities to serve and helping communities to feed, power, and educate themselves; by saving the world's children from preventable deaths; and by realizing the promise of an AIDS-free generation.

Above all, America must remain a beacon to all who seek freedom during this period of historic change. I saw the power of hope last year in Rangoon – when Aung San Suu Kyi welcomed an American President into the home where she had been imprisoned for years; when thousands of Burmese lined the streets, waving American flags, including a man who said, "There is justice and law in the United States. I want our country to be like that."

In defense of freedom, we will remain the anchor of strong alliances from the Americas to Africa; from Europe to Asia. In the Middle East, we will stand with citizens as they demand their universal rights, and support stable transitions to democracy. The process will be messy, and we cannot presume to dictate the course of change in countries like Egypt; but we can – and will – insist on respect for the fundamental rights of all people. We will keep the pressure on a Syrian regime that has murdered its own people, and support opposition leaders that respect the rights of every Syrian. And we will stand steadfast with Israel in pursuit of security and a lasting peace. These are the messages I will deliver when I travel to the Middle East next month.

And all this work depends on the courage and sacrifice of those who serve in dangerous places at great personal risk: our diplomats, our intelligence officers, and the men and women of the United States Armed Forces. As long as I'm Commander-in-Chief, we will do whatever we must to protect those who serve their country abroad, and we will maintain the best military the world has ever known. We'll invest in new capabilities, even as we reduce waste and wartime spending. We will ensure equal treatment for all service members, and equal benefits for their families, gay and straight. We will draw upon the courage and skills of our sisters and daughters and moms, because women have proven under fire that they are ready for combat. We will keep faith with our veterans, investing in world-class care, including mental health care, for our wounded warriors; supporting our military families; giving our veterans the benefits, education, and job opportunities that they have earned. And I want to thank my wife Michelle and Dr. Jill Biden for their continued dedication to serving our military families as well as they have serve us. Thank you, honey. Thank you, Jill.

Defending our freedom, though, is not just the job of our military alone. We must all do our part to make sure our God-given rights are protected here at home. That includes one of the most fundamental right of a democracy: the right to vote. Now, when any American – no matter where they live or what their party – are denied that right because they can't afford to wait for five, six, seven hours just to cast their ballot, we are betraying our ideals. So tonight I'm announcing a non-partisan commission to improve the voting experience in America, and it definitely needs improvement. And I'm asking two long-time experts in the field, who, by the way, recently served as the top attorneys for my campaign and for Governor Romney's campaign, to lead it. We can fix this, and we will. The American people demand it, and so does our democracy.

Of course, what I've said tonight matters little if we don't come together to protect our most precious resource: our children.

It has been two months since Newtown. I know this is not the first time this country has debated how to reduce gun violence. But this time is different. Overwhelming majorities of Americans – Americans who believe in the 2nd Amendment – have come together around commonsense reform, like background checks that will make it harder for criminals to get their hands on a gun. Senators of both parties are working together on tough new laws to prevent anyone from buying guns for resale to criminals. Police chiefs are asking our help to get weapons of war and massive ammunition magazines off our streets, because these police chiefs, they're tired of seeing their guys and gals being outgunned.

Each of these proposals deserves a vote in Congress. Now if you want to vote no, that's your choice. But these proposals deserve a vote. Because in the two months since Newtown, more than a thousand birthdays, graduations, anniversaries have been stolen from our lives by a bullet from a gun. More than a thousand.

One of those we lost was a young girl named Hadiya Pendleton. She was fifteen years old. She loved Fig Newtons and lip gloss. She was a majorette. She was so good to her friends, they all thought they were her best friend. Just three weeks ago, she was here, in Washington, with her classmates, performing for her country at my inauguration. And a week later, she was shot and killed in a Chicago park after school, just a mile away from my house. Hadiya's parents, Nate and Cleo, are in this chamber tonight, along with more than two dozen Americans whose lives have been torn apart by gun violence. They deserve a vote. They deserve a vote.

Gabby Giffords deserves a vote.

The families of Newtown deserve a vote.

The families of Aurora deserve a vote.

The families of Oak Creek, and Tucson, and Blacksburg, and the countless other communities ripped open by gun violence – they deserve a simple vote.

Our actions will not prevent every senseless act of violence in this country. Indeed, no laws, no initiatives, no administrative acts will perfectly solve all the challenges I've outlined tonight. But we were never sent here to be perfect. We were sent here to make what difference we can, to secure this nation, expand opportunity, and uphold our ideals through the hard, often frustrating, but absolutely necessary work of self-government. We were sent here to look out for our fellow Americans the same way they look out for one another, every single day, usually without fanfare, all across this country. We should follow their example.

We should follow the example of a New York City nurse named Menchu Sanchez. When Hurricane Sandy plunged her hospital into darkness, she wasn't thinking about how her own home was faring – they were with the twenty precious newborns in her care and the rescue plan she devised that kept them all safe.

We should follow the example of a North Miami woman named Desiline Victor. When she arrived at her polling place, she was told the wait to vote might be six hours. And as time ticked by, her concern was not with her tired body or aching feet, but whether folks like her would get to have their say. Hour after hour, a throng of people stayed in line in support of her. Because Desiline is 102 years old. And they erupted in cheers when she finally put on a sticker that read "I Voted."

We should follow the example of a police officer named Brian Murphy. When a gunman opened fire on a Sikh temple in Wisconsin, and Brian was the first to arrive, he did not consider his own safety. He fought back until help arrived, and ordered his fellow officers to protect the safety of the fellow Americans worshiping inside – even as he lay bleeding from twelve bullet wounds. And when asked how he did that, Brian said, "That's just the way we're made." That's just the way we're made. We may do different jobs, and wear different uniforms, and hold different views than the person beside us. But as Americans, we all share the same proud title:

We are citizens.

It's a word that doesn't just describe our nationality or our legal status. It describes the way we're made. It describes what we believe. It captures the enduring idea that this country only works when we accept certain obligations to one another and to future generations; that our rights are wrapped up in the rights of others; and that well into our third century as a nation, it remains the task of us all, as citizens of these United States, to be the authors of the next great chapter of our American story.

Thank you, God bless you, and God bless the United States of America.

1.6.1   Notes

[1] "State Of The Union 2013: Obama Invited To Deliver Address On Feb. 12," Donna Cassata, *The Huffington Post*, 11 January 2013

1.7   Barack Obama's Sixth State of the Union Address

Mr. Speaker, Mr. Vice President, Members of Congress, my fellow Americans:

Today in America, a teacher spent extra time with a student who needed it, and did her part to lift America's graduation rate to its highest level in more than three decades.

An entrepreneur flipped on the lights in her tech startup, and did her part to add to the more than eight million new jobs our businesses have created over the past four years.

An autoworker fine-tuned some of the best, most fuel-efficient cars in the world, and did his part to help America wean itself off foreign oil.

A farmer prepared for the spring after the strongest five-year stretch of farm exports in our history. A rural doctor gave a young child the first prescription to treat asthma that his mother could afford. A man took the bus home from the graveyard shift, bone-tired but dreaming big dreams for his son. And in tight-knit communities across America, fathers and mothers will tuck in their kids, put an arm around their spouse, remember fallen comrades, and give thanks for being home from a war that, after twelve long years, is finally coming to an end.

Tonight, this chamber speaks with one voice to the people we represent: it is you, our citizens, who make the state of our union strong.

Here are the results of your efforts: The lowest unemployment rate in over five years. A rebounding housing market. A manufacturing sector that's adding jobs for the first time since the 1990s. More oil produced at home than we buy from the rest of the world – the first time that's happened in nearly twenty years. Our deficits – cut by more than half. And for the first time in over a decade, business leaders around the world have declared that China is no longer the world's number one place to invest; America is.

That's why I believe this can be a breakthrough year for America. After five years of grit and determined effort, the United States is better-positioned for the 21st century than any other nation on Earth.

The question for everyone in this chamber, running through every decision we make this year, is whether we are going to help or hinder this progress. For several years now, this town has been consumed by a rancorous argument over the proper size of the federal government. It's an important debate – one that dates back to our very founding. But when that debate prevents us from carrying out even the most basic functions of our democracy – when our differences shut down government or threaten the full faith and credit of the United States – then we are not doing right by the American people.

As President, I'm committed to making Washington work better, and rebuilding the trust of the people who sent us here. I believe most of you are, too. Last month, thanks to the work of Democrats and Republicans, this Congress finally produced a budget that undoes some of last year's severe cuts to priorities like education. Nobody got everything they wanted, and we can still do more to invest in this country's future while bringing down our deficit in a balanced way. But the budget compromise should leave us freer to focus on creating new jobs, not creating new crises.

In the coming months, let's see where else we can make progress together. Let's make this a year of action. That's what most Americans want – for all of us in this chamber to focus on their lives, their hopes, their aspirations. And what I believe unites the people of this nation, regardless of race or region or party, young or old, rich or poor, is the simple, profound belief in opportunity for all – the notion that if you work hard and take responsibility, you can get ahead.

Let's face it: that belief has suffered some serious blows. Over more than three decades, even before the Great Recession hit, massive shifts in technology and global competition had eliminated a lot of good, middle-class jobs, and weakened the economic foundations that families depend on.

Today, after four years of economic growth, corporate profits and stock prices have rarely been higher, and those at the top have never done better. But average wages have barely budged. Inequality has deepened. Upward mobility has stalled.

The cold, hard fact is that even in the midst of recovery, too many Americans are working more than ever just to get by – let alone get ahead. And too many still aren't working at all.

Our job is to reverse these trends. It won't happen right away, and we won't agree on everything. But what I offer tonight is a set of concrete, practical proposals to speed up growth, strengthen the middle class, and build new ladders of opportunity into the middle class. Some require Congressional action, and I'm eager to work with all of you. But America does not stand still – and neither will I. So wherever and whenever I can take steps without legislation to expand opportunity for more American families, that's what I'm going to do.

As usual, our First Lady sets a good example. Michelle's Let's Move partnership with schools, businesses, and local leaders has helped bring down childhood obesity rates for the first time in thirty years – an achievement that will improve lives and reduce health care costs for decades to come. The Joining Forces alliance that Michelle and Jill Biden launched has already encouraged employers to hire or train nearly 400,000 veterans and military spouses. Taking a page from that playbook, the White House just organized a College Opportunity Summit where already, 150 universities, businesses, and nonprofits have made concrete commitments to reduce inequality in access to higher education – and help every hardworking kid go to college and succeed when they get to campus. Across the country, we're partnering with mayors, governors, and state legislatures on issues from homelessness to marriage equality.

The point is, there are millions of Americans outside Washington who are tired of stale political arguments, and are moving this country forward. They believe, and I believe, that here in America, our success should depend not on accident of birth, but the strength of our work ethic and the scope of our dreams. That's what drew our forebears here. It's how the daughter of a factory worker is CEO of America's largest automaker; how the son of a barkeeper is Speaker of the House; how the son of a single mom can be President of the greatest nation on Earth.

Opportunity is who we are. And the defining project of our generation is to restore that promise.

We know where to start: the best measure of opportunity is access to a good job. With the economy picking up speed, companies say they intend to hire more people this year. And over half of big manufacturers say they're thinking of insourcing jobs from abroad.

So let's make that decision easier for more companies. Both Democrats and Republicans have argued that our tax code is riddled with wasteful, complicated loopholes that punish businesses investing here, and reward companies that keep profits abroad. Let's flip that equation. Let's work together to close those loopholes, end those incentives to ship jobs overseas, and lower tax rates for businesses that create jobs here at home.

Moreover, we can take the money we save with this transition to tax reform to create jobs rebuilding our roads, upgrading our ports, unclogging our commutes – because in today's global economy, first-class jobs gravitate to first-class infrastructure. We'll need Congress to protect more than three million jobs by finishing transportation and waterways bills this summer. But I will act on my own to slash bureaucracy and streamline the permitting process for key projects, so we can get more construction workers on the job as fast as possible.

We also have the chance, right now, to beat other countries in the race for the next wave of high-tech manufacturing jobs. My administration has launched two hubs for high-tech manufacturing in Raleigh and Youngstown, where we've connected businesses to research universities that can help America lead the world in advanced technologies. Tonight, I'm announcing we'll launch six more this year. Bipartisan bills in both houses could double the number of these hubs and the jobs they create. So get those bills to my desk and put more Americans back to work.

Let's do more to help the entrepreneurs and small business owners who create most new jobs in America. Over the past five years, my administration has made more loans to small business owners than any other. And when ninety-eight percent of our exporters are small businesses, new trade partnerships with Europe and the Asia-Pacific will help them create more jobs. We need to work together on tools like bipartisan trade promotion authority to protect our workers, protect our environment, and open new markets to new goods stamped "Made in the USA." China and Europe aren't standing on the sidelines. Neither should we.

We know that the nation that goes all-in on innovation today will own the global economy tomorrow. This is an edge America cannot surrender. Federally-funded research helped lead to the ideas and inventions behind Google and smartphones. That's why Congress should undo the damage done by last year's cuts to basic research so we can unleash the next great American discovery – whether it's vaccines that stay ahead of drug-resistant bacteria, or paper-thin material that's stronger than steel. And let's pass a patent reform bill that allows our businesses to stay focused on innovation, not costly, needless litigation.

Now, one of the biggest factors in bringing more jobs back is our commitment to American energy. The all-of-the-above energy strategy I announced a few years ago is working, and today, America is closer to energy independence than we've been in decades.

One of the reasons why is natural gas – if extracted safely, it's the bridge fuel that can power our economy with less of the carbon pollution that causes climate change. Businesses plan to invest almost $100 billion in new factories that use natural gas. I'll cut red tape to help states get those factories built, and this Congress can help by putting people to work building fueling stations that shift more cars and trucks from foreign oil to American natural gas. My administration will keep working with the industry to sustain production and job growth while strengthening protection of our air, our water, and our communities. And while we're at it, I'll use my authority to protect more of our pristine federal lands for future generations.

It's not just oil and natural gas production that's booming; we're becoming a global leader in solar, too. Every four minutes, another American home or business goes solar; every panel pounded into place by a worker whose job can't be outsourced. Let's continue that progress with a smarter tax policy that stops giving $4 billion a year to fossil fuel industries that don't need it, so that we can invest more in fuels of the future that do.

And even as we've increased energy production, we've partnered with businesses, builders, and local communities to reduce the energy we consume. When we rescued our automakers, for example, we worked with them to set higher fuel efficiency standards for our cars. In the coming months, I'll build on that success by setting new standards for our trucks, so we can keep driving down oil imports and what we pay at the pump.

Taken together, our energy policy is creating jobs and leading to a cleaner, safer planet. Over the past eight years, the United States has reduced our total carbon pollution more than any other nation on Earth. But we have to act with more urgency – because a changing climate is already harming western communities struggling with drought, and coastal cities dealing with floods. That's why I directed my administration to work with states, utilities, and others to set new standards on the amount of carbon pollution our power plants are allowed to dump into the air. The shift to a cleaner energy economy won't happen overnight, and it will require tough choices along the way. But the debate is settled. Climate change is a fact. And when our children's children look us in the eye and ask if we did all we could to leave them a safer, more stable world, with new sources of energy, I want us to be able to say yes, we did.

Finally, if we are serious about economic growth, it is time to heed the call of business leaders, labor leaders, faith leaders, and law enforcement – and fix our broken immigration system. Republicans and Democrats in the Senate have acted. I know that members of both parties in the House want to do the same. Independent economists say immigration reform will grow our economy and shrink our deficits by almost $1 trillion in the next two decades. And for good reason: when people come here to fulfill their dreams – to study, invent, and contribute to our culture – they make our country a more attractive place for businesses to locate and create jobs for everyone. So let's get immigration reform done this year.

The ideas I've outlined so far can speed up growth and create more jobs. But in this rapidly-changing economy, we have to make sure that every American has the skills to fill those jobs.

The good news is, we know how to do it. Two years ago, as the auto industry came roaring back, Andra Rush opened up a manufacturing firm in Detroit. She knew that Ford needed parts for the best-selling truck in America, and she knew how to make them. She just needed the workforce. So she dialed up what we call an American Job Center – places where folks can walk in to get the help or training they need to find a new job, or better job. She was flooded with new workers. And today, Detroit Manufacturing Systems has more than 700 employees.

What Andra and her employees experienced is how it should be for every employer – and every job seeker. So tonight, I've asked Vice President Biden to lead an across-the-board reform of America's training programs to make sure they have one mission: train Americans with the skills employers need, and match them to good jobs that need to be filled right now. That means more on-the-job training, and more apprenticeships that set a young worker on an upward trajectory for life. It means connecting companies to community colleges that can help design training to fill their specific needs. And if Congress wants to help, you can concentrate funding on proven programs that connect more ready-to-work Americans with ready-to-be-filled jobs.

I'm also convinced we can help Americans return to the workforce faster by reforming unemployment insurance so that it's more effective in today's economy. But first, this Congress needs to restore the unemployment insurance you just let expire for 1.6 million people.

Let me tell you why.

Misty DeMars is a mother of two young boys. She'd been steadily employed since she was a teenager. She put herself through college. She'd never collected unemployment benefits. In May, she and her husband used their life savings to buy their first home. A week later, budget cuts claimed the job she loved. Last month, when their unemployment insurance was cut off, she sat down and wrote me a letter – the kind I get every day. "We are the face of the unemployment crisis," she wrote. "I am not dependent on the government...Our country depends on people like us who build careers, contribute to society...care about our neighbors...I am confident that in time I will find a job...I will pay my taxes, and we will raise our children in their own home in the community we love. Please give us this chance."

Congress, give these hardworking, responsible Americans that chance. They need our help, but more important, this country needs them in the game. That's why I've been asking CEOs to give more long-term unemployed workers a fair shot at that new job and new chance to support their families; this week, many will come to the White House to make that commitment real. Tonight, I ask every business leader in America to join us and to do the same – because we are stronger when America fields a full team.

Of course, it's not enough to train today's workforce. We also have to prepare tomorrow's workforce, by guaranteeing every child access to a world-class education.

Estiven Rodriguez couldn't speak a word of English when he moved to New York City at age nine. But last month, thanks to the support of great teachers and an innovative tutoring program, he led a march of his classmates – through a crowd of cheering parents and neighbors – from their high school to the post office, where they mailed off their college applications. And this son of a factory worker just found out he's going to college this fall.

Five years ago, we set out to change the odds for all our kids. We worked with lenders to reform student loans, and today, more young people are earning college degrees than ever before. Race to the Top, with the help of governors from both parties, has helped states raise expectations and performance. Teachers and principals in schools from Tennessee to Washington, D.C. are making big strides in preparing students with skills for the new economy – problem solving, critical thinking, science, technology, engineering, and math. Some of this change is hard. It requires everything from more challenging curriculums and more demanding parents to better support for teachers and new ways to measure how well our kids think, not how well they can fill in a bubble on a test. But it's worth it – and it's working.

The problem is we're still not reaching enough kids, and we're not reaching them in time. That has to change.

Research shows that one of the best investments we can make in a child's life is high-quality early education. Last year, I asked this Congress to help states make high-quality pre-K available to every four year-old. As a parent as well as a President, I repeat that request tonight. But in the meantime, thirty states have raised pre-k funding on their own. They know we can't wait. So just as we worked with states to reform our schools, this year, we'll invest in new partnerships with states and communities across the country in a race to the top for our youngest children. And as Congress decides what it's going to do, I'm going to pull together a coalition of elected officials, business leaders, and philanthropists willing to help more kids access the high-quality pre-K they need.

Last year, I also pledged to connect 99 percent of our students to high-speed broadband over the next four years. Tonight, I can announce that with the support of the FCC and companies like Apple, Microsoft, Sprint, and Verizon, we've got a down payment to start connecting more than 15,000 schools and twenty million students over the next two years, without adding a dime to the deficit.

We're working to redesign high schools and partner them with colleges and employers that offer the real-world education and hands-on training that can lead directly to a job and career. We're shaking up our system of higher education to give parents more information, and colleges more incentives to offer better value, so that no middle-class kid is priced out of a college education. We're offering millions the opportunity to cap their monthly student loan payments to ten percent of their income, and I want to work with Congress to see how we can help even more Americans who feel trapped by student loan debt. And I'm reaching out to some of America's leading foundations and corporations on a new initiative to help more young men of color facing tough odds stay on track and reach their full potential.

The bottom line is, Michelle and I want every child to have the same chance this country gave us. But we know our opportunity agenda won't be complete – and too many young people entering the workforce today will see the American Dream as an empty promise – unless we do more to make sure our economy honors the dignity of work, and hard work pays off for every single American.

Today, women make up about half our workforce. But they still make 77 cents for every dollar a man earns. That is wrong, and in 2014, it's an embarrassment. A woman deserves equal pay for equal work. She deserves to have a baby without sacrificing her job. A mother deserves a day off to care for a sick child or sick parent without running into hardship – and you know what, a father does, too. It's time to do away with workplace policies that belong in a "Mad Men" episode. This year, let's all come together – Congress, the White House, and businesses from Wall Street to Main Street – to give every woman the opportunity she deserves. Because I firmly believe when women succeed, America succeeds.

Now, women hold a majority of lower-wage jobs – but they're not the only ones stifled by stagnant wages. Americans understand that some people will earn more than others, and we don't resent those who, by virtue of their efforts, achieve incredible success. But Americans overwhelmingly agree that no one who works full time should ever have to raise a family in poverty.

In the year since I asked this Congress to raise the minimum wage, five states have passed laws to raise theirs. Many businesses have done it on their own. Nick Chute is here tonight with his boss, John Soranno. John's an owner of Punch Pizza in Minneapolis, and Nick helps make the dough. Only now he makes more of it: John just gave his employees a raise, to ten bucks an hour – a decision that eased their financial stress and boosted their morale.

Tonight, I ask more of America's business leaders to follow John's lead and do what you can to raise your employees' wages. To every mayor, governor, and state legislator in America, I say, you don't have to wait for Congress to act; Americans will support you if you take this on. And as a chief executive, I intend to lead by example. Profitable corporations like Costco see higher wages as the smart way to boost productivity and reduce turnover. We should too. In the coming weeks, I will issue an Executive Order requiring federal contractors to pay their federally-funded employees a fair wage of at least $10.10 an hour – because if you cook our troops' meals or wash their dishes, you shouldn't have to live in poverty.

Of course, to reach millions more, Congress needs to get on board. Today, the federal minimum wage is worth about twenty percent less than it was when Ronald Reagan first stood here. Tom Harkin and George Miller have a bill to fix that by lifting the minimum wage to $10.10. This will help families. It will give businesses customers with more money to spend. It doesn't involve any new bureaucratic program. So join the rest of the country. Say yes. Give America a raise.

There are other steps we can take to help families make ends meet, and few are more effective at reducing inequality and helping families pull themselves up through hard work than the Earned Income Tax Credit. Right now, it helps about half of all parents at some point. But I agree with Republicans like Senator Rubio that it doesn't do enough for single workers who don't have kids. So let's work together to strengthen the credit, reward work, and help more Americans get ahead.

Let's do more to help Americans save for retirement. Today, most workers don't have a pension. A Social Security check often isn't enough on its own. And while the stock market has doubled over the last five years, that doesn't help folks who don't have 401ks. That's why, tomorrow, I will direct the Treasury to create a new way for working Americans to start their own retirement savings: MyRA. It's a new savings bond that encourages folks to build a nest egg. MyRA guarantees a decent return with no risk of losing what you put in. And if this Congress wants to help, work with me to fix an upside-down tax code that gives big tax breaks to help the wealthy save, but does little to nothing for middle-class Americans. Offer every American access to an automatic IRA on the job, so they can save at work just like everyone in this chamber can. And since the most important investment many families make is their home, send me legislation that protects taxpayers from footing the bill for a housing crisis ever again, and keeps the dream of homeownership alive for future generations of Americans.

One last point on financial security. For decades, few things exposed hard-working families to economic hardship more than a broken health care system. And in case you haven't heard, we're in the process of fixing that.

A pre-existing condition used to mean that someone like Amanda Shelley, a physician assistant and single mom from Arizona, couldn't get health insurance. But on January 1st, she got covered. On January 3rd, she felt a sharp pain. On January 6th, she had emergency surgery. Just one week earlier, Amanda said, that surgery would've meant bankruptcy.

That's what health insurance reform is all about – the peace of mind that if misfortune strikes, you don't have to lose everything.

Already, because of the Affordable Care Act, more than three million Americans under age 26 have gained coverage under their parents' plans.

More than nine million Americans have signed up for private health insurance or Medicaid coverage.

And here's another number: zero. Because of this law, no American can ever again be dropped or denied coverage for a preexisting condition like asthma, back pain, or cancer. No woman can ever be charged more just because she's a woman. And we did all this while adding years to Medicare's finances, keeping Medicare premiums flat, and lowering prescription costs for millions of seniors.

Now, I don't expect to convince my Republican friends on the merits of this law. But I know that the American people aren't interested in refighting old battles. So again, if you have specific plans to cut costs, cover more people, and increase choice – tell America what you'd do differently. Let's see if the numbers add up. But let's not have another forty-something votes to repeal a law that's already helping millions of Americans like Amanda. The first forty were plenty. We got it. We all owe it to the American people to say what we're for, not just what we're against.

And if you want to know the real impact this law is having, just talk to Governor Steve Beshear of Kentucky, who's here tonight. Kentucky's not the most liberal part of the country, but he's like a man possessed when it comes to covering his commonwealth's families. "They are our friends and neighbors," he said. "They are people we shop and go to church with...farmers out on the tractors...grocery clerks...they are people who go to work every morning praying they don't get sick. No one deserves to live that way."

Steve's right. That's why, tonight, I ask every American who knows someone without health insurance to help them get covered by March 31st. Moms, get on your kids to sign up. Kids, call your mom and walk her through the application. It will give her some peace of mind – plus, she'll appreciate hearing from you.

After all, that's the spirit that has always moved this nation forward. It's the spirit of citizenship – the recognition that through hard work and responsibility, we can pursue our individual dreams, but still come together as one American family to make sure the next generation can pursue its dreams as well.

Citizenship means standing up for everyone's right to vote. Last year, part of the Voting Rights Act was weakened. But conservative Republicans and liberal Democrats are working together to strengthen it; and the bipartisan commission I appointed last year has offered reforms so that no one has to wait more than a half hour to vote. Let's support these efforts. It should be the power of our vote, not the size of our bank account, that drives our democracy.

Citizenship means standing up for the lives that gun violence steals from us each day. I have seen the courage of parents, students, pastors, and police officers all over this country who say "we are not afraid," and I intend to keep trying, with or without Congress, to help stop more tragedies from visiting innocent Americans in our movie theaters, shopping malls, or schools like Sandy Hook.

Citizenship demands a sense of common cause; participation in the hard work of self-government; an obligation to serve to our communities. And I know this chamber agrees that few Americans give more to their country than our diplomats and the men and women of the United States Armed Forces.

Tonight, because of the extraordinary troops and civilians who risk and lay down their lives to keep us free, the United States is more secure. When I took office, nearly 180,000 Americans were serving in Iraq and Afghanistan. Today, all our troops are out of Iraq. More than 60,000 of our troops have already come home from Afghanistan. With Afghan forces now in the lead for their own security, our troops have moved to a support role. Together with our allies, we will complete our mission there by the end of this year, and America's longest war will finally be over.

After 2014, we will support a unified Afghanistan as it takes responsibility for its own future. If the Afghan government signs a security agreement that we have negotiated, a small force of Americans could remain in Afghanistan with NATO allies to carry out two narrow missions: training and assisting Afghan forces, and counterterrorism operations to pursue any remnants of al Qaeda. For while our relationship with Afghanistan will change, one thing will not: our resolve that terrorists do not launch attacks against our country.

The fact is, that danger remains. While we have put al Qaeda's core leadership on a path to defeat, the threat has evolved, as al Qaeda affiliates and other extremists take root in different parts of the world. In Yemen, Somalia, Iraq, and Mali, we have to keep working with partners to disrupt and disable these networks. In Syria, we'll support the opposition that rejects the agenda of terrorist networks. Here at home, we'll keep strengthening our defenses, and combat new threats like cyberattacks. And as we reform our defense budget, we have to keep faith with our men and women in uniform, and invest in the capabilities they need to succeed in future missions.

We have to remain vigilant. But I strongly believe our leadership and our security cannot depend on our military alone. As Commander-in-Chief, I have used force when needed to protect the American people, and I will never hesitate to do so as long as I hold this office. But I will not send our troops into harm's way unless it's truly necessary; nor will I allow our sons and daughters to be mired in open-ended conflicts. We must fight the battles that need to be fought, not those that terrorists prefer from us – large-scale deployments that drain our strength and may ultimately feed extremism.

So, even as we aggressively pursue terrorist networks – through more targeted efforts and by building the capacity of our foreign partners – America must move off a permanent war footing. That's why I've imposed prudent limits on the use of drones – for we will not be safer if people abroad believe we strike within their countries without regard for the consequence. That's why, working with this Congress, I will reform our surveillance programs – because the vital work of our intelligence community depends on public confidence, here and abroad, that the privacy of ordinary people is not being violated. And with the Afghan war ending, this needs to be the year Congress lifts the remaining restrictions on detainee transfers and we close the prison at Guantanamo Bay – because we counter terrorism not just through intelligence and military action, but by remaining true to our Constitutional ideals, and setting an example for the rest of the world.

You see, in a world of complex threats, our security and leadership depends on all elements of our power – including strong and principled diplomacy. American diplomacy has rallied more than fifty countries to prevent nuclear materials from falling into the wrong hands, and allowed us to reduce our own reliance on Cold War stockpiles. American diplomacy, backed by the threat of force, is why Syria's chemical weapons are being eliminated, and we will continue to work with the international community to usher in the future the Syrian people deserve – a future free of dictatorship, terror and fear. As we speak, American diplomacy is supporting Israelis and Palestinians as they engage in difficult but necessary talks to end the conflict there; to achieve dignity and an independent state for Palestinians, and lasting peace and security for the State of Israel – a Jewish state that knows America will always be at their side.

And it is American diplomacy, backed by pressure, that has halted the progress of Iran's nuclear program – and rolled parts of that program back – for the very first time in a decade. As we gather here tonight, Iran has begun to eliminate its stockpile of higher levels of enriched uranium. It is not installing advanced centrifuges. Unprecedented inspections help the world verify, every day, that Iran is not building a bomb. And with our allies and partners, we're engaged in negotiations to see if we can peacefully achieve a goal we all share: preventing Iran from obtaining a nuclear weapon.

These negotiations will be difficult. They may not succeed. We are clear-eyed about Iran's support for terrorist organizations like Hezbollah, which threaten our allies; and the mistrust between our nations cannot be wished away. But these negotiations do not rely on trust; any long-term deal we agree to must be based on verifiable action that convinces us and the international community that Iran is not building a nuclear bomb. If John F. Kennedy and Ronald Reagan could negotiate with the Soviet Union, then surely a strong and confident America can negotiate with less powerful adversaries today.

The sanctions that we put in place helped make this opportunity possible. But let me be clear: if this Congress sends me a new sanctions bill now that threatens to derail these talks, I will veto it. For the sake of our national security, we must give diplomacy a chance to succeed. If Iran's leaders do not seize this opportunity, then I will be the first to call for more sanctions, and stand ready to exercise all options to make sure Iran does not build a nuclear weapon. But if Iran's leaders do seize the chance, then Iran could take an important step to rejoin the community of nations, and we will have resolved one of the leading security challenges of our time without the risks of war.

Finally, let's remember that our leadership is defined not just by our defense against threats, but by the enormous opportunities to do good and promote understanding around the globe – to forge greater cooperation, to expand new markets, to free people from fear and want. And no one is better positioned to take advantage of those opportunities than America.

Our alliance with Europe remains the strongest the world has ever known. From Tunisia to Burma, we're supporting those who are willing to do the hard work of building democracy. In Ukraine, we stand for the principle that all people have the right to express themselves freely and peacefully, and have a say in their country's future. Across Africa, we're bringing together businesses and governments to double access to electricity and help end extreme poverty. In the Americas, we are building new ties of commerce, but we're also expanding cultural and educational exchanges among young people. And we will continue to focus on the Asia-Pacific, where we support our allies, shape a future of greater security and prosperity, and extend a hand to those devastated by disaster – as we did in the Philippines, when our Marines and civilians rushed to aid those battered by a typhoon, and were greeted with words like, "We will never forget your kindness" and "God bless America!"

We do these things because they help promote our long-term security. And we do them because we believe in the inherent dignity and equality of every human being, regardless of race or religion, creed or sexual orientation. And next week, the world will see one expression of that commitment – when Team USA marches the red, white, and blue into the Olympic Stadium – and brings home the gold.

My fellow Americans, no other country in the world does what we do. On every issue, the world turns to us, not simply because of the size of our economy or our military might – but because of the ideals we stand for, and the burdens we bear to advance them.

No one knows this better than those who serve in uniform. As this time of war draws to a close, a new generation of heroes returns to civilian life. We'll keep slashing that backlog so our veterans receive the benefits they've earned, and our wounded warriors receive the health care – including the mental health care – that they need. We'll keep working to help all our veterans translate their skills and leadership into jobs here at home. And we all continue to join forces to honor and support our remarkable military families.

Let me tell you about one of those families I've come to know.

I first met Cory Remsburg, a proud Army Ranger, at Omaha Beach on the 65th anniversary of D-Day. Along with some of his fellow Rangers, he walked me through the program – a strong, impressive young man, with an easy manner, sharp as a tack. We joked around, and took pictures, and I told him to stay in touch.

A few months later, on his tenth deployment, Cory was nearly killed by a massive roadside bomb in Afghanistan. His comrades found him in a canal, face down, underwater, shrapnel in his brain.

For months, he lay in a coma. The next time I met him, in the hospital, he couldn't speak; he could barely move. Over the years, he's endured dozens of surgeries and procedures, and hours of grueling rehab every day.

Even now, Cory is still blind in one eye. He still struggles on his left side. But slowly, steadily, with the support of caregivers like his dad Craig, and the community around him, Cory has grown stronger. Day by day, he's learned to speak again and stand again and walk again – and he's working toward the day when he can serve his country again.

"My recovery has not been easy," he says. "Nothing in life that's worth anything is easy."

Cory is here tonight. And like the Army he loves, like the America he serves, Sergeant First Class Cory Remsburg never gives up, and he does not quit.

My fellow Americans, men and women like Cory remind us that America has never come easy. Our freedom, our democracy, has never been easy. Sometimes we stumble; we make mistakes; we get frustrated or discouraged. But for more than two hundred years, we have put those things aside and placed our collective shoulder to the wheel of progress – to create and build and expand the possibilities of individual achievement; to free other nations from tyranny and fear; to promote justice, and fairness, and equality under the law, so that the words set to paper by our founders are made real for every citizen. The America we want for our kids – a rising America where honest work is plentiful and communities are strong; where prosperity is widely shared and opportunity for all lets us go as far as our dreams and toil will take us – none of it is easy. But if we work together; if we summon what is best in us, with our feet planted firmly in today but our eyes cast towards tomorrow – I know it's within our reach.

Believe it.

God bless you, and God bless the United States of America.

1.7.1 Notes

[1] "FULL TRANSCRIPT: Obama's 2014 State of the Union address", *The Washington Post*

1.8   Barack Obama's Seventh State of the Union Address

Mr. Speaker, Mr. Vice President, Members of Congress, my fellow Americans:

We are fifteen years into this new century. Fifteen years that dawned with terror touching our shores; that unfolded with a new generation fighting two long and costly wars; that saw a vicious recession spread across our nation and the world. It has been, and still is, a hard time for many.

But tonight, we turn the page.

Tonight, after a breakthrough year for America, our economy is growing and creating jobs at the fastest pace since 1999. Our unemployment rate is now lower than it was before the financial crisis. More of our kids are graduating than ever before; more of our people are insured than ever before; we are as free from the grip of foreign oil as we've been in almost 30 years.

Tonight, for the first time since 9/11, our combat mission in Afghanistan is over. Six years ago, nearly 180,000 American troops served in Iraq and Afghanistan. Today, fewer than 15,000 remain. And we salute the courage and sacrifice of every man and woman in this 9/11 Generation who has served to keep us safe. We are humbled and grateful for your service.

America, for all that we've endured; for all the grit and hard work required to come back; for all the tasks that lie ahead, know this:

The shadow of crisis has passed, and the State of the Union is strong.

At this moment -- with a growing economy, shrinking deficits, bustling industry, and booming energy production -- we have risen from recession freer to write our own future than any other nation on Earth. It's now up to us to choose who we want to be over the next fifteen years, and for decades to come.

Will we accept an economy where only a few of us do spectacularly well? Or will we commit ourselves to an economy that generates rising incomes and chances for everyone who makes the effort?

Will we approach the world fearful and reactive, dragged into costly conflicts that strain our military and set back our standing? Or will we lead wisely, using all elements of our power to defeat new threats and protect our planet?

Will we allow ourselves to be sorted into factions and turned against one another -- or will we recapture the sense of common purpose that has always propelled America forward?

In two weeks, I will send this Congress a budget filled with ideas that are practical, not partisan. And in the months ahead, I'll crisscross the country making a case for those ideas.

So tonight, I want to focus less on a checklist of proposals, and focus more on the values at stake in the choices before us.

It begins with our economy.

Seven years ago, Rebekah and Ben Erler of Minneapolis were newlyweds. She waited tables. He worked construction. Their first child, Jack, was on the way.

They were young and in love in America, and it doesn't get much better than that.

"If only we had known," Rebekah wrote to me last spring, "what was about to happen to the housing and construction market."

As the crisis worsened, Ben's business dried up, so he took what jobs he could find, even if they kept him on the road for long stretches of time. Rebekah took out student loans, enrolled in community college, and retrained for a new career. They sacrificed for each other. And slowly, it paid off. They bought their first home. They had a second son, Henry. Rebekah got a better job, and then a raise. Ben is back in construction -- and home for dinner every night.

"It is amazing," Rebekah wrote, "what you can bounce back from when you have to...we are a strong, tight-knit family who has made it through some very, very hard times."

We are a strong, tight-knit family who has made it through some very, very hard times.

America, Rebekah and Ben's story is our story. They represent the millions who have worked hard, and scrimped, and sacrificed, and retooled. You are the reason I ran for this office. You're the people I was thinking of six years ago today, in the darkest months of the crisis, when I stood on the steps of this Capitol and promised we would rebuild our economy on a new foundation. And it's been your effort and resilience that has made it possible for our country to emerge stronger.

We believed we could reverse the tide of outsourcing, and draw new jobs to our shores. And over the past five years, our businesses have created more than 11 million new jobs.

We believed we could reduce our dependence on foreign oil and protect our planet. And today, America is number one in oil and gas. America is number one in wind power. Every three weeks, we bring online as much solar power as we did in all of 2008. And thanks to lower gas prices and higher fuel standards, the typical family this year should save $750 at the pump.

We believed we could prepare our kids for a more competitive world. And today, our younger students have earned the highest math and reading scores on record. Our high school graduation rate has hit an all-time high. And more Americans finish college than ever before.

We believed that sensible regulations could prevent another crisis, shield families from ruin, and encourage fair competition. Today, we have new tools to stop taxpayer-funded bailouts, and a new consumer watchdog to protect us from predatory lending and abusive credit card practices. And in the past year alone, about ten million uninsured Americans finally gained the security of health coverage.

At every step, we were told our goals were misguided or too ambitious; that we would crush jobs and explode deficits. Instead, we've seen the fastest economic growth in over a decade, our deficits cut by two-thirds, a stock market that has doubled, and health care inflation at its lowest rate in fifty years.

So the verdict is clear. Middle-class economics works. Expanding opportunity works. And these policies will continue to work, as long as politics don't get in the way. We can't slow down businesses or put our economy at risk with government shutdowns or fiscal showdowns. We can't put the security of families at risk by taking away their health insurance, or unraveling the new rules on Wall Street, or refighting past battles on immigration when we've got a system to fix. And if a bill comes to my desk that tries to do any of these things, it will earn my veto.

Today, thanks to a growing economy, the recovery is touching more and more lives. Wages are finally starting to rise again. We know that more small business owners plan to raise their employees' pay than at any time since 2007. But here's the thing -- those of us here tonight, we need to set our sights higher than just making sure government doesn't halt the progress we're making. We need to do more than just do no harm. Tonight, together, let's do more to restore the link between hard work and growing opportunity for every American.

Because families like Rebekah's still need our help. She and Ben are working as hard as ever, but have to forego vacations and a new car so they can pay off student loans and save for retirement. Basic childcare for Jack and Henry costs more than their mortgage, and almost as much as a year at the University of Minnesota. Like millions of hardworking Americans, Rebekah isn't asking for a handout, but she is asking that we look for more ways to help families get ahead.

In fact, at every moment of economic change throughout our history, this country has taken bold action to adapt to new circumstances, and to make sure everyone gets a fair shot. We set up worker protections, Social Security, Medicare, and Medicaid to protect ourselves from the harshest adversity. We gave our citizens schools and colleges, infrastructure and the internet -- tools they needed to go as far as their effort will take them.

That's what middle-class economics is -- the idea that this country does best when everyone gets their fair shot, everyone does their fair share, and everyone plays by the same set of rules. We don't just want everyone to share in America's success -- we want everyone to contribute to our success.

So what does middle-class economics require in our time?

First -- middle-class economics means helping working families feel more secure in a world of constant change. That means helping folks afford childcare, college, health care, a home, retirement -- and my budget will address each of these issues, lowering the taxes of working families and putting thousands of dollars back into their pockets each year.

Here's one example. During World War II, when men like my grandfather went off to war, having women like my grandmother in the workforce was a national security priority -- so this country provided universal childcare. In today's economy, when having both parents in the workforce is an economic necessity for many families, we need affordable, high-quality childcare more than ever. It's not a nice-to-have -- it's a must-have. It's time we stop treating childcare as a side issue, or a women's issue, and treat it like the national economic priority that it is for all of us. And that's why my

plan will make quality childcare more available, and more affordable, for every middle-class and low-income family with young children in America -- by creating more slots and a new tax cut of up to $3,000 per child, per year.

Here's another example. Today, we're the only advanced country on Earth that doesn't guarantee paid sick leave or paid maternity leave to our workers. Forty-three million workers have no paid sick leave. Forty-three million. Think about that. And that forces too many parents to make the gut-wrenching choice between a paycheck and a sick kid at home. So I'll be taking new action to help states adopt paid leave laws of their own. And since paid sick leave won where it was on the ballot last November, let's put it to a vote right here in Washington. Send me a bill that gives every worker in America the opportunity to earn seven days of paid sick leave. It's the right thing to do.

Of course, nothing helps families make ends meet like higher wages. That's why this Congress still needs to pass a law that makes sure a woman is paid the same as a man for doing the same work. Really. It's 2015. It's time. We still need to make sure employees get the overtime they've earned. And to everyone in this Congress who still refuses to raise the minimum wage, I say this: If you truly believe you could work full-time and support a family on less than $15,000 a year, go try it. If not, vote to give millions of the hardest-working people in America a raise.

These ideas won't make everybody rich, or relieve every hardship. That's not the job of government. To give working families a fair shot, we'll still need more employers to see beyond next quarter's earnings and recognize that investing in their workforce is in their company's long-term interest. We still need laws that strengthen rather than weaken unions, and give American workers a voice. But things like child care and sick leave and equal pay; things like lower mortgage premiums and a higher minimum wage -- these ideas will make a meaningful difference in the lives of millions of families. That is a fact. And that's what all of us -- Republicans and Democrats alike -- were sent here to do.

Second, to make sure folks keep earning higher wages down the road, we have to do more to help Americans upgrade their skills.

America thrived in the 20th century because we made high school free, sent a generation of GIs to college, and trained the best workforce in the world. But in a 21st century economy that rewards knowledge like never before, we need to do more.

By the end of this decade, two in three job openings will require some higher education. Two in three. And yet, we still live in a country where too many bright, striving Americans are priced out of the education they need. It's not fair to them, and it's not smart for our future.

That's why I am sending this Congress a bold new plan to lower the cost of community college -- to zero.

Forty percent of our college students choose community college. Some are young and starting out. Some are older and looking for a better job. Some are veterans and single parents trying to transition back into the job market. Whoever you are, this plan is your chance to graduate ready for the new economy, without a load of debt. Understand, you've got to earn it -- you've got to keep your grades up and graduate on time. Tennessee, a state with Republican leadership, and Chicago, a city with Democratic leadership, are showing that free community college is possible. I want to spread that idea all across America, so that two years of college becomes as free and universal in America as high school is today. And I want to work with this Congress, to make sure Americans already burdened with student loans can reduce their monthly payments, so that student debt doesn't derail anyone's dreams.

Thanks to Vice President Biden's great work to update our job training system, we're connecting community colleges with local employers to train workers to fill high-paying jobs like coding, and nursing, and robotics. Tonight, I'm also asking more businesses to follow the lead of companies like CVS and UPS, and offer more educational benefits and paid apprenticeships -- opportunities that give workers the chance to earn higher-paying jobs even if they don't have a higher education.

And as a new generation of veterans comes home, we owe them every opportunity to live the American Dream they helped defend. Already, we've made strides towards ensuring that every veteran has access to the highest quality care. We're slashing the backlog that had too many veterans waiting years to get the benefits they need, and we're making it easier for vets to translate their training and experience into civilian jobs. Joining Forces, the national campaign launched by Michelle and Jill Biden, has helped nearly 700,000 veterans and military spouses get new jobs. So to every CEO in America, let me repeat: If you want somebody who's going to get the job done, hire a veteran.

Finally, as we better train our workers, we need the new economy to keep churning out high-wage jobs for our workers to fill.

Since 2010, America has put more people back to work than Europe, Japan, and all advanced economies combined. Our manufacturers have added almost 800,000 new jobs. Some of our bedrock sectors, like our auto industry, are booming. But there are also millions of Americans who work in jobs that didn't even exist ten or twenty years ago -- jobs at companies like Google, and eBay, and Tesla.

So no one knows for certain which industries will generate the jobs of the future. But we do know we want them here in America. That's why the third part of middle-class economics is about building the most competitive economy anywhere, the place where businesses want to locate and hire.

21st century businesses need 21st century infrastructure -- modern ports, stronger bridges, faster trains and the fastest internet. Democrats and Republicans used to agree on this. So let's set our sights higher than a single oil pipeline. Let's pass a bipartisan infrastructure plan that could create more than thirty times as many jobs per year, and make this country stronger for decades to come.

21st century businesses, including small businesses, need to sell more American products overseas. Today, our businesses export more than ever, and exporters tend to pay their workers higher wages. But as we speak, China wants to write the rules for the world's fastest-growing region. That would put our workers and businesses at a disadvantage. Why would we let that happen? We should write those rules. We should level the playing field. That's why I'm asking both parties to give me trade promotion authority to protect American workers, with strong new trade deals from Asia to Europe that aren't just free, but fair.

Look, I'm the first one to admit that past trade deals haven't always lived up to the hype, and that's why we've gone after countries that break the rules at our expense. But ninety-five percent of the world's customers live outside our borders, and we can't close ourselves off from those opportunities. More than half of manufacturing executives have said they're actively looking at bringing jobs back from China. Let's give them one more reason to get it done.

21st century businesses will rely on American science, technology, research and development. I want the country that eliminated polio and mapped the human genome to lead a new era of medicine -- one that delivers the right treatment at the right time. In some patients with cystic fibrosis, this approach has reversed a disease once thought unstoppable. Tonight, I'm launching a new Precision Medicine Initiative to bring us closer to curing diseases like cancer and diabetes -- and to give all of us access to the personalized information we need to keep ourselves and our families healthier.

I intend to protect a free and open internet, extend its reach to every classroom, and every community, and help folks build the fastest networks, so that the next generation of digital innovators and entrepreneurs have the platform to keep reshaping our world.

I want Americans to win the race for the kinds of discoveries that unleash new jobs -- converting sunlight into liquid fuel; creating revolutionary prosthetics, so that a veteran who gave his arms for his country can play catch with his kid; pushing out into the Solar System not just to visit, but to stay. Last month, we launched a new spacecraft as part of a re-energized space program that will send American astronauts to Mars. In two months, to prepare us for those missions, Scott Kelly will begin a year-long stay in space. Good luck, Captain -- and make sure to Instagram it.

Now, the truth is, when it comes to issues like infrastructure and basic research, I know there's bipartisan support in this chamber. Members of both parties have told me so. Where we too often run onto the rocks is how to pay for these investments. As Americans, we don't mind paying our fair share of taxes, as long as everybody else does, too. But for far too long, lobbyists have rigged the tax code with loopholes that let some corporations pay nothing while others pay full freight. They've riddled it with giveaways the superrich don't need, denying a break to middle class families who do.

This year, we have an opportunity to change that. Let's close loopholes so we stop rewarding companies that keep profits abroad, and reward those that invest in America. Let's use those savings to rebuild our infrastructure and make it more attractive for companies to bring jobs home. Let's simplify the system and let a small business owner file based on her actual bank statement, instead of the number of accountants she can afford. And let's close the loopholes that lead to inequality by allowing the top one percent to avoid paying taxes on their accumulated wealth. We can use that money to help more families pay for childcare and send their kids to college. We need a tax code that truly helps working Americans trying to get a leg up in the new economy, and we can achieve that together.

Helping hardworking families make ends meet. Giving them the tools they need for good-paying jobs in this new economy. Maintaining the conditions for growth and competitiveness. This is where America needs to go. I believe it's where the American people want to go. It will make our economy stronger a year from now, fifteen years from now, and deep into the century ahead.

Of course, if there's one thing this new century has taught us, it's that we cannot separate our work at home from challenges beyond our shores.

My first duty as Commander-in-Chief is to defend the United States of America. In doing so, the question is not whether America leads in the world, but how. When we make rash decisions, reacting to the headlines instead of using our heads; when the first response to a challenge is to send in our military -- then we risk getting drawn into unnecessary conflicts, and neglect the broader strategy we need for a safer, more prosperous world. That's what our enemies want us to do.

I believe in a smarter kind of American leadership. We lead best when we combine military power with strong diplomacy; when we leverage our power with coalition building; when we don't let our fears blind us to the opportunities that this new century presents. That's exactly what we're doing right now -- and around the globe, it is making a difference.

First, we stand united with people around the world who've been targeted by terrorists -- from a school in Pakistan to the streets of Paris. We will continue to hunt down terrorists and dismantle their networks, and we reserve the right to act unilaterally, as we've done relentlessly since I took office to take out terrorists who pose a direct threat to us and our allies.

At the same time, we've learned some costly lessons over the last thirteen years.

Instead of Americans patrolling the valleys of Afghanistan, we've trained their security forces, who've now taken the lead, and we've honored our troops' sacrifice by supporting that country's first democratic transition. Instead of sending large ground forces overseas, we're partnering with nations from South Asia to North Africa to deny safe haven to terrorists who threaten America. In Iraq and Syria, American leadership -- including our military power -- is stopping ISIL's advance. Instead of getting dragged into another ground war in the Middle East, we are leading a broad coalition, including Arab nations, to degrade and ultimately destroy this terrorist group. We're also supporting a moderate opposition in Syria that can help us in this effort, and assisting people everywhere who stand up to the bankrupt ideology of violent extremism. This effort will take time. It will require focus. But we will succeed. And tonight, I call on this Congress to show the world that we are united in this mission by passing a resolution to authorize the use of force against ISIL.

Second, we are demonstrating the power of American strength and diplomacy. We're upholding the principle that bigger nations can't bully the small -- by opposing Russian aggression, supporting Ukraine's democracy, and reassuring our NATO allies. Last year, as we were doing the hard work of imposing sanctions along with our allies, some suggested that Mr. Putin's aggression was a masterful display of strategy and strength. Well, today, it is America that stands strong and united with our allies, while Russia is isolated, with its economy in tatters.

That's how America leads -- not with bluster, but with persistent, steady resolve.

In Cuba, we are ending a policy that was long past its expiration date. When what you're doing doesn't work for fifty years, it's time to try something new. Our shift in Cuba policy has the potential to end a legacy of mistrust in our hemisphere; removes a phony excuse for restrictions in Cuba; stands up for democratic values; and extends the hand of friendship to the Cuban people. And this year, Congress should begin the work of ending the embargo. As His Holiness, Pope Francis, has said, diplomacy is the work of "small steps." These small steps have added up to new hope for the future in Cuba. And after years in prison, we're overjoyed that Alan Gross is back where he belongs. Welcome home, Alan.

Our diplomacy is at work with respect to Iran, where, for the first time in a decade, we've halted the progress of its nuclear program and reduced its stockpile of nuclear material. Between now and this spring, we have a chance to negotiate a comprehensive agreement that prevents a nuclear-armed Iran; secures America and our allies -- including Israel; while avoiding yet another Middle East conflict. There are no guarantees that negotiations will succeed, and I keep all options on the table to prevent a nuclear Iran. But new sanctions passed by this Congress, at this moment in time, will all but guarantee that diplomacy fails -- alienating America from its allies; and ensuring that Iran starts up its nuclear program again. It doesn't make sense. That is why I will veto any new sanctions bill that threatens to undo this progress. The American people expect us to only go to war as a last resort, and I intend to stay true to that wisdom.

Third, we're looking beyond the issues that have consumed us in the past to shape the coming century.

No foreign nation, no hacker, should be able to shut down our networks, steal our trade secrets, or invade the privacy of American families, especially our kids. We are making sure our government integrates intelligence to combat cyber threats, just as we have done to combat terrorism. And tonight, I urge this Congress to finally pass the legislation we need to better meet the evolving threat of cyber-attacks, combat identity theft, and protect our children's information. If we don't act, we'll leave our nation and our economy vulnerable. If we do, we can continue to protect the technologies that have unleashed untold opportunities for people around the globe.

In West Africa, our troops, our scientists, our doctors, our nurses and healthcare workers are rolling back Ebola -- saving countless lives and stopping the spread of disease. I couldn't be prouder of them, and I thank this Congress for your bipartisan support of their efforts. But the job is not yet done -- and the world needs to use this lesson to build a more effective global effort to prevent the spread of future pandemics, invest in smart development, and eradicate extreme poverty.

In the Asia Pacific, we are modernizing alliances while making sure that other nations play by the rules -- in how they trade, how they resolve maritime disputes, and how they participate in meeting common international challenges like nonproliferation and disaster relief. And no challenge -- no challenge -- poses a greater threat to future generations than climate change.

2014 was the planet's warmest year on record. Now, one year doesn't make a trend, but this does -- 14 of the 15 warmest years on record have all fallen in the first 15 years of this century.

I've heard some folks try to dodge the evidence by saying they're not scientists; that we don't have enough information to act. Well, I'm not a scientist, either. But you know what -- I know a lot of really good scientists at NASA, and NOAA, and at our major universities. The best scientists in the world are all telling us that our activities are changing the climate, and if we do not act forcefully, we'll continue to see rising oceans, longer, hotter heat waves, dangerous droughts and floods, and massive disruptions that can trigger greater migration, conflict, and hunger around the globe. The Pentagon says that climate change poses immediate risks to our national security. We should act like it.

That's why, over the past six years, we've done more than ever before to combat climate change, from the way we produce energy, to the way we use it. That's why we've set aside more public lands and waters than any administration in history. And that's why I will not let this Congress endanger the health of our children by turning back the clock on our efforts. I am determined to make sure American leadership drives international action. In Beijing, we made an historic announcement -- the United States will double the pace at which we cut carbon pollution, and China committed, for the first time, to limiting their emissions. And because the world's two largest economies came together, other nations are now stepping up, and offering hope that, this year, the world will finally reach an agreement to protect the one planet we've got.

There's one last pillar to our leadership -- and that's the example of our values.

As Americans, we respect human dignity, even when we're threatened, which is why I've prohibited torture, and worked to make sure our use of new technology like drones is properly constrained. It's why we speak out against the deplorable anti-Semitism that has resurfaced in certain parts of the world. It's why we continue to reject offensive stereotypes of Muslims -- the vast majority of whom share our commitment to peace. That's why we defend free speech, and advocate for political prisoners, and condemn the persecution of women, or religious minorities, or people who are lesbian, gay, bisexual, or transgender. We do these things not only because they're right, but because they make us safer.

As Americans, we have a profound commitment to justice -- so it makes no sense to spend three million dollars per prisoner to keep open a prison that the world condemns and terrorists use to recruit. Since I've been President, we've worked responsibly to cut the population of GTMO in half. Now it's time to finish the job. And I will not relent in my determination to shut it down. It's not who we are.

As Americans, we cherish our civil liberties -- and we need to uphold that commitment if we want maximum cooperation from other countries and industry in our fight against terrorist networks. So while some have moved on from the debates over our surveillance programs, I haven't. As promised, our intelligence agencies have worked hard, with the recommendations of privacy advocates, to increase transparency and build more safeguards against potential abuse. And next month, we'll issue a report on how we're keeping our promise to keep our country safe while strengthening privacy.

Looking to the future instead of the past. Making sure we match our power with diplomacy, and use force wisely. Building coalitions to meet new challenges and opportunities. Leading -- always -- with the example of our values. That's what makes us exceptional. That's what keeps us strong. And that's why we must keep striving to hold ourselves to the highest of standards -- our own.

You know, just over a decade ago, I gave a speech in Boston where I said there wasn't a liberal America, or a conservative America; a black America or a white America -- but a United States of America. I said this because I had seen it in my own life, in a nation that gave someone like me a chance; because I grew up in Hawaii, a melting pot of races and customs; because I made Illinois my home -- a state of small towns, rich farmland, and one of the world's great cities; a microcosm of the country where Democrats and Republicans and Independents, good people of every ethnicity and every faith, share certain bedrock values.

Over the past six years, the pundits have pointed out more than once that my presidency hasn't delivered on this vision. How ironic, they say, that our politics seems more divided than ever. It's held up as proof not just of my own flaws -- of which there are many -- but also as proof that the vision itself is misguided, and naïve, and that there are too many people in this town who actually benefit from partisanship and gridlock for us to ever do anything about it.

I know how tempting such cynicism may be. But I still think the cynics are wrong.

I still believe that we are one people. I still believe that together, we can do great things, even when the odds are long. I believe this because over and over in my six years in office, I have seen America at its best. I've seen the hopeful faces of young graduates from New York to California; and our newest officers at West Point, Annapolis, Colorado Springs, and New London. I've mourned with grieving families in Tucson and Newtown; in Boston, West, Texas, and West Virginia. I've watched Americans beat back adversity from the Gulf Coast to the Great Plains; from Midwest assembly lines to the Mid-Atlantic seaboard. I've seen something like gay marriage go from a wedge issue used to drive us apart to a story of freedom across our country, a civil right now legal in states that seven in ten Americans call home.

So I know the good, and optimistic, and big-hearted generosity of the American people who, every day, live the idea that we are our brother's keeper, and our sister's keeper. And I know they expect those of us who serve here to set a better example.

So the question for those of us here tonight is how we, all of us, can better reflect America's hopes. I've served in Congress with many of you. I know many of you well. There are a lot of good people here, on both sides of the aisle. And many of you have told me that this isn't what you signed up for -- arguing past each other on cable shows, the constant fundraising, always looking over your shoulder at how the base will react to every decision.

Imagine if we broke out of these tired old patterns. Imagine if we did something different.

Understand -- a better politics isn't one where Democrats abandon their agenda or Republicans simply embrace mine.

A better politics is one where we appeal to each other's basic decency instead of our basest fears.

A better politics is one where we debate without demonizing each other; where we talk issues, and values, and principles, and facts, rather than "gotcha" moments, or trivial gaffes, or fake controversies that have nothing to do with people's daily lives.

A better politics is one where we spend less time drowning in dark money for ads that pull us into the gutter, and spend more time lifting young people up, with a sense of purpose and possibility, and asking them to join in the great mission of building America.

If we're going to have arguments, let's have arguments -- but let's make them debates worthy of this body and worthy of this country.

We still may not agree on a woman's right to choose, but surely we can agree it's a good thing that teen pregnancies and abortions are nearing all-time lows, and that every woman should have access to the health care she needs.

Yes, passions still fly on immigration, but surely we can all see something of ourselves in the striving young student, and agree that no one benefits when a hardworking mom is taken from her child, and that it's possible to shape a law that upholds our tradition as a nation of laws and a nation of immigrants.

We may go at it in campaign season, but surely we can agree that the right to vote is sacred; that it's being denied to too many; and that, on this 50th anniversary of the great march from Selma to Montgomery and the passage of the Voting Rights Act, we can come together, Democrats and Republicans, to make voting easier for every single American.

We may have different takes on the events of Ferguson and New York. But surely we can understand a father who fears his son can't walk home without being harassed. Surely we can understand the wife who won't rest until the police officer she married walks through the front door at the end of his shift. Surely we can agree it's a good thing that for the first time in 40 years, the crime rate and the incarceration rate have come down together, and use that as a starting point for Democrats and Republicans, community leaders and law enforcement, to reform America's criminal justice system so that it protects and serves us all.

That's a better politics. That's how we start rebuilding trust. That's how we move this country forward. That's what the American people want. That's what they deserve.

I have no more campaigns to run. (*responding to Republican members of Congress:* I know, because I won both of them.)

My only agenda for the next two years is the same as the one I've had since the day I swore an oath on the steps of this Capitol -- to do what I believe is best for America. If you share the broad vision I outlined tonight, join me in the work at hand. If you disagree with parts of it, I hope you'll at least work with me where you do agree. And I commit to every Republican here tonight that I will not only seek out your ideas, I will seek to work with you to make this country stronger.

Because I want this chamber, this city, to reflect the truth -- that for all our blind spots and shortcomings, we are a people with the strength and generosity of spirit to bridge divides, to unite in common effort, and help our neighbors, whether down the street or on the other side of the world.

I want our actions to tell every child, in every neighborhood: your life matters, and we are as committed to improving your life chances as we are for our own kids.

I want future generations to know that we are a people who see our differences as a great gift, that we are a people who value the dignity and worth of every citizen -- man and woman, young and old, black and white, Latino and Asian, immigrant and Native American, gay and straight, Americans with mental illness or physical disability.

I want them to grow up in a country that shows the world what we still know to be true: that we are still more than a collection of red states and blue states; that we are the United States of America.

I want them to grow up in a country where a young mom like Rebekah can sit down and write a letter to her President with a story to sum up these past six years:

"It is amazing what you can bounce back from when you have to...we are a strong, tight-knit family who has made it through some very, very hard times."

My fellow Americans, we too are a strong, tight-knit family. We, too, have made it through some hard times. Fifteen years into this new century, we have picked ourselves up, dusted ourselves off, and begun again the work of remaking America. We've laid a new foundation. A brighter future is ours to write. Let's begin this new chapter -- together -- and let's start the work right now.

Thank you, God bless you, and God bless this country we love.

1.8.1 Notes

[1] "State of the Union 2015: Full transcript", *Cable News Network*

Chapter 2

President Barack Obama's Inaugural Addresses

2.1   Barack Obama's First Inaugural Address

Barack Obama being sworn in as President of the United States by Chief Justice of the United States John G. Roberts

My fellow citizens:

I stand here today humbled by the task before us, grateful for the trust you have bestowed, mindful of the sacrifices borne

Video of the Inaugural Address
(83.2MB, 21m 21s, help, file info or download)

by our ancestors. I thank President Bush for his service to our nation, as well as the generosity and cooperation he has shown throughout this transition.

Forty-four Americans have now taken the presidential oath.[1] The words have been spoken during rising tides of prosperity and the still waters of peace. Yet, every so often the oath is taken amidst gathering clouds and raging storms. At these moments, America has carried on not simply because of the skill or vision of those in high office, but because We the People have remained faithful to the ideals of our forbearers, and true to our founding documents.

So it has been. So it must be with this generation of Americans.

That we are in the midst of crisis is now well understood. Our nation is at war, against a far-reaching network of violence and hatred. Our economy is badly weakened, a consequence of greed and irresponsibility on the part of some, but also our collective failure to make hard choices and prepare the nation for a new age. Homes have been lost; jobs shed; businesses shuttered. Our health care is too costly; our schools fail too many; and each day brings further evidence that the ways we use energy strengthen our adversaries and threaten our planet.

These are the indicators of crisis, subject to data and statistics. Less measurable but no less profound is a sapping of confidence across our land — a nagging fear that America's decline is inevitable, and that the next generation must lower its sights.

Today I say to you that the challenges we face are real. They are serious and they are many. They will not be met easily or in a short span of time. But know this, America — they will be met. On this day, we gather because we have chosen hope over fear, unity of purpose over conflict and discord. On this day, we come to proclaim an end to the petty grievances and false promises, the recriminations and worn-out dogmas, that for far too long have strangled our politics.

We remain a young nation, but in the words of Scripture, the time has come to set aside childish things. The time has come to reaffirm our enduring spirit; to choose our better history; to carry forward that precious gift, that noble idea, passed on from generation to generation: the God-given promise that all are equal, all are free, and all deserve a chance to pursue their full measure of happiness.

In reaffirming the greatness of our nation, we understand that greatness is never a given. It must be earned. Our journey has never been one of short-cuts or settling-for-less. It has not been the path for the faint-hearted — for those who prefer leisure over work, or seek only the pleasures of riches and fame. Rather, it has been the risk-takers, the doers, the makers of things — some celebrated but more often men and women obscure in their labor, who have carried us up the long, rugged path towards prosperity and freedom.

For us, they packed up their few worldly possessions and traveled across oceans in search of a new life.

For us, they toiled in sweatshops and settled the West; endured the lash of the whip and plowed the hard earth.

For us, they fought and died, in places like Concord and Gettysburg; Normandy and Khe Sanh. Time and again these men and women struggled and sacrificed and worked till their hands were raw so that we might live a better life. They saw America as bigger than the sum of our individual ambitions; greater than all the differences of birth or wealth or faction.

This is the journey we continue today. We remain the most prosperous, powerful nation on Earth. Our workers are no less productive than when this crisis began. Our minds are no less inventive, our goods and services no less needed than they were last week or last month or last year. Our capacity remains undiminished. But our time of standing pat, of protecting narrow interests and putting off unpleasant decisions — that time has surely passed. Starting today, we must pick ourselves up, dust ourselves off, and begin again the work of remaking America.

For everywhere we look, there is work to be done. The state of the economy calls for action, bold and swift, and we will act — not only to create new jobs, but to lay a new foundation for growth. We will build the roads and bridges, the electric grids and digital lines that feed our commerce and bind us together. We will restore science to its rightful place, and wield technology's wonders to raise health care's quality and lower its cost. We will harness the sun and the winds and the soil to fuel our cars and run our factories. And we will transform our schools and colleges and universities to meet the demands of a new age. All this we can do. All this we will do.

Now, there are some who question the scale of our ambitions — who suggest that our system cannot tolerate too many big plans. Their memories are short. For they have forgotten what this country has already done; what free men and women can achieve when imagination is joined to common purpose, and necessity to courage.

What the cynics fail to understand is that the ground has shifted beneath them — that the stale political arguments that have consumed us for so long no longer apply. The question we ask today is not whether our government is too big or too small, but whether it works — whether it helps families find jobs at a decent wage, care they can afford, a retirement that is dignified. Where the answer is *yes*, we intend to move forward. Where the answer is *no*, programs will end. And those of us who manage the public's dollars will be held to account — to spend wisely, reform bad habits, and do our business in the light of day — because only then can we restore the vital trust between a people and their government.

Nor is the question before us whether the market is a force for good or ill. Its power to generate wealth and expand freedom is unmatched, but this crisis has reminded us that without a watchful eye, the market can spin out of control — and that a nation cannot prosper long when it favors only the prosperous. The success of our economy has always depended not just on the size of our Gross Domestic Product, but on the reach of our prosperity; on our ability to extend opportunity to every willing heart — not out of charity, but because it is the surest route to our common good.

As for our common defense, we reject as false the choice between our safety and our ideals. Our Founding Fathers, faced with perils we can scarcely imagine, drafted a charter to assure the rule of law and the rights of man, a charter expanded by the blood of generations. Those ideals still light the world, and we will not give them up for expedience's sake. And so to all the other peoples and governments who are watching today, from the grandest capitals to the small village where my father was born: know that America is a friend of each nation and every man, woman, and child who seeks a future of peace and dignity, and that we are ready to lead once more.

Recall that earlier generations faced down fascism and communism not just with missiles and tanks, but with sturdy alliances and enduring convictions. They understood that our power alone cannot protect us, nor does it entitle us to do as we please. Instead, they knew that our power grows through its prudent use; our security emanates from the justness of our cause, the force of our example, the tempering qualities of humility and restraint.

We are the keepers of this legacy. Guided by these principles once more, we can meet those new threats that demand even greater effort — even greater cooperation and understanding between nations. We will begin to responsibly leave Iraq to its people, and forge a hard-earned peace in Afghanistan. With old friends and former foes, we will work tirelessly to lessen the nuclear threat, and roll back the specter of a warming planet. We will not apologize for our way of life, nor will we waver in its defense, and for those who seek to advance their aims by inducing terror and slaughtering innocents, we say to you now that our spirit is stronger and cannot be broken; you cannot outlast us, and we will defeat you.

For we know that our patchwork heritage is a strength, not a weakness. We are a nation of Christians and Muslims, Jews and Hindus — and non-believers. We are shaped by every language and culture, drawn from every end of this Earth; and because we have tasted the bitter swill of civil war and segregation, and emerged from that dark chapter stronger and more united, we cannot help but believe that the old hatreds shall someday pass; that the lines of tribe shall soon dissolve; that as the world grows smaller, our common humanity shall reveal itself; and that America must play its role in ushering in a new era of peace.

To the Muslim world, we seek a new way forward, based on mutual interest and mutual respect.

To those leaders around the globe who seek to sow conflict, or blame their society's ills on the West — know that your people will judge you on what you can build, not what you destroy. To those who cling to power through corruption and deceit and the silencing of dissent, know that you are on the wrong side of history; but that we will extend a hand if you are willing to unclench your fist.

To the people of poor nations, we pledge to work alongside you to make your farms flourish and let clean waters flow; to nourish starved bodies and feed hungry minds. And to those nations like ours that enjoy relative plenty, we say we can no longer afford indifference to the suffering outside our borders; nor can we consume the world's resources without regard to effect. For the world has changed, and we must change with it.

As we consider the road that unfolds before us, we remember with humble gratitude those brave Americans who, at this very hour, patrol far-off deserts and distant mountains. They have something to tell us, just as the fallen heroes who lie in Arlington whisper through the ages.

We honor them not only because they are guardians of our liberty, but because they embody the spirit of service; a willingness to find meaning in something greater than themselves. And yet, at this moment — a moment that will define a generation — it is precisely this spirit that must inhabit us all.

For as much as government can do and must do, it is ultimately the faith and determination of the American people upon which this nation relies. It is the kindness to take in a stranger when the levees break, the selflessness of workers who would rather cut their hours than see a friend lose their job which sees us through our darkest hours. It is the firefighter's courage to storm a stairway filled with smoke, but also a parent's willingness to nurture a child, that finally decides our fate.

Our challenges may be new. The instruments with which we meet them may be new. But those values upon which our success depends — honesty and hard work, courage and fair play, tolerance and curiosity, loyalty and patriotism — these things are old. These things are true. They have been the quiet force of progress throughout our history. What is demanded then is a return to these truths. What is required of us now is a new era of responsibility — a recognition, on the part of every American, that we have duties to ourselves, our nation, and the world — duties that we do not grudgingly accept but rather seize gladly, firm in the knowledge that there is nothing so satisfying to the spirit, so defining of our character, than giving our all to a difficult task.

This is the price and the promise of citizenship.

This is the source of our confidence — the knowledge that God calls on us to shape an uncertain destiny.

This is the meaning of our liberty and our creed — why men and women and children of every race and every faith can join in celebration across this magnificent mall, and why a man whose father less than sixty years ago might not have been served at a local restaurant can now stand before you to take a most sacred oath.

So let us mark this day with remembrance, of who we are and how far we have traveled. In the year of America's birth, in the coldest of months, a small band of patriots huddled by dying campfires on the shores of an icy river. The capital was abandoned. The enemy was advancing. The snow was stained with blood. At a moment when the outcome of our revolution was most in doubt, the father of our nation ordered these words be read to the people:[2]

> "Let it be told to the future world...that in the depth of winter, when nothing but hope and virtue could survive...that the city and the country, alarmed at one common danger, came forth to meet [it]."[3]

America, in the face of our common dangers, in this winter of our hardship, let us remember these timeless words. With hope and virtue, let us brave once more the icy currents, and endure what storms may come. Let it be said by our children's children that when we were tested we refused to let this journey end, that we did not turn back nor did we falter; and with eyes fixed on the horizon and God's grace upon us, we carried forth that great gift of freedom and delivered it safely to future generations.

Thank you. God bless you. And God bless the United States of America.

2.1.1   Notes

[1] While Obama was the 44th person to serve as president, only 43 people had taken the presidential oath as of 2009; Grover Cleveland is counted as the 22nd and 24th President due to his non-consecutive terms (in 1885 and 1893), .

[2] The Crisis No. I from The American Crisis by Thomas Paine was printed in the Pennsylvania Journal on December 19, 1776. Within a day of its publication, General Washington ordered it be read to his dispirited and suffering troops before his crossing of the Delaware River. Its opening sentence *These are the times that try men's souls* was adopted as the watchword of the Battle of Trenton on December 26 and is believed to have inspired much of the courage which won that victory. The American Crisis/Editor's Preface

[3] Obama's quote is the fifth paragraph from the bottom of Paine's writing with three words (bolded) omitted: "Let it be told to the future world, that in the depth of winter, when nothing but hope and virtue could survive, that the city and the country, alarmed at one common danger, came forth to meet **and to repulse** it.". The Crisis No. I

2.2   Barack Obama's Second Inaugural Address

Vice President Biden, Mr. Chief Justice, Members of the United States Congress, distinguished guests, and fellow citizens:

Each time we gather to inaugurate a president, we bear witness to the enduring strength of our Constitution. We affirm the promise of our democracy. We recall that what binds this nation together is not the colors of our skin or the tenets of our faith or the origins of our names. What makes us exceptional – what makes us American – is our allegiance to an idea, articulated in a declaration made more than two centuries ago:

"We hold these truths to be self-evident, that all men are created equal, that they are endowed by their Creator with certain unalienable rights, that among these are Life, Liberty, and the pursuit of Happiness."

Today we continue a never-ending journey, to bridge the meaning of those words with the realities of our time. For history tells us that while these truths may be self-evident, they have never been self-executing; that while freedom is a gift from God, it must be secured by His people here on Earth. The patriots of 1776 did not fight to replace the tyranny of a king with the privileges of a few or the rule of a mob. They gave to us a Republic, a government of, and by, and for the people, entrusting each generation to keep safe our founding creed.

For more than two hundred years, we have. Through blood drawn by lash and blood drawn by sword, we learned that no union founded on the principles of liberty and equality could survive half-slave and half-free. We made ourselves anew, and vowed to move forward together.

Together, we determined that a modern economy requires railroads and highways to speed travel and commerce; schools and colleges to train our workers. Together, we discovered that a free market only thrives when there are rules to ensure competition and fair play. Together, we resolved that a great nation must care for the vulnerable, and protect its people from life's worst hazards and misfortune. Through it all, we have never relinquished our skepticism of central authority, nor have we succumbed to the fiction that all society's ills can be cured through government alone. Our celebration of initiative and enterprise; our insistence on hard work and personal responsibility, these are constants in our character.

But we have always understood that when times change, so must we; that fidelity to our founding principles requires new responses to new challenges; that preserving our individual freedoms ultimately requires collective action. For the American people can no more meet the demands of today's world by acting alone than American soldiers could have met the forces of fascism or communism with muskets and militias. No single person can train all the math and science teachers we'll need to equip our children for the future, or build the roads and networks and research labs that will bring new jobs and businesses to our shores. Now, more than ever, we must do these things together, as one nation, and one people.

This generation of Americans has been tested by crises that steeled our resolve and proved our resilience. A decade of war is now ending. An economic recovery has begun. America's possibilities are limitless, for we possess all the qualities that this world without boundaries demands: youth and drive; diversity and openness; an endless capacity for risk and a gift for reinvention. My fellow Americans, we are made for this moment, and we will seize it – so long as we seize it together.

For we, the people, understand that our country cannot succeed when a shrinking few do very well and a growing many barely make it. We believe that America's prosperity must rest upon the broad shoulders of a rising middle class. We know that America thrives when every person can find independence and pride in their work; when the wages of honest labor liberate families from the brink of hardship. We are true to our creed when a little girl born into the bleakest poverty knows that she has the same chance to succeed as anybody else, because she is an American, she is free, and she is equal, not just in the eyes of God but also in our own.

We understand that outworn programs are inadequate to the needs of our time. We must harness new ideas and technology to remake our government, revamp our tax code, reform our schools, and empower our citizens with the skills they need to work harder, learn more, and reach higher. But while the means will change, our purpose endures: a nation that rewards the effort and determination of every single American. That is what this moment requires. That is what will give real meaning to our creed.

We, the people, still believe that every citizen deserves a basic measure of security and dignity. We must make the hard choices to reduce the cost of health care and the size of our deficit. But we reject the belief that America must choose between caring for the generation that built this country and investing in the generation that will build its future. For we remember the lessons of our past, when twilight years were spent in poverty, and parents of a child with a disability had nowhere to turn. We do not believe that in this country, freedom is reserved for the lucky, or happiness for the few. We recognize that no matter how responsibly we live our lives, any one of us, at any time, may face a job loss, or a sudden illness, or a home swept away in a terrible storm. The commitments we make to each other – through Medicare, and Medicaid, and Social Security – these things do not sap our initiative; they strengthen us. They do not make us a nation of takers; they free us to take the risks that make this country great.

We, the people, still believe that our obligations as Americans are not just to ourselves, but to all posterity. We will respond to the threat of climate change, knowing that the failure to do so would betray our children and future generations. Some may still deny the overwhelming judgment of science, but none can avoid the devastating impact of raging fires, and crippling drought, and more powerful storms.

The path towards sustainable energy sources will be long and sometimes difficult. But America cannot resist this transition; we must lead it. We cannot cede to other nations the technology that will power new jobs and new industries – we must claim its promise. That is how we will maintain our economic vitality and our national treasure – our forests and waterways; our croplands and snowcapped peaks. That is how we will preserve our planet, commanded to our care by God. That's what will lend meaning to the creed our fathers once declared.

We, the people, still believe that enduring security and lasting peace do not require perpetual war. Our brave men and women in uniform, tempered by the flames of battle, are unmatched in skill and courage. Our citizens, seared by the memory of those we have lost, know too well the price that is paid for liberty. The knowledge of their sacrifice will keep us forever vigilant against those who would do us harm. But we are also heirs to those who won the peace and not just the war, who turned sworn enemies into the surest of friends, and we must carry those lessons into this time as well.

We will defend our people and uphold our values through strength of arms and rule of law. We will show the courage to try and resolve our differences with other nations peacefully – not because we are naïve about the dangers we face, but because engagement can more durably lift suspicion and fear. America will remain the anchor of strong alliances in every corner of the globe; and we will renew those institutions that extend our capacity to manage crisis abroad, for no one has a greater stake in a peaceful world than its most powerful nation. We will support democracy from Asia to Africa; from the Americas to the Middle East, because our interests and our conscience compel us to act on behalf of those who long for freedom. And we must be a source of hope to the poor, the sick, the marginalized, the victims of prejudice – not out of mere charity, but because peace in our time requires the constant advance of those principles that our common creed describes: tolerance and opportunity; human dignity and justice.

We, the people, declare today that the most evident of truths – that all of us are created equal – is the star that guides us still; just as it guided our forebears through Seneca Falls, and Selma, and Stonewall; just as it guided all those men and women, sung and unsung, who left footprints along this great Mall, to hear a preacher say that we cannot walk alone; to hear a King proclaim that our individual freedom is inextricably bound to the freedom of every soul on Earth.

It is now our generation's task to carry on what those pioneers began. For our journey is not complete until our wives, our mothers, and daughters can earn a living equal to their efforts. Our journey is not complete until our gay brothers and sisters are treated like anyone else under the law – for if we are truly created equal, then surely the love we commit to one another must be equal as well. Our journey is not complete until no citizen is forced to wait for hours to exercise the right to vote. Our journey is not complete until we find a better way to welcome the striving, hopeful immigrants who still see America as a land of opportunity; until bright young students and engineers are enlisted in our workforce rather than expelled from our country. Our journey is not complete until all our children, from the streets of Detroit to the hills of Appalachia to the quiet lanes of Newtown, know that they are cared for, and cherished, and always safe from harm.

That is our generation's task – to make these words, these rights, these values – of Life, and Liberty, and the Pursuit of Happiness – real for every American. Being true to our founding documents does not require us to agree on every contour of life; it does not mean we will all define liberty in exactly the same way, or follow the same precise path to happiness. Progress does not compel us to settle centuries-long debates about the role of government for all time – but it does require us to act in our time.

For now decisions are upon us, and we cannot afford delay. We cannot mistake absolutism for principle, or substitute spectacle for politics, or treat name-calling as reasoned debate. We must act, knowing that our work will be imperfect. We must act, knowing that today's victories will be only partial, and that it will be up to those who stand here in four years, and forty years, and four hundred years hence to advance the timeless spirit once conferred to us in a spare Philadelphia hall.

My fellow Americans, the oath I have sworn before you today, like the one recited by others who serve in this Capitol, was an oath to God and country, not party or faction – and we must faithfully execute that pledge during the duration of our service. But the words I spoke today are not so different from the oath that is taken each time a soldier signs up for duty, or an immigrant realizes her dream. My oath is not so different from the pledge we all make to the flag that waves above and that fills our hearts with pride.

They are the words of citizens, and they represent our greatest hope. You and I, as citizens, have the power to set this country's course. You and I, as citizens, have the obligation to shape the debates of our time – not only with the votes we cast, but with the voices we lift in defense of our most ancient values and enduring ideals. Let each of us now embrace, with solemn duty and awesome joy, what is our lasting birthright. With common effort and common purpose, with passion and dedication, let us answer the call of history, and carry into an uncertain future that precious light of freedom.

Thank you, God bless you, and may He forever bless these United States of America.

2.2.1   Notes

[1] "2013 inaugural ceremony to be pushed back a day," David Jackson, *USA Today*, 28 March 2012

The honor of your presence
is requested at the ceremonies attending the
Inauguration of the

President and Vice President of the United States

The Capitol of the United States of America
City of Washington
January twentieth
Two thousand nine
by the
Joint Congressional
Committee on Inaugural Ceremonies

Dianne Feinstein, Chairman,
Harry Reid, Robert F. Bennett,
Nancy Pelosi, Steny H. Hoyer, John A. Boehner

MALL STANDING AREA · SILVER

Admit Bearer to Mall Standing Area
(see back for entrance gates)

Ticket Holders Will be Required to
Pass Through Security Screening.

Please Arrive Early Due to Large Crowds

This Card Does Not Admit to
Capitol Building

Gates Open–9:00 a.m.
Musical Prelude–10:30 a.m.
Ceremonies–11:30 a.m.

Silver ticket for the inaugural ceremony distributed to the general public by the U.S. Congress

Chapter 3

President Barack Obama's 2014 / 2015 Speeches

3.1 Statement by the President on the Passing of Leonard Nimoy

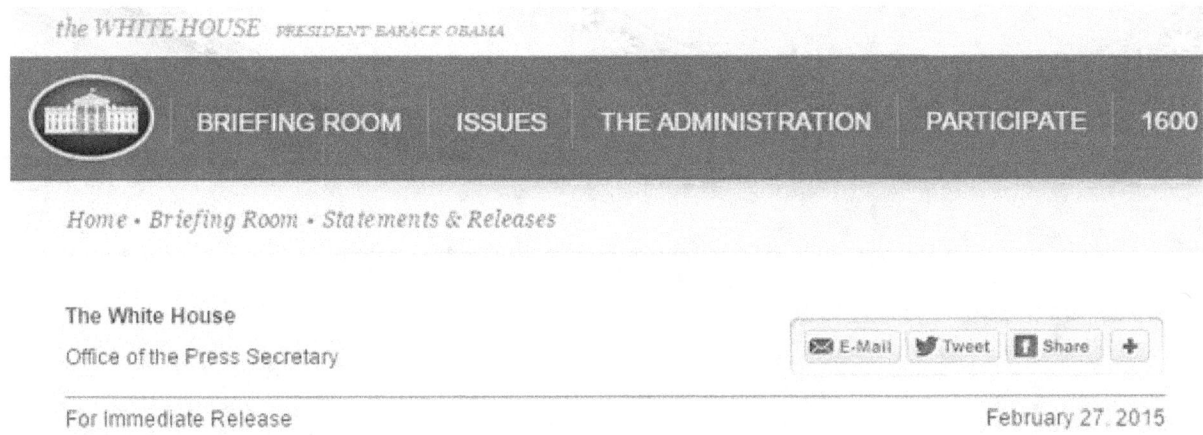

The White House

Office of the Press Secretary

E-Mail   Tweet   Share   +

For Immediate Release   February 27, 2015

Statement by the President on the Passing of Leonard Nimoy

Long before being nerdy was cool, there was Leonard Nimoy. Leonard was a lifelong lover of the arts and humanities, a supporter of the sciences, generous with his talent and his time. And of course, Leonard was Spock. Cool, logical, big-eared and level-headed, the center of Star Trek's optimistic, inclusive vision of humanity's future.

I loved Spock.

In 2007, I had the chance to meet Leonard in person. It was only logical to greet him with the Vulcan salute, the universal sign for "Live long and prosper." And after 83 years on this planet – and on his visits to many others – it's clear Leonard Nimoy did just that. Michelle and I join his family, friends, and countless fans who miss him so dearly today.

Statement by the President on the Passing of Leonard Nimoy

Administration of Barack Obama, 2015

Statement on the Death of Leonard S. Nimoy
February 27, 2015

Long before being nerdy was cool, there was Leonard Nimoy. Leonard was a lifelong lover of the arts and humanities, a supporter of the sciences, generous with his talent and his time. And of course, Leonard was Spock: cool, logical, big eared, and level headed, the center of Star Trek's optimistic, inclusive vision of humanity's future. I loved Spock.

In 2007, I had the chance to meet Leonard in person. It was only logical to greet him with the Vulcan salute, the universal sign for "Live long and prosper." And after 83 years on this planet—and on his visits to many others—it's clear Leonard Nimoy did just that. Michelle and I join his family, friends, and countless fans who miss him so dearly today.

Categories: Statements by the President : Deaths :: Nimoy, Leonard S.

Names: Obama, Michelle.

Subjects: Deaths : Nimoy, Leonard S.

DCPD Number: DCPD201500133.

1

Statement on the Death of Leonard S Nimoy

Statement by the President on the Passing of Leonard Nimoy

The White House

Office of the Press Secretary

February 27, 2015

Statement by the President on the Passing of Leonard Nimoy

Long before being nerdy was cool, there was Leonard Nimoy. Leonard was a lifelong lover of the arts and humanities, a supporter of the sciences, generous with his talent and his time. And of course, Leonard was Spock. Cool, logical, big-eared and level-headed, the center of Star Trek's optimistic, inclusive vision of humanity's future.

I loved Spock.

In 2007, I had the chance to meet Leonard in person. It was only logical to greet him with the Vulcan salute, the universal sign for "Live long and prosper." And after 83 years on this planet – and on his visits to many others – it's clear Leonard Nimoy did just that. Michelle and I join his family, friends, and countless fans who miss him so dearly today.

3.2   Statement by the President on the Murder of Boris Nemtsov

The White House

Office of the Press Secretary

For immediate release
February 27, 2015

Statement by the President on the Murder of Boris Nemtsov

The United States condemns the brutal murder of Boris Nemtsov, and we call upon the Russian government to conduct a prompt, impartial, and transparent investigation into the circumstances of his murder and ensure that those responsible for this vicious killing are brought to justice. Nemtsov was a tireless advocate for his country, seeking for his fellow Russian citizens the rights to which all people are entitled. I admired Nemtsov's courageous dedication to the struggle against corruption in Russia and appreciated his willingness to share his candid views with me when we met in Moscow in 2009. We offer our sincere condolences to Boris Efimovich's family, and to the Russian people, who have lost one of the most dedicated and eloquent defenders of their rights.

3.3   President Obama Delivers Remarks on the 50th Anniversary of the Selma Marches

Former President George W. Bush listens as President Obama delivers remarks at the foot of the Edmund Pettus Bridge

President Obama Delivers Remarks on the 50th Anniversary of the Selma Marches

The White House

Office of the Press Secretary

March 7, 2015

For Immediate Release

March 07, 2015

Remarks by the President at the 50th Anniversary of the Selma to Montgomery Marches

Edmund Pettus Bridge

Selma, Alabama

2:17 P.M. CST

AUDIENCE MEMBER: We love you, President Obama!

THE PRESIDENT: Well, you know I love you back. (Applause.)

It is a rare honor in this life to follow one of your heroes. And John Lewis is one of my heroes.

Now, I have to imagine that when a younger John Lewis woke up that morning 50 years ago and made his way to Brown

Chapel, heroics were not on his mind. A day like this was not on his mind. Young folks with bedrolls and backpacks were milling about. Veterans of the movement trained newcomers in the tactics of non-violence; the right way to protect yourself when attacked. A doctor described what tear gas does to the body, while marchers scribbled down instructions for contacting their loved ones. The air was thick with doubt, anticipation and fear. And they comforted themselves with the final verse of the final hymn they sung:

"No matter what may be the test, God will take care of you; Lean, weary one, upon His breast, God will take care of you."

And then, his knapsack stocked with an apple, a toothbrush, and a book on government -- all you need for a night behind bars -- John Lewis led them out of the church on a mission to change America.

President and Mrs. Bush, Governor Bentley, Mayor Evans, Sewell, Reverend Strong, members of Congress, elected officials, foot soldiers, friends, fellow Americans:

As John noted, there are places and moments in America where this nation's destiny has been decided. Many are sites of war -- Concord and Lexington, Appomattox, Gettysburg. Others are sites that symbolize the daring of America's character -- Independence Hall and Seneca Falls, Kitty Hawk and Cape Canaveral.

Selma is such a place. In one afternoon 50 years ago, so much of our turbulent history -- the stain of slavery and anguish of civil war; the yoke of segregation and tyranny of Jim Crow; the death of four little girls in Birmingham; and the dream of a Baptist preacher -- all that history met on this bridge.

It was not a clash of armies, but a clash of wills; a contest to determine the true meaning of America. And because of men and women like John Lewis, Joseph Lowery, Hosea Williams, Amelia Boynton, Diane Nash, Ralph Abernathy, C.T. Vivian, Andrew Young, Fred Shuttlesworth, Dr. Martin Luther King, Jr., and so many others, the idea of a just America and a fair America, an inclusive America, and a generous America -- that idea ultimately triumphed.

As is true across the landscape of American history, we cannot examine this moment in isolation. The march on Selma was part of a broader campaign that spanned generations; the leaders that day part of a long line of heroes.

We gather here to celebrate them. We gather here to honor the courage of ordinary Americans willing to endure billy clubs and the chastening rod; tear gas and the trampling hoof; men and women who despite the gush of blood and splintered bone would stay true to their North Star and keep marching towards justice.

They did as Scripture instructed: "Rejoice in hope, be patient in tribulation, be constant in prayer." And in the days to come, they went back again and again. When the trumpet call sounded for more to join, the people came — black and white, young and old, Christian and Jew, waving the American flag and singing the same anthems full of faith and hope. A white newsman, Bill Plante, who covered the marches then and who is with us here today, quipped that the growing number of white people lowered the quality of the singing. (Laughter.) To those who marched, though, those old gospel songs must have never sounded so sweet.

In time, their chorus would well up and reach President Johnson. And he would send them protection, and speak to the nation, echoing their call for America and the world to hear: "We shall overcome." (Applause.) What enormous faith these men and women had. Faith in God, but also faith in America.

The Americans who crossed this bridge, they were not physically imposing. But they gave courage to millions. They held no elected office. But they led a nation. They marched as Americans who had endured hundreds of years of brutal violence, countless daily indignities — but they didn't seek special treatment, just the equal treatment promised to them almost a century before. (Applause.)

What they did here will reverberate through the ages. Not because the change they won was preordained; not because their victory was complete; but because they proved that nonviolent change is possible, that love and hope can conquer hate.

As we commemorate their achievement, we are well-served to remember that at the time of the marches, many in power condemned rather than praised them. Back then, they were called Communists, or half-breeds, or outside agitators, sexual and moral degenerates, and worse — they were called everything but the name their parents gave them. Their faith was questioned. Their lives were threatened. Their patriotism challenged.

And yet, what could be more American than what happened in this place? (Applause.) What could more profoundly vindicate the idea of America than plain and humble people — unsung, the downtrodden, the dreamers not of high station, not born to wealth or privilege, not of one religious tradition but many, coming together to shape their country's course?

What greater expression of faith in the American experiment than this, what greater form of patriotism is there than the belief that America is not yet finished, that we are strong enough to be self-critical, that each successive generation can look upon our imperfections and decide that it is in our power to remake this nation to more closely align with our highest ideals? (Applause.)

That's why Selma is not some outlier in the American experience. That's why it's not a museum or a static monument to behold from a distance. It is instead the manifestation of a creed written into our founding documents: "We the People...in order to form a more perfect union." "We hold these truths to be self-evident, that all men are created equal." (Applause.)

These are not just words. They're a living thing, a call to action, a roadmap for citizenship and an insistence in the capacity of free men and women to shape our own destiny. For founders like Franklin and Jefferson, for leaders like Lincoln and FDR, the success of our experiment in self-government rested on engaging all of our citizens in this work. And that's what we celebrate here in Selma. That's what this movement was all about, one leg in our long journey toward freedom. (Applause.)

The American instinct that led these young men and women to pick up the torch and cross this bridge, that's the same instinct that moved patriots to choose revolution over tyranny. It's the same instinct that drew immigrants from across oceans and the Rio Grande; the same instinct that led women to reach for the ballot, workers to organize against an unjust status quo; the same instinct that led us to plant a flag at Iwo Jima and on the surface of the Moon. (Applause.)

It's the idea held by generations of citizens who believed that America is a constant work in progress; who believed that loving this country requires more than singing its praises or avoiding uncomfortable truths. It requires the occasional disruption, the willingness to speak out for what is right, to shake up the status quo. That's America. (Applause.)

That's what makes us unique. That's what cements our reputation as a beacon of opportunity. Young people behind the Iron Curtain would see Selma and eventually tear down that wall. Young people in Soweto would hear Bobby Kennedy talk about ripples of hope and eventually banish the scourge of apartheid. Young people in Burma went to prison rather than submit to military rule. They saw what John Lewis had done. From the streets of Tunis to the Maidan in Ukraine, this generation of young people can draw strength from this place, where the powerless could change the world's greatest power and push their leaders to expand the boundaries of freedom.

They saw that idea made real right here in Selma, Alabama. They saw that idea manifest itself here in America.

Because of campaigns like this, a Voting Rights Act was passed. Political and economic and social barriers came down. And the change these men and women wrought is visible here today in the presence of African Americans who run boardrooms, who sit on the bench, who serve in elected office from small towns to big cities; from the Congressional Black Caucus all the way to the Oval Office. (Applause.)

Because of what they did, the doors of opportunity swung open not just for black folks, but for every American. Women marched through those doors. Latinos marched through those doors. Asian Americans, gay Americans, Americans with disabilities -- they all came through those doors. (Applause.) Their endeavors gave the entire South the chance to rise again, not by reasserting the past, but by transcending the past.

What a glorious thing, Dr. King might say. And what a solemn debt we owe. Which leads us to ask, just how might we repay that debt?

First and foremost, we have to recognize that one day's commemoration, no matter how special, is not enough. If Selma taught us anything, it's that our work is never done. (Applause.) The American experiment in self-government gives work and purpose to each generation.

Selma teaches us, as well, that action requires that we shed our cynicism. For when it comes to the pursuit of justice, we can afford neither complacency nor despair.

Just this week, I was asked whether I thought the Department of Justice's Ferguson report shows that, with respect to race, little has changed in this country. And I understood the question; the report's narrative was sadly familiar. It evoked the kind of abuse and disregard for citizens that spawned the Civil Rights Movement. But I rejected the notion that nothing's changed. What happened in Ferguson may not be unique, but it's no longer endemic. It's no longer sanctioned by law or by custom. And before the Civil Rights Movement, it most surely was. (Applause.)

We do a disservice to the cause of justice by intimating that bias and discrimination are immutable, that racial division is inherent to America. If you think nothing's changed in the past 50 years, ask somebody who lived through the Selma or Chicago or Los Angeles of the 1950s. Ask the female CEO who once might have been assigned to the secretarial pool if nothing's changed. Ask your gay friend if it's easier to be out and proud in America now than it was thirty years ago. To deny this progress, this hard-won progress -- our progress — would be to rob us of our own agency, our own capacity, our responsibility to do what we can to make America better.

Of course, a more common mistake is to suggest that Ferguson is an isolated incident; that racism is banished; that the work that drew men and women to Selma is now complete, and that whatever racial tensions remain are a consequence of those seeking to play the "race card" for their own purposes. We don't need the Ferguson report to know that's not true. We just need to open our eyes, and our ears, and our hearts to know that this nation's racial history still casts its long shadow upon us.

We know the march is not yet over. We know the race is not yet won. We know that reaching that blessed destination where we are judged, all of us, by the content of our character requires admitting as much, facing up to the truth. "We are capable of bearing a great burden," James Baldwin once wrote, "once we discover that the burden is reality and arrive where reality is."

There's nothing America can't handle if we actually look squarely at the problem. And this is work for all Americans, not just some. Not just whites. Not just blacks. If we want to honor the courage of those who marched that day, then all of us are called to possess their moral imagination. All of us will need to feel as they did the fierce urgency of now. All of us need to recognize as they did that change depends on our actions, on our attitudes, the things we teach our children. And if we make such an effort, no matter how hard it may sometimes seem, laws can be passed, and consciences can be stirred, and consensus can be built. (Applause.)

With such an effort, we can make sure our criminal justice system serves all and not just some. Together, we can raise the level of mutual trust that policing is built on — the idea that police officers are members of the community they risk their lives to protect, and citizens in Ferguson and New York and Cleveland, they just want the same thing young people here marched for 50 years ago -- the protection of the law. (Applause.) Together, we can address unfair sentencing and overcrowded prisons, and the stunted circumstances that rob too many boys of the chance to become men, and rob the nation of too many men who could be good dads, and good workers, and good neighbors. (Applause.)

With effort, we can roll back poverty and the roadblocks to opportunity. Americans don't accept a free ride for anybody, nor do we believe in equality of outcomes. But we do expect equal opportunity. And if we really mean it, if we're not just giving lip service to it, but if we really mean it and are willing to sacrifice for it, then, yes, we can make sure every child gets an education suitable to this new century, one that expands imaginations and lifts sights and gives those children the skills they need. We can make sure every person willing to work has the dignity of a job, and a fair wage, and a real voice, and sturdier rungs on that ladder into the middle class.

And with effort, we can protect the foundation stone of our democracy for which so many marched across this bridge — and that is the right to vote. (Applause.) Right now, in 2015, 50 years after Selma, there are laws across this country designed to make it harder for people to vote. As we speak, more of such laws are being proposed. Meanwhile, the Voting Rights Act, the culmination of so much blood, so much sweat and tears, the product of so much sacrifice in the face of wanton violence, the Voting Rights Act stands weakened, its future subject to political rancor.

How can that be? The Voting Rights Act was one of the crowning achievements of our democracy, the result of Republican and Democratic efforts. (Applause.) President Reagan signed its renewal when he was in office. President George W. Bush signed its renewal when he was in office. (Applause.) One hundred members of Congress have come here today to honor people who were willing to die for the right to protect it. If we want to honor this day, let that hundred go back to Washington and gather four hundred more, and together, pledge to make it their mission to restore that law this year. That's how we honor those on this bridge. (Applause.)

Of course, our democracy is not the task of Congress alone, or the courts alone, or even the President alone. If every new voter-suppression law was struck down today, we would still have, here in America, one of the lowest voting rates among free peoples. Fifty years ago, registering to vote here in Selma and much of the South meant guessing the number of jellybeans in a jar, the number of bubbles on a bar of soap. It meant risking your dignity, and sometimes, your life.

What's our excuse today for not voting? How do we so casually discard the right for which so many fought? (Applause.) How do we so fully give away our power, our voice, in shaping America's future? Why are we pointing to somebody else when we could take the time just to go to the polling places? (Applause.) We give away our power.

Fellow marchers, so much has changed in 50 years. We have endured war and we've fashioned peace. We've seen technological wonders that touch every aspect of our lives. We take for granted conveniences that our parents could have scarcely imagined. But what has not changed is the imperative of citizenship; that willingness of a 26-year-old deacon, or a Unitarian minister, or a young mother of five to decide they loved this country so much that they'd risk everything to realize its promise.

That's what it means to love America. That's what it means to believe in America. That's what it means when we say America is exceptional.

For we were born of change. We broke the old aristocracies, declaring ourselves entitled not by bloodline, but endowed by our Creator with certain inalienable rights. We secure our rights and responsibilities through a system of self-government, of and by and for the people. That's why we argue and fight with so much passion and conviction -- because we know our efforts matter. We know America is what we make of it.

Look at our history. We are Lewis and Clark and Sacajawea, pioneers who braved the unfamiliar, followed by a stampede of farmers and miners, and entrepreneurs and hucksters. That's our spirit. That's who we are.

We are Sojourner Truth and Fannie Lou Hamer, women who could do as much as any man and then some. And we're Susan B. Anthony, who shook the system until the law reflected that truth. That is our character.

We're the immigrants who stowed away on ships to reach these shores, the huddled masses yearning to breathe free -- Holocaust survivors, Soviet defectors, the Lost Boys of Sudan. We're the hopeful strivers who cross the Rio Grande because we want our kids to know a better life. That's how we came to be. (Applause.)

We're the slaves who built the White House and the economy of the South. (Applause.) We're the ranch hands and cowboys who opened up the West, and countless laborers who laid rail, and raised skyscrapers, and organized for workers' rights.

We're the fresh-faced GIs who fought to liberate a continent. And we're the Tuskeegee Airmen, and the Navajo code-talkers, and the Japanese Americans who fought for this country even as their own liberty had been denied.

We're the firefighters who rushed into those buildings on 9/11, the volunteers who signed up to fight in Afghanistan and Iraq. We're the gay Americans whose blood ran in the streets of San Francisco and New York, just as blood ran down this bridge. (Applause.)

We are storytellers, writers, poets, artists who abhor unfairness, and despise hypocrisy, and give voice to the voiceless, and tell truths that need to be told.

We're the inventors of gospel and jazz and blues, bluegrass and country, and hip-hop and rock and roll, and our very own sound with all the sweet sorrow and reckless joy of freedom.

We are Jackie Robinson, enduring scorn and spiked cleats and pitches coming straight to his head, and stealing home in the World Series anyway. (Applause.)

We are the people Langston Hughes wrote of who "build our temples for tomorrow, strong as we know how." We are the people Emerson wrote of, "who for truth and honor's sake stand fast and suffer long;" who are "never tired, so long as we can see far enough."

That's what America is. Not stock photos or airbrushed history, or feeble attempts to define some of us as more American than others. (Applause.) We respect the past, but we don't pine for the past. We don't fear the future; we grab for it. America is not some fragile thing. We are large, in the words of Whitman, containing multitudes. We are boisterous and diverse and full of energy, perpetually young in spirit. That's why someone like John Lewis at the ripe old age of 25 could lead a mighty march.

And that's what the young people here today and listening all across the country must take away from this day. You are America. Unconstrained by habit and convention. Unencumbered by what is, because you're ready to seize what ought to be.

For everywhere in this country, there are first steps to be taken, there's new ground to cover, there are more bridges to be crossed. And it is you, the young and fearless at heart, the most diverse and educated generation in our history, who the nation is waiting to follow.

Because Selma shows us that America is not the project of any one person. Because the single-most powerful word in our democracy is the word "We." "We The People." "We Shall Overcome." "Yes We Can." (Applause.) That word is owned by no one. It belongs to everyone. Oh, what a glorious task we are given, to continually try to improve this great nation of ours.

Fifty years from Bloody Sunday, our march is not yet finished, but we're getting closer. Two hundred and thirty-nine years after this nation's founding our union is not yet perfect, but we are getting closer. Our job's easier because somebody already got us through that first mile. Somebody already got us over that bridge. When it feels the road is too hard, when the torch we've been passed feels too heavy, we will remember these early travelers, and draw strength from their example, and hold firmly the words of the prophet Isaiah: "Those who hope in the Lord will renew their strength. They will soar on [the] wings like eagles. They will run and not grow weary. They will walk and not be faint." (Applause.)

We honor those who walked so we could run. We must run so our children soar. And we will not grow weary. For we believe in the power of an awesome God, and we believe in this country's sacred promise.

May He bless those warriors of justice no longer with us, and bless the United States of America. Thank you, everybody. (Applause.)

END

2:50 P.M. CST

3.4 Remarks by the President at the 2015 Gridiron Dinner

Remarks by the President at the 2015 Gridiron Dinner

Washington Renaissance Hotel

Washington, DC

March 14, 2015

Remarks by the President at the 2015 Gridiron Dinner

10:05 P.M. EDT

THE PRESIDENT: Thank you! (Applause.) Thank you so much. Thank you. Please have a seat. Thank you so much. What a beautiful evening. Everybody looks wonderful. It's like Downton Abbey, except less funny. (Laughter.) This is my third appearance at this dinner as President. And I predict you will laugh harder than ever. I'm not saying I'm any funnier. I'm saying weed is now legal in D.C. (Laughter and applause.) I know that's how you guys are getting through this dinner. That's why you ate the food. (Laughter.)

This is also my first gridiron with a new press secretary, Josh Earnest, who's doing a great job. (Applause.) The other day, Josh came into the Oval and he said, "I've got good news and bad news. The good news is that people are finally rallying around their charismatic African-American president. The bad news — it's Clarence Page." (Laughter.)

Clarence and I go way back.

MR. PAGE: Way back.

THE PRESIDENT: Way back. Before he took office, he felt comfortable asking me for tips on a being a successful black president. (Laughter.) And I told him, you want to keep your birth certificate handy. (Laughter and applause.)

Now, let's face it, being President does age you. I mean, look at me. (Laughter.) I was hoping Fred Thompson would be the Republican speaker so I could buy a reverse mortgage. (Laughter and applause.) You start getting crankier as you get older. Next week, I'm signing an executive order to get off my lawn. (Laughter.) And getting older changes you. For example, coffee really disagrees with me these days — which is why John Boehner just invited coffee to address the joint House. (Laughter.)

It is amazing, though, how time flies. Just a few years ago, I could never imagine ever being in my fifties. And when it comes to my approval ratings, I still can't. (Laughter.) I mean, think about how things have changed since 2008. Back then, I was the young, tech-savvy candidate of the future. Now I'm yesterday's news and Hillary has got a server in her house. (Laughter.) I didn't even know you could have one of those in your house. (Laughter and applause.) I am so far behind. Did you know that? I would have gotten one.

On the bright side, by the time I'm done with this job, I will finally have enough life experience for a memoir. (Laughter.)

My Vice President isn't here tonight. He told me, "If I want to hear people talking for five hours straight, I'll just stay home alone." (Laughter.) And, by the way, this is just a quick aside — Joe rubs my shoulders too. (Laughter.) I just wanted everybody to know. He does. It's not bad, it feels pretty good. I don't let him give me a pedicure, but — (laughter.)

Of course, I want to acknowledge my fellow speakers tonight. Give it up for Terry McAuliffe — (applause) — the Governor of Virginia and the mayor of "This Town." Terry loves fundraising. He's the first person who's actually been upset to learn you can't ask people for tons of money once you become the Governor of Virginia. Well, except maybe the previous Governor of Virginia. (Laughter.)

I also want to congratulate Scott Walker. He did a great job tonight. Give it up for him. (Applause.) Governor Perry, don't you think he did a great job tonight? I noticed you weren't clapping that much.

This lame duck stuff is fun. (Laughter.)

Despite a great performance tonight, Scott has had a few recent stumbles. The other week he said he didn't know whether or not I was a Christian. And I was taken aback, but fortunately my faith teaches us forgiveness. So, Governor Walker, as-salamu alaykum. (Laughter and applause.)

Scott also recently punted on a question of evolution, which I do think is a problem. I absolutely believe in the theory of evolution — when it comes to gay marriage.

And, finally, Governor Walker got some heat for staying silent when Rudy Giuliani said I don't love America — which I also think is a problem. Think about it, Scott — if I did not love America, I wouldn't have moved here from Kenya. (Laughter and applause.) Still trying to deal with the overstaying the visa thing. But hopefully the court is okay with the immigration initiatives.

Governors Walker and Perry are not the only possible 2016-ers here tonight. We also have Dr. Ben Carson. He wants to make it clear that being here was a choice. The fact is, Doctor, embracing homosexuality is not something you do because you go to prison. It's something you do because your Vice President can't keep a secret on "Meet the Press." (Laughter.)

But for all the gaffes, all the slip-ups, I think 2016 will come down to the issues. For example, equal pay. Did you know that the average male presidential candidate earns $150,000 less per speech than a woman doing the same job? (Laughter.) It's terrible. We got to fix that.

And we can't just focus on 2016, people. We just had an election. This new Congress is just getting started, which is why I want to acknowledge the leader of the House Republicans — as soon as I figure out who that is. (Laughter.)

The fact is, I really genuinely like John Boehner. But from your press reports, I gather he may be in real trouble. Over the past several weeks, many of you have been writing about a possible conservative coup — or as Bill O'Reilly calls it, "reporting from the war zone." He's been sniffing around. The good news is, Bill has an eyewitness who can back up some of his claims. The bad news, of course, is that it's Brian Williams.

And as much as I like to make fun of my friends in the GOP and the media, it's not like this is an easy time to be a Democrat. They're turning last year's midterms into a movie; it's called "50 Shades of Red."

But, as was noted, we are determined to bounce back. The Democratic Party recently analyzed the midterm elections, and concluded we have to spend more time focused on older white voters — which is why I'm here. (Laughter and applause.)

Staying focused, moving forward — it's not always easy in this climate. I mean, you guys are always picking us apart. Recently, I made some comments about the Crusades, and people started blowing it all out of proportion, scrutinizing every single word. What is this, the Spanish Inquisition? (Laughter.)

And then I got flak for appearing on a video for BuzzFeed, trying to reach younger voters. What nonsense. You know, you don't diminish your office by taking a selfie. You do it by sending a poorly written letter to Iran. (Laughter and applause.) Really, that wasn't a joke.

Now, as with everyone else, I want to end the night by saying something a little more serious. We are producing and consuming news in ways that we couldn't have imagined a few years ago, let alone a few decades ago. But I believe that having access to more information than ever hasn't diminished people's hunger for understanding that news, and processing it. And they want to see an even deeper sense of what's going on in their world because of so much change.

And as much as politicians and the press go at it sometimes, I think that without the outstanding work that so many of you do every single day, then our need for understanding will not be met and our democracy will be poor.

When there's a crisis playing out around the world, or a milestone in our history like the one that we commemorated at Selma last week, we count on you to provide context, to see past the superficial, and in some cases, to risk everything in pursuit of the true story, and to hold us — those of us in power — to account.

So while the world of media may be changing, I am confident that our democracy will always be able to rely on the tradition represented by the reporters in this room: your persistence, your dedication, and your lifelong commitment to helping all of us better understand this world. That's how our democracy works. And we are very grateful for the job that you do.

So thank you, God bless you. And God bless one of the many countries that I love. (Laughter and applause.) Thank you.

3.5 President Obama Delivers Eulogy for the Honorable Reverend Clementa Pinckney

President Obama Delivers Eulogy for the Honorable Reverend Clementa Pinckney

The White House

Office of the Press Secretary

June 26, 2015

For Immediate Release

June 26, 2015

Remarks by the President in Eulogy for the Honorable Reverend Clementa Pinckney

College of Charleston Charleston, South Carolina

2:49 P.M. EDT

Creating President Obama Delivers Eulogy for the Honorable Reverend Clementa Pinckney

THE PRESIDENT: Giving all praise and honor to God. (Applause.)

The Bible calls us to hope. To persevere, and have faith in things not seen.

"They were still living by faith when they died," Scripture tells us. "They did not receive the things promised; they only saw them and welcomed them from a distance, admitting that they were foreigners and strangers on Earth."

We are here today to remember a man of God who lived by faith. A man who believed in things not seen. A man who believed there were better days ahead, off in the distance. A man of service who persevered, knowing full well he would not receive all those things he was promised, because he believed his efforts would deliver a better life for those who followed.

To Jennifer, his beloved wife; to Eliana and Malana, his beautiful, wonderful daughters; to the Mother Emanuel family and the people of Charleston, the people of South Carolina.

I cannot claim to have the good fortune to know Reverend Pinckney well. But I did have the pleasure of knowing him and meeting him here in South Carolina, back when we were both a little bit younger. (Laughter.) Back when I didn't have visible grey hair. (Laughter.) The first thing I noticed was his graciousness, his smile, his reassuring baritone, his deceptive sense of humor -- all qualities that helped him wear so effortlessly a heavy burden of expectation.

Friends of his remarked this week that when Clementa Pinckney entered a room, it was like the future arrived; that even from a young age, folks knew he was special. Anointed. He was the progeny of a long line of the faithful -- a family of preachers who spread God's word, a family of protesters who sowed change to expand voting rights and desegregate the South. Clem heard their instruction, and he did not forsake their teaching.

He was in the pulpit by 13, pastor by 18, public servant by 23. He did not exhibit any of the cockiness of youth, nor youth's insecurities; instead, he set an example worthy of his position, wise beyond his years, in his speech, in his conduct, in his love, faith, and purity.

As a senator, he represented a sprawling swath of the Lowcountry, a place that has long been one of the most neglected in America. A place still wracked by poverty and inadequate schools; a place where children can still go hungry and the sick can go without treatment. A place that needed somebody like Clem. (Applause.)

His position in the minority party meant the odds of winning more resources for his constituents were often long. His calls for greater equity were too often unheeded, the votes he cast were sometimes lonely. But he never gave up. He stayed true to his convictions. He would not grow discouraged. After a full day at the capitol, he'd climb into his car and head to the church to draw sustenance from his family, from his ministry, from the community that loved and needed him. There he would fortify his faith, and imagine what might be.

Reverend Pinckney embodied a politics that was neither mean, nor small. He conducted himself quietly, and kindly, and diligently. He encouraged progress not by pushing his ideas alone, but by seeking out your ideas, partnering with you to make things happen. He was full of empathy and fellow feeling, able to walk in somebody else's shoes and see through their eyes. No wonder one of his senate colleagues remembered Senator Pinckney as "the most gentle of the 46 of us -- the best of the 46 of us."

Clem was often asked why he chose to be a pastor and a public servant. But the person who asked probably didn't know the history of the AME church. (Applause.) As our brothers and sisters in the AME church know, we don't make those distinctions. "Our calling," Clem once said, "is not just within the walls of the congregation, but...the life and community in which our congregation resides." (Applause.)

He embodied the idea that our Christian faith demands deeds and not just words; that the "sweet hour of prayer" actually lasts the whole week long -- (applause) -- that to put our faith in action is more than individual salvation, it's about our collective salvation; that to feed the hungry and clothe the naked and house the homeless is not just a call for isolated charity but the imperative of a just society.

What a good man. Sometimes I think that's the best thing to hope for when you're eulogized -- after all the words and recitations and resumes are read, to just say someone was a good man. (Applause.)

You don't have to be of high station to be a good man. Preacher by 13. Pastor by 18. Public servant by 23. What a life Clementa Pinckney lived. What an example he set. What a model for his faith. And then to lose him at 41 -- slain in his sanctuary with eight wonderful members of his flock, each at different stages in life but bound together by a common commitment to God.

Cynthia Hurd. Susie Jackson. Ethel Lance. DePayne Middleton-Doctor. Tywanza Sanders. Daniel L. Simmons. Sharonda Coleman-Singleton. Myra Thompson. Good people. Decent people. God-fearing people. (Applause.) People so full of life and so full of kindness. People who ran the race, who persevered. People of great faith.

To the families of the fallen, the nation shares in your grief. Our pain cuts that much deeper because it happened in a church. The church is and always has been the center of African-American life -- (applause) -- a place to call our own in a too often hostile world, a sanctuary from so many hardships.

Over the course of centuries, black churches served as "hush harbors" where slaves could worship in safety; praise houses where their free descendants could gather and shout hallelujah -- (applause) -- rest stops for the weary along the Underground Railroad; bunkers for the foot soldiers of the Civil Rights Movement. They have been, and continue to be, community centers where we organize for jobs and justice; places of scholarship and network; places where children are loved and fed and kept out of harm's way, and told that they are beautiful and smart -- (applause) -- and taught that they matter. (Applause.) That's what happens in church.

That's what the black church means. Our beating heart. The place where our dignity as a people is inviolate. When there's no better example of this tradition than Mother Emanuel -- (applause) -- a church built by blacks seeking liberty, burned to the ground because its founder sought to end slavery, only to rise up again, a Phoenix from these ashes. (Applause.)

When there were laws banning all-black church gatherings, services happened here anyway, in defiance of unjust laws. When there was a righteous movement to dismantle Jim Crow, Dr. Martin Luther King, Jr. preached from its pulpit, and marches began from its steps. A sacred place, this church. Not just for blacks, not just for Christians, but for every American who cares about the steady expansion -- (applause) -- of human rights and human dignity in this country; a foundation stone for liberty and justice for all. That's what the church meant. (Applause.)

We do not know whether the killer of Reverend Pinckney and eight others knew all of this history. But he surely sensed the meaning of his violent act. It was an act that drew on a long history of bombs and arson and shots fired at churches, not random, but as a means of control, a way to terrorize and oppress. (Applause.) An act that he imagined would incite fear and recrimination; violence and suspicion. An act that he presumed would deepen divisions that trace back to our nation's original sin.

Oh, but God works in mysterious ways. (Applause.) God has different ideas. (Applause.)

He didn't know he was being used by God. (Applause.) Blinded by hatred, the alleged killer could not see the grace surrounding Reverend Pinckney and that Bible study group -- the light of love that shone as they opened the church doors and invited a stranger to join in their prayer circle. The alleged killer could have never anticipated the way the families of the fallen would respond when they saw him in court -- in the midst of unspeakable grief, with words of forgiveness. He couldn't imagine that. (Applause.)

The alleged killer could not imagine how the city of Charleston, under the good and wise leadership of Mayor Riley -- (applause) -- how the state of South Carolina, how the United States of America would respond -- not merely with revulsion at his evil act, but with big-hearted generosity and, more importantly, with a thoughtful introspection and self-examination that we so rarely see in public life.

Blinded by hatred, he failed to comprehend what Reverend Pinckney so well understood -- the power of God's grace. (Applause.)

This whole week, I've been reflecting on this idea of grace. (Applause.) The grace of the families who lost loved ones. The grace that Reverend Pinckney would preach about in his sermons. The grace described in one of my favorite hymnals -- the one we all know: Amazing grace, how sweet the sound that saved a wretch like me. (Applause.) I once was lost, but now I'm found; was blind but now I see. (Applause.)

According to the Christian tradition, grace is not earned. Grace is not merited. It's not something we deserve. Rather, grace is the free and benevolent favor of God -- (applause) -- as manifested in the salvation of sinners and the bestowal of blessings. Grace.

As a nation, out of this terrible tragedy, God has visited grace upon us, for he has allowed us to see where we've been blind. (Applause.) He has given us the chance, where we've been lost, to find our best selves. (Applause.) We may not have earned it, this grace, with our rancor and complacency, and short-sightedness and fear of each other -- but we got it all the same. He gave it to us anyway. He's once more given us grace. But it is up to us now to make the most of it, to receive it with gratitude, and to prove ourselves worthy of this gift.

For too long, we were blind to the pain that the Confederate flag stirred in too many of our citizens. (Applause.) It's true, a flag did not cause these murders. But as people from all walks of life, Republicans and Democrats, now acknowledge -- including Governor Haley, whose recent eloquence on the subject is worthy of praise -- (applause) -- as we all have to acknowledge, the flag has always represented more than just ancestral pride. (Applause.) For many, black and white, that flag was a reminder of systemic oppression and racial subjugation. We see that now.

Removing the flag from this state's capitol would not be an act of political correctness; it would not be an insult to the valor of Confederate soldiers. It would simply be an acknowledgment that the cause for which they fought -- the cause of slavery -- was wrong -- (applause) -- the imposition of Jim Crow after the Civil War, the resistance to civil rights for all people was wrong. (Applause.) It would be one step in an honest accounting of America's history; a modest but meaningful balm for so many unhealed wounds. It would be an expression of the amazing changes that have transformed this state and this country for the better, because of the work of so many people of goodwill, people of all races striving to form a more perfect union. By taking down that flag, we express God's grace. (Applause.)

But I don't think God wants us to stop there. (Applause.) For too long, we've been blind to the way past injustices continue to shape the present. Perhaps we see that now. Perhaps this tragedy causes us to ask some tough questions about how we can permit so many of our children to languish in poverty, or attend dilapidated schools, or grow up without prospects for a job or for a career. (Applause.)

Perhaps it causes us to examine what we're doing to cause some of our children to hate. (Applause.) Perhaps it softens hearts towards those lost young men, tens and tens of thousands caught up in the criminal justice system -- (applause) -- and leads us to make sure that that system is not infected with bias; that we embrace changes in how we train and equip our police so that the bonds of trust between law enforcement and the communities they serve make us all safer and more secure. (Applause.)

Maybe we now realize the way racial bias can infect us even when we don't realize it, so that we're guarding against not just racial slurs, but we're also guarding against the subtle impulse to call Johnny back for a job interview but not Jamal.

(Applause.) So that we search our hearts when we consider laws to make it harder for some of our fellow citizens to vote. (Applause.) By recognizing our common humanity by treating every child as important, regardless of the color of their skin or the station into which they were born, and to do what's necessary to make opportunity real for every American -- by doing that, we express God's grace. (Applause.)

For too long --

AUDIENCE: For too long!

THE PRESIDENT: For too long, we've been blind to the unique mayhem that gun violence inflicts upon this nation. (Applause.) Sporadically, our eyes are open: When eight of our brothers and sisters are cut down in a church basement, 12 in a movie theater, 26 in an elementary school. But I hope we also see the 30 precious lives cut short by gun violence in this country every single day; the countless more whose lives are forever changed -- the survivors crippled, the children traumatized and fearful every day as they walk to school, the husband who will never feel his wife's warm touch, the entire communities whose grief overflows every time they have to watch what happened to them happen to some other place.

The vast majority of Americans -- the majority of gun owners -- want to do something about this. We see that now. (Applause.) And I'm convinced that by acknowledging the pain and loss of others, even as we respect the traditions and ways of life that make up this beloved country -- by making the moral choice to change, we express God's grace. (Applause.)

We don't earn grace. We're all sinners. We don't deserve it. (Applause.) But God gives it to us anyway. (Applause.) And we choose how to receive it. It's our decision how to honor it.

None of us can or should expect a transformation in race relations overnight. Every time something like this happens, somebody says we have to have a conversation about race. We talk a lot about race. There's no shortcut. And we don't need more talk. (Applause.) None of us should believe that a handful of gun safety measures will prevent every tragedy. It will not. People of goodwill will continue to debate the merits of various policies, as our democracy requires -- this is a big, raucous place, America is. And there are good people on both sides of these debates. Whatever solutions we find will necessarily be incomplete.

But it would be a betrayal of everything Reverend Pinckney stood for, I believe, if we allowed ourselves to slip into a comfortable silence again. (Applause.) Once the eulogies have been delivered, once the TV cameras move on, to go back to business as usual -- that's what we so often do to avoid uncomfortable truths about the prejudice that still infects our society. (Applause.) To settle for symbolic gestures without following up with the hard work of more lasting change -- that's how we lose our way again.

It would be a refutation of the forgiveness expressed by those families if we merely slipped into old habits, whereby those who disagree with us are not merely wrong but bad; where we shout instead of listen; where we barricade ourselves behind preconceived notions or well-practiced cynicism.

Reverend Pinckney once said, "Across the South, we have a deep appreciation of history -- we haven't always had a deep appreciation of each other's history." (Applause.) What is true in the South is true for America. Clem understood that justice grows out of recognition of ourselves in each other. That my liberty depends on you being free, too. (Applause.) That history can't be a sword to justify injustice, or a shield against progress, but must be a manual for how to avoid repeating the mistakes of the past -- how to break the cycle. A roadway toward a better world. He knew that the path of grace involves an open mind -- but, more importantly, an open heart.

That's what I've felt this week -- an open heart. That, more than any particular policy or analysis, is what's called upon right now, I think -- what a friend of mine, the writer Marilyn Robinson, calls "that reservoir of goodness, beyond, and of another kind, that we are able to do each other in the ordinary cause of things."

That reservoir of goodness. If we can find that grace, anything is possible. (Applause.) If we can tap that grace, everything can change. (Applause.)

Amazing grace. Amazing grace.

(Begins to sing) -- Amazing grace -- (applause) -- how sweet the sound, that saved a wretch like me; I once was lost, but now I'm found; was blind but now I see. (Applause.)

Clementa Pinckney found that grace.

Cynthia Hurd found that grace.

Susie Jackson found that grace.

Ethel Lance found that grace.

DePayne Middleton-Doctor found that grace.

Tywanza Sanders found that grace.

Daniel L. Simmons, Sr. found that grace.

Sharonda Coleman-Singleton found that grace.

Myra Thompson found that grace.

Through the example of their lives, they've now passed it on to us. May we find ourselves worthy of that precious and extraordinary gift, as long as our lives endure. May grace now lead them home. May God continue to shed His grace on the United States of America. (Applause.)

END 3:28 P.M. EDT

3.6   Cool clock, Ahmed. Want to bring it to the White House?

President Obama @POTUS · Sep 16

Cool clock, Ahmed. Want to bring it to the White House? We should inspire more kids like you to like science. It's what makes America great.

440K   440K

President Obama tweet to student Ahmed Mohamed

Cool clock, Ahmed. Want to bring it to the White House?

POTUS

The White House

President Barack Obama

September 16, 2015

Cool clock, Ahmed. Want to bring it to the White House? We should inspire more kids like you to like science. It's what makes America great.

This work is in the **public domain** in the United States because it is a work of the United States *federal* government (see 17 U.S.C. 105).

3.7 Statement by the President on the Shootings at Umpqua Community College, Roseburg, Oregon

Statement by the President on the Shootings at Umpqua Community College, Roseburg, Oregon

The White House

Office of the Press Secretary

President Barack Obama

October 1, 2015

Statement by the President on the Shootings at Umpqua Community College, Roseburg, Oregon:

James S. Brady Press Briefing Room

6:22 P.M. EDT

THE PRESIDENT: There's been another mass shooting in America -- this time, in a community college in Oregon.

That means there are more American families -- moms, dads, children -- whose lives have been changed forever. That means there's another community stunned with grief, and communities across the country forced to relieve their own anguish, and parents across the country who are scared because they know it might have been their families or their children.

I've been to Roseburg, Oregon. There are really good people there. I want to thank all the first responders whose bravery likely saved some lives today. Federal law enforcement has been on the scene in a supporting role, and we've offered to stay and help as much as Roseburg needs, for as long as they need.

In the coming days, we'll learn about the victims -- young men and women who were studying and learning and working hard, their eyes set on the future, their dreams on what they could make of their lives. And America will wrap everyone who's grieving with our prayers and our love.

But as I said just a few months ago, and I said a few months before that, and I said each time we see one of these mass shootings, our thoughts and prayers are not enough. It's not enough. It does not capture the heartache and grief and anger that we should feel. And it does nothing to prevent this carnage from being inflicted someplace else in America -- next week, or a couple of months from now.

We don't yet know why this individual did what he did. And it's fair to say that anybody who does this has a sickness in their minds, regardless of what they think their motivations may be. But we are not the only country on Earth that has people with mental illnesses or want to do harm to other people. We are the only advanced country on Earth that sees these kinds of mass shootings every few months.

Earlier this year, I answered a question in an interview by saying, "The United States of America is the one advanced nation on Earth in which we do not have sufficient common-sense gun-safety laws -- even in the face of repeated mass killings." And later that day, there was a mass shooting at a movie theater in Lafayette, Louisiana. That day! Somehow this has become routine. The reporting is routine. My response here at this podium ends up being routine. The conversation in the aftermath of it. We've become numb to this.

We talked about this after Columbine and Blacksburg, after Tucson, after Newtown, after Aurora, after Charleston. It cannot be this easy for somebody who wants to inflict harm on other people to get his or her hands on a gun.

And what's become routine, of course, is the response of those who oppose any kind of common-sense gun legislation. Right now, I can imagine the press releases being cranked out: We need more guns, they'll argue. Fewer gun safety laws.

Does anybody really believe that? There are scores of responsible gun owners in this country --they know that's not true. We know because of the polling that says the majority of Americans understand we should be changing these laws -- including the majority of responsible, law-abiding gun owners.

There is a gun for roughly every man, woman, and child in America. So how can you, with a straight face, make the argument that more guns will make us safer? We know that states with the most gun laws tend to have the fewest gun deaths. So the notion that gun laws don't work, or just will make it harder for law-abiding citizens and criminals will still get their guns is not borne out by the evidence.

We know that other countries, in response to one mass shooting, have been able to craft laws that almost eliminate mass shootings. Friends of ours, allies of ours -- Great Britain, Australia, countries like ours. So we know there are ways to prevent it.

And, of course, what's also routine is that somebody, somewhere will comment and say, Obama politicized this issue. Well, this is something we should politicize. It is relevant to our common life together, to the body politic. I would ask news organizations -- because I won't put these facts forward -- have news organizations tally up the number of Americans who've been killed through terrorist attacks over the last decade and the number of Americans who've been killed by gun violence, and post those side-by-side on your news reports. This won't be information coming from me; it will be coming from you. We spend over a trillion dollars, and pass countless laws, and devote entire agencies to preventing terrorist attacks on our soil, and rightfully so. And yet, we have a Congress that explicitly blocks us from even collecting data on how we could potentially reduce gun deaths. How can that be?

This is a political choice that we make to allow this to happen every few months in America. We collectively are answerable to those families who lose their loved ones because of our inaction. When Americans are killed in mine disasters, we work to make mines safer. When Americans are killed in floods and hurricanes, we make communities safer. When roads are unsafe, we fix them to reduce auto fatalities. We have seatbelt laws because we know it saves lives. So the notion that gun violence is somehow different, that our freedom and our Constitution prohibits any modest regulation of how we use a deadly weapon, when there are law-abiding gun owners all across the country who could hunt and protect their families and do everything they do under such regulations doesn't make sense.

So, tonight, as those of us who are lucky enough to hug our kids a little closer are thinking about the families who aren't so fortunate, I'd ask the American people to think about how they can get our government to change these laws, and to save lives, and to let young people grow up. And that will require a change of politics on this issue. And it will require that the American people, individually, whether you are a Democrat or a Republican or an independent, when you decide to vote for somebody, are making a determination as to whether this cause of continuing death for innocent people should be a relevant factor in your decision. If you think this is a problem, then you should expect your elected officials to reflect your views.

And I would particularly ask America's gun owners -- who are using those guns properly, safely, to hunt, for sport, for protecting their families -- to think about whether your views are properly being represented by the organization that suggests it's speaking for you.

And each time this happens I'm going to bring this up. Each time this happens I am going to say that we can actually do something about it, but we're going to have to change our laws. And this is not something I can do by myself. I've got to have a Congress and I've got to have state legislatures and governors who are willing to work with me on this.

I hope and pray that I don't have to come out again during my tenure as President to offer my condolences to families in these circumstances. But based on my experience as President, I can't guarantee that. And that's terrible to say. And it can change.

May God bless the memories of those who were killed today. May He bring comfort to their families, and courage to the injured as they fight their way back. And may He give us the strength to come together and find the courage to change.

Thank you.

END

6:35 P.M. EDT

3.8   Remarks by the President at the 2015 White House Astronomy Night

The White House
Office of the Press Secretary

For Immediate Release
October 20, 2015

Remarks by the President at Astronomy Night

South Lawn

7:27 P.M. EDT

THE PRESIDENT: Hello, everybody! (Applause.) Yay! (Applause.) Everybody, have a seat. Welcome to the White House. I love Astronomy Night. (Applause.) And we've got a very clear night to enjoy Astronomy Night. This is some of the most fun that I have on this job. They never let me tinker with the telescopes. They don't let me hold the moon rocks when you guys aren't around. Michelle is dying to know how they grow lettuce on the International Space Station. (Laughter.) But when you guys come, I get to have some fun.

And we've got some space buffs here tonight. We have a number of members of Congress, including former astronaut, Senator Bill Nelson, from the great state of Florida. (Applause.) My science advisor, John Holdren, is here. Where is he? John -- there he is. (Applause.) See, John is a superstar in this crowd. (Laughter.) The head of NASA, Charlie Bolden -- (applause) -- along with 11 of his fellow astronauts. Mae Jameson, the first African-American woman in space is here. (Applause.) We've got Bill Nye the Science Guy. (Applause.) We've got the Mythbusters in the house. (Applause.)

But the most important thing we have here, in addition to this guy, is the young people who are here. (Applause.) Young people from across the country who are already focused on some of the greatest mysteries of the universe.

And I'm going to begin with a quick story. A long time ago, in a galaxy far, far away-- (laughter) -- actually, it was in Brooklyn -- a 14-year-old asked his parents, "What are the stars?" His parents replied, "They're lights in the sky, kid." The answer did not satisfy that young man, so he set out to answer his endless questions about the stars and the planets and possibilities of extraterrestrial life. And Carl Sagan grew up to become an astronomer who enlarged this country's imagination and sense of wonder about the depths of outer space.

We've got some young Americans here tonight with that same kind of adventurous spirit.

When Pranav Sivakumar was six years old, he found an encyclopedia about famous scientists lying around the house. At least he thinks it was lying around there. Actually, his parents probably were setting it out -- (laughter) -- hoping he was going to run into it. And he's been fascinated with outer space ever since. For years, every Saturday morning, his parents drove him an hour to an astrophysics lab for "Ask-A-Scientist" class. And before long, he teamed up with researchers he met there to study the "gravitational lensing of quasars." That is not what I was thinking about at his age. Pranav was a global finalist in the Google Science Fair -- not once, but twice. So you know he's going to do some important things. Give him a big round of applause. (Applause.)

With the help from their coaches, the RCS Rocketry Champions of Russellville, Alabama -- where are you? You're back there. There you go. Stand up, guys. (Applause.) They built a rocket that flies eggs -- well, at least one egg -- nearly one thousand feet into the air, and returns to the earth, unbroken, in under a minute. They beat hundreds of other teams to take first place in the America and International Rocketry Challenges. We are very proud of you gentlemen, and ladies. Great job. (Applause.)

From the time she was young, Phoebe Kinzelman spent nights like tonight on her grandfather's driveway, staring at the stars through his telescope. She spent a summer at Space Camp at NASA's Johnson Space Center, and her dream is to become an astronaut. I think she speaks for many of us when she says that one of her favorite Instagram accounts is Scott Kelly's. "Space is this humbling thing," Phoebe says, "you can't get too eager to rule the entire universe." But Phoebe is on her way. Where's Phoebe? Stand up, Phoebe, so everybody can you give you a big round of applause. (Applause.)

And where's Pranav? Because I was talking about him, and I didn't -- there you go. Give Pranav a big round of applause. (Applause.)

So these are examples of the extraordinary young people that we have here today. Phoebe has given pretty wise advice for a 17-year-old. Young people like Phoebe should encourage all of us to help our young people set their sights as high as they want. We need teachers to light a spark of curiosity in young minds. And we've got some outstanding teachers here today. We need parents to leave encyclopedias of famous scientists lying around the house, or help turn a bedroom into an ideas laboratory. We need to inspire more young people to ask about the stars, and begin that lifetime quest to become the next great scientist, or inventor, or engineer, or astronaut.

And we have to watch for, and cultivate, and encourage those glimmers of curiosity and possibility, and not suppress them, not squelch them -- because not only are the young people's futures at stake, but our own is at stake.

That's one of the reasons that my administration has worked so hard to encourage kids to enter STEM fields, especially young women who are too often underrepresented in these fields. (Applause.) We are halfway to my goal of training 100,000 new STEM teachers by the end of the decade. We're on track to connect 99 percent of our students to high-speed Internet before the end of the decade. And over the past six years, our "Educate to Innovate" campaign has raised $1 billion to support STEM programs nationwide, including 80 other Astronomy Nights happening right now, all across the country.

So tonight, I'm proud to announce new commitments, by cities and organizations all over the country, to expose even more students and their parents to STEM education.

Bayer is launching a national effort to help 100,000 American parents and children work on science and engineering projects together. More than 300 foundations, museums, libraries and schools across the country are partnering to bring hands-on science programming to students who don't have it. Eight observatories in Hawaii will offer all of the residents of that state free, guided tours. They didn't do that when I was in high school. (Laughter.) Wish we had thought that up earlier.

But these are just a few examples of the work that's being done all across the country. And I hope that more are going to follow the leads of these outstanding organizations, because that's how we're going to make sure our next generation of explorers take us even farther than we're going today.

A few hours ago, I got a chance to talk to the astronauts up on the International Space Station, where Scott Kelly is living for an entire year. Last month, NASA found water flowing on Mars. Earlier this year, we mapped Pluto in high-resolution. In recent years, we've discovered the first Earth-sized planet orbiting a star in a distant galaxy. And we've even slipped the outermost grasp of our solar system with Voyager 1 -- the first human-made object to venture into interstellar space. In 2017, with the help of American space companies, our astronauts will once again launch to space directly from American soil. And today, NASA is developing the capabilities to send humans to Mars in the 2030s. (Applause.) That means that some of the young people who are here tonight might be working on that project. Some of you might be on your way to mars.

America can do anything. We just got to keep on encouraging every new generation to explore, and invent, and create, and discover. We got to keep encouraging some young kid in Brooklyn, or a budding rocket scientist in Alabama, or that young girl who's dreaming to become an astronaut. Because as long as young people, like so many of you who are here tonight, keep seeking answers to the great questions, America can do anything. Which is why I'm so excited to have you all tonight. You make me feel hopeful about our future. Because I know that you're not satisfied with being home to the last great discovery -- you want to be home to the next great discovery.

And when I look out in the faces of these young people, I am absolutely confident that there are new frontiers that we're going to be busting through in my lifetime and beyond. So thank you for that. You make me excited and you make me inspired. (Applause.)

So enough talk. Let's have some fun with this telescope. It looks pretty big. My understanding is, is that we've got another young lady, Sofy. We need you to come up here and help me with this telescope, because I don't know what I'm doing. (Laughter.) Where are you? Where are you? Save me. Here we go. Okay. I don't want to break it.

How are you? I'm very proud of you. Let's grab a mic here. All right, introduce yourself.

MS. ALVAREZ: Hello, I'm Sofy Alvarez, and I'm a student at Brooklyn International High School, and I'm from Paraguay.

THE PRESIDENT: Well, it's great to see you, Sofy. So what are we going to do with this big telescope here?

MS. ALVAREZ: Well, we're going to see the moon.

THE PRESIDENT: Well, let's do that. I see it there, but you think I'm going to get a better view through this big telescope?

MS. ALVAREZ: Probably.

THE PRESIDENT: You think so?

MS. ALVAREZ: Yeah.

THE PRESIDENT: Okay. So, is it already set up for me?

MS. ALVAREZ: Oh, yeah. So I just wanted to tell you more about it and how it works.

THE PRESIDENT: Please do.

MS. ALVAREZ: So this is a reflecting telescope, so it has three parts. There are two mirrors, and one of them right now is capturing the light of the moon. And then the other mirror is just making it focus. And there is an eye-piece lens, which right now is making it -- magnifying the image of the moon. And that's how you're going to be able to see the moon, like it's right in front of you.

So do you want to try?

THE PRESIDENT: Should I just go ahead and try it?

MS. ALVAREZ: Yes.

THE PRESIDENT: Okay. Does it matter which eye?

MS. ALVAREZ: The one you see the best with.

THE PRESIDENT: I'm teasing. (Laughter.) All right. Wow.

MS. ALVAREZ: So right now what you're seeing, they're the black smooth parts, the dark smooth parts. They're called "marias" -- "maria" or "seas." And they're lava flows, and they're on the craters. They're the result of heavy bombardments with other gigantic space stuff with the moon.

THE PRESIDENT: Is "space stuff" a scientific term? (Laughter.)

MS. ALVAREZ: Yes, I think so. (Laughter.)

THE PRESIDENT: Can I just say -- this looks spectacular.

MS. ALVAREZ: It does.

THE PRESIDENT: You guys are going to get a chance to see through this. But as good as it looks out there, it sure looks better here.

Now, the interesting thing is, the image is inverted.

MS. ALVAREZ: It is?

THE PRESIDENT: Yes, it is. (Laughter.) See, if you look up, the right side -- my right side -- is lit up. But if you look through the telescope, it's the left side that's lit up.

MS. ALVAREZ: Well, it has a mirror. It's a reflecting lens. So is it that --

THE PRESIDENT: I was trying to make a point -- (laughter) --

MS. ALVAREZ: Yes, yes.

THE PRESIDENT: -- about optics. (Laughter.) Well, this is spectacular.

So, Sofy, what year are you in school?

MS. ALVAREZ: I'm sorry?

THE PRESIDENT: What year are you in school? What grade?

MS. ALVAREZ: I'm a senior in high school.

THE PRESIDENT: You're a senior?

MS. ALVAREZ: Yeah.

THE PRESIDENT: So what do you want to do next year?

MS. ALVAREZ: Well, I want to follow photography. I'm also interested in Korean studies. And I also like astronomy, so I want to do something with those three, if possible.

THE PRESIDENT: Wow.

MS. ALVAREZ: If possible.

THE PRESIDENT: Anything is possible with you. You're a spectacular young lady. Give Sofy a big round of applause. (Applause.)

MS. ALVAREZ: Thank you.

THE PRESIDENT: All right, everybody, we are setting you loose. We've got some incredible exhibits all over the place -- not just this telescope, but I know that we've got a mini planetarium and virtual reality, and real reality. (Laughter.) So there's all kinds of good stuff. I hope you guys have a wonderful time tonight. And I hope that all of you are inspired the way I am by science and by space.

Thank you, everybody. (Applause.)

END

7:41 P.M. EDT

3.9 Remarks by Barack Obama in Address to the People of India

Namaste! Thank you so much. Thank you so much, Neha, for what a wonderful introduction. Everybody, please have a seat. Nothing fills me with more hope than when I hear incredible young people like Neha and all the outstanding work that she's doing on behalf of India's youth and for representing this nation's energy and its optimism and its idealism. She makes me very, very proud. And I'm sure -- I think they may be her -- is that somebody related to you? Okay. Because we just had a chance to meet, and she's beaming with pride right now sitting next to you. Give Neha a big round of applause once again.

Distinguished guests, ladies and gentlemen, to all the students and young people who are here today, to the people of India watching and listening across this vast nation -- I bring the friendship and the greetings of the American people. On behalf of myself and Michelle, thank you so much for welcoming us back to India. Bahoot dhanyavad.

It has been a great honor to be the first American President to join you for Republic Day. With the tricolor waving above us, we celebrated the strength of your constitution. We paid tribute to India's fallen heroes. In yesterday's parade, we saw the pride and the diversity of this nation -- including the Dare Devils on their Royal Enfields, which was very impressive. Secret Service does not let me ride motorcycles. Especially not on my head.

I realize that the sight of an American President as your chief guest on Republic Day would have once seemed unimaginable. But my visit reflects the possibilities of a new moment. As I've said many times, I believe that the relationship between India and the United States can be one of the defining partnerships of this century. When I spoke to your Parliament on my last visit, I laid out my vision for how our two nations can build that partnership. And today, I want to speak directly to you -- the people of India -- about what I believe we can achieve together, and how we can do it.

My commitment to a new chapter between our countries flows from the deep friendship between our people. And Michelle and I have felt it ourselves. I recognized India with the first state visit of my presidency -- where we also danced to some pretty good Bhangra. For the first time, we brought Diwali to the White House. On our last celebration here, we celebrated the Festival of Lights in Mumbai. We danced with some children. Unfortunately, we were not able to schedule any dancing this visit. Senorita, bade-bade deshon mein. You know what I mean. Everybody said, by the way, how much better a dance Michelle was than me -- -- which hurt my feelings a little bit.

On a more personal level, India represents an intersection of two men who have always inspired me. When Reverend Dr. Martin Luther King, Jr. was protesting racial segregation in the United States, he said that his guiding light was Mahatma Gandhi. When Dr. King came to India, he said that being here -- in "Gandhi's land" -- reaffirmed his conviction that in the struggle for justice and human dignity, the most potent weapon of all is non-violent resistance. And those two great souls are why we can gather here together today, Indians and Americans, equal and free.

And there is another link that binds us. More than 100 years ago, America welcomed a son of India -- Swami Vivekananda. And Swami Vivekananda, he helped bring Hinduism and yoga to our country. And he came to my hometown of Chicago. And there, at a great gathering of religious leaders, he spoke of his faith and the divinity in every soul, and the purity of love. And he began his speech with a simple greeting: "Sisters and brothers of America."

So today, let me say: Sisters and brothers of India -- -- my confidence in what our nations can achieve together is rooted in the values we share. For we may have our different histories and speak different languages, but when we look at each other, we see a reflection of ourselves.

Having thrown off colonialism, we created constitutions that began with the same three words -- "we the people." As societies that celebrate knowledge and innovation, we transformed ourselves into high-tech hubs of the global economy. Together, we unlock new discoveries -- from the particles of creation to outer space -- two nations to have gone to both the Moon and to Mars. And here in India, this dynamism has resulted in a stunning achievement. You've lifted countless millions from poverty and built one of the world's largest middle classes.

And nobody embodies this progress and this sense of possibility more than our young people. Empowered by technology, you are connecting and collaborating like never before -- on Facebook and WhatsApp and Twitter. And chances are, you're talking to someone in America -- your friends, your cousins. The United States has the largest Indian diaspora in the world, including some three million proud Indian-Americans. And they make America stronger, and they tie us together -- bonds of family and friendship that allow us to share in each other's success.

For all these reasons, India and the United States are not just natural partners. I believe America can be India's best partner. I believe that. Of course, only Indians can decide India's role in the world. But I'm here because I'm absolutely convinced that both our peoples will have more jobs and opportunity, and our nations will be more secure, and the world will be a safer and a more just place when our two democracies -- the world's largest democracy and the world's oldest democracy -- stand together. I believe that.

So here in New Delhi, Prime Minister Modi and I have begun this work anew. And here's what I think we can do together. America wants to be your partner as you lift up the lives of the Indian people and provide greater opportunity. So working together, we're giving farmers new techniques and data -- from our satellites to their cell phones -- to increase yields and boost incomes. We're joining you in your effort to empower every Indian with a bank account.

And with the breakthroughs we achieved on this visit, we can finally move toward fully implementing our civil nuclear agreement, which will mean more reliable electricity for Indians and cleaner, non-carbon energy that helps fight climate change. And I don't have to describe for you what more electricity means. Students being able to study at night; businesses being able to stay open longer and hire more workers; farmers being able to use mechanized tools that increase their productivity; whole communities seeing more prosperity. In recent years, India has lifted more people out of poverty than any other country. And now we have a historic opportunity with India leading the way to end the injustice of extreme poverty all around the world.

America wants to be your partner as you protect the health of your people and the beauty of this land, from the backwaters of Kerala to the banks of Ganges. As we deliver more energy, more electricity, let's do it with clean, renewable energy, like solar and wind. And let's put cleaner vehicles on the road and more filtration systems on farms and villages. Because every child should be able to drink clean water, and every child should be able to breathe clean air. We need our young people healthy for their futures. And we can do it. We have the technology to do it.

America wants to be your partner in igniting the next wave of Indian growth. As India pursues more trade and investment, we want to be first in line. We're ready to join you in building new infrastructure -- the roads and the airports, the ports, the bullet trains to propel India into the future. We're ready to help design "smart cities" that serve citizens better, and we want to develop more advanced technologies with India, as we do with our closest allies.

We believe we can be even closer partners in ensuring our mutual security. And both our nations have known the anguish of terrorism, and we stand united in the defense of our people. And now we're deepening our defense cooperation against new challenges. The United States welcomes a greater role for India in the Asia Pacific, where the freedom of navigation must be upheld and disputes must be resolved peacefully. And even as we acknowledge the world as it is, we must never stop working for the world as it should be -- a world without nuclear weapons. That should be a goal for all of us.

I believe that if we're going to be true global partners, then our two nations must do more around the world together. So to ensure international security and peace, multilateral institutions created in the 20th century have to be updated for the 21st. And that's why I support a reformed United Nations Security Council that includes India as a permanent member.

Of course, as I've said before, with power comes responsibility. In this region, India can play a positive role in helping countries forge a better future, from Burma to Sri Lanka, where today there's new hope for democracy. With your experience in elections, you can help other countries with theirs. With your expertise in science and medicine, India can do more around the world to fight disease and develop new vaccines, and help us end the moral outrage of even a single child dying from a preventable disease. Together, we can stand up against human trafficking and work to end the scourge of modern day slavery.

And being global partners means confronting the urgent global challenge of climate change. With rising seas, melting Himalayan glaciers, more unpredictable monsoons, cyclones getting stronger -- few countries will be more affected by a warmer planet than India. And the United States recognizes our part in creating this problem, so we're leading the global effort to combat it. And today, I can say that America's carbon pollution is near its lowest level in almost two decades.

I know the argument made by some that it's unfair for countries like the United States to ask developing nations and emerging economies like India to reduce your dependence on the same fossil fuels that helped power our growth for more than a century. But here's the truth: Even if countries like the United States curb our emissions, if countries that are growing rapidly like India -- with soaring energy needs -- don't also embrace cleaner fuels, then we don't stand a chance against climate change.

So we welcome India's ambitious targets for generating more clean energy. We'll continue to help India deal with the impacts of climate change -- because you shouldn't have to bear that burden alone. As we keep working for a strong global agreement on climate change, it's young people like you who have to speak up, so we can protect this planet for your generation. I'll be gone when the worst effects happen. It's your generation and your children that are going to be impacted. That's why it's urgent that we begin this work right now.

Development that lifts up the lives and health of our people. Trade and economic partnerships that reduce poverty and create opportunity. Leadership in the world that defends our security, and advances human dignity, and protects our planet -- that's what I believe India and America can do together. So with the rest of my time, I want to discuss how we can do it. Because in big and diverse societies like ours, progress ultimately depends on something more basic, and that is how we see each other. And we know from experience what makes nations strong. And Neha I think did a great job of describing the essence of what's important here.

We are strongest when we see the inherent dignity in every human being. Look at our countries -- the incredible diversity even here in this hall. India is defined by countless languages and dialects, and every color and caste and creed, gender and orientations. And likewise, in America, we're black and white, and Latino and Asian, and Indian-American, and Native American. Your constitution begins with the pledge to uphold "the dignity of the individual." And our Declaration of Independence proclaims that "all men are created equal."

In both our countries, generations have worked to live up to these ideals. When he came to India, Martin Luther King, Jr. was introduced to some schoolchildren as a "fellow untouchable." My grandfather was a cook for the British army in Kenya. The distant branches of Michelle's family tree include both slaves and slave owners. When we were born, people who looked like us still couldn't vote in some parts of the country. Even as America has blessed us with extraordinary opportunities, there were moments in my life where I've been treated differently because of the color of my skin.

Many countries, including the United States, grapple with questions of identity and inequality, and how we treat each other, people who are different than us, how we deal with diversity of beliefs and of faiths. Right now, in crowded neighborhoods not far from here, a man is driving an auto-rickshaw, or washing somebody else's clothes, or doing the hard work no one else will do. And a woman is cleaning somebody else's house. And a young man is on a bicycle delivering lunch. A little girl is hauling a heavy bucket of water. And I believe their dreams, their hopes, are just as important, just as beautiful, just as worthy as ours. And so even as we live in a world of terrible inequality, we're also proud to live in countries where even the grandson of a cook can become President, or even a Dalit can help write a constitution, and even a tea seller can become Prime Minister.

The point is, is that the aim of our work must be not to just have a few do well, but to have everybody have a chance, everybody who is willing to work for it have the ability to dream big and then reach those dreams.

Our nations are strongest when we uphold the equality of all our people -- and that includes our women. Now, you may have noticed, I'm married to a very strong and talented woman. Michelle is not afraid to speak her mind, or tell me when I'm wrong -- which happens frequently. And we have two beautiful daughters, so I'm surrounded by smart, strong women. And in raising our girls, we've tried to instill in them basic values -- a sense of compassion for others, and respect for themselves, and the confidence that they can go as far as their imaginations and abilities will carry them. And as part of Michelle's work as First Lady, she's met with women and girls around the world, including here in India, to let them know that America believes in them, too.

In the United States, we're still working to make sure that women and girls have all the opportunities they deserve, and that they're treated equally. And we have some great role models, including here today the former speaker of our House of Representatives -- Nancy Pelosi -- -- the first woman speaker of the House, and my great partner.

And here in India, it's the wives and the mothers who so often hold families and communities together. Indian women have shown that they can succeed in every field -- including government, where many of your leaders are women. And the young women who are here today are part of a new generation that is making your voice heard, and standing up and determined to play your part in India's progress.

And here's what we know. We know from experience that nations are more successful when their women are successful. When girls go to school -- this is one of the most direct measures of whether a nation is going to develop effectively is how it treats its women. When a girl goes to school, it doesn't just open up her young mind, it benefits all of us -- because maybe someday she'll start her own business, or invent a new technology, or cure a disease. And when women are able to work, families are healthier, and communities are wealthier, and entire countries are more prosperous. And when young women are educated, then their children are going to be well educated and have more opportunity.

So if nations really want to succeed in today's global economy, they can't simply ignore the talents of half their people. And as husbands and fathers and brothers, we have to step up -- because every girl's life matters. Every daughter deserves the same chance as our sons. Every woman should be able to go about her day -- to walk the streets or ride the bus -- and be safe, and be treated with respect and dignity. She deserves that.

And one of the favorite things about this trip for me has been to see all these incredible Indian women in the armed forces, including the person who commanded the Guard that greeted me when I arrived. It's remarkable, and it's a sign of great strength and great progress.

Our nations are strongest when we see that we are all God's children -- all equal in His eyes and worthy of His love. Across our two great countries we have Hindus and Muslims, Christians and Sikhs, and Jews and Buddhists and Jains and so many faiths. And we remember the wisdom of Gandhiji, who said, "for me, the different religions are beautiful flowers from the same garden, or they are branches of the same majestic tree." Branches of the same majestic tree.

Our freedom of religion is written into our founding documents. It's part of America's very first amendment. Your Article 25 says that all people are "equally entitled to freedom of conscience and the right freely to profess, practice and propagate religion." In both our countries -- in all countries -- upholding this fundamental freedom is the responsibility of government, but it's also the responsibility of every person.

In our lives, Michelle and I have been strengthened by our Christian faith. But there have been times where my faith has been questioned -- by people who don't know me -- or they've said that I adhere to a different religion, as if that were somehow a bad thing. Around the world, we've seen intolerance and violence and terror perpetrated by those who profess to be standing up for their faith, but, in fact, are betraying it. No society is immune from the darkest impulses of man. And too often religion has been used to tap into those darker impulses as opposed to the light of God. Three years ago in our state of Wisconsin, back in the United States, a man went to a Sikh temple and, in a terrible act of violence, killed six innocent people -- Americans and Indians. And in that moment of shared grief, our two countries reaffirmed a basic truth, as we must again today -- that every person has the right to practice their faith how they choose, or to practice no faith at all, and to do so free of persecution and fear and discrimination.

The peace we seek in the world begins in human hearts. And it finds its glorious expression when we look beyond any differences in religion or tribe, and rejoice in the beauty of every soul. And nowhere is that more important than India. Nowhere is it going to be more necessary for that foundational value to be upheld. India will succeed so long as it is not splintered along the lines of religious faith -- so long as it's not splintered along any lines -- and is unified as one nation. And it's when all Indians, whatever your faith, go to the movies and applaud actors like Shah Rukh Khan. And when you celebrate athletes like Milkha Singh or Mary Kom. And every Indian can take pride in the courage of a humanitarian who liberates boys and girls from forced labor and exploitation -- who is here today -- Kailash Satyarthi. Our most recent winner of the Nobel Prize for Peace.

So that's what unifies us: Do we act with compassion and empathy. Are we measured by our efforts -- by what Dr. King called "the content of our character" rather than the color of our skin or the manner in which we worship our God. In both our countries, in India and in America, our diversity is our strength. And we have to guard against any efforts to divide ourselves along sectarian lines or any other lines. And if we do that well, if America shows itself as an example of its diversity and yet the capacity to live together and work together in common effort, in common purpose; if India, as massive as it is, with so much diversity, so many differences is able to continually affirm its democracy, that is an example for every other country on Earth. That's what makes us world leaders -- not just the size of our economy or the number of weapons we have, but our ability to show the way in how we work together, and how much respect we show each other.

And, finally, our nations are strongest when we empower our young people — because ultimately, you're the one who has to break down these old stereotypes and these old barriers, these old ways of thinking. Prejudices and stereotypes and assumptions -- those are what happens to old minds like mine. I'm getting gray hair now. I was more youthful when I first started this office. And that's why young people are so important in these efforts.

Here in India, most people are under 35 years old. And India is on track to become the world's most populous country. So young Indians like you aren't just going to define the future of this nation, you're going to shape the world. Like young people everywhere, you want to get an education, and find a good job, and make your mark. And it's not easy, but in our two countries, it's possible.

Remember, Michelle and I don't come from wealthy backgrounds or famous families. Our families didn't have a lot of money. We did have parents and teachers and communities that cared about us. And with the help of scholarships and student loans, we were able to attend some of best schools of the world. Without that education, we wouldn't be here today. So whether it's in America, or here in India, or around the world, we believe young people like you ought to have every chance to pursue your dreams, as well.

So as India builds new community colleges, we'll link you with our own, so more young people graduate with the skills and training to succeed. We'll increase collaborations between our colleges and universities, and help create the next India institute of technology. We'll encourage young entrepreneurs who want to start a business. And we'll increase exchanges, because I want more American students coming to India, and more Indian students coming to America. And that way, we can learn from each other and we can go further. Because one other thing we have in common Indians and Americans are some of the hardest working people on Earth.

And I've seen that -- Michelle and I have seen that in a family here in India. I just want to tell you a quick story. On our last visit here, we visited Humayun's Tomb. And while we were there, we met some of the laborers who are the backbone of this nation's progress. We met their children and their families as well -- and some wonderful young children with bright smiles, sparks in their eyes. And one of the children we met was a boy named Vishal.

And today, Vishal is 16 years old. And he and his family live in South Delhi, in the village of Mor Band. And his mother works hard in their modest home, and his sister is now in university; she wants to become a teacher. His brother is a construction worker earning his daily wage. And his father works as a stone layer, farther away, but sends home what little he makes so Vishal can go to school. And Vishal loves math, and mostly, he studies. And when he's not studying, he likes watching kabaddi. And he dreams of someday joining the Indian armed forces. And we're grateful that Vishal and his family joined us today. We're very proud of him, because he's an example of the talent that's here. And Vishal's dreams are as important as Malia and Sasha's dreams, our daughters. And we want him to have the same opportunities.

Sisters and brothers of India, we are not perfect countries. And we've known tragedy and we've known triumph. We're home to glittering skyscrapers, but also terrible poverty; and new wealth, but also rising inequality. We have many challenges in front of us. But the reason I stand here today, and am so optimistic about our future together, is that, despite our imperfections, our two nations possess the keys to progress in the century ahead. We vote in free elections. We work and we build and we innovate. We lift up the least among us. We reach for heights previous generations could not even imagine. We respect human rights and human dignity, and it is recorded in our constitutions. And we keep striving to live up to those ideals put to paper all those years ago.

And we do these things because they make our lives better and safer and more prosperous. But we also do them because our moral imaginations extend beyond the limits of our own lives. And we believe that the circumstances of our birth need not dictate the arc of our lives. We believe in the father working far from home sending money back so his family might have a better life. We believe in the mother who goes without so that her children might have something more. We believe in the laborer earning his daily wage, and the student pursuing her degree. And we believe in a young boy who knows that if he just keeps studying, if he's just given the chance, his hopes might be realized, too.

We are all "beautiful flowers from the same garden...branches of the same majestic tree." And I'm the first American President to come to your country twice, but I predict I will not be the last. Because, as Americans, we believe in the promise of India. We believe in the people of India. We are proud to be your friend. We are proud to be your partner as you build the country of your dreams.

Jai Hind! Thank you.

3.9.1 References

1. *Remarks by President Obama in Address to the People of India* - 27 January 2015.

3.10 President Obama's Statement on Keeping the Internet Open and Free

3.10.1 President Obama's Statement on Keeping the Internet Open and Free

The President's Statement

The White House

Washington

An open Internet is essential to the American economy, and increasingly to our very way of life. By lowering the cost of launching a new idea, igniting new political movements, and bringing communities closer together, it has been one of the most significant democratizing influences the world has ever known.

"Net neutrality" has been built into the fabric of the Internet since its creation — but it is also a principle that we cannot take for granted. We cannot allow Internet service providers (ISPs) to restrict the best access or to pick winners and losers in the online marketplace for services and ideas. That is why today, I am asking the Federal Communications Commission (FCC) to answer the call of almost 4 million public comments, and implement the strongest possible rules to protect net neutrality.

When I was a candidate for this office, I made clear my commitment to a free and open Internet, and my commitment remains as strong as ever. Four years ago, the FCC tried to implement rules that would protect net neutrality with little to no impact on the telecommunications companies that make important investments in our economy. After the rules were challenged, the court reviewing the rules agreed with the FCC that net neutrality was essential for preserving an environment that encourages new investment in the network, new online services and content, and everything else that makes up the Internet as we now know it. Unfortunately, the court ultimately struck down the rules — not because it disagreed with the need to protect net neutrality, but because it believed the FCC had taken the wrong legal approach.

The FCC is an independent agency, and ultimately this decision is theirs alone. I believe the FCC should create a new set of rules protecting net neutrality and ensuring that neither the cable company nor the phone company will be able to act as a gatekeeper, restricting what you can do or see online. The rules I am asking for are simple, common-sense steps that reflect the Internet you and I use every day, and that some ISPs already observe. These bright-line rules include:

- **No blocking.** If a consumer requests access to a website or service, and the content is legal, your ISP should not be permitted to block it. That way, every player — not just those commercially affiliated with an ISP — gets a fair shot at your business.

- **No throttling.** Nor should ISPs be able to intentionally slow down some content or speed up others — through a process often called "throttling" — based on the type of service or your ISP's preferences.

- **Increased transparency.** The connection between consumers and ISPs — the so-called "last mile" — is not the only place some sites might get special treatment. So, I am also asking the FCC to make full use of the transparency authorities the court recently upheld, and if necessary to apply net neutrality rules to points of interconnection between the ISP and the rest of the Internet.

- **No paid prioritization.** Simply put: No service should be stuck in a "slow lane" because it does not pay a fee. That kind of gatekeeping would undermine the level playing field essential to the Internet's growth. So, as I have before, I am asking for an explicit ban on paid prioritization and any other restriction that has a similar effect.

If carefully designed, these rules should not create any undue burden for ISPs, and can have clear, monitored exceptions for reasonable network management and for specialized services such as dedicated, mission-critical networks serving a hospital. But combined, these rules mean everything for preserving the Internet's openness.

The rules also have to reflect the way people use the Internet today, which increasingly means on a mobile device. I believe the FCC should make these rules fully applicable to mobile broadband as well, while recognizing the special challenges that come with managing wireless networks.

To be current, these rules must also build on the lessons of the past. For almost a century, our law has recognized that companies who connect you to the world have special obligations not to exploit the monopoly they enjoy over access in and out of your home or business. That is why a phone call from a customer of one phone company can reliably reach a customer of a different one, and why you will not be penalized solely for calling someone who is using another provider. It is common sense that the same philosophy should guide any service that is based on the transmission of information — whether a phone call, or a packet of data.

So the time has come for the FCC to recognize that broadband service is of the same importance and must carry the same obligations as so many of the other vital services do. To do that, I believe the FCC should reclassify consumer broadband service under Title II of the Telecommunications Act — while at the same time forbearing from rate regulation and other provisions less relevant to broadband services. This is a basic acknowledgment of the services ISPs provide to American homes and businesses, and the straightforward obligations necessary to ensure the network works for everyone — not just one or two companies.

Investment in wired and wireless networks has supported jobs and made America the center of a vibrant ecosystem of digital devices, apps, and platforms that fuel growth and expand opportunity. Importantly, network investment remained strong under the previous net neutrality regime, before it was struck down by the court; in fact, the court agreed that protecting net neutrality helps foster more investment and innovation. If the FCC appropriately forbears from the Title II regulations that are not needed to implement the principles above — principles that most ISPs have followed for years — it will help ensure new rules are consistent with incentives for further investment in the infrastructure of the Internet.

The Internet has been one of the greatest gifts our economy — and our society — has ever known. The FCC was chartered to promote competition, innovation, and investment in our networks. In service of that mission, there is no higher calling than protecting an open, accessible, and free Internet. I thank the Commissioners for having served this cause with distinction and integrity, and I respectfully ask them to adopt the policies I have outlined here, to preserve this technology's promise for today, and future generations to come.

US President Barack Obama (2009)

The President Delivers a Statement on the Shooting in Oregon

President Obama speaks at 2015 White House Astronomy Night.

President Obama's Statement on Keeping the Internet Open and Free

Chapter 4

Notable Legislation Enacted

4.1 Lilly Ledbetter Fair Pay Act of 2009

111TH UNITED STATES CONGRESS
1ST SESSION

An Act

To amend title VII of the Civil Rights Act of 1964 and the Age Discrimination in Employment Act of 1967, and to modify the operation of the Americans with Disabilities Act of 1990 and the Rehabilitation Act of 1973, to clarify that a discriminatory compensation decision or other practice that is unlawful under such Acts occurs each time compensation is paid pursuant to the discriminatory compensation decision or other practice, and for other purposes.

Be it enacted by the Senate and House of Representatives of the United States of America in Congress assembled,

Section 1. Short Title.

This title may be cited as the ``**Lilly Ledbetter Fair Pay Act of 2009**´´.

Sec. 2. Findings.

Congress finds the following:

> (1) The Supreme Court in *Ledbetter v. Goodyear Tire & Rubber Co.*, 550 U.S. 618 (2007), significantly impairs statutory protections against discrimination in compensation that Congress established and that have been bedrock principles of American law for decades. The Ledbetter decision undermines those statutory protections by unduly restricting the time period in which victims of discrimination can challenge and recover for discriminatory compensation decisions or other practices, contrary to the intent of Congress.

> (2) The limitation imposed by the Court on the filing of discriminatory compensation claims ignores the reality of wage discrimination and is at odds with the robust application of the civil rights laws that Congress intended.

> (3) With regard to any charge of discrimination under any law, nothing in this Act is intended to preclude or limit an aggrieved person's right to introduce evidence of an unlawful employment practice that has occurred outside the time for filing a charge of discrimination.

(4) Nothing in this Act is intended to change current law treatment of when pension distributions are considered paid.

Sec. 3. Discrimination in Compensation Because of Race, Color, Religion, Sex, or National Origin.

Section 706(e) of the Civil Rights Act of 1964 (42 U.S.C. 2000e-5(e)) is amended by adding at the end the following:

``(3)(A) For purposes of this section, an unlawful employment practice occurs, with respect to discrimination in compensation in violation of this title, when a discriminatory compensation decision or other practice is adopted, when an individual becomes subject to a discriminatory compensation decision or other practice, or when an individual is affected by application of a discriminatory compensation decision or other practice, including each time wages, benefits, or other compensation is paid, resulting in whole or in part from such a decision or other practice.

``(B) In addition to any relief authorized by section 1977A of the Revised Statutes (42 U.S.C. 1981a), liability may accrue and an aggrieved person may obtain relief as provided in subsection (g)(1), including recovery of back pay for up to two years preceding the filing of the charge, where the unlawful employment practices that have occurred during the charge filing period are similar or related to unlawful employment practices with regard to discrimination in compensation that occurred outside the time for filing a charge.''.

Sec. 4. Discrimination in Compensation Because of Age.

Section 7(d) of the Age Discrimination in Employment Act of 1967 (29 U.S.C. 626(d)) is amended—

(1) in the first sentence—

(A) by redesignating paragraphs (1) and (2) as subparagraphs (A) and (B), respectively; and

(B) by striking ``(d)'' and inserting ``(d)(1)'';

(2) in the third sentence, by striking ``Upon'' and inserting the following:

``(2) Upon''; and

(3) by adding at the end the following:

``(3) For purposes of this section, an unlawful practice occurs, with respect to discrimination in compensation in violation of this Act, when a discriminatory compensation decision or other practice is adopted, when a person becomes subject to a discriminatory compensation decision or other practice, or when a person is affected by application of a discriminatory compensation decision or other practice, including each time wages, benefits, or other compensation is paid, resulting in whole or in part from such a decision or other practice.''.

Sec. 5. Application to Other Laws.

(a) Americans With Disabilities Act of 1990.—

The amendments made by section 3 shall apply to claims of discrimination in compensation brought under title I and section 503 of the Americans with Disabilities Act of 1990 (42 U.S.C. 12111 et seq., 12203), pursuant to section 107(a) of such Act (42 U.S.C. 12117(a)), which adopts the powers, remedies, and procedures set forth in section 706 of the Civil Rights Act of 1964 (42 U.S.C. 2000e-5).

(b) Rehabilitation Act of 1973.—

The amendments made by section 3 shall apply to claims of discrimination in compensation brought under sections 501 and 504 of the Rehabilitation Act of 1973 (29 U.S.C. 791, 794), pursuant to—

(1) sections 501(g) and 504(d) of such Act (29 U.S.C. 791(g), 794(d)), respectively, which adopt the standards applied under title I of the Americans with Disabilities Act of 1990 for determining whether a violation has occurred in a complaint alleging employment discrimination; and

(2) paragraphs (1) and (2) of section 505(a) of such Act (29 U.S.C. 794a(a)) (as amended by subsection (c)).

(c) Conforming Amendments.—

(1) Rehabilitation Act of 1973.—
Section 505(a) of the Rehabilitation Act of 1973 (29 U.S.C. 794a(a)) is amended—

(A) in paragraph (1), by inserting after ``(42 U.S.C. 2000e-5 (f) through (k))″ the following: ``(and the application of section 706(e)(3) (42 U.S.C. 2000e-5(e)(3)) to claims of discrimination in compensation)″; and

(B) in paragraph (2), by inserting after ``1964″ the following: ``(42 U.S.C. 2000d et seq.) (and in subsection (e)(3) of section 706 of such Act (42 U.S.C. 2000e-5), applied to claims of discrimination in compensation)″.

(2) Civil Rights Act of 1964.—
Section 717 of the Civil Rights Act of 1964 (42 U.S.C. 2000e-16) is amended by adding at the end the following:

``(f) Section 706(e)(3) shall apply to complaints of discrimination in compensation under this section.″.

(3) Age Discrimination in Employment Act of 1967.—
Section 15(f) of the Age Discrimination in Employment Act of 1967 (29 U.S.C. 633a(f)) is amended by striking ``of section″ and inserting ``of sections 7(d)(3) and″.

Sec. 6. Effective Date.

This Act, and the amendments made by this Act, take effect as if enacted on May 28, 2007 and apply to all claims of discrimination in compensation under title VII of the Civil Rights Act of 1964 (42 U.S.C. 2000e et seq.), the Age Discrimination in Employment Act of 1967 (29 U.S.C. 621 et seq.), title I and section 503 of the Americans with Disabilities Act of 1990, and sections 501 and 504 of the Rehabilitation Act of 1973, that are pending on or after that date.

Approved January 29, 2009.

4.1.1 Legislative History

- S. 181, (H.R. 11)
    - HOUSE REPORTS:
        - No. 111-5 (Comm. on Rules)
    - CONGRESSIONAL RECORD, Vol. 155 (2009):
        - Jan. 15, 21, 22, considered and passed Senate.
        - Jan. 27, considered and passed House.
    - DAILY COMPILATION OF PRESIDENTIAL DOCUMENTS (2009):
        - Jan. 29, Presidential remarks.

4.2   Children's Health Insurance Program Reauthorization Act of 2009

111TH UNITED STATES CONGRESS
1ST SESSION

An Act
To amend title XXI of the Social Security Act to extend and improve the Children's Health Insurance Program, and for other purposes.

Be it enacted by the Senate and House of Representatives of the United States of America in Congress assembled,

SECTION 1. SHORT TITLE; AMENDMENTS TO SOCIAL SECURITY ACT; REFERENCES; TABLE OF CONTENTS.

(a) SHORT TITLE.—

This Act may be cited as the "**Children's Health Insurance Program Reauthorization Act of 2009**".

(b) AMENDMENTS TO SOCIAL SECURITY ACT.—

Except as otherwise specifically provided, whenever in this Act an amendment is expressed in terms of an amendment to or repeal of a section or other provision, the reference shall be considered to be made to that section or other provision of the Social Security Act.

(c) REFERENCES TO CHIP; MEDICAID; SECRETARY.—

In this Act:

(1) CHIP.—

The term "CHIP" means the State Children's Health Insurance Program established under title XXI of the Social Security Act (42 U.S.C. 1397aa et seq.).

(2) MEDICAID.—

The term "Medicaid" means the program for medical assistance established under title XIX of the Social Security Act (42 U.S.C. 1396 et seq.).

(3) SECRETARY.—

The term "Secretary" means the Secretary of Health and Human Services.

(d) TABLE OF CONTENTS.—

The table of contents of this Act is as follows:

Subtitle A—Outreach and Enrollment Activities

Sec. 201. Grants and enhanced administrative funding for outreach and enrollment.
Sec. 202. Increased outreach and enrollment of Indians.
Sec. 203. State option to rely on findings from an Express Lane agency to
conduct simplified eligibility determinations.

Subtitle B—Reducing Barriers to Enrollment

Sec. 211. Verification of declaration of citizenship or nationality for purposes
of eligibility for Medicaid and CHIP.
Sec. 212. Reducing administrative barriers to enrollment.
Sec. 213. Model of Interstate coordinated enrollment and coverage process.
Sec. 214. Permitting States to ensure coverage without a 5-year delay of certain
children and pregnant women under the Medicaid program and CHIP.

TITLE III—REDUCING BARRIERS TO PROVIDING PREMIUM ASSISTANCE

Subtitle A—Additional State Option for Providing Premium Assistance

Sec. 301. Additional State option for providing premium assistance.
Sec. 302. Outreach, education, and enrollment assistance.

Subtitle B—Coordinating Premium Assistance With Private Coverage

Sec. 311. Special enrollment period under group health plans in case of termination of Medicaid or CHIP coverage or eligibility for assistance in purchase
of employment-based coverage; coordination of coverage.

TITLE IV—STRENGTHENING QUALITY OF CARE AND HEALTH OUTCOMES

Sec. 401. Child health quality improvement activities for children enrolled in
Medicaid or CHIP.
Sec. 402. Improved availability of public information regarding enrollment of
children in CHIP and Medicaid.
Sec. 403. Application of certain managed care quality safeguards to CHIP.

TITLE V—IMPROVING ACCESS TO BENEFITS

Sec. 501. Dental benefits.
Sec. 502. Mental health parity in CHIP plans.
Sec. 503. Application of prospective payment system for services provided by
Federally-qualified health centers and rural health clinics.
Sec. 504. Premium grace period.
Sec. 505. Clarification of coverage of services provided through school-based
health centers.
Sec. 506. Medicaid and CHIP Payment and Access Commission.

TITLE VI—PROGRAM INTEGRITY AND OTHER MISCELLANEOUS PROVISIONS

Subtitle A—Program Integrity and Data Collection

SEC. 2. PURPOSE.

It is the purpose of this Act to provide dependable and stable funding for children's health insurance under titles XXI and XIX of the Social Security Act in order to enroll all six million uninsured children who are eligible, but not enrolled, for coverage today through such titles.

SEC. 3. GENERAL EFFECTIVE DATE; EXCEPTION FOR STATE LEGISLATION; CONTINGENT EFFECTIVE DATE; RELIANCE ON LAW.

(a) GENERAL EFFECTIVE DATE.—

Unless otherwise provided in this Act, subject to subsections (b) through (d), this Act (and the amendments made by this Act) shall take effect on April 1, 2009, and shall apply to child health assistance and medical assistance provided on or after that date.

(b) EXCEPTION FOR STATE LEGISLATION.—

In the case of a State plan under title XIX or State child health plan under XXI of the Social Security Act, which the Secretary of Health and Human Services determines requires State legislation in order for the respective plan to meet one or more additional requirements imposed by amendments made by this Act, the respective plan shall not be regarded as failing to comply with the requirements of such title solely on the basis of its failure to meet such an additional requirement before the first day of the first calendar quarter beginning after the close of the first regular session of the State legislature that begins after the date of enactment of this Act. For purposes of the previous sentence, in the case of a State that has a 2-year legislative session, each year of the session shall be considered to be a separate regular session of the State legislature.

(c) COORDINATION OF CHIP FUNDING FOR FISCAL YEAR 2009.—

Notwithstanding any other provision of law, insofar as funds have been appropriated under section 2104(a)(11), 2104(k), or 2104(l) of the Social Security Act, as amended by section 201 of Public Law 110-173, to provide allotments to States under CHIP for fiscal year 2009—

> (1) any amounts that are so appropriated that are not so allotted and obligated before April 1, 2009, are rescinded; and
>
> (2) any amount provided for CHIP allotments to a State under this Act (and the amendments made by this Act) for such fiscal year shall be reduced by the amount of such appropriations so allotted and obligated before such date.

(d) RELIANCE ON LAW.—

With respect to amendments made by this Act (other than title VII) that become effective as of a date—

> (1) such amendments are effective as of such date whether or not regulations implementing such amendments have been issued; and
>
> (2) Federal financial participation for medical assistance or child health assistance furnished under title XIX or XXI, respectively, of the Social Security Act on or after such date by a State in good faith reliance on such amendments before the date of promulgation of final regulations, if any, to carry out such amendments (or before the date of guidance, if any, regarding the implementation of such amendments) shall not be denied on the basis of the State's failure to comply with such regulations or guidance.

Approved February 4, 2009.

4.2.1   Legislative History

- H.R. 2, (S. 896)
  - HOUSE REPORTS:
    - No. 111-1 (Comm. on Rules)
  - CONGRESSIONAL RECORD, Vol. 155 (2009):
    - Jan. 14, considered and passed House.
    - Jan. 26-29, considered and passed Senate, amended.
    - Feb. 4, House concurred in Senate amendment.
  - DAILY COMPILATION OF PRESIDENTIAL DOCUMENTS, Vol. 44 (2009):
    - Feb. 4, Presidential remarks.

4.3   DTV Delay Act

111TH UNITED STATES CONGRESS
1ST SESSION

An Act

To postpone the DTV transition date.

Be it enacted by the Senate and House of Representatives of the United States of America in Congress assembled,

Section 1. Short Title.

This Act may be cited as the ``**DTV Delay Act**´´.

Sec. 2. Postponement of DTV Transition Date.

(a) In General.—

Section 3002(b) of the Digital Television Transition and Public Safety Act of 2005 (47 U.S.C. 309 note) is amended—

(1) by striking ``February 18, 2009;´´ in paragraph (1) and inserting ``June 13, 2009;´´; and

(2) by striking ``February 18, 2009,´´ in paragraph (2) and inserting ``that date´´.

(b) Conforming Amendments.—

(1) Section 3008(a)(1) of that Act (47 U.S.C. 309 note) is amended by striking ``February 17, 2009.´´ and inserting ``June 12, 2009.´´.

(2) Section 309(j)(14)(A) of the Communications Act of 1934 (47 U.S.C. 309(j)(14)(A)) is amended by striking ``February 17, 2009.´´ and inserting ``June 12, 2009.´´.

(3) Section 337(e)(1) of the Communications Act of 1934 (47 U.S.C. 337(e)(1)) is amended by striking ``February 17, 2009.´´ and inserting ``June 12, 2009.´´.

(c) License Terms.—

(1) EXTENSION.—
The Federal Communications Commission shall extend the terms of the licenses for the recovered spectrum, including the license period and construction requirements associated with those licenses, for a 116-day period.

(2) DEFINITION.—
In this subsection, the term ``recovered spectrum´´ means—

(A) the recovered analog spectrum, as such term is defined in section 309(j)(15)(C)(vi) of the Communications Act of 1934; and

(B) the spectrum excluded from the definition of recovered analog spectrum by subclauses (I) and (II) of such section.

Sec. 3. Modification of Digital-to-Analog Converter Box Program.

(a) Extension of Coupon Program.—

Section 3005(c)(1)(A) of the Digital Television Transition and Public Safety Act of 2005 (47 U.S.C. 309 note) is amended by striking ``March 31, 2009,'' and inserting ``July 31, 2009,''.

(b) Treatment of Expired Coupons.—

Section 3005(c)(1) of the Digital Television Transition and Public Safety Act of 2005 (47 U.S.C. 309 note) is amended by adding at the end the following:

``(D) EXPIRED COUPONS.— The Assistant Secretary may issue to a household, upon request by the household, one replacement coupon for each coupon that was issued to such household and that expired without being redeemed.''.

(c) Conforming Amendment.—

Section 3005(c)(1)(A) of the Digital Television Transition and Public Safety Act of 2005 (47 U.S.C. 309 note) is amended by striking ``receives, via the United States Postal Service,'' and inserting ``redeems''.

(d) Condition of Modifications.—

The amendments made by this section shall not take effect until the enactment of additional budget authority after the date of enactment of this Act to carry out the analog-to-digital converter box program under section 3005 of the Digital Television Transition and Public Safety Act of 2005.

Sec. 4. Implementation.

(a) Permissive Early Termination Under Existing Requirements.—

Nothing in this Act is intended to prevent a licensee of a television broadcast station from terminating the broadcasting of such station's analog television signal (and continuing to broadcast exclusively in the digital television service) prior to the date established by law under section 3002(b) of the Digital Television Transition and Public Safety Act of 2005 for termination of all licenses for full-power television stations in the analog television service (as amended by section 2 of this Act) so long as such prior termination is conducted in accordance with the Federal Communications Commission's requirements in effect on the date of enactment of this Act, including the flexible procedures established in the Matter of Third Periodic Review of the Commission's Rules and Policies Affecting the Conversion to Digital Television (FCC 07-228, MB Docket No. 07-91, released December 31, 2007).

(b) Public Safety Radio Services.—

Nothing in this Act, or the amendments made by this Act, shall prevent a public safety service licensee from commencing operations consistent with the terms of its license on spectrum recovered as a result of the voluntary cessation of broadcasting in the analog or digital television service pursuant to subsection (a). Any such public safety use shall be subject to the relevant Federal Communications Commission rules and regulations in effect on the date of enactment of this Act, including section 90.545 of the Commission's rules (47 C.F.R. 90.545).

(c) Expedited Rulemaking.—

Notwithstanding any other provision of law, the Federal Communications Commission and the National Telecommunications and Information Administration shall, not later than 30 days after the date of enactment of this Act, each adopt or revise its rules, regulations, or orders or take such other actions as may be necessary or appropriate to implement the provisions, and carry out the purposes, of this Act and the amendments made by this Act.

Sec. 5. Extension of Commission Auction Authority.

Section 309(j)(11) of the Communications Act of 1934 (47 U.S.C. 309(j)(11)) is amended by striking ``2011.'' and inserting ``2012.''.

Approved February 11, 2009.

4.3.1 Legislative History

- S. 352, (S. 328)

  - HOUSE REPORTS:
    - No. 111-11 (Comm. on Rules)
  - CONGRESSIONAL RECORD, Vol. 155 (2009):
    - Jan. 29, considered and passed Senate.
    - Feb. 4, considered and passed House.

4.3.2 See also

- Digital Television Transition and Public Safety Act of 2005

- DTV Transition Assistance Act

4.4 American Recovery and Reinvestment Act of 2009

111TH UNITED STATES CONGRESS
1ST SESSION

An Act
Making supplemental appropriations for job preservation and creation, infrastructure investment, energy efficiency and science, assistance to the unemployed, and State and local fiscal stabilization, for the fiscal year ending September 30, 2009, and for other purposes.

Be it enacted by the Senate and House of Representatives of the United States of America in Congress assembled,

Section 1. Short Title.

This Act may be cited as the ``**American Recovery and Reinvestment Act of 2009**''.

Sec. 2. Table of Contents.

The table of contents for this Act is as follows:

DIVISION A—APPROPRIATIONS PROVISIONS

DIVISION B—TAX, UNEMPLOYMENT, HEALTH, STATE FISCAL RELIEF, AND OTHER PROVISIONS

Sec. 3. Purposes and Principles.

(a) Statement of Purposes.—

The purposes of this Act include the following:

(1) To preserve and create jobs and promote economic recovery.
(2) To assist those most impacted by the recession.
(3) To provide investments needed to increase economic efficiency by spurring technological advances in science and health.
(4) To invest in transportation, environmental protection, and other infrastructure that will provide long-term economic benefits.
(5) To stabilize State and local government budgets, in order to minimize and avoid reductions in essential services and counterproductive state and local tax increases.

(b) General Principles Concerning Use of Funds.—

The President and the heads of Federal departments and agencies shall manage and expend the funds made available in this Act so as to achieve the purposes specified in subsection (a), including commencing expenditures and activities as quickly as possible consistent with prudent management.

Sec. 4. References.

Except as expressly provided otherwise, any reference to "this Act" contained in any division of this Act shall be treated as referring only to the provisions of that division.

Sec. 5. Emergency Designations.

(a) In General.—

Each amount in this Act is designated as an emergency requirement and necessary to meet emergency needs pursuant to section 204(a) of S.Con.Res. 21 (110th Congress) and section 301(b)(2) of S.Con.Res. 70 (110th Congress), the concurrent resolutions on the budget for fiscal years 2008 and 2009.

(b) Pay-as-You-Go.—

All applicable provisions in this Act are designated as an emergency for purposes of pay-as-you-go principles.

Approved February 17, 2009.

4.4.1 Legislative History

- H.R. 1, (S. 336, S. 350, S. 1)
    - SENATE REPORTS:
        - No. 111-3 accompanying S. 336 (Comm. on Appropriations).
    - HOUSE REPORTS:
        - No. 111-4 (Comm. on Appropriations)
        - No. 111-6 (Comm. on Rules)
        - No. 111-7 (Comm. on Energy and Commmerce)
        - No. 111-8 (Comm. on Ways and Means)
        - No. 111-9 (Comm. on Rules)
        - No. 111-17 (Comm. on Rules)
    - CONFERENCE REPORTS:
        - No. 111-16 (Comm. of Conference)
    - CONGRESSIONAL RECORD, Vol. 155 (2009):
        - Jan. 27, 28, considered and passed House.
        - Feb. 2-7, 9, 10, considered and passed Senate, amended.
        - Feb. 13, House and Senate agreed to conference report.
    - DAILY COMPILATION OF PRESIDENTIAL DOCUMENTS (2009):
        - Feb. 17, Presidential remarks and statement.

4.4.2 Alternative Table of Contents for Division A

The table of contents for Division A that follows was *not part of the Act*, and iss added here as an extra feature on Wikisource.

This work is in the **public domain** in the United States because it is a work of the United States *federal* government (see 17 U.S.C. 105).

4.5 Omnibus Public Land Management Act of 2009

111TH UNITED STATES CONGRESS
1ST SESSION

An Act
To designate certain land as components of the National Wilderness Preservation System, to authorize certain programs and activities in the Department of the Interior and the Department of Agriculture, and for other purposes.

Be it enacted by the Senate and House of Representatives of the United States of America in Congress assembled,

SECTION 1. SHORT TITLE; TABLE OF CONTENTS.

(a) Short Title- This Act may be cited as the `**Omnibus Public Land Management Act of 2009**'.

(b) Table of Contents- The table of contents of this Act is as follows:

TITLE III—FOREST SERVICE AUTHORIZATIONS

TITLE XI—UNITED STATES GEOLOGICAL SURVEY AUTHORIZATIONS

TITLE XII—OCEANS

4.5.1 Legislative History

- H.R. 146

  - CONGRESSIONAL RECORD, Vol. 155 (2009):
    - Mar. 2, 3, considered and passed House.
    - Mar. 17-19, considered and passed Senate, amended.
    - Mar. 25, House concurred in Senate amendments.
  - DAILY COMPILATION OF PRESIDENTIAL DOCUMENTS (2009):
    - Mar. 30, Presidential remarks and statement.

4.6 Edward M. Kennedy Serve America Act

111TH UNITED STATES CONGRESS
1ST SESSION

An Act
Entitled The Edward M. Kennedy Serve America Act, an Act to reauthorize and reform the national service laws.

Be it enacted by the Senate and House of Representatives of the United States of America in Congress assembled,

SECTION 1. SHORT TITLE; TABLE OF CONTENTS.

(a) Short Title—

    This Act may be cited as the ``**Serve America Act**´´.

(b) Table of Contents—

    The table of contents of this Act is as follows:

Sec. 1. Short title; table of contents.

TITLE I—AMENDMENTS TO NATIONAL AND COMMUNITY SERVICE ACT OF 1990

Sec. 1001.References.

Subtitle A—Amendments to Subtitle A (General Provisions)
Sec. 1101. Purposes.
Sec. 1102. Definitions.

Subtitle B—Amendments to Subtitle B (Learn and Serve America)
Sec. 1201. School-based allotments.
Sec. 1202. Higher education provisions.
Sec. 1203. Campuses of Service.
Sec. 1204. Innovative programs and research.
Sec. 1205. Service-learning impact study.

Subtitle C—Amendments to Subtitle C (National Service Trust Program)
Sec. 1301. Prohibition on grants to Federal agencies; limits on Corporation costs.
Sec. 1302. Eligible national service programs.
Sec. 1303. Types of positions.
Sec. 1304. Conforming repeal relating to training and technical assistance.
Sec. 1305. Assistance to State Commissions; challenge grants.
Sec. 1306. Allocation of assistance to States and other eligible entities.
Sec. 1307. Additional authority.
Sec. 1308. State selection of programs.
Sec. 1309. National service program assistance requirements.
Sec. 1310. Prohibited activities and ineligible organizations.
Sec. 1311. Consideration of applications.
Sec. 1312. Description of participants.
Sec. 1313. Selection of national service participants.
Sec. 1314. Terms of service.
Sec. 1315. Adjustments to living allowance.

Subtitle D—Amendments to Subtitle D (National Service Trust and Provision of National Service Educational Awards)
Sec. 1401. Availability of funds in the National Service Trust.
Sec. 1402. Individuals eligible to receive an educational award from the Trust.
Sec. 1403. Certifications.
Sec. 1404. Determination of the amount of the educational award.
Sec. 1405. Disbursement of educational awards.
Sec. 1406. Approval process for approved positions.

Subtitle E—Amendments to Subtitle E (National Civilian Community Corps)
Sec. 1501. Purpose.
Sec. 1502. Program components.
Sec. 1503. Eligible participants.
Sec. 1504. Summer national service program.
Sec. 1505. National Civilian Community Corps.
Sec. 1506. Training.

TITLE III—TECHNICAL AMENDMENTS TO TABLES OF CONTENTS

TITLE IV—AMENDMENTS TO OTHER LAWS

TITLE V—VOLUNTEERS FOR PROSPERITY PROGRAM

TITLE VI—EFFECTIVE DATE

Approved April 21, 2009.

4.6.1 Legislative History

- H.R. 1388, (S. 277)

- HOUSE REPORTS:

  - No. 111-37 (Comm. on Education and Labor).

- CONGRESSIONAL RECORD, Vol. 155 (2009):

  - Mar. 18, considered and passed House.

  - Mar. 24-26, considered and passed Senate, amended.

  - Mar. 31, House concurred in Senate amendments.

- DAILY COMPILATION OF PRESIDENTIAL DOCUMENTS (2009):

  - Apr. 21, Presidential remarks.

4.6.2 See Also

- Domestic Volunteer Service Act of 1973 (Public Law 93-113)

- National and Community Service Act of 1990: (Public Law 101-610)

  - American Conservation and Youth Service Corps Act of 1990 (Title I / Subtitle C)

  - National and Community Service Act (Title I / Subtitle D)

  - The Points of Light Foundation Act (Title III)

- National and Community Service Technical Amendments Act of 1991 (Public Law 102-10)

- National and Community Service Technical Amendment Act of 1992 (Public Law 102-384)

- National and Community Service Trust Act of 1993 (Public Law 103-82)

- King Holiday and Service Act of 1994 (Public Law 103-304)

- Unity in the Spirit of America Act or the USA Act (Public Law 107-117)

- Strengthen AmeriCorps Program Act (Public Law 108-45)

- Executive Order 13254 (Establishing the USA Freedom Corps)

    - Later amended by Executive Order 13286

- Executive Order 13317 (Volunteers for Prosperity)

    - Later amended by Executive Order 13418

- Executive Order 13331 (National and Community Service Programs)

4.7   Fraud Enforcement and Recovery Act of 2009

111TH UNITED STATES CONGRESS
1ST SESSION

An Act
To improve enforcement of mortgage fraud, securities and commodities fraud, financial institution fraud, and other frauds related
to Federal assistance and relief programs, for the recovery of funds lost to these frauds, and for other purposes.

Be it enacted by the Senate and House of Representatives of the United States of America in Congress assembled,

Section 1. Short Title.

This Act may be cited as the ``**Fraud Enforcement and Recovery Act of 2009**´´ or ``**FERA**´´.

Sec. 2. Amendments to Improve Mortgage, Securities, Commodities, and Financial Fraud Recovery and Enforcement.

(a) Definition of Financial Institution Amended to Include Mortgage Lending Business.—

Section 20 of title 18, United States Code, is amended—

(1) in paragraph (8), by striking ``or´´ after the semicolon;

(2) in paragraph (9), by striking the period and inserting ``; or´´; and

(3) by inserting at the end the following:

``(10) a mortgage lending business (as defined in section 27 of this title) or any person or entity that makes in whole or in part a federally related mortgage loan as defined in section 3 of the Real Estate Settlement Procedures Act of 1974.´´.

(b) Mortgage Lending Business Defined.—

(1) In General.—

Chapter 1 of title 18, United States Code, is amended by inserting after section 26 the following:

``§ 27. Mortgage Lending Business Defined

``In this title, the term 'mortgage lending business' means an organization which finances or refinances any debt secured by an interest in real estate, including private mortgage companies and any subsidiaries of such organizations, and whose activities affect interstate or foreign commerce.´´.

(2) Chapter Analysis.—

The chapter analysis for chapter 1 of title 18, United States Code, is amended by adding at the end the following:

``§ 27. Mortgage Lending Business Defined.´´.

(c) False Statements in Mortgage Applications Amended to Include False Statements by Mortgage Brokers and Agents of Mortgage Lending Businesses.—

Section 1014 of title 18, United States Code, is amended by—

(1) striking ``or´´ after ``the International Banking Act of 1978),´´; and

(2) inserting after ``section 25(a) of the Federal Reserve Act´´ the following: ``, or a mortgage lending business, or any person or entity that makes in whole or in part a federally related mortgage loan as defined in section 3 of the Real Estate Settlement Procedures Act of 1974´´.

(d) Major Fraud Against the Government Amended to Include Economic Relief and Troubled Asset Relief Program Funds.—

Section 1031(a) of title 18, United States Code, is amended by—

(1) inserting after ``or promises, in´´ the following: ``any grant, contract, subcontract, subsidy, loan, guarantee, insurance, or other form of Federal assistance, including through the Troubled Asset Relief Program, an economic stimulus, recovery or rescue plan provided by the Government, or the Government's purchase of any troubled asset as defined in the Emergency Economic Stabilization Act of 2008, or in´´;

(2) striking ``the contract, subcontract´´ and inserting ``such grant, contract, subcontract, subsidy, loan, guarantee, insurance, or other form of Federal assistance´´; and

(3) striking ``for such property or services´´.

(e) Securities Fraud Amended to Include Fraud Involving Options and Futures in Commodities.—

(1) In General.—

Section 1348 of title 18, United States Code, is amended—

(A) in the caption, by inserting ``and commodities´´ after ``Securities´´;

(B) in paragraph (1), by inserting ``any commodity for future delivery, or any option on a commodity for future delivery, or´´ after ``any person in connection with´´; and

(C) in paragraph (2), by inserting ``any commodity for future delivery, or any option on a commodity for future delivery, or´´ after ``in connection with the purchase or sale of´´.

(2) Chapter Analysis.—

The item for section 1348 in the chapter analysis for chapter 63 of title 18, United States Code, is amended by inserting ``and commodities´´ after ``Securities´´.

(f) Money Laundering Amended to Define Proceeds of Specified Unlawful Activity.—

(1) Money Laundering.—

Section 1956(c) of title 18, United States Code, is amended—

(A) in paragraph (8), by striking the period and inserting ``; and´´; and

(B) by inserting at the end the following:

``(9) the term 'proceeds' means any property derived from or obtained or retained, directly or indirectly, through some form of unlawful activity, including the gross receipts of such activity.´´.

(2) Monetary Transactions.—

Section 1957(f) of title 18, United States Code, is amended by striking paragraph (3) and inserting the following:

``(3) the terms 'specified unlawful activity' and 'proceeds' shall have the meaning given those terms in section 1956 of this title.´´.

(g) Sense of the Congress and Report Concerning Required Approval for Merger Cases.—

(1) Sense of Congress.—

It is the sense of the Congress that no prosecution of an offense under section 1956 or 1957 of title 18, United States Code, should be undertaken in combination with the prosecution of any other offense, without prior approval of the Attorney General, the Deputy Attorney General, the Assistant Attorney General in charge of the Criminal Division, a Deputy Assistant Attorney General in the Criminal Division, or the relevant United States Attorney, if the conduct to be charged as ``specified unlawful activity´´ in connection with the offense under section 1956 or 1957 is so closely connected with the conduct to be charged as the other offense that there is no clear delineation between the two offenses.

(2) Report.—

One year after the date of the enactment of this Act, and at the end of each of the four succeeding one-year periods, the Attorney General shall report to the House and Senate Committees on the Judiciary on efforts undertaken by the Department of Justice to ensure that the review and approval described in paragraph (1) takes place in all appropriate cases. The report shall include the following:

(A) The number of prosecutions described in paragraph (1) that were undertaken during the previous one-year period after prior approval by an official described in paragraph (1), classified by type of offense and by the approving official.

(B) The number of prosecutions described in paragraph (1) that were undertaken during the previous one-year period without such prior approval, classified by type of offense, and the reasons why such prior approval was not obtained.

(C) The number of times during the previous year in which an approval described in paragraph (1) was denied.

Sec. 3. Authorization of Additional Funding to Combat Mortgage Fraud, Securities and Commodities Fraud, and Other Frauds Involving Federal Economic Assistance.

(a) Authorization of Additional Appropriations for the Department of Justice.—

(1) In General.—

There is authorized to be appropriated to the Attorney General, $165,000,000 for each of the fiscal years 2010 and 2011, for the purposes of investigations and prosecutions and civil and administrative proceedings involving Federal assistance programs and financial institutions, including financial institutions to which this Act and amendments made by this Act apply.

(2) Allocations.—

With respect to fiscal years 2010 and 2011, the amounts authorized to be appropriated under paragraph (1) shall be allocated as follows:

(A) Federal Bureau of Investigation: $75,000,000 for fiscal year 2010 and $65,000,000 for fiscal year 2011, an appropriate percentage of which amounts shall be used to investigate mortgage fraud.

(B) The offices of the United States Attorneys: $50,000,000 for each fiscal year.

(C) The criminal division of the Department of Justice: $20,000,000 for each fiscal year.

(D) The civil division of the Department of Justice: $15,000,000 for each fiscal year.

(E) The tax division of the Department of Justice: $5,000,000 for each fiscal year.

(b) Authorization of Additional Appropriations for the Postal Inspection Service.—

There is authorized to be appropriated to the Postal Inspection Service of the United States Postal Service, $30,000,000 for each of the fiscal years 2010 and 2011 for investigations involving Federal assistance programs and financial institutions, including financial institutions to which this Act and amendments made by this Act apply.

(c) Authorization of Additional Appropriations for the Inspector General for the Department of Housing and Urban Development.—

There is authorized to be appropriated to the Inspector General of the Department of Housing and Urban Development, $30,000,000 for each of the fiscal years 2010 and 2011 for investigations involving Federal assistance programs and financial institutions, including financial institutions to which this Act and amendments made by this Act apply.

(d) Authorization of Additional Appropriations for the United States Secret Service.—

There is authorized to be appropriated to the United States Secret Service of the Department of Homeland Security, $20,000,000 for each of the fiscal years 2010 and 2011 for investigations involving Federal assistance programs and financial institutions, including financial institutions to which this Act and amendments made by this Act apply.

(e) Authorization of Additional Appropriations for the Securities and Exchange Commission.—

(1) In General.—

There is authorized to be appropriated to the Securities and Exchange Commission, $20,000,000 for each of the fiscal years 2010 and 2011 for investigations and enforcement proceedings involving financial institutions, including financial institutions to which this Act and amendments made by this Act apply.

(2) Inspector General.—

There is authorized to be appropriated to the Securities and Exchange Commission, $1,000,000 for each of the fiscal years 2010 and 2011 for the salaries and expenses of the Office of the Inspector General of the Securities and Exchange Commission.

(f) Use of Funds.—

(1) In General.—

The funds appropriated pursuant to authorization under this section shall be limited to covering the costs of each listed agency or department for investigating possible criminal, civil, or administrative violations and for criminal, civil, or administrative proceedings involving financial crimes and crimes against Federal assistance programs, including mortgage fraud, securities and commodities fraud, financial institution fraud, and other frauds related to Federal assistance and relief programs.

(2) Funds for Training and Research.—

Funds authorized to be appropriated under this section may be used and expended for programs for improving the detection, investigation, and prosecution of economic crime including financial fraud and mortgage fraud. Funds allocated under this section may be allocated to programs which assist State and local criminal justice agencies to develop, establish, and maintain intelligence-focused policing strategies and related information sharing; provide training and investigative support services to State and local criminal justice agencies to provide such agencies with skills and resources needed to investigate and prosecute such criminal activities and related criminal activities; provide research support, establish partnerships, and provide other resources to aid State and local criminal justice agencies to prevent, investigate, and prosecute such criminal activities and related problems; provide information and research to the general public to facilitate the prevention of such criminal activities; and any other programs specified by the Attorney General as furthering the purposes of this Act.

(g) Additional Nature of Authorizations; Availability.—

The amounts authorized under this section are in addition to amounts otherwise authorized in other Acts and shall remain available until expended.

(h) Report to Congress.—

Following the final expenditure of all funds appropriated pursuant to authorization under this section, the Attorney General, in consultation with the United States Postal Inspection Service, the Inspector General for the Department of Housing and Urban Development, the Secretary of Homeland Security, and the Commissioner of the Securities and Exchange Commission, shall submit a report to Congress identifying—

(1) the amounts expended under each of subsections (a), (b), (c), (d), and (e) and a certification of compliance with the requirements listed in subsection (f); and

(2) the amounts recovered as a result of criminal or civil restitution, fines, penalties, and other monetary recoveries resulting from criminal, civil, or administrative proceedings and settlements undertaken with funds authorized by this Act.

Sec. 4. Clarifications to the False Claims Act to Reflect the Original Intent of the Law.

(a) Clarification of the False Claims Act.—

Section 3729 of title 31, United States Code, is amended—

(1) by striking subsection (a) and inserting the following:

``(a) Liability for Certain Acts.—

``(1) In general.—Subject to paragraph (2), any person who—

``(A) knowingly presents, or causes to be presented, a false or fraudulent claim for payment or approval;

``(B) knowingly makes, uses, or causes to be made or used, a false record or statement material to a false or fraudulent claim;

``(C) conspires to commit a violation of subparagraph (A), (B), (D), (E), (F), or (G);

``(D) has possession, custody, or control of property or money used, or to be used, by the Government and knowingly delivers, or causes to be delivered, less than all of that money or property;

``(E) is authorized to make or deliver a document certifying receipt of property used, or to be used, by the Government and, intending to defraud the Government, makes or delivers the receipt without completely knowing that the information on the receipt is true;

``(F) knowingly buys, or receives as a pledge of an obligation or debt, public property from an officer or employee of the Government, or a member of the Armed Forces, who lawfully may not sell or pledge property; or

``(G) knowingly makes, uses, or causes to be made or used, a false record or statement material to an obligation to pay or transmit money or property to the Government, or knowingly conceals or knowingly and improperly avoids or decreases an obligation to pay or transmit money or property to the Government, is liable to the United States Government for a civil penalty of not less than $5,000 and not more than $10,000, as adjusted by the Federal Civil Penalties Inflation Adjustment Act of 1990 (28 U.S.C. 2461 note; Public Law 101-410), plus 3 times the amount of damages which the Government sustains because of the act of that person.

``(2) Reduced damages.—If the court finds that—

``(A) the person committing the violation of this subsection furnished officials of the United States responsible for investigating false claims violations with all information known to such person about the violation within 30 days after the date on which the defendant first obtained the information;

``(B) such person fully cooperated with any Government investigation of such violation; and

``(C) at the time such person furnished the United States with the information about the violation, no criminal prosecution, civil action, or administrative action had commenced under this title with respect to such violation, and the person did not have actual knowledge of the existence of an investigation into such violation, the court may assess not less than 2 times the amount of damages which the Government sustains because of the act of that person.

``(3) Costs of civil actions.—A person violating this subsection shall also be liable to the United States Government for the costs of a civil action brought to recover any such penalty or damages.'';

(2) by striking subsections (b) and (c) and inserting the following:

``(b) Definitions.—For purposes of this section—

``(1) the terms 'knowing' and 'knowingly'—

``(A) mean that a person, with respect to information—

    ``(i) has actual knowledge of the information;

    ``(ii) acts in deliberate ignorance of the truth or falsity of the information; or

    ``(iii) acts in reckless disregard of the truth or falsity of the information; and

``(B) require no proof of specific intent to defraud;

``(2) the term 'claim'—

    ``(A) means any request or demand, whether under a contract or otherwise, for money or property and whether or not the United States has title to the money or property, that—

        ``(i) is presented to an officer, employee, or agent of the United States; or

        ``(ii) is made to a contractor, grantee, or other recipient, if the money or property is to be spent or used on the Government's behalf or to advance a Government program or interest, and if the United States Government—

            ``(I) provides or has provided any portion of the money or property requested or demanded; or

            ``(II) will reimburse such contractor, grantee, or other recipient for any portion of the money or property which is requested or demanded; and

    ``(B) does not include requests or demands for money or property that the Government has paid to an individual as compensation for Federal employment or as an income subsidy with no restrictions on that individual's use of the money or property;

``(3) the term 'obligation' means an established duty, whether or not fixed, arising from an express or implied contractual, grantor-grantee, or licensor-licensee relationship, from a fee-based or similar relationship, from statute or regulation, or from the retention of any overpayment; and

``(4) the term 'material' means having a natural tendency to influence, or be capable of influencing, the payment or receipt of money or property.´´;

(3) by redesignating subsections (d) and (e) as subsections (c) and (d), respectively; and

(4) in subsection (c), as redesignated, by striking ``subparagraphs (A) through (C) of subsection (a)´´ and inserting ``subsection (a)(2)´´.

(b) Intervention by the Government.—

    Section 3731(b) of title 31, United States Code, is amended—

        (1) by redesignating subsection (c) as subsection (d);

        (2) by redesignating subsection (d) as subsection (e); and

        (3) by inserting the new subsection (c):

``(c) If the Government elects to intervene and proceed with an action brought under 3730(b), the Government may file its own complaint or amend the complaint of a person who has brought an action under section 3730(b) to clarify or add detail to the claims in which the Government is intervening and to add any additional claims with respect to which the Government contends it is entitled to relief. For statute of limitations purposes, any such Government pleading shall relate back to the filing date of the complaint of the person who originally brought the action, to the extent that the claim of the Government arises out of the conduct, transactions, or occurrences set forth, or attempted to be set forth, in the prior complaint of that person.´´.

(c) Civil Investigative Demands.—

    Section 3733 of title 31, United States Code, is amended—

        (1) in subsection (a)—

            (A) in paragraph (1)—

                (i) in the matter preceding subparagraph (A)—

                    (I) by inserting ``, or a designee (for purposes of this section),´´ after ``Whenever the Attorney General´´; and

                    (II) by striking ``the Attorney General may, before commencing a civil proceeding under section 3730 or other false claims law,´´ and inserting ``the Attorney General, or a designee, may, before commencing a civil proceeding under section 3730(a) or other false claims law, or making an election under section 3730(b),´´; and

                (ii) in the matter following subparagraph (D)—

                    (I) by striking ``may not delegate´´ and inserting ``may delegate´´; and

                    (II) by adding at the end the following: ``Any information obtained by the Attorney General or a designee of the Attorney General under this section may be shared with any qui tam relator if the Attorney General or designee determine it is necessary as part of any false claims act investigation.´´; and

            (B) in paragraph (2)(G), by striking the second sentence;

        (2) in subsection (i)(2)—

    (A) in subparagraph (B), by striking ``, who is authorized for such use under regulations which the Attorney General shall issue''; and

    (B) in subparagraph (C), by striking ``Disclosure of information to any such other agency shall be allowed only upon application, made by the Attorney General to a United States district court, showing substantial need for the use of the information by such agency in furtherance of its statutory responsibilities.''; and

(3) in subsection (l)—

    (A) in paragraph (6), by striking ``and'' after the semicolon;

    (B) in paragraph (7), by striking the period and inserting ``; and''; and

    (C) by adding at the end the following:

``(8) the term 'official use' means any use that is consistent with the law, and the regulations and policies of the Department of Justice, including use in connection with internal Department of Justice memoranda and reports; communications between the Department of Justice and a Federal, State, or local government agency, or a contractor of a Federal, State, or local government agency, undertaken in furtherance of a Department of Justice investigation or prosecution of a case; interviews of any qui tam relator or other witness; oral examinations; depositions; preparation for and response to civil discovery requests; introduction into the record of a case or proceeding; applications, motions, memoranda and briefs submitted to a court or other tribunal; and communications with Government investigators, auditors, consultants and experts, the counsel of other parties, arbitrators and mediators, concerning an investigation, case or proceeding.''.

(d) Relief from Retaliatory Actions.—

Section 3730(h) of title 31, United States Code, is amended to read as follows:

``(h) Relief From Retaliatory Actions.—

    ``(1) In general.—Any employee, contractor, or agent shall be entitled to all relief necessary to make that employee, contractor, or agent whole, if that employee, contractor, or agent is discharged, demoted, suspended, threatened, harassed, or in any other manner discriminated against in the terms and conditions of employment because of lawful acts done by the employee, contractor, or agent or associated others in furtherance of other efforts to stop 1 or more violations of this subchapter.

    ``(2) Relief.—Relief under paragraph (1) shall include reinstatement with the same seniority status that employee, contractor, or agent would have had but for the discrimination, 2 times the amount of back pay, interest on the back pay, and compensation for any special damages sustained as a result of the discrimination, including litigation costs and reasonable attorneys' fees. An action under this subsection may be brought in the appropriate district court of the United States for the relief provided in this subsection.''.

(e) False Claims Jurisdiction.—

Section 3732 of title 31, United States Code, is amended by adding at the end the following new subsection:

``(c) Service on State or Local Authorities.—With respect to any State or local government that is named as a co-plaintiff with the United States in an action brought under subsection (b), a seal on the action ordered by the court under section 3730(b) shall not preclude the Government or the person bringing the action from serving the complaint, any other pleadings, or the written disclosure of substantially all material evidence and information possessed by the person bringing the action on the law enforcement authorities that are authorized under the law of that State or local government to investigate and prosecute such actions on behalf of such governments, except that such seal applies to the law enforcement authorities so served to the same extent as the seal applies to other parties in the action.''.

(f) Effective Date and Application.—

The amendments made by this section shall take effect on the date of enactment of this Act and shall apply to conduct on or after the date of enactment, except that—

(1) subparagraph (B) of section 3729(a)(1) of title 31, United States Code, as added by subsection (a)(1), shall take effect as if enacted on June 7, 2008, and apply to all claims under the False Claims Act (31 U.S.C. 3729 et seq.) that are pending on or after that date; and

(2) section 3731(b) of title 31, as amended by subsection (b); section 3733, of title 31, as amended by subsection (c); and section 3732 of title 31, as amended by subsection (e); shall apply to cases pending on the date of enactment.

Sec. 5. Financial Crisis Inquiry Commission.

(a) Establishment of Commission.—

There is established in the legislative branch the Financial Crisis Inquiry Commission (in this section referred to as the ``Commission'') to examine the causes, domestic and global, of the current financial and economic crisis in the United States.

(b) Composition of the Commission.—

(1) Members.—
The Commission shall be composed of 10 members, of whom—

(A) 3 members shall be appointed by the majority leader of the Senate, in consultation with relevant Committees;

(B) 3 members shall be appointed by the Speaker of the House of Representatives, in consultation with relevant Committees;

(C) 2 members shall be appointed by the minority leader of the Senate, in consultation with relevant Committees; and

(D) 2 members shall be appointed by the minority leader of the House of Representatives, in consultation with relevant Committees.

(2) Qualifications; Limitation.—

(A) In General.—

It is the sense of the Congress that individuals appointed to the Commission should be prominent United States citizens with national recognition and significant depth of experience in such fields as banking, regulation of markets, taxation, finance, economics, consumer protection, and housing.

(B) Limitation.—

No person who is a member of Congress or an officer or employee of the Federal Government or any State or local government may serve as a member of the Commission.

(3) Chairperson; Vice Chairperson.—

(A) In General.—

Subject to the requirements of subparagraph (B), the Chairperson of the Commission shall be selected jointly by the Majority Leader of the Senate and the Speaker of the House of Representatives, and the Vice Chairperson shall be selected jointly by the Minority Leader of the Senate and the Minority Leader of the House of Representatives.

(B) Political party affiliation.—

The Chairperson and Vice Chairperson of the Commission may not be from the same political party.

(4) Meetings, quorum; vacancies.—

(A) Meetings.—

(i) Initial Meeting.—

The initial meeting of the Commission shall be as soon as possible after a quorum of members have been appointed.

(ii) Subsequent Meetings.—

After the initial meeting of the Commission, the Commission shall meet upon the call of the Chairperson or a majority of its members.

(B) Quorum.—

6 members of the Commission shall constitute a quorum.

(C) Vacancies.—

Any vacancy on the Commission shall—

(i) not affect the powers of the Commission; and

(ii) be filled in the same manner in which the original appointment was made.

(c) Functions of the Commission.—

The functions of the Commission are—

(1) to examine the causes of the current financial and economic crisis in the United States, specifically the role of—

(A) fraud and abuse in the financial sector, including fraud and abuse towards consumers in the mortgage sector;

(B) Federal and State financial regulators, including the extent to which they enforced, or failed to enforce statutory, regulatory, or supervisory requirements;

(C) the global imbalance of savings, international capital flows, and fiscal imbalances of various governments;

(D) monetary policy and the availability and terms of credit;

(E) accounting practices, including, mark-to-market and fair value rules, and treatment of off-balance sheet vehicles;

(F) tax treatment of financial products and investments;

(G) capital requirements and regulations on leverage and liquidity, including the capital structures of regulated and non-regulated financial entities;

(H) credit rating agencies in the financial system, including, reliance on credit ratings by financial institutions and Federal financial regulators, the use of credit ratings in financial regulation, and the use of credit ratings in the securitization markets;

(I) lending practices and securitization, including the originate-to-distribute model for extending credit and transferring risk;

(J) affiliations between insured depository institutions and securities, insurance, and other types of nonbanking companies;

(K) the concept that certain institutions are "too-big-to-fail" and its impact on market expectations;

(L) corporate governance, including the impact of company conversions from partnerships to corporations;

(M) compensation structures;

(N) changes in compensation for employees of financial companies, as compared to compensation for others with similar skill sets in the labor market;

(O) the legal and regulatory structure of the United States housing market;

(P) derivatives and unregulated financial products and practices, including credit default swaps;

(Q) short-selling;

(R) financial institution reliance on numerical models, including risk models and credit ratings;

(S) the legal and regulatory structure governing financial institutions, including the extent to which the structure creates the opportunity for financial institutions to engage in regulatory arbitrage;

(T) the legal and regulatory structure governing investor and mortgagor protection;

(U) financial institutions and government-sponsored enterprises; and

(V) the quality of due diligence undertaken by financial institutions;

(2) to examine the causes of the collapse of each major financial institution that failed (including institutions that were acquired to prevent their failure) or was likely to have failed if not for the receipt of exceptional Government assistance from the Secretary of the Treasury during the period beginning in August 2007 through April 2009;

(3) to submit a report under subsection (h);

(4) to refer to the Attorney General of the United States and any appropriate State attorney general any person that the Commission finds may have violated the laws of the United States in relation to such crisis; and

(5) to build upon the work of other entities, and avoid unnecessary duplication, by reviewing the record of the Committee on Banking, Housing, and Urban Affairs of the Senate, the Committee on Financial Services of the House of Representatives, other congressional committees, the Government Accountability Office, other legislative panels, and any other department, agency, bureau, board, commission, office, independent establishment, or instrumentality of the United States (to the fullest extent permitted by law) with respect to the current financial and economic crisis.

(d) Powers of the Commission.—

(1) Hearings and Evidence.—
The Commission may, for purposes of carrying out this section—

(A) hold hearings, sit and act at times and places, take testimony, receive evidence, and administer oaths; and

(B) require, by subpoena or otherwise, the attendance and testimony of witnesses and the production of books, records, correspondence, memoranda, papers, and documents.

(2) Subpoenas.—

(A) Service.—

Subpoenas issued under paragraph (1)(B) may be served by any person designated by the Commission.

(B) Enforcement.—

(i) In General.—

In the case of contumacy or failure to obey a subpoena issued under paragraph (1)(B), the United States district court for the judicial district in which the subpoenaed person resides, is served, or may be found, or where the subpoena is returnable, may issue an order requiring such person to appear at any designated place to testify or to produce documentary or other evidence. Any failure to obey the order of the court may be punished by the court as a contempt of that court.

(ii) Additional Enforcement.—

Sections 102 through 104 of the Revised Statutes of the United States (2 U.S.C. 192 through 194) shall apply in the case of any failure of any witness to comply with any subpoena or to testify when summoned under the authority of this section.

(iii) Issuance.—

A subpoena may be issued under this subsection only—

(I) by the agreement of the Chairperson and the Vice Chairperson; or

(II) by the affirmative vote of a majority of the Commission, including an affirmative vote of at least one member appointed under subparagraph (C) or (D) of subsection (b)(1), a majority being present.

(3) Contracting.—

The Commission may enter into contracts to enable the Commission to discharge its duties under this section.

(4) Information from Federal agencies and other entities.—

(A) In General.—

The Commission may secure directly from any department, agency, bureau, board, commission, office, independent establishment, or instrumentality of the United States any information related to any inquiry of the Commission conducted under this section, including information of a confidential nature (which the Commission shall maintain in a secure manner). Each such department, agency, bureau, board, commission, office, independent establishment, or instrumentality shall furnish such information directly to the Commission upon request.

(B) Other Entities.—

It is the sense of the Congress that the Commission should seek testimony or information from principals and other representatives of government agencies and private entities that were significant participants in the United States and global financial and housing markets during the time period examined by the Commission.

(5) Administrative Support Services.—

Upon the request of the Commission—

(A) the Administrator of General Services shall provide to the Commission, on a reimbursable basis, the administrative support services necessary for the Commission to carry out its responsibilities under this Act; and

(B) other Federal departments and agencies may provide to the Commission any administrative support services as may be determined by the head of such department or agency to be advisable and authorized by law.

(6) Donations of Goods and Services.—

The Commission may accept, use, and dispose of gifts or donations of services or property.

(7) Postal Services.—

The Commission may use the United States mails in the same manner and under the same conditions as departments and agencies of the United States.

(8) Powers of Subcommittees, Members, and Agents.—

Any subcommittee, member, or agent of the Commission may, if authorized by the Commission, take any action which the Commission is authorized to take by this section.

(e) Staff of the Commission.—

(1) Director.—

The Commission shall have a Director who shall be appointed by the Chairperson and the Vice Chairperson, acting jointly.

(2) Staff.—

The Chairperson and the Vice Chairperson may jointly appoint additional personnel, as may be necessary, to enable the Commission to carry out its functions.

(3) Applicability of certain civil service laws.—

The Director and staff of the Commission may be appointed without regard to the provisions of title 5, United States Code, governing appointments in the competitive service, and may be paid without regard to the provisions of chapter 51 and subchapter III of chapter 53 of such title relating to classification and General Schedule pay rates, except that no rate of pay fixed under this paragraph may exceed the equivalent of that payable for a position at level V of the Executive Schedule under section 5316 of title 5, United States Code. Any individual appointed under paragraph (1) or (2) shall be treated as an employee for purposes of chapters 63, 81, 83, 84, 85, 87, 89, 89A, 89B, and 90 of that title.

(4) Detailees.—

Any Federal Government employee may be detailed to the Commission without reimbursement from the Commission, and such detailee shall retain the rights, status, and privileges of his or her regular employment without interruption.

(5) Consultant Services.—

The Commission is authorized to procure the services of experts and consultants in accordance with section 3109 of title 5, United States Code, but at rates not to exceed the daily rate paid a person occupying a position at level IV of the Executive Schedule under section 5315 of title 5, United States Code.

(f) Compensation and Travel Expenses.—

(1) Compensation.—

Each member of the Commission may be compensated at a rate not to exceed the daily equivalent of the annual rate of basic pay in effect for a position at level IV of the Executive Schedule under section 5315 of title 5, United States Code, for each day during which that member is engaged in the actual performance of the duties of the Commission.

(2) Travel Expenses.—

While away from their homes or regular places of business in the performance of services for the Commission, members of the Commission shall be allowed travel expenses, including per diem in lieu of subsistence, in the same manner as persons employed intermittently in the Government service are allowed expenses under section 5703(b) of title 5, United States Code.

(g) Nonapplicability of Federal Advisory Committee Act.—

The Federal Advisory Committee Act (5 U.S.C. App.) shall not apply to the Commission.

(h) Report of the Commission; Appearance Before and Consultations with Congress.—

(1) Report.—

On December 15, 2010, the Commission shall submit to the President and to the Congress a report containing the findings and conclusions of the Commission on the causes of the current financial and economic crisis in the United States.

(2) Institution-specific Reports Authorized.—

At the discretion of the chairperson of the Commission, the report under paragraph (1) may include reports or specific findings on any financial institution examined by the Commission under subsection (c)(2).

(3) Appearance Before the Congress.—

The chairperson of the Commission shall, not later than 120 days after the date of submission of the final reports under paragraph (1), appear before the Committee on Banking, Housing, and Urban Affairs of the Senate and the Committee on Financial Services of the House of Representatives regarding such reports and the findings of the Commission.

(4) Consultations with the Congress.—

The Commission shall consult with the Committee on Banking, Housing, and Urban Affairs of the Senate, the Committee on Financial Services of the House of Representatives, and other relevant committees of the Congress, for purposes of informing the Congress on the work of the Commission.

(i) Termination of Commission.—

(1) In General.—

The Commission, and all the authorities of this section, shall terminate 60 days after the date on which the final report is submitted under subsection (h).

(2) Administrative activities before termination.—

The Commission may use the 60-day period referred to in paragraph (1) for the purpose of concluding the activities of the Commission, including providing testimony to committees of the Congress concerning reports of the Commission and disseminating the final report submitted under subsection (h).

(j) Authorization of Appropriation.—

There is authorized to be appropriated to the Secretary of the Treasury such sums as are necessary to cover the costs of the Commission.

Approved May 20, 2009.

4.7.1 Legislative History

- S. 386, (H.R. 1748)

  - SENATE REPORTS:
    - No. 111-10 (Comm. on the Judiciary)
  - CONGRESSIONAL RECORD, Vol. 155 (2009):
    - Apr. 22, 23, 27, 28, considered and passed Senate.
    - May 6, considered and passed House, amended.
    - May 14, Senate concurred in House amendments with an amendment.
    - May 19, House concurred in Senate amendment.
  - WEEKLY COMPILATION OF PRESIDENTIAL DOCUMENTS (2009):
    - May 20, Presidential remarks and statement.

4.8 Division A

==DIVISION A — PREVENTING MORTGAGE FORECLOSURES==

Section 1. Short Title; Table of Contents.

(a) Short Title.—

This division may be cited as the ``**Helping Families Save Their Homes Act of 2009**´´.

(b) Table of Contents.—

The table of contents of this division is the following:

Sec. 1. Short Title; Table of Contents.

4.9   Weapon Systems Acquisition Reform Act of 2009

111TH UNITED STATES CONGRESS
1ST SESSION

An Act
To improve the organization and procedures of the Department of Defense for the acquisition of major weapon systems, and for other purposes.

Be it enacted by the Senate and House of Representatives of the United States of America in Congress assembled,

SECTION 1. SHORT TITLE; TABLE OF CONTENTS.

(a) Short Title—

This Act may be cited as the ``**Weapon Systems Acquisition Reform Act of 2009**´´.

(b) Table of Contents—

The table of contents for this Act is as follows:

SEC. 2. DEFINITIONS.

In this Act:

(1) The term ``congressional defense committees'' has the meaning given that term in section 101(a)(16) of title 10, United States Code.

(2) The term ``major defense acquisition program'' has the meaning given that term in section 2430 of title 10, United States Code.

(3) The term ``major weapon system'' has the meaning given that term in section 2379(d) of title 10, United States Code.

4.9.1 TITLE I—ACQUISITION ORGANIZATION

SEC. 101. COST ASSESSMENT AND PROGRAM EVALUATION.

(a) Director of Cost Assessment and Program Evaluation-

(1) IN GENERAL—

Chapter 4 of title 10, United States Code, is amended by inserting after section 139b the following new section:

``Sec. 139c. Director of Cost Assessment and Program Evaluation

``(a) Appointment- There is a Director of Cost Assessment and Program Evaluation in the Department of Defense, appointed by the President, by and with the advice and consent of the Senate.

``(b) Independent Advice to Secretary of Defense- (1) The Director of Cost Assessment and Program Evaluation is the principal advisor to the Secretary of Defense and other senior officials of the Department of Defense, and shall provide independent analysis and advice to such officials, on the following matters:

``(A) Matters assigned to the Director pursuant to this section and section 2334 of this title.

``(B) Matters assigned to the Director by the Secretary pursuant to section 113 of this title.

``(2) The Director may communicate views on matters within the responsibility of the Director directly to the Secretary of Defense and the Deputy Secretary of Defense without obtaining the approval or concurrence of any other official within the Department of Defense.

``(c) Deputy Directors- There are two Deputy Directors within the Office of the Director of Cost Assessment and Program Evaluation, as follows:

``(1) The Deputy Director for Cost Assessment.

``(2) The Deputy Director for Program Evaluation.

``(d) Responsibilities- The Director of Cost Assessment and Program Evaluation shall serve as the principal official within the senior management of the Department of Defense for the following:

``(1) Cost estimation and cost analysis for acquisition programs of the Department of Defense, and carrying out the duties assigned pursuant to section 2334 of this title.

``(2) Analysis and advice on matters relating to the planning and programming phases of the Planning, Programming, Budgeting and Execution system, and the preparation of materials and guidance for such system, as directed by the Secretary of Defense, working in coordination with the Under Secretary of Defense (Comptroller).

``(3) Analysis and advice for resource discussions relating to requirements under consideration in the Joint Requirements Oversight Council pursuant to section 181 of this title.

``(4) Formulation of study guidance for analyses of alternatives for major defense acquisition programs and performance of such analyses, as directed by the Secretary of Defense

``(5) Review, analysis, and evaluation of programs for executing approved strategies and policies, ensuring that information on programs is presented accurately and completely, and assessing the effect of spending by the Department of Defense on the United States economy.

``(6) Assessments of special access and compartmented intelligence programs, in coordination with the Under Secretary of Defense for Acquisition, Technology, and Logistics and the Under Secretary of Defense for Intelligence and in accordance with applicable policies.

``(7) Assessments of alternative plans, programs, and policies with respect to the acquisition programs of the Department of Defense.

``(8) Leading the development of improved analytical skills and competencies within the cost assessment and program evaluation workforce of the Department of Defense and improved tools, data, and methods to promote performance, economy, and efficiency in analyzing national security planning and the allocation of defense resources.''.

(2) CLERICAL AMENDMENT- The table of sections at the beginning of chapter 4 of such title is amended by inserting after the item relating to section 139b the following new item:

``139c. Director of Cost Assessment and Program Evaluation.''.

(3) EXECUTIVE SCHEDULE LEVEL IV- Section 5315 of title 5, United States Code, is amended by inserting after the item relating to the Director of Operational Test and Evaluation, Department of Defense the following new item:

``Director of Cost Assessment and Program Evaluation, Department of Defense.''.

(b) Independent Cost Estimation and Cost Analysis-

(1) IN GENERAL—

Chapter 137 of title 10, United States Code, is amended by adding at the end the following new section:

``Sec. 2334. Independent cost estimation and cost analysis

``(a) In General- The Director of Cost Assessment and Program Evaluation shall ensure that the cost estimation and cost analysis processes of the Department of Defense provide accurate information and realistic estimates of cost for the acquisition programs of the Department of Defense. In carrying out that responsibility, the Director shall—

``(1) prescribe, by authority of the Secretary of Defense, policies and procedures for the conduct of cost estimation and cost analysis for the acquisition programs of the Department of Defense;

``(2) provide guidance to and consult with the Secretary of Defense, the Under Secretary of Defense for Acquisition, Technology, and Logistics, the Under Secretary of Defense (Comptroller), the Secretaries of the military departments, and the heads of the Defense Agencies with respect to cost estimation in the Department of Defense in general and with respect to specific cost estimates and cost analyses to be conducted in connection with a major defense acquisition program under chapter 144 of this title or a major automated information system program under chapter 144A of this title;

``(3) issue guidance relating to the proper selection of confidence levels in cost estimates generally, and specifically, for the proper selection of confidence levels in cost estimates for major defense acquisition programs and major automated information system programs;

``(4) issue guidance relating to full consideration of life-cycle management and sustainability costs in major defense acquisition programs and major automated information system programs;

``(5) review all cost estimates and cost analyses conducted in connection with major defense acquisition programs and major automated information system programs;

``(6) conduct independent cost estimates and cost analyses for major defense acquisition programs and major automated information system programs for which the Under Secretary of Defense for Acquisition, Technology, and Logistics is the Milestone Decision Authority—

``(A) in advance of—

``(i) any certification under section 2366a or 2366b of this title;

``(ii) any decision to enter into low-rate initial production or full-rate production;

``(iii) any certification under section 2433a of this title; and

``(iv) any report under section 2445c(f) of this title; and

``(B) at any other time considered appropriate by the Director or upon the request of the Under Secretary of Defense for Acquisition, Technology, and Logistics; and

``(7) periodically assess and update the cost indexes used by the Department to ensure that such indexes have a sound basis and meet the Department's needs for realistic cost estimation.

``(b) Review of Cost Estimates, Cost Analyses, and Records of the Military Departments and Defense Agencies- The Secretary of Defense shall ensure that the Director of Cost Assessment and Program Evaluation—

``(1) promptly receives the results of all cost estimates and cost analyses conducted by the military departments and Defense Agencies, and all studies conducted by the military departments and Defense Agencies in connection with such cost estimates and cost analyses, for major defense acquisition programs and major automated information system programs of the military departments and Defense Agencies; and

``(2) has timely access to any records and data in the Department of Defense (including the records and data of each military department and Defense Agency and including classified and proprietary information) that the Director considers necessary to review in order to carry out any duties under this section.

``(c) Participation, Concurrence, and Approval in Cost Estimation- The Director of Cost Assessment and Program Evaluation may—

``(1) participate in the discussion of any discrepancies between an independent cost estimate and the cost estimate of a military department or Defense Agency for a major defense acquisition program or major automated information system program of the Department of Defense;

``(2) comment on deficiencies in the methodology or execution of any cost estimate or cost analysis developed by a military department or Defense Agency for a major defense acquisition program or major automated information system program;

``(3) concur in the choice of a cost estimate within the baseline description or any other cost estimate (including the confidence level for any such cost estimate) for use at any event specified in subsection (a)(6); and

``(4) participate in the consideration of any decision to request authorization of a multiyear procurement contract for a major defense acquisition program.

``(d) Disclosure of Confidence Levels for Baseline Estimates of Major Defense Acquisition Programs- The Director of Cost Assessment and Program Evaluation, and the Secretary of the military department concerned or the head of the Defense Agency concerned (as applicable), shall each—

``(1) disclose in accordance with paragraph (2) the confidence level used in establishing a cost estimate for a major defense acquisition program or major automated information system program, the rationale for selecting such confidence level, and, if such confidence level is less than 80 percent, the justification for selecting a confidence level of less than 80 percent; and

``(2) include the disclosure required by paragraph (1)—

``(A) in any decision documentation approving a cost estimate within the baseline description or any other cost estimate for use at any event specified in subsection (a)(6); and

``(B) in the next Selected Acquisition Report pursuant to section 2432 of this title in the case of a major defense acquisition program, or the next quarterly report pursuant to section 2445c of this title in the case of a major automated information system program.

``(e) Annual Report on Cost Assessment Activities- (1) The Director of Cost Assessment and Program Evaluation shall prepare an annual report summarizing the cost estimation and cost analysis activities of the Department of Defense during the previous year and assessing the progress of the Department in improving the accuracy of its cost estimates and analyses. Each report shall include, for the year covered by such report, an assessment of—

``(A) the extent to which each of the military departments and Defense Agencies have complied with policies, procedures, and guidance issued by the Director with regard to the preparation of cost estimates for major defense acquisition programs and major automated information systems;

``(B) the overall quality of cost estimates prepared by each of the military departments and Defense Agencies for major defense acquisition programs and major automated information system programs; and

``(C) any consistent differences in methodology or approach among the cost estimates prepared by the military departments, the Defense Agencies, and the Director.

``(2) Each report under this subsection shall be submitted concurrently to the Secretary of Defense, the Under Secretary of Defense for Acquisition, Technology, and Logistics, the Under Secretary of Defense (Comptroller), and the congressional defense committees not later than 10 days after the transmittal to Congress of the budget of the President for the next fiscal year (as submitted pursuant to section 1105 of title 31).

``(3)(A) Each report submitted to the congressional defense committees under this subsection shall be submitted in unclassified form, but may include a classified annex.

``(B) The Director shall ensure that a report submitted under this subsection does not include any information, such as proprietary or source selection sensitive information, that could undermine the integrity of the acquisition process.

``(C) The unclassified version of each report submitted to the congressional defense committees under this subsection shall be posted on an Internet website of the Department of Defense that is available to the public.

``(4) The Secretary of Defense may comment on any report of the Director to the congressional defense committees under this subsection.

``(f) Staff- The Secretary of Defense shall ensure that the Director of Cost Assessment and Program Evaluation has sufficient professional staff of military and civilian personnel to enable the Director to carry out the duties and responsibilities of the Director under this section.``.

(2) CLERICAL AMENDMENT- The table of sections at the beginning of chapter 137 of such title is amended by adding at the end the following new item:

``2334. Independent cost estimation and cost analysis.``.

(c) Transfer of Personnel and Functions-

(1) TRANSFER OF FUNCTIONS—

The functions of the Office of Program Analysis and Evaluation of the Department of Defense, including the functions of the Cost Analysis Improvement Group, are hereby transferred to the Office of the Director of Cost Assessment and Program Evaluation.

(2) TRANSFER OF PERSONNEL TO DEPUTY DIRECTOR FOR INDEPENDENT COST ASSESSMENT—

The personnel of the Cost Analysis Improvement Group are hereby transferred to the Deputy Director for Cost Assessment in the Office of the Director of Cost Assessment and Program Evaluation.

(3) TRANSFER OF PERSONNEL TO DEPUTY DIRECTOR FOR PROGRAM ANALYSIS AND EVALUATION—

The personnel (other than the personnel transferred under paragraph (2)) of the Office of Program Analysis and Evaluation are hereby transferred to the Deputy Director for Program Evaluation in the Office of the Director of Cost Assessment and Program Evaluation.

(d) Conforming Amendments-

(1) Section 181(d) of title 10, United States Code, is amended by striking ``Director of the Office of Program Analysis and Evaluation`` and inserting ``Director of Cost Assessment and Program Evaluation``.

(2) Section 2306b(i)(1)(B) of such title is amended by striking ``Cost Analysis Improvement Group of the Department of Defense`` and inserting ``Director of Cost Assessment and Program Analysis``.

(3) Section 2366a(a)(4) of such title is amended by inserting ``, with the concurrence of the Director of Cost Assessment and Program Evaluation,`` after ``has been submitted``.

(4) Section 2366b(a)(1)(C) of such title is amended by inserting ``, with the concurrence of the Director of Cost Assessment and Program Evaluation,`` after ``have been developed to execute``.

(5) Subparagraph (A) of section 2434(b)(1) of such title is amended to read as follows:

``(A) be prepared or approved by the Director of Cost Assessment and Program Evaluation; and``.

(6) Section 2445c(f)(3) of such title is amended by striking ``are reasonable`` and inserting ``have been determined, with the concurrence of the Director of Cost Assessment and Program Evaluation, to be reasonable``.

(e) Report on Monitoring of Operating and Support Costs for Major Defense Acquisition Programs-

(1) REPORT TO SECRETARY OF DEFENSE—

Not later than one year after the date of the enactment of this Act, the Director of Cost Assessment and Program Evaluation under section 139c of title 10 United States Code (as added by subsection (a)), shall review existing systems and methods of the Department of Defense for tracking and assessing operating and support costs on major defense acquisition programs and submit to the Secretary of Defense a report on the finding and recommendations of the Director as a result of the review, including an assessment by the Director of the feasibility and advisability of establishing baselines for operating and support costs under section 2435 of title 10, United States Code.

(2) TRANSMITTAL TO CONGRESS—

Not later than 30 days after receiving the report required by paragraph (1), the Secretary shall transmit the report to the congressional defense committees, together with any comments on the report the Secretary considers appropriate.

SEC. 102. DIRECTORS OF DEVELOPMENTAL TEST AND EVALUATION AND SYSTEMS ENGINEERING.

(a) In General-

(1) ESTABLISHMENT OF POSITIONS—

Chapter 4 of title 10, United States Code, as amended by section 101(a) of this Act, is further amended by inserting after section 139c the following new section:
``Sec. 139d. Director of Developmental Test and Evaluation; Director of Systems Engineering: joint guidance

``(a) Director of Developmental Test and Evaluation-

``(1) APPOINTMENT- There is a Director of Developmental Test and Evaluation, who shall be appointed by the Secretary of Defense from among individuals with an expertise in test and evaluation.

``(2) PRINCIPAL ADVISOR FOR DEVELOPMENTAL TEST AND EVALUATION- The Director shall be the principal advisor to the Secretary of Defense and the Under Secretary of Defense for Acquisition, Technology, and Logistics on developmental test and evaluation in the Department of Defense.

``(3) SUPERVISION- The Director shall be subject to the supervision of the Under Secretary of Defense for Acquisition, Technology, and Logistics and shall report to the Under Secretary.

``(4) COORDINATION WITH DIRECTOR OF SYSTEMS ENGINEERING- The Director of Developmental Test and Evaluation shall closely coordinate with the Director of Systems Engineering to ensure that the developmental test and evaluation activities of the Department of Defense are fully integrated into and consistent with the systems engineering and development planning processes of the Department.

``(5) DUTIES- The Director shall—

``(A) develop policies and guidance for—

``(i) the conduct of developmental test and evaluation in the Department of Defense (including integration and developmental testing of software);

``(ii) in coordination with the Director of Operational Test and Evaluation, the integration of developmental test and evaluation with operational test and evaluation;

``(iii) the conduct of developmental test and evaluation conducted jointly by more than one military department or Defense Agency;

``(B) review and approve the developmental test and evaluation plan within the test and evaluation master plan for each major defense acquisition program of the Department of Defense;

``(C) monitor and review the developmental test and evaluation activities of the major defense acquisition programs;

``(D) provide advocacy, oversight, and guidance to elements of the acquisition workforce responsible for developmental test and evaluation;

``(E) periodically review the organizations and capabilities of the military departments with respect to developmental test and evaluation and identify needed changes or improvements to such organizations and capabilities, and provide input regarding needed changes or improvements for the test and evaluation strategic plan developed in accordance with section 196(d) of this title; and

``(F) perform such other activities relating to the developmental test and evaluation activities of the Department of Defense as the Under Secretary of Defense for Acquisition, Technology, and Logistics may prescribe.

``(6) ACCESS TO RECORDS- The Secretary of Defense shall ensure that the Director has access to all records and data of the Department of Defense (including the records and data of each military department and including classified and propriety information, as appropriate) that the Director considers necessary in order to carry out the Director's duties under this subsection.

``(7) CONCURRENT SERVICE AS DIRECTOR OF DEPARTMENT OF DEFENSE TEST RESOURCES MANAGEMENT CENTER- The individual serving as the Director of Developmental Test and Evaluation may also serve concurrently as the Director of the Department of Defense Test Resource Management Center under section 196 of this title.

``(b) Director of Systems Engineering-

``(1) APPOINTMENT- There is a Director of Systems Engineering, who shall be appointed by the Secretary of Defense from among individuals with an expertise in systems engineering and development planning.

``(2) PRINCIPAL ADVISOR FOR SYSTEMS ENGINEERING AND DEVELOPMENT PLANNING- The Director shall be the principal advisor to the Secretary of Defense and the Under Secretary of Defense for Acquisition, Technology, and Logistics on systems engineering and development planning in the Department of Defense.

``(3) SUPERVISION- The Director shall be subject to the supervision of the Under Secretary of Defense for Acquisition, Technology, and Logistics and shall report to the Under Secretary.

``(4) COORDINATION WITH DIRECTOR OF DEVELOPMENTAL TEST AND EVALUATION- The Director of Systems Engineering shall closely coordinate with the Director of Developmental Test and Evaluation to ensure that the developmental test and evaluation activities of the Department of Defense are fully integrated into and consistent with the systems engineering and development planning processes of the Department.

``(5) DUTIES- The Director shall—

``(A) develop policies and guidance for—

``(i) the use of systems engineering principles and best practices, generally;

``(ii) the use of systems engineering approaches to enhance reliability, availability, and maintainability on major defense acquisition programs;

``(iii) the development of systems engineering master plans for major defense acquisition programs including systems engineering considerations in support of lifecycle management and sustainability; and

``(iv) the inclusion of provisions relating to systems engineering and reliability growth in requests for proposals;

``(B) review and approve the systems engineering master plan for each major defense acquisition program;

``(C) monitor and review the systems engineering and development planning activities of the major defense acquisition programs;

``(D) provide advocacy, oversight, and guidance to elements of the acquisition workforce responsible for systems engineering, development planning, and lifecycle management and sustainability functions;

``(E) provide input on the inclusion of systems engineering requirements in the process for consideration of joint military requirements by the Joint Requirements Oversight Council pursuant to section 181 of this title, including specific input relating to each capabilities development document;

``(F) periodically review the organizations and capabilities of the military departments with respect to systems engineering, development planning, and lifecycle management and sustainability, and identify needed changes or improvements to such organizations and capabilities; and

``(G) perform such other activities relating to the systems engineering and development planning activities of the Department of Defense as the Under Secretary of Defense for Acquisition, Technology, and Logistics may prescribe.

``(6) ACCESS TO RECORDS- The Director shall have access to any records or data of the Department of Defense (including the records and data of each military department and including classified and proprietary information as appropriate) that the Director considers necessary to review in order to carry out the Director's duties under this subsection.

``(c) Joint Annual Report- Not later than March 31 each year, beginning in 2010, the Director of Developmental Test and Evaluation and the Director of Systems Engineering shall jointly submit to the congressional defense committees a report on the activities undertaken pursuant to subsections (a) and (b) during the preceding year. Each report shall include a section on activities relating to the major defense acquisition programs which shall set forth, at a minimum, the following:

``(1) A discussion of the extent to which the major defense acquisition programs are fulfilling the objectives of their systems engineering master plans and developmental test and evaluation plans.

``(2) A discussion of the waivers of and deviations from requirements in test and evaluation master plans, systems engineering master plans, and other testing requirements that occurred during the preceding year with respect to such programs, any concerns raised by such waivers or deviations, and the actions that have been taken or are planned to be taken to address such concerns.

``(3) An assessment of the organization and capabilities of the Department of Defense for systems engineering, development planning, and developmental test and evaluation with respect to such programs.

``(4) Any comments on such report that the Secretary of Defense considers appropriate.

``(d) Joint Guidance- The Director of Developmental Test and Evaluation and the Director of Systems Engineering shall jointly, in coordination with the official designated by the Secretary of Defense under section 103 of the Weapon Systems Acquisition Reform Act of 2009, issue guidance on the following:

``(1) The development and tracking of detailed measurable performance criteria as part of the systems engineering master plans and the developmental test and evaluation plans within the test and evaluation master plans of major defense acquisition programs.

``(2) The use of developmental test and evaluation to measure the achievement of specific performance objectives within a systems engineering master plan.

``(3) A system for storing and tracking information relating to the achievement of the performance criteria and objectives specified pursuant to this subsection.

``(e) Major Defense Acquisition Program Defined- In this section, the term ``major defense acquisition program˝ has the meaning given that term in section 2430 of this title.˝.

(2) CLERICAL AMENDMENT- The table of sections at the beginning of chapter 4 of such title, as amended by section 101(a) of this Act, is further amended by inserting after the item relating to section 139c the following new item:

``139d. Director of Developmental Test and Evaluation; Director of Systems Engineering: joint guidance.˝.

(b) Developmental Test and Evaluation and Systems Engineering in the Military Departments and Defense Agencies-

(1) PLANS—

The service acquisition executive of each military department and each Defense Agency with responsibility for a major defense acquisition program shall develop and implement plans to ensure the military department or Defense Agency concerned has provided appropriate resources for each of the following:

(A) Developmental testing organizations with adequate numbers of trained personnel in order to—

(i) ensure that developmental testing requirements are appropriately addressed in the translation of operational requirements into contract specifications, in the source selection process, and in the preparation of requests for proposals on all major defense acquisition programs;

(ii) participate in the planning of developmental test and evaluation activities, including the preparation and approval of a developmental test and evaluation plan within the test and evaluation master plan for each major defense acquisition program; and

(iii) participate in and oversee the conduct of developmental testing, the analysis of data, and the preparation of evaluations and reports based on such testing.

(B) Development planning and systems engineering organizations with adequate numbers of trained personnel in order to—

(i) support key requirements, acquisition, and budget decisions made for each major defense acquisition program prior to Milestone A approval and Milestone B approval through a rigorous systems analysis and systems engineering process;

(ii) include a robust program for improving reliability, availability, maintainability, and sustainability as an integral part of design and development within the systems engineering master plan for each major defense acquisition program; and

(iii) identify systems engineering requirements, including reliability, availability, maintainability, and lifecycle management and sustainability requirements, during the Joint Capabilities Integration Development System process, and incorporate such systems engineering requirements into contract requirements for each major defense acquisition program.

(2) REPORTS BY SERVICE ACQUISITION EXECUTIVES—

Not later than 180 days after the date of the enactment of this Act, the service acquisition executive of each military department and each Defense Agency with responsibility for a major defense acquisition program shall submit to the Director of Developmental Test and Evaluation and the Director of Systems Engineering a report on the extent to which—

(A) such military department or Defense Agency has implemented, or is implementing, the plan required by paragraph (1); and

(B) additional authorities or resources are needed to attract, develop, retain, and reward developmental test and evaluation personnel and systems engineers with appropriate levels of hands-on experience and technical expertise to meet the needs of such military department or Defense Agency.

(3) ASSESSMENT OF REPORTS BY DIRECTORS OF DEVELOPMENTAL TEST AND EVALUATION AND SYSTEMS ENGINEERING—

The first annual report submitted to Congress by the Director of Developmental Test and Evaluation and the Director of Systems Engineering under section 139d(c) of title 10, United States Code (as added by subsection (a)), shall include an assessment by the Directors of the reports submitted by the service acquisition executives to the Directors under paragraph (2).

SEC. 103. PERFORMANCE ASSESSMENTS AND ROOT CAUSE ANALYSES FOR MAJOR DEFENSE ACQUISITION PROGRAMS.

(a) Designation of Senior Official Responsibility for Performance Assessments and Root Cause Analyses-

(1) IN GENERAL—

The Secretary of Defense shall designate a senior official in the Office of the Secretary of Defense as the principal official of the Department of Defense responsible for conducting and overseeing performance assessments and root cause analyses for major defense acquisition programs.

(2) NO PROGRAM EXECUTION RESPONSIBILITY—

The Secretary shall ensure that the senior official designated under paragraph (1) is not responsible for program execution.

(3) STAFF AND RESOURCES—

The Secretary shall assign to the senior official designated under paragraph (1) appropriate staff and resources necessary to carry out official's function under this section.

(b) Responsibilities—

The senior official designated under subsection (a) shall be responsible for the following:

(1) Carrying out performance assessments of major defense acquisition programs in accordance with the requirements of subsection (c) periodically or when requested by the Secretary of Defense, the Under Secretary of Defense for Acquisition, Technology and Logistics, the Secretary of a military department, or the head of a Defense Agency.

(2) Conducting root cause analyses for major defense acquisition programs in accordance with the requirements of subsection (d) when required by section 2433a(a)(1) of title 10, United States Code (as added by section 206(a) of this Act), or when requested by the Secretary of Defense, the Under Secretary of Defense for Acquisition, Technology and Logistics, the Secretary of a military department, or the head of a Defense Agency.

(3) Issuing policies, procedures, and guidance governing the conduct of performance assessments and root cause analyses by the military departments and the Defense Agencies.

(4) Evaluating the utility of performance metrics used to measure the cost, schedule, and performance of major defense acquisition programs, and making such recommendations to the Secretary of Defense as the official considers appropriate to improve such metrics.

(5) Advising acquisition officials on performance issues regarding a major defense acquisition program that may arise—

  (A) prior to certification under section 2433a of title 10, United States Code (as so added);
  (B) prior to entry into full-rate production; or
  (C) in the course of consideration of any decision to request authorization of a multiyear procurement contract for the program.

(c) Performance Assessments—

For purposes of this section, a performance assessment with respect to a major defense acquisition program is an evaluation of the following:

(1) The cost, schedule, and performance of the program, relative to current metrics, including performance requirements and baseline descriptions.

(2) The extent to which the level of program cost, schedule, and performance predicted relative to such metrics is likely to result in the timely delivery of a level of capability to the warfighter that is consistent with the level of resources to be expended and provides superior value to alternative approaches that may be available to meet the same military requirement.

(d) Root Cause Analyses—

For purposes of this section and section 2433a of title 10, United States Code (as so added), a root cause analysis with respect to a major defense acquisition program is an assessment of the underlying cause or causes of shortcomings in cost, schedule, or performance of the program, including the role, if any, of—

(1) unrealistic performance expectations;

(2) unrealistic baseline estimates for cost or schedule;

(3) immature technologies or excessive manufacturing or integration risk;

(4) unanticipated design, engineering, manufacturing, or technology integration issues arising during program performance;

(5) changes in procurement quantities;

(6) inadequate program funding or funding instability;

(7) poor performance by government or contractor personnel responsible for program management; or

(8) any other matters.

(e) Support of Applicable Capabilities and Expertise—

The Secretary of Defense shall ensure that the senior official designated under subsection (a) has the support of other Department of Defense officials with relevant capabilities and expertise needed to carry out the requirements of this section.

(f) Annual Report—

Not later than March 1 each year, beginning in 2010, the official responsible for conducting and overseeing performance assessments and root cause analyses for major defense acquisition programs shall submit to the congressional defense committees a report on the activities undertaken under this section during the preceding year.

SEC. 104. ASSESSMENT OF TECHNOLOGICAL MATURITY OF CRITICAL TECHNOLOGIES OF MAJOR DEFENSE ACQUISITION PROGRAMS BY THE DIRECTOR OF DEFENSE RESEARCH AND ENGINEERING.

(a) Assessment by Director of Defense Research and Engineering-

(1) IN GENERAL—

Section 139a of title 10, United States Code, is amended by adding at the end the following new subsection:

"(c)(1) The Director of Defense Research and Engineering, in consultation with the Director of Developmental Test and Evaluation, shall periodically review and assess the technological maturity and integration risk of critical technologies of the major defense acquisition programs of the Department of Defense and report on the findings of such reviews and assessments to the Under Secretary of Defense for Acquisition, Technology, and Logistics.

"(2) The Director shall submit to the Secretary of Defense and to the congressional defense committees by March 1 of each year a report on the technological maturity and integration risk of critical technologies of the major defense acquisition programs of the Department of Defense.".

(2) FIRST ANNUAL REPORT—

The first annual report under subsection (c)(2) of section 139a of title 10, United States Code (as added by paragraph (1)), shall be submitted to the congressional defense committees not later than March 1, 2010, and shall address the results of reviews and assessments conducted by the Director of Defense Research and Engineering pursuant to subsection (c)(1) of such section (as so added) during the preceding calendar year.

(b) Report on Resources for Implementation—

Not later than 120 days after the date of the enactment of this Act, the Director of Defense Research and Engineering shall submit to the congressional defense committees a report describing any additional resources that may be required by the Director, and by other research and engineering elements of the Department of Defense, to carry out the following:

(1) The requirements under the amendment made by subsection (a)(1).

(2) The technological maturity assessments required by section 2366b(a) of title 10, United States Code.

(3) The requirements of Department of Defense Instruction 5000, as revised.

(c) Technological Maturity Standards—

Not later than 180 days after the date of the enactment of this Act, the Director of Defense Research and Engineering, in consultation with the Director of Developmental Test and Evaluation, shall develop knowledge-based standards against which to measure the technological maturity and integration risk of critical technologies at key stages in the acquisition process for purposes of conducting the reviews and assessments of major defense acquisition programs required by subsection (c) of section 139a of title 10, United States Code (as so added).

SEC. 105. ROLE OF THE COMMANDERS OF THE COMBATANT COMMANDS IN IDENTIFYING JOINT MILITARY REQUIREMENTS.

(a) In General—

Section 181(d) of title 10, United States Code, as amended by section 101(d) of this Act, is further amended—

(1) by inserting ``(1)´´ before ``The Under Secretary´´; and

(2) by adding at the end the following new paragraph:

> ``(2) The Council shall seek and consider input from the commanders of the combatant commands in carrying out its mission under paragraphs (1) and (2) of subsection (b) and in conducting periodic reviews in accordance with the requirements of subsection (e).´´.

(b) Input From Commanders of Combatant Commands—

The Joint Requirements Oversight Council in the Department of Defense shall seek and consider input from the commanders of combatant commands, in accordance with section 181(d) of title 10, United States Code (as amended by subsection (a)). Such input may include, but is not limited to, an assessment of the following:

(1) Any current or projected missions or threats in the theater of operations of the commander of a combatant command that would inform the assessment of a new joint military requirement.

(2) The necessity and sufficiency of a proposed joint military requirement in terms of current and projected missions or threats.

(3) The relative priority of a proposed joint military requirement in comparison with other joint military requirements within the theater of operations of the commander of a combatant command.

(4) The ability of partner nations in the theater of operations of the commander of a combatant command to assist in meeting the joint military requirement or the benefit, if any, of a partner nation assisting in development or use of technologies developed to meet the joint military requirement.

(c) Comptroller General of the United States Review of Implementation-

(1) REQUIREMENT—

Not later than two years after the date of the enactment of this Act, the Comptroller General of the United States shall submit to the Committees on Armed Services of the Senate and the House of Representatives a report on the implementation of the requirements of—

(A) subsection (d)(2) of section 181 of title 10, United States Code (as amended by subsection (a)), for the Joint Requirements Oversight Council to solicit and consider input from the commanders of the combatant commands;

(B) the amendments to subsection (b) of section 181 of title 10, United States Code, made by section 942 of the National Defense Authorization Act for Fiscal Year 2008 (Public Law 110-181; 122 Stat. 287) and by section 201(b) of this Act; and

(C) the requirements of section 201(c) of this Act.

(2) MATTERS COVERED—

The report shall include, at a minimum, an assessment of—

(A) the extent to which the Council has effectively sought, and the commanders of the combatant commands have provided, meaningful input on proposed joint military requirements;

(B) the quality and effectiveness of efforts to estimate the level of resources needed to fulfill joint military requirements; and

(C) the extent to which the Council has considered trade-offs among cost, schedule, and performance objectives.

4.9.2 TITLE II—ACQUISITION POLICY

SEC. 201. CONSIDERATION OF TRADE-OFFS AMONG COST, SCHEDULE, AND PERFORMANCE OBJECTIVES IN DEPARTMENT OF DEFENSE ACQUISITION PROGRAMS.

(a) Consideration of Trade-Offs-

(1) IN GENERAL—

The Secretary of Defense shall ensure that mechanisms are developed and implemented to require consideration of trade-offs among cost, schedule, and performance objectives as part of the process for developing requirements for Department of Defense acquisition programs.

(2) ELEMENTS—

The mechanisms required under this subsection shall ensure, at a minimum, that—
(A) Department of Defense officials responsible for acquisition, budget, and cost estimating functions are provided an appropriate opportunity to develop estimates and raise cost and schedule matters before performance objectives are established for capabilities for which the Chairman of the Joint Requirements Oversight Council is the validation authority; and
(B) the process for developing requirements is structured to enable incremental, evolutionary, or spiral acquisition approaches, including the deferral of technologies that are not yet mature and capabilities that are likely to significantly increase costs or delay production until later increments or spirals.

(b) Duties of Joint Requirements Oversight Council—

Section 181(b) of title 10, United States Code, is amended—
(1) in paragraph (1)—

(A) by striking ``and´´ at the end of subparagraph (A);
(B) by inserting ``and´´ at the end of subparagraph (B) after the semicolon; and
(C) by adding at the end the following new subparagraph:

``(C) in ensuring the consideration of trade-offs among cost, schedule, and performance objectives for joint military requirements in consultation with the advisors specified in subsection (d);´´.

(2) in paragraph (3)—

(A) by inserting ``, in consultation with the Under Secretary of Defense (Comptroller), the Under Secretary of Defense for Acquisition, Technology, and Logistics, and the Director of Cost Assessment and Performance Evaluation,´´ after ``assist the Chairman´´; and
(B) by striking ``and´´ after the semicolon at the end;

(3) in paragraph (4), by striking the period at the end and inserting ``; and´´; and

(4) by adding at the end the following new paragraph:

``(5) assist the Chairman, in consultation with the commanders of the combatant commands and the Under Secretary of Defense for Acquisition, Technology, and Logistics, in establishing an objective for the overall period of time within which an initial operational capability should be delivered to meet each joint military requirement.´´.

(c) Review of Joint Military Requirements—

The Secretary of Defense shall ensure that each new joint military requirement recommended by the Joint Requirements Oversight Council is reviewed to ensure that the Joint Requirements Oversight Council has, in making such recommendation—

(1) taken appropriate action to seek and consider input from the commanders of the combatant commands, in accordance with the requirements of section 181(d) of title 10, United States Code (as amended by section 105(a) of this Act);

(2) engaged in consideration of trade-offs among cost, schedule, and performance objectives in accordance with the requirements of section 181(b)(1)(C) of title 10, United States Code (as added by subsection (b)); and

(3) engaged in consideration of issues of joint portfolio management, including alternative material and non-material solutions, as provided in Department of Defense instructions for the development of joint military requirements.

(d) Study Guidance for Analyses of Alternatives—

The Director of Cost Assessment and Program Evaluation shall take the lead in the development of study guidance for an analysis of alternatives for each joint military requirement for which the Chairman of the Joint Requirements Oversight Council is the validation authority. In developing the guidance, the Director shall solicit the advice of appropriate officials within the Department of Defense and ensure that the guidance requires, at a minimum—

(1) full consideration of possible trade-offs among cost, schedule, and performance objectives for each alternative considered; and

(2) an assessment of whether or not the joint military requirement can be met in a manner that is consistent with the cost and schedule objectives recommended by the Joint Requirements Oversight Council.

(e) Analysis of Alternatives in Certification for Milestone A—

Section 2366a(a) of title 10, United States Code, as amended by section 101(d)(3) of this Act, is further amended—

(1) by striking ``and'' at the end of paragraph (3);

(2) by redesignating paragraph (4) as paragraph (5); and

(3) by inserting after paragraph (3) the following new paragraph (4):

> ``(4) that an analysis of alternatives has been performed consistent with study guidance developed by the Director of Cost Assessment and Program Evaluation; and''.

(f) Duties of Milestone Decision Authority—

Section 2366b(a)(1)(B) of such title is amended by inserting ``appropriate trade-offs among cost, schedule, and performance objectives have been made to ensure that'' before ``the program is affordable''.

SEC. 202. ACQUISITION STRATEGIES TO ENSURE COMPETITION THROUGHOUT THE LIFECYCLE OF MAJOR DEFENSE ACQUISITION PROGRAMS.

(a) Acquisition Strategies To Ensure Competition—

The Secretary of Defense shall ensure that the acquisition strategy for each major defense acquisition program includes—

(1) measures to ensure competition, or the option of competition, at both the prime contract level and the subcontract level (at such tier or tiers as are appropriate) of such program throughout the life-cycle of such program as a means to improve contractor performance; and

(2) adequate documentation of the rationale for the selection of the subcontract tier or tiers under paragraph (1).

(b) Measures To Ensure Competition—

The measures to ensure competition, or the option of competition, for purposes of subsection (a)(1) may include measures to achieve the following, in appropriate cases if such measures are cost-effective:

(1) Competitive prototyping.

(2) Dual-sourcing.

(3) Unbundling of contracts.

(4) Funding of next-generation prototype systems or subsystems.

(5) Use of modular, open architectures to enable competition for upgrades.

(6) Use of build-to-print approaches to enable production through multiple sources.

(7) Acquisition of complete technical data packages.

(8) Periodic competitions for subsystem upgrades.

(9) Licensing of additional suppliers.

(10) Periodic system or program reviews to address long-term competitive effects of program decisions.

(c) Additional Measures To Ensure Competition at Subcontract Level—

The Secretary shall take actions to ensure fair and objective ``make-buy'' decisions by prime contractors on major defense acquisition programs by—

(1) requiring prime contractors to give full and fair consideration to qualified sources other than the prime contractor for the development or construction of major subsystems and components of major weapon systems;

(2) providing for government surveillance of the process by which prime contractors consider such sources and determine whether to conduct such development or construction in-house or through a subcontract; and

(3) providing for the assessment of the extent to which a contractor has given full and fair consideration to qualified sources other than the contractor in sourcing decisions as a part of past performance evaluations.

(d) Consideration of Competition Throughout Operation and Sustainment of Major Weapon Systems—

Whenever a decision regarding source of repair results in a plan to award a contract for performance of maintenance and sustainment of a major weapon system, the Secretary shall take actions to ensure that, to the maximum extent practicable and consistent with statutory requirements, contracts for such maintenance and sustainment are awarded on a competitive basis and give full consideration to all sources (including sources that partner or subcontract with public or private sector repair activities).

(e) Applicability-

(1) STRATEGY AND MEASURES TO ENSURE COMPETITION—

The requirements of subsections (a) and (b) shall apply to any acquisition plan for a major defense acquisition program that is developed or revised on or after the date that is 60 days after the date of the enactment of this Act.

(2) ADDITIONAL ACTIONS—

The actions required by subsections (c) and (d) shall be taken within 180 days after the date of the enactment of this Act.

SEC. 203. PROTOTYPING REQUIREMENTS FOR MAJOR DEFENSE ACQUISITION PROGRAMS.

(a) Competitive Prototyping—

Not later than 90 days after the date of the enactment of this Act, the Secretary of Defense shall modify the guidance of the Department of Defense relating to the operation of the acquisition system with respect to competitive prototyping for major defense acquisition programs to ensure the following:

(1) That the acquisition strategy for each major defense acquisition program provides for competitive prototypes before Milestone B approval (or Key Decision Point B approval in the case of a space program) unless the Milestone Decision Authority for such program waives the requirement pursuant to paragraph (2).

(2) That the Milestone Decision Authority may waive the requirement in paragraph (1) only—

(A) on the basis that the cost of producing competitive prototypes exceeds the expected life-cycle benefits (in constant dollars) of producing such prototypes, including the benefits of improved performance and increased technological and design maturity that may be achieved through competitive prototyping; or
(B) on the basis that, but for such waiver, the Department would be unable to meet critical national security objectives.

(3) That whenever a Milestone Decision Authority authorizes a waiver pursuant to paragraph (2), the Milestone Decision Authority—

(A) shall require that the program produce a prototype before Milestone B approval (or Key Decision Point B approval in the case of a space program) if the expected life-cycle benefits (in constant dollars) of producing such prototype exceed its cost and its production is consistent with achieving critical national security objectives; and
(B) shall notify the congressional defense committees in writing not later than 30 days after the waiver is authorized and include in such notification the rationale for the waiver and the plan, if any, for producing a prototype.

(4) That prototypes may be required under paragraph (1) or (3) for the system to be acquired or, if prototyping of the system is not feasible, for critical subsystems of the system.

(b) Comptroller General Review of Certain Waivers-

(1) NOTICE TO COMPTROLLER GENERAL—

Whenever a Milestone Decision Authority authorizes a waiver of the requirement for prototypes pursuant to paragraph (2) of subsection (a) on the basis of excessive cost, the Milestone Decision Authority shall submit the notification of the waiver, together with the rationale, to the Comptroller General of the United States at the same time it is submitted to the congressional defense committees.

(2) COMPTROLLER GENERAL REVIEW—

Not later than 60 days after receipt of a notification of a waiver under paragraph (1), the Comptroller General shall—
(A) review the rationale for the waiver; and
(B) submit to the congressional defense committees a written assessment of the rationale for the waiver.

SEC. 204. ACTIONS TO IDENTIFY AND ADDRESS SYSTEMIC PROBLEMS IN MAJOR DEFENSE ACQUISITION PROGRAMS PRIOR TO MILESTONE B APPROVAL.

(a) Modification to Certification Requirement—

Subsection (a) of section 2366a of title 10, United States Code, is amended by striking ``may not receive Milestone A approval, or Key Decision Point A approval in the case of a space program,´´ and inserting ``may not receive Milestone A approval, or Key Decision Point A approval in the case of a space program, or otherwise be initiated prior to Milestone B approval, or Key Decision Point B approval in the case of a space program,´´.

(b) Modification to Notification Requirement—

Subsection (b) of such section is amended—

(1) by inserting ``(1)´´ before ``With respect to´´;

(2) in paragraph (1), as so designated, by striking ``by at least 25 percent,´´ and inserting ``by at least 25 percent, or the program manager determines that the period of time required for the delivery of an initial operational capability is likely to exceed the schedule objective established pursuant to section 181(b)(5) of this title by more than 25 percent,´´; and

(3) by adding at the end the following new paragraph:

> ``(2) Not later than 30 days after a program manager submits a notification to the Milestone Decision Authority pursuant to paragraph (1) with respect to a major defense acquisition program, the Milestone Decision Authority shall submit to the congressional defense committees a report that—
>
> > ``(A) identifies the root causes of the cost or schedule growth in accordance with applicable policies, procedures, and guidance;
> > ``(B) identifies appropriate acquisition performance measures for the remainder of the development of the program; and
> > ``(C) includes one of the following:
> > > ``(i) A written certification (with a supporting explanation) stating that—
> > > > ``(I) the program is essential to national security;
> > > > ``(II) there are no alternatives to the program that will provide acceptable military capability at less cost;
> > > > ``(III) new estimates of the development cost or schedule, as appropriate, are reasonable; and
> > > > ``(IV) the management structure for the program is adequate to manage and control program development cost and schedule.
> > > ``(ii) A plan for terminating the development of the program or withdrawal of Milestone A approval, or Key Decision Point A approval in the case of a space program, if the Milestone Decision Authority determines that such action is in the interest of national defense.´´.

(c) Application to Ongoing Programs-

(1) IN GENERAL—

Each major defense acquisition program described in paragraph (2) shall be certified in accordance with the requirements of section 2366a of title 10, United States Code (as amended by this section), within one year after the date of the enactment of this Act.

(2) COVERED PROGRAMS—

The requirement in paragraph (1) shall apply to any major defense acquisition program that—

(A) was initiated before the date of the enactment of this Act; and

(B) as of the date of certification under paragraph (1) has not otherwise been certified pursuant to either section 2366a (as so amended) or 2366b of title 10, United States Code.

SEC. 205. ADDITIONAL REQUIREMENTS FOR CERTAIN MAJOR DEFENSE ACQUISITION PROGRAMS.

(a) Additional Requirements Relating to Milestone B Approval—

Section 2366b of title 10, United States Code, is amended—

(1) in subsection (d)—

(A) by inserting ``(1)´´ before ``The milestone decision authority may´´; and

(B) by striking the second sentence and inserting the following:

``(2) Whenever the milestone decision authority makes such a determination and authorizes such a waiver—

``(A) the waiver, the determination, and the reasons for the determination shall be submitted in writing to the congressional defense committees within 30 days after the waiver is authorized; and

``(B) the milestone decision authority shall review the program not less often than annually to determine the extent to which such program currently satisfies the certification components specified in paragraphs (1) and (2) of subsection (a) until such time as the milestone decision authority determines that the program satisfies all such certification components.´´;

(2) by redesignating subsections (e) and (f) as subsections (f) and (g), respectively, and inserting after subsection (d) the following new subsection (e):

``(e) Designation of Certification Status in Budget Documentation- Any budget request, budget justification material, budget display, reprogramming request, Selected Acquisition Report, or other budget documentation or performance report submitted by the Secretary of Defense to the President regarding a major defense acquisition program receiving a waiver pursuant to subsection (d) shall prominently and clearly indicate that such program has not fully satisfied the certification requirements of this section until such time as the milestone decision authority makes the determination that such program has satisfied all such certification components.´´; and

(3) in subsection (a)—

(A) in paragraph (1), by striking ``and´´ at the end;

(B) by redesignating paragraph (2) as paragraph (3);

(C) by inserting after paragraph (1) the following new paragraph (2):

``(2) has received a preliminary design review and conducted a formal post-preliminary design review assessment, and certifies on the basis of such assessment that the program demonstrates a high likelihood of accomplishing its intended mission; and´´; and

(D) in paragraph (3), as redesignated by subparagraph (B) of this paragraph—

(i) in subparagraph (D), by striking the semicolon and inserting ``, as determined by the Milestone Decision Authority on the basis of an independent review and assessment by the Director of Defense Research and Engineering; and´´;

(ii) by striking subparagraph (E); and

(iii) by redesignating subparagraph (F) as subparagraph (E).

(b) Certification and Review of Programs Entering Development Prior to Enactment of Section 2366b of Title 10-

(1) DETERMINATION—

Not later than 270 days after the date of the enactment of this Act, for each major defense acquisition program that received Milestone B approval before January 6, 2006, and has not received Milestone C approval, and for each space program that received Key Decision Point B approval before January 6, 2006, and has not received Key Decision Point C approval, the Milestone Decision Authority shall determine whether or not such program satisfies all of the certification components specified in paragraphs (1) and (2) of subsection (a) of section 2366b of title 10, United States Code (as amended by subsection (a) of this section).

(2) ANNUAL REVIEW—

The Milestone Decision Authority shall review any program determined pursuant to paragraph (1) not to satisfy any of the certification components of subsection (a) of section 2366b of title 10, United States Code (as so amended), not less often than annually thereafter to determine the extent to which such program currently satisfies such certification components until such time as the Milestone Decision Authority determines that such program satisfies all such certification components.

(3) DESIGNATION OF CERTIFICATION STATUS IN BUDGET DOCUMENTATION—

Any budget request, budget justification material, budget display, reprogramming request, Selected Acquisition Report, or other budget documentation or performance report submitted by the Secretary of Defense to the President regarding a major defense acquisition program which the Milestone Decision Authority determines under paragraph (1) does not satisfy all of the certification components of subsection (a) of section 2366b of title 10, United States Code, (as so amended) shall prominently and clearly indicate that such program has not fully satisfied such certification components until such time as the Milestone Decision Authority makes the determination that such program has satisfied all such certification components.

(c) Reviews of Programs Restructured After Experiencing Critical Cost Growth—

The official designated to perform oversight of performance assessment pursuant to section 103 of this Act, shall assess the performance of each major defense acquisition program that has exceeded critical cost growth thresholds established pursuant to section 2433(e) of title 10, United States Code, but has not been terminated in accordance with section 2433a of such title (as added by section 206(a) of this Act) not less often than semi-annually until one year after the date on which such program receives a new milestone approval, in accordance with section 2433a(c)(3) of such title (as so added). The results of reviews performed under this subsection shall be reported to the Under Secretary of Defense for Acquisition, Technology, and Logistics and summarized in the next annual report of such designated official.

SEC. 206. CRITICAL COST GROWTH IN MAJOR DEFENSE ACQUISITION PROGRAMS.

(a) Actions Following Critical Cost Growth-

(1) IN GENERAL—

Chapter 144 of title 10, United States Code, is amended by inserting after section 2433 the following new section:

``Sec. 2433a. Critical cost growth in major defense acquisition programs

``(a) Reassessment of Program- If the program acquisition unit cost or procurement unit cost of a major defense acquisition program or designated subprogram (as determined by the Secretary under section 2433(d) of this title) increases by a percentage equal to or greater than the critical cost growth threshold for the program or subprogram, the Secretary of Defense, after consultation with the Joint Requirements Oversight Council regarding program requirements, shall—

``(1) determine the root cause or causes of the critical cost growth in accordance with applicable statutory requirements and Department of Defense policies, procedures, and guidance; and

``(2) in consultation with the Director of Cost Assessment and Program Evaluation, carry out an assessment of—

> ``(A) the projected cost of completing the program if current requirements are not modified;
>
> ``(B) the projected cost of completing the program based on reasonable modification of such requirements;
>
> ``(C) the rough order of magnitude of the costs of any reasonable alternative system or capability; and
>
> ``(D) the need to reduce funding for other programs due to the growth in cost of the program.

``(b) Presumption of Termination- (1) After conducting the reassessment required by subsection (a) with respect to a major defense acquisition program, the Secretary shall terminate the program unless the Secretary submits to Congress, before the end of the 60-day period beginning on the day the Selected Acquisition Report containing the information described in section 2433(g) of this title is required to be submitted under section 2432(f) of this title, a written certification in accordance with paragraph (2).

``(2) A certification described by this paragraph with respect to a major defense acquisition program is a written certification that—

> ``(A) the continuation of the program is essential to the national security;
>
> ``(B) there are no alternatives to the program which will provide acceptable capability to meet the joint military requirement (as defined in section 181(g)((1) of this title) at less cost;
>
> ``(C) the new estimates of the program acquisition unit cost or procurement unit cost have been determined by the Director of Cost Assessment and Program Evaluation to be reasonable;
>
> ``(D) the program is a higher priority than programs whose funding must be reduced to accommodate the growth in cost of the program; and
>
> ``(E) the management structure for the program is adequate to manage and control program acquisition unit cost or procurement unit cost.

``(3) A written certification under paragraph (2) shall be accompanied by a report presenting the root cause analysis and assessment carried out pursuant to subsection (a) and the basis for each determination made in accordance with subparagraphs (A) through (E) of paragraph (2), together with supporting documentation.

``(c) Actions if Program Not Terminated- (1) If the Secretary elects not to terminate a major defense acquisition program pursuant to subsection (b), the Secretary shall—

> ``(A) restructure the program in a manner that addresses the root cause or causes of the critical cost growth, as identified pursuant to subsection (a), and ensures that the program has an appropriate management structure as set forth in the certification submitted pursuant to subsection (b)(2)(E);
>
> ``(B) rescind the most recent Milestone approval, or Key Decision Point approval in the case of a space program, for the program and withdraw any associated certification under section 2366a or 2366b of this title;

``(C) require a new Milestone approval, or Key Decision Point approval in the case of a space program, for the program before taking any contract action to enter a new contract, exercise an option under an existing contract, or otherwise extend the scope of an existing contract under the program, except to the extent determined necessary by the Milestone Decision Authority, on a non-delegable basis, to ensure that the program can be restructured as intended by the Secretary without unnecessarily wasting resources;

``(D) include in the report specified in paragraph (2) a description of all funding changes made as a result of the growth in cost of the program, including reductions made in funding for other programs to accommodate such cost growth; and

``(E) conduct regular reviews of the program in accordance with the requirements of section 205 of the Weapon Systems Acquisition Reform Act of 2009.

``(2) For purposes of paragraph (1)(D), the report specified in this paragraph is the first Selected Acquisition Report for the program submitted pursuant to section 2432 of this title after the President submits a budget pursuant to section 1105 of title 31, in the calendar year following the year in which the program was restructured.

``(d) Actions if Program Terminated- If a major defense acquisition program is terminated pursuant to subsection (b), the Secretary shall submit to Congress a written report setting forth—

``(1) an explanation of the reasons for terminating the program;

``(2) the alternatives considered to address any problems in the program; and

``(3) the course the Department plans to pursue to meet any continuing joint military requirements otherwise intended to be met by the program.´´.

(2) CLERICAL AMENDMENT- The table of sections at the beginning of chapter 144 of such title is amended by inserting after the item relating to section 2433 the following new item:

``2433a. Critical cost growth in major defense acquisition programs.´´.

(3) CONFORMING AMENDMENT- Paragraph (2) of section 2433(e) of such title 10 is amended to read as follows:

``(2) If the program acquisition unit cost or procurement unit cost of a major defense acquisition program or designated major subprogram (as determined by the Secretary under subsection (d)) increases by a percentage equal to or greater than the critical cost growth threshold for the program or subprogram, the Secretary of Defense shall take actions consistent with the requirements of section 2433a of this title.´´.

(b) Treatment as MDAP—

Section 2430 of such title is amended—

(1) in subsection (a)(2), by inserting ``, including all planned increments or spirals,´´ after ``an eventual total expenditure for procurement´´; and

(2) by adding at the end the following new subsection:

``(c) For purposes of subsection (a)(2), the Secretary shall consider, as applicable, the following:

``(1) The estimated level of resources required to fulfill the relevant joint military requirement, as determined by the Joint Requirements Oversight Council pursuant to section 181 of this title.

``(2) The cost estimate referred to in section 2366a(a)(4) of this title.
``(3) The cost estimate referred to in section 2366b(a)(1)(C) of this title.
``(4) The cost estimate within a baseline description as required by section 2435 of this title.''.

SEC. 207. ORGANIZATIONAL CONFLICTS OF INTEREST IN MAJOR DEFENSE ACQUISITION PROGRAMS.

(a) Revised Regulations Required—

Not later than 270 days after the date of the enactment of this Act, the Secretary of Defense shall revise the Defense Supplement to the Federal Acquisition Regulation to provide uniform guidance and tighten existing requirements for organizational conflicts of interest by contractors in major defense acquisition programs.

(b) Elements—

The revised regulations required by subsection (a) shall, at a minimum—

(1) address organizational conflicts of interest that could arise as a result of—

(A) lead system integrator contracts on major defense acquisition programs and contracts that follow lead system integrator contracts on such programs, particularly contracts for production;

(B) the ownership of business units performing systems engineering and technical assistance functions, professional services, or management support services in relation to major defense acquisition programs by contractors who simultaneously own business units competing to perform as either the prime contractor or the supplier of a major subsystem or component for such programs;

(C) the award of major subsystem contracts by a prime contractor for a major defense acquisition program to business units or other affiliates of the same parent corporate entity, and particularly the award of subcontracts for software integration or the development of a proprietary software system architecture; or

(D) the performance by, or assistance of, contractors in technical evaluations on major defense acquisition programs;

(2) ensure that the Department of Defense receives advice on systems architecture and systems engineering matters with respect to major defense acquisition programs from federally funded research and development centers or other sources independent of the prime contractor;

(3) require that a contract for the performance of systems engineering and technical assistance functions for a major defense acquisition program contains a provision prohibiting the contractor or any affiliate of the contractor from participating as a prime contractor or a major subcontractor in the development or construction of a weapon system under the program; and

(4) establish such limited exceptions to the requirement in paragraphs (2) and (3) as may be necessary to ensure that the Department of Defense has continued access to advice on systems architecture and systems engineering matters from highly-qualified contractors with domain experience and expertise, while ensuring that such advice comes from sources that are objective and unbiased.

(c) Consultation in Revision of Regulations-

(1) RECOMMENDATIONS OF PANEL ON CONTRACTING INTEGRITY—

Not later than 90 days after the date of the enactment of this Act, the Panel on Contracting Integrity established pursuant to section 813 of the John Warner National Defense Authorization Act for Fiscal Year 2007 (Public Law 109-364; 120 Stat. 2320) shall present recommendations to the Secretary of Defense on measures to eliminate or mitigate organizational conflicts of interest in major defense acquisition programs.

(2) CONSIDERATION OF RECOMMENDATIONS—

In developing the revised regulations required by subsection (a), the Secretary shall consider the following:

(A) The recommendations presented by the Panel on Contracting Integrity pursuant to paragraph (1).

(B) Any findings and recommendations of the Administrator for Federal Procurement Policy and the Director of the Office of Government Ethics pursuant to section 841(b) of the Duncan Hunter National Defense Authorization Act for Fiscal Year 2009 (Public Law 110-417; 122 Stat. 4539).

(d) Extension of Panel on Contracting Integrity—

Subsection (e) of section 813 of the John Warner National Defense Authorization Act for Fiscal Year 2007 is amended to read as follows:

``(e) Termination-

``(1) IN GENERAL- Subject to paragraph (2), the panel shall continue to serve until the date that is 18 months after the date on which the Secretary of Defense notifies the congressional defense committees of an intention to terminate the panel based on a determination that the activities of the panel no longer justify its continuation and that concerns about contracting integrity have been mitigated.

``(2) MINIMUM CONTINUING SERVICE- The panel shall continue to serve at least until December 31, 2011.´´.

4.9.3   TITLE III—ADDITIONAL ACQUISITION PROVISIONS

SEC. 301. AWARDS FOR DEPARTMENT OF DEFENSE PERSONNEL FOR EXCELLENCE IN THE ACQUISITION OF PRODUCTS AND SERVICES.

(a) In General—

Not later than 180 days after the date of the enactment of this Act, the Secretary of Defense shall commence carrying out a program to recognize excellent performance by individuals and teams of members of the Armed Forces and civilian personnel of the Department of Defense in the acquisition of products and services for the Department of Defense.

(b) Elements—

The program required by subsection (a) shall include the following:

(1) Procedures for the nomination by the personnel of the military departments and the Defense Agencies of individuals and teams of members of the Armed Forces and civilian personnel of the Department of Defense for eligibility for recognition under the program.

(2) Procedures for the evaluation of nominations for recognition under the program by one or more panels of individuals from the Government, academia, and the private sector who have such expertise, and are appointed in such manner, as the Secretary shall establish for purposes of the program.

(c) Award of Cash Bonuses—

As part of the program required by subsection (a), the Secretary may award to any individual recognized pursuant to the program a cash bonus authorized by any other provision of law to the extent that the performance of such individual so recognized warrants the award of such bonus under such provision of law.

SEC. 302. EARNED VALUE MANAGEMENT.

(a) Modification of Elements in Report on Implementation—

Subsection (a) of section 887 of the Duncan Hunter National Defense Authorization Act for Fiscal Year 2009 (Public Law 110-417; 122 Stat. 4562) is amended by striking paragraph (7) and inserting the following new paragraphs:

> ``(7) A discussion of the methodology used to establish appropriate baselines for earned value management at the award of a contract or commencement of a program, whichever is earlier.
> ``(8) A discussion of the manner in which the Department ensures that personnel responsible for administering and overseeing earned value management systems have the training and qualifications needed to perform that responsibility.
> ``(9) A discussion of mechanisms to ensure that contractors establish and use approved earned value management systems, including mechanisms such as the consideration of the quality of contractor earned value management performance in past performance evaluations.
> ``(10) Recommendations for improving earned value management and its implementation within the Department, including—
>
> > ``(A) a discussion of the merits of possible alternatives; and
> > ``(B) a plan for implementing any improvements the Secretary determines to be appropriate.``.

(b) Modification of Report Date—

Subsection (b) of such section is amended by striking ``270 days after the date of the enactment of this Act`` and inserting ``October 14, 2009``.

SEC. 303. EXPANSION OF NATIONAL SECURITY OBJECTIVES OF THE NATIONAL TECHNOLOGY AND INDUSTRIAL BASE.

(a) In General—

Section 2501(a) of title 10, United States Code, is amended by adding at the end the following new paragraph:

> ``(6) Maintaining critical design skills to ensure that the armed forces are provided with systems capable of ensuring technological superiority over potential adversaries.``.

(b) Assessment of Effect of Termination of Major Defense Acquisition Programs on Technology and Industrial Capabilities—

Section 2505(b) of such title is amended—

(1) in paragraph (2), by striking ``and`` at the end;

(2) in paragraph (3), by striking the period at the end and inserting ``; and``; and

(3) by adding at the end the following new paragraph:

> ``(4) consider the effects of the termination of major defense acquisition programs (as the term is defined in section 2430 of this title) in the previous fiscal year on the sectors and capabilities in the assessment.``.

**SEC. 304. COMPTROLLER GENERAL OF THE UNITED STATES REPORTS ON COSTS AND FINAN-
CIAL INFORMATION REGARDING MAJOR DEFENSE ACQUISITION PROGRAMS.**

(a) Review of Operating and Support Costs of Major Weapon Systems-

(1) IN GENERAL—

Not later than one year after the date of the enactment of this Act, the Comptroller
General of the United States shall submit to the congressional defense committees a
report on growth in operating and support costs for major weapon systems.

(2) ELEMENTS—

In preparing the report required by paragraph (1), the Comptroller General shall, at a
minimum—
(A) identify the original estimates for operating and support costs for major weapon
systems selected by the Comptroller General for purposes of the report;
(B) assess the actual operating and support costs for such major weapon systems;
(C) analyze the rate of growth for operating and support costs for such major weapon
systems;
(D) for such major weapon systems that have experienced the highest rate of growth in
operating and support costs, assess the factors contributing to such growth;
(E) assess measures taken by the Department of Defense to reduce operating and support
costs for major weapon systems; and
(F) make such recommendations as the Comptroller General considers appropriate.

(b) Review of Financial Information Relating to Major Defense Acquisition Programs-

(1) REVIEW—

The Comptroller General of the United States shall perform a review of weaknesses in
operations affecting the reliability of financial information on the systems and assets to
be acquired under major defense acquisition programs.

(2) ELEMENTS—

The review required under paragraph (1) shall—
(A) identify any weaknesses in operations under major defense acquisition programs
that hinder the capacity to assemble reliable financial information on the systems and
assets to be acquired under such programs in accordance with applicable accounting
standards;
(B) identify any mechanisms developed by the Department of Defense to address weaknesses in operations under major defense acquisition programs identified pursuant to
subparagraph (A); and
(C) assess the implementation of the mechanisms set forth pursuant to subparagraph
(B), including—

(i) the actions taken, or planned to be taken, to implement such mechanisms;
(ii) the schedule for carrying out such mechanisms; and
(iii) the metrics, if any, instituted to assess progress in carrying out such mechanisms.

(3) CONSULTATION—

In performing the review required by paragraph (1), the Comptroller General shall seek
and consider input from each of the following:
(A) The Chief Management Officer of the Department of Defense.
(B) The Chief Management Officer of the Department of the Army.
(C) The Chief Management Officer of the Department of the Navy.
(D) The Chief Management Officer of the Department of the Air Force.

(4) REPORT—

Not later than one year after the date of enactment of this Act, the Comptroller General shall submit to the congressional defense committees a report on the results of the review required by paragraph (1).

Approved May 22, 2009.

4.9.4 Legislative History

- S. 454, (H.R. 2101)

- HOUSE REPORTS:

    - No. 111-101 accompanying H.R. 2101 (Comm. on Armed Services)
    - No. 111-124 (Comm. of Conference)

- CONGRESSIONAL RECORD, Vol. 155 (2009):

    - May 6, 7, considered and passed Senate.
    - May 13, considered and passed House, amended, in lieu of H.R. 2101 pursuant to H. Res. 432.
    - May 20, Senate agreed to conference report.
    - May 21, House agreed to conference report.

- WEEKLY COMPILATION OF PRESIDENTIAL DOCUMENTS (2009):

    - May 22, Presidential remarks.

4.10 Credit Card Accountability Responsibility and Disclosure Act of 2009

111TH UNITED STATES CONGRESS
1ST SESSION

An Act
To amend the Truth in Lending Act to establish fair and transparent practices relating to the extension of credit under an open end consumer credit plan, and for other purposes.

Be it enacted by the Senate and House of Representatives of the United States of America in Congress assembled,

Section 1. Short Title; Table of Contents.

(a) Short Title.—

This Act may be cited as the ``**Credit Card Accountability Responsibility and Disclosure Act of 2009**´´ or the ``**Credit CARD Act of 2009**´´.

(b) Table of Contents.—

The table of contents for this Act is as follows:

Sec. 1. Short Title; Table of Contents.
Sec. 2. Regulatory Authority.
Sec. 3. Effective Date.

TITLE I — CONSUMER PROTECTION

Sec. 2. Regulatory Authority.

The Board of Governors of the Federal Reserve System (in this Act referred to as the ``Board´´) may issue such rules and publish such model forms as it considers necessary to carry out this Act and the amendments made by this Act.

Sec. 3. Effective Date.

This Act and the amendments made by this Act shall become effective 9 months after the date of enactment of this Act, except as otherwise specifically provided in this Act.

Approved May 22, 2009.

4.10.1   Legislative History

- H.R. 627, (S. 414)

    - HOUSE REPORTS:

        - No. 111-88 (Comm. on Financial Services)

    - SENATE REPORTS:

        - No. 111-16 accompanying S. 414 (Comm. on Banking, Housing, and Urban Affairs)

    - CONGRESSIONAL RECORD, Vol. 155 (2009):

        - Apr. 29, 30, considered and passed House.
        - May 11-14, 19, considered and passed Senate, amended.
        - May 20, House concurred in Senate amendment.

    - DAILY COMPILATION OF PRESIDENTIAL DOCUMENTS (2009):

        - May 22, Presidential remarks.

4.11   Division A

DIVISION A—FAMILY SMOKING PREVENTION AND TOBACCO CONTROL ACT

SECTION 1. SHORT TITLE; TABLE OF CONTENTS.

(a) Short Title.—

This division may be cited as the ``**Family Smoking Prevention and Tobacco Control Act**´´.

(b) Table of Contents.—

The table of contents of this division is as follows:

Sec. 1. Short title; table of contents.
Sec. 2. Findings.
Sec. 3. Purpose.
Sec. 4. Scope and effect.
Sec. 5. Severability.
Sec. 6. Modification of deadlines for Secretarial action.

TITLE I—AUTHORITY OF THE FOOD AND DRUG ADMINISTRATION

SEC. 2. FINDINGS.

The Congress finds the following:

(1) The use of tobacco products by the Nation's children is a pediatric disease of considerable proportions that results in new generations of tobacco-dependent children and adults.

(2) A consensus exists within the scientific and medical communities that tobacco products are inherently dangerous and cause cancer, heart disease, and other serious adverse health effects.

(3) Nicotine is an addictive drug.

(4) Virtually all new users of tobacco products are under the minimum legal age to purchase such products.

(5) Tobacco advertising and marketing contribute significantly to the use of nicotine-containing tobacco products by adolescents.

(6) Because past efforts to restrict advertising and marketing of tobacco products have failed adequately to curb tobacco use by adolescents, comprehensive restrictions on the sale, promotion, and distribution of such products are needed.

(7) Federal and State governments have lacked the legal and regulatory authority and resources they need to address comprehensively the public health and societal problems caused by the use of tobacco products.

(8) Federal and State public health officials, the public health community, and the public at large recognize that the tobacco industry should be subject to ongoing oversight.

(9) Under article I, section 8 of the Constitution, the Congress is vested with the responsibility for regulating interstate commerce and commerce with Indian tribes.

(10) The sale, distribution, marketing, advertising, and use of tobacco products are activities in and substantially affecting interstate commerce because they are sold, marketed, advertised, and distributed in interstate commerce on a nationwide basis, and have a substantial effect on the Nation's economy.

(11) The sale, distribution, marketing, advertising, and use of such products substantially affect interstate commerce through the health care and other costs attributable to the use of tobacco products.

(12) It is in the public interest for Congress to enact legislation that provides the Food and Drug Administration with the authority to regulate tobacco products and the advertising and promotion of such products. The benefits to the American people from enacting such legislation would be significant in human and economic terms.

(13) Tobacco use is the foremost preventable cause of premature death in America. It causes over 400,000 deaths in the United States each year, and approximately 8,600,000 Americans have chronic illnesses related to smoking.

(14) Reducing the use of tobacco by minors by 50 percent would prevent well over 10,000,000 of today's children from becoming regular, daily smokers, saving over 3,000,000 of them from premature death due to tobacco-induced disease. Such a reduction in youth smoking would also result in approximately $75,000,000,000 in savings attributable to reduced health care costs.

(15) Advertising, marketing, and promotion of tobacco products have been especially directed to attract young persons to use tobacco products, and these efforts have resulted in increased use of such products by youth. Past efforts to oversee these activities have not been successful in adequately preventing such increased use.

(16) In 2005, the cigarette manufacturers spent more than $13,000,000,000 to attract new users, retain current users, increase current consumption, and generate favorable long-term attitudes toward smoking and tobacco use.

(17) Tobacco product advertising often misleadingly portrays the use of tobacco as socially acceptable and healthful to minors.

(18) Tobacco product advertising is regularly seen by persons under the age of 18, and persons under the age of 18 are regularly exposed to tobacco product promotional efforts.

(19) Through advertisements during and sponsorship of sporting events, tobacco has become strongly associated with sports and has become portrayed as an integral part of sports and the healthy lifestyle associated with rigorous sporting activity.

(20) Children are exposed to substantial and unavoidable tobacco advertising that leads to favorable beliefs about tobacco use, plays a role in leading young people to overestimate the prevalence of tobacco use, and increases the number of young people who begin to use tobacco.

(21) The use of tobacco products in motion pictures and other mass media glamorizes its use for young people and encourages them to use tobacco products.

(22) Tobacco advertising expands the size of the tobacco market by increasing consumption of tobacco products including tobacco use by young people.

(23) Children are more influenced by tobacco marketing than adults: more than 80 percent of youth smoke three heavily marketed brands, while only 54 percent of adults, 26 and older, smoke these same brands.

(24) Tobacco company documents indicate that young people are an important and often crucial segment of the tobacco market. Children, who tend to be more price sensitive than adults, are influenced by advertising and promotion practices that result in drastically reduced cigarette prices.

(25) Comprehensive advertising restrictions will have a positive effect on the smoking rates of young people.

(26) Restrictions on advertising are necessary to prevent unrestricted tobacco advertising from undermining legislation prohibiting access to young people and providing for education about tobacco use.

(27) International experience shows that advertising regulations that are stringent and comprehensive have a greater impact on overall tobacco use and young people's use than weaker or less comprehensive ones.

(28) Text only requirements, although not as stringent as a ban, will help reduce underage use of tobacco products while preserving the informational function of advertising.

(29) It is in the public interest for Congress to adopt legislation to address the public health crisis created by actions of the tobacco industry.

(30) The final regulations promulgated by the Secretary of Health and Human Services in the August 28, 1996, issue of the Federal Register (61 Fed. Reg. 44615–44618) for inclusion as part 897 of title 21, Code of Federal Regulations, are consistent with the first amendment to the United States Constitution and with the standards set forth in the amendments made by this subtitle for the regulation of tobacco products by the Food and Drug Administration, and the restriction on the sale and distribution of, including access to and the advertising and promotion of, tobacco products contained in such regulations are substantially related to accomplishing the public health goals of this division.

(31) The regulations described in paragraph (30) will directly and materially advance the Federal Government's substantial interest in reducing the number of children and adolescents who use cigarettes and smokeless tobacco and in preventing the life-threatening health consequences associated with tobacco use. An overwhelming majority of Americans who use tobacco products begin using such products while they are minors and become addicted to the nicotine in those products before reaching the age of 18. Tobacco advertising and promotion play a crucial role in the decision of these minors to begin using tobacco products. Less restrictive and less comprehensive approaches have not and will not be effective in reducing the problems addressed by such regulations. The reasonable restrictions on the advertising and promotion of tobacco products contained in such regulations will lead to a significant decrease in the number of minors using and becoming addicted to those products.

(32) The regulations described in paragraph (30) impose no more extensive restrictions on communication by tobacco manufacturers and sellers than are necessary to reduce the number of children and adolescents who use cigarettes and smokeless tobacco and to prevent the life-threatening health consequences associated with tobacco use. Such regulations are narrowly tailored to restrict those advertising and promotional practices which are most likely to be seen or heard by youth and most likely to entice them into tobacco use, while affording tobacco manufacturers and sellers ample opportunity to convey information about their products to adult consumers.

(33) Tobacco dependence is a chronic disease, one that typically requires repeated interventions to achieve long-term or permanent abstinence.

(34) Because the only known safe alternative to smoking is cessation, interventions should target all smokers to help them quit completely.

(35) Tobacco products have been used to facilitate and finance criminal activities both domestically and internationally. Illicit trade of tobacco products has been linked to organized crime and terrorist groups.

(36) It is essential that the Food and Drug Administration review products sold or distributed for use to reduce risks or exposures associated with tobacco products and that it be empowered to review any advertising and labeling for such products. It is also essential that manufacturers, prior to marketing such products, be required to demonstrate that such products will meet a series of rigorous criteria, and will benefit the health of the population as a whole, taking into account both users of tobacco products and persons who do not currently use tobacco products.

(37) Unless tobacco products that purport to reduce the risks to the public of tobacco use actually reduce such risks, those products can cause substantial harm to the public health to the extent that the individuals, who would otherwise not consume tobacco products or would consume such products less, use tobacco products purporting to reduce risk. Those who use products sold or distributed as modified risk products that do not in fact reduce risk, rather than quitting or reducing their use of tobacco products, have a substantially increased likelihood of suffering disability and premature death. The costs to society of the widespread use of products sold or distributed as modified risk products that do not in fact reduce risk or that increase risk include thousands of unnecessary deaths and injuries and huge costs to our health care system.

(38) As the National Cancer Institute has found, many smokers mistakenly believe that "low tar" and "light" cigarettes cause fewer health problems than other cigarettes. As the

National Cancer Institute has also found, mistaken beliefs about the health consequences of smoking "low tar" and "light" cigarettes can reduce the motivation to quit smoking entirely and thereby lead to disease and death.

(39) Recent studies have demonstrated that there has been no reduction in risk on a population-wide basis from "low tar" and "light" cigarettes, and such products may actually increase the risk of tobacco use.

(40) The dangers of products sold or distributed as modified risk tobacco products that do not in fact reduce risk are so high that there is a compelling governmental interest in ensuring that statements about modified risk tobacco products are complete, accurate, and relate to the overall disease risk of the product.

(41) As the Federal Trade Commission has found, consumers have misinterpreted advertisements in which one product is claimed to be less harmful than a comparable product, even in the presence of disclosures and advisories intended to provide clarification.

(42) Permitting manufacturers to make unsubstantiated statements concerning modified risk tobacco products, whether express or implied, even if accompanied by disclaimers would be detrimental to the public health.

(43) The only way to effectively protect the public health from the dangers of unsubstantiated modified risk tobacco products is to empower the Food and Drug Administration to require that products that tobacco manufacturers sold or distributed for risk reduction be reviewed in advance of marketing, and to require that the evidence relied on to support claims be fully verified.

(44) The Food and Drug Administration is a regulatory agency with the scientific expertise to identify harmful substances in products to which consumers are exposed, to design standards to limit exposure to those substances, to evaluate scientific studies supporting claims about the safety of products, and to evaluate the impact of labels, labeling, and advertising on consumer behavior in order to reduce the risk of harm and promote understanding of the impact of the product on health. In connection with its mandate to promote health and reduce the risk of harm, the Food and Drug Administration routinely makes decisions about whether and how products may be marketed in the United States.

(45) The Federal Trade Commission was created to protect consumers from unfair or deceptive acts or practices, and to regulate unfair methods of competition. Its focus is on those marketplace practices that deceive or mislead consumers, and those that give some competitors an unfair advantage. Its mission is to regulate activities in the marketplace. Neither the Federal Trade Commission nor any other Federal agency except the Food and Drug Administration possesses the scientific expertise needed to implement effectively all provisions of the Family Smoking Prevention and Tobacco Control Act.

(46) If manufacturers state or imply in communications directed to consumers through the media or through a label, labeling, or advertising, that a tobacco product is approved or inspected by the Food and Drug Administration or complies with Food and Drug Administration standards, consumers are likely to be confused and misled. Depending upon the particular language used and its context, such a statement could result in consumers being misled into believing that the product is endorsed by the Food and Drug Administration for use or in consumers being misled about the harmfulness of the product because of such regulation, inspection, approval, or compliance.

(47) In August 2006 a United States district court judge found that the major United States cigarette companies continue to target and market to youth. USA v. Philip Morris, USA, Inc., et al. (Civil Action No. 99–2496 (GK), August 17, 2006).

(48) In August 2006 a United States district court judge found that the major United States cigarette companies dramatically increased their advertising and promotional spending in ways that encourage youth to start smoking subsequent to the signing of the Master Settlement Agreement in 1998. USA v. Philip Morris, USA, Inc., et al. (Civil Action No. 99–2496 (GK), August 17, 2006).

(49) In August 2006 a United States district court judge found that the major United States cigarette companies have designed their cigarettes to precisely control nicotine delivery levels and provide doses of nicotine sufficient to create and sustain addiction while also concealing much of their nicotine-related research. USA v. Philip Morris, USA, Inc., et al. (Civil Action No. 99–2496 (GK), August 17, 2006).

SEC. 3. PURPOSE.

The purposes of this division are—

(1) to provide authority to the Food and Drug Administration to regulate tobacco products under the Federal Food, Drug, and Cosmetic Act (21 U.S.C. 301 et seq.), by recognizing it as the primary Federal regulatory authority with respect to the manufacture, marketing, and distribution of tobacco products as provided for in this division;

(2) to ensure that the Food and Drug Administration has the authority to address issues of particular concern to public health officials, especially the use of tobacco by young people and dependence on tobacco;

(3) to authorize the Food and Drug Administration to set national standards controlling the manufacture of tobacco products and the identity, public disclosure, and amount of ingredients used in such products;

(4) to provide new and flexible enforcement authority to ensure that there is effective oversight of the tobacco industry's efforts to develop, introduce, and promote less harmful tobacco products;

(5) to vest the Food and Drug Administration with the authority to regulate the levels of tar, nicotine, and other harmful components of tobacco products;

(6) in order to ensure that consumers are better informed, to require tobacco product manufacturers to disclose research which has not previously been made available, as well as research generated in the future, relating to the health and dependency effects or safety of tobacco products;

(7) to continue to permit the sale of tobacco products to adults in conjunction with measures to ensure that they are not sold or accessible to underage purchasers;

(8) to impose appropriate regulatory controls on the tobacco industry;

(9) to promote cessation to reduce disease risk and the social costs associated with tobacco-related diseases; and

(10) to strengthen legislation against illicit trade in tobacco products.

SEC. 4. SCOPE AND EFFECT.

(a) Intended effect.—

Nothing in this division (or an amendment made by this division) shall be construed to—

(1) establish a precedent with regard to any other industry, situation, circumstance, or legal action; or

(2) affect any action pending in Federal, State, or tribal court, or any agreement, consent decree, or contract of any kind.

(b) Agricultural activities.—

The provisions of this division (or an amendment made by this division) which authorize the Secretary to take certain actions with regard to tobacco and tobacco products shall not be construed to affect any authority of the Secretary of Agriculture under existing law regarding the growing, cultivation, or curing of raw tobacco.

(c) Revenue activities.—

The provisions of this division (or an amendment made by this division) which authorize the Secretary to take certain actions with regard to tobacco products shall not be construed to affect any authority of the Secretary of the Treasury under chapter 52 of the Internal Revenue Code of 1986.

SEC. 5. SEVERABILITY.

If any provision of this division, of the amendments made by this division, or of the regulations promulgated under this division (or under such amendments), or the application of any such provision to any person or circumstance is held to be invalid, the remainder of this division, such amendments and such regulations, and the application of such provisions to any other person or circumstance shall not be affected and shall continue to be enforced to the fullest extent possible.

SEC. 6. MODIFICATION OF DEADLINES FOR SECRETARIAL ACTION.

(a) Delayed commencement of dates for Secretarial action.—

    (1) In general.—

    Except as provided in subsection (c), with respect to any time periods specified in this division (or in an amendment made by this division) that begin on the date of enactment of this Act, within which the Secretary of Health and Human Services is required to carry out and complete specified activities, the calculation of such time periods shall commence on the date described in subsection (b).

    (2) Limitation.—

    Subsection (a) shall only apply with respect to obligations of the Secretary of Health and Human Services that must be completed within a specified time period and shall not apply to the obligations of any other person or to any other provision of this division (including the amendments made by this division) that do not create such obligations of the Secretary and are not contingent on actions by the Secretary.

(b) Date described.—

The date described in this subsection is the first day of the first fiscal quarter following the initial 2 consecutive fiscal quarters of fiscal year 2010 for which the Secretary of Health and Human Services has collected fees under section 919 of the Federal Food, Drug, and Cosmetic Act (as added by section 101).

(c) Exception.—

Subsection (a) shall not apply to any time period (or date) contained—

    (1) in section 102, except that the reference to "180 days" in subsection (a)(1) of such section shall be deemed to be "270 days"; and
    (2) in sections 201 through 204 (or the amendments made by any such sections).

(d) Adjustment.—

The Secretary of Health and Human Services may extend or reduce the duration of one or more time periods to which subsection (a) applies if the Secretary determines appropriate, except that no such period shall be extended for more than 90 days.

4.12   Enhanced Partnership with Pakistan Act of 2009

111TH UNITED STATES CONGRESS
1ST SESSION

An Act
To authorize appropriations for fiscal years 2010 through 2014 to promote an enhanced strategic partnership with Pakistan and its people, and for other purposes.

Be it enacted by the Senate and House of Representatives of the United States of America in Congress assembled,

Section 1. Short Title; Table of Contents.

(a) Short Title.—

This Act may be cited as the ``**Enhanced Partnership with Pakistan Act of 2009**´´.

(b) Table of Contents.—

The table of contents for this Act is as follows:

Sec. 2. Definitions.

In this Act:

(1) APPROPRIATE CONGRESSIONAL COMMITTEES.—
Except as otherwise provided in this Act, the term "appropriate congressional committees" means the Committees on Appropriations and Foreign Relations of the Senate and the Committees on Appropriations and Foreign Affairs of the House of Representatives.

(2) COUNTERINSURGENCY.—

The term "counterinsurgency" means efforts to defeat organized movements that seek to overthrow the duly constituted Governments of Pakistan and Afghanistan through violent means.

(3) COUNTERTERRORISM.—

The term "counterterrorism" means efforts to combat al Qaeda and other foreign terrorist organizations that are designated by the Secretary of State in accordance with section 219 of the Immigration and Nationality Act (8 U.S.C. 1189), or other individuals and entities engaged in terrorist activity or support for such activity.

(4) FATA.—

The term "FATA" means the Federally Administered Tribal Areas of Pakistan.

(5) FRONTIER CRIMES REGULATION.—

The term "Frontier Crimes Regulation" means the Frontier Crimes Regulation, codified under British law in 1901, and applicable to the FATA.

(6) IMPACT EVALUATION RESEARCH.—

The term "impact evaluation research" means the application of research methods and statistical analysis to measure the extent to which change in a population-based outcome can be attributed to program intervention instead of other environmental factors.

(7) MAJOR DEFENSE EQUIPMENT.—

The term "major defense equipment" has the meaning given the term in section 47(6) of the Arms Export Control Act (22 U.S.C. 2794(6)).

(8) NWFP.—

The term "NWFP" means the North West Frontier Province of Pakistan, which has Peshawar as its provincial capital.

(9) OPERATIONS RESEARCH.—

The term "operations research" means the application of social science research methods, statistical analysis, and other appropriate scientific methods to judge, compare, and improve policies and program outcomes, from the earliest stages of defining and designing programs through their development and implementation, with the objective of the rapid dissemination of conclusions and concrete impact on programming.

(10) SECURITY FORCES OF PAKISTAN.—

The term "security forces of Pakistan" means the military and intelligence services of the Government of Pakistan, including the Armed Forces, Inter-Services Intelligence Directorate, Intelligence Bureau, police forces, levies, Frontier Corps, and Frontier Constabulary.

(11) SECURITY-RELATED ASSISTANCE.—

The term "security-related assistance"—

  (A) means—

(i) grant assistance to carry out section 23 of the Arms Export Control Act (22 U.S.C. 2763); and

(ii) assistance under chapter 2 of part II of the Foreign Assistance Act of 1961 (22 U.S.C. 2311 et. seq); but

(B) does not include—
(i) assistance authorized to be appropriated or otherwise made available under any provision of law that is funded from accounts within budget function 050 (National Defense); and

(ii) amounts appropriated or otherwise available to the Pakistan Counterinsurgency Capability Fund established under the Supplemental Appropriations Act, 2009 (Public Law 111-32).

Sec. 3. Findings.

Congress finds the following:

(1) The people of the Islamic Republic of Pakistan and the United States share a long history of friendship and comity, and the interests of both nations are well-served by strengthening and deepening this friendship.

(2) Since 2001, the United States has contributed more than $15,000,000,000 to Pakistan, of which more than $10,000,000,000 has been security-related assistance and direct payments.

(3) With the free and fair election of February 18, 2008, Pakistan returned to civilian rule, reversing years of political tension and mounting popular concern over military rule and Pakistan's own democratic reform and political development.

(4) Pakistan is a major non-NATO ally of the United States and has been a valuable partner in the battle against al Qaeda and the Taliban, but much more remains to be accomplished by both nations.

(5) The struggle against al Qaeda, the Taliban, and affiliated terrorist groups has led to the deaths of several thousand Pakistani civilians and members of the security forces of Pakistan over the past seven years.

(6) Despite killing or capturing hundreds of al Qaeda operatives and other terrorists—including major al Qaeda leaders, such as Khalid Sheikh Muhammad, Ramzi bin al-Shibh, and Abu Faraj al-Libi—the FATA, parts of the NWFP, Quetta in Balochistan, and Muridke in Punjab remain a sanctuary for al Qaeda, the Afghan Taliban, the Terikh-e Taliban and affiliated groups from which these groups organize terrorist actions against Pakistan and other countries.

(7) The security forces of Pakistan have struggled to contain a Taliban-backed insurgency, recently taking direct action against those who threaten Pakistan's security and stability, including military operations in the FATA and the NWFP.

(8) On March 27, 2009, President Obama noted, "Multiple intelligence estimates have warned that al Qaeda is actively planning attacks on the United States homeland from its safe-haven in Pakistan.".

(9) According to a Government Accountability Office report (GAO–08–622), "since 2003, the [A]dministration's national security strategies and Congress have recognized that a comprehensive plan that includes all elements of national power—diplomatic, military, intelligence, development assistance, economic, and law enforcement support—was needed to address the terrorist threat emanating from the FATA" and that such a strategy was also mandated by section 7102(b)(3) of the Intelligence Reform and Terrorism Prevention Act of 2004 (Public Law 108-458; 22 U.S.C. 2656f note) and section 2042(b)(2) of the Implementing the Recommendations of the 9/11 Commission Act of 2007 (Public Law 110-53; 22 U.S.C. 2375 note).

(10) During 2008 and 2009, the people of Pakistan have been especially hard hit by rising food and commodity prices and severe energy shortages, with 2/3 of the population living on less than $2 a day and 1/5 of the population living below the poverty line according to the United Nations Development Program.

(11) Economic growth is a fundamental foundation for human security and national stability in Pakistan, a country with more than 175,000,000 people, an annual population growth rate of two percent, and a ranking of 136 out of 177 countries in the United Nations Human Development Index.

(12) The 2009 Pakistani military offensive in the NWFP and the FATA displaced millions of residents in one of the gravest humanitarian crises Pakistan has faced, and despite the heroic efforts of Pakistanis to respond to the needs of the displaced millions and facilitate the return of many, it has highlighted the need for Pakistan to develop an effective national counterinsurgency strategy.

Sec. 4. Statement of Principles.

Congress declares that the relationship between the United States and Pakistan should be based on the following principles:

(1) Pakistan is a critical friend and ally to the United States, both in times of strife and in times of peace, and the two countries share many common goals, including combating terrorism and violent radicalism, solidifying democracy and rule of law in Pakistan, and promoting the social and economic development of Pakistan.

(2) United States assistance to Pakistan is intended to supplement, not supplant, Pakistan's own efforts in building a stable, secure, and prosperous Pakistan.

(3) The United States requires a balanced, integrated, countrywide strategy for Pakistan that provides assistance throughout the country and does not disproportionately focus on security-related assistance or one particular area or province.

(4) The United States supports Pakistan's struggle against extremist elements and recognizes the profound sacrifice made by Pakistan in the fight against terrorism, including the loss of more than 1,900 soldiers and police since 2001 in combat with al Qaeda, the Taliban, and other extremist and terrorist groups.

(5) The United States intends to work with the Government of Pakistan—

(A) to build mutual trust and confidence by actively and consistently pursuing a sustained, long-term, multifaceted relationship between the two countries, devoted to strengthening the mutual security, stability, and prosperity of both countries;

(B) to support the people of Pakistan and their democratic government in their efforts to consolidate democracy, including strengthening Pakistan's parliament, helping Pakistan reestablish an independent and transparent judicial system, and working to extend the rule of law in all areas in Pakistan;

(C) to promote sustainable long-term development and infrastructure projects, including in healthcare, education, water management, and energy programs, in all areas of Pakistan, that are sustained and supported by each successive democratic government in Pakistan;

(D) to ensure that all the people of Pakistan, including those living in areas governed by the Frontier Crimes Regulation, have access to public, modernized education and vocational training to enable them to provide for themselves, for their families, and for a more prosperous future for their children;

(E) to support the strengthening of core curricula and the quality of schools across Pakistan, including madrassas, in order to improve the prospects for Pakistani children's futures and eliminate incitements to violence and intolerance;

(F) to encourage and promote public-private partnerships in Pakistan in order to bolster ongoing development efforts and strengthen economic prospects, especially with respect to opportunities to build civic responsibility and professional skills of the people of Pakistan, including support for institutions of higher learning with international accreditation;

(G) to expand people-to-people engagement between the two countries, through increased educational, technical, and cultural exchanges and other methods;

(H) to encourage the development of local analytical capacity to measure program effectiveness and progress on an integrated basis, especially across the areas of United States assistance and payments to Pakistan, and increase accountability for how such assistance and payments are being spent;

(I) to assist Pakistan's efforts to improve counterterrorism financing and anti-money laundering regulatory structure in order to achieve international standards and encourage Pakistan to apply for "Financial Action Task Force" observer status and adhere to the United Nations International Convention for the Suppression of the Financing of Terrorism;

(J) to strengthen Pakistan's counterinsurgency and counterterrorism strategy to help prevent any territory of Pakistan from being used as a base or conduit for terrorist attacks in Pakistan or elsewhere;

(K) to strengthen Pakistan's efforts to develop strong and effective law enforcement and national defense forces under civilian leadership;

(L) to achieve full cooperation in matters of counter-proliferation of nuclear materials and related networks;

(M) to strengthen Pakistan's efforts to gain control of its under-governed areas and address the threat posed by any person or group that conducts violence, sabotage, or other terrorist activities in Pakistan or its neighboring countries; and

(N) to explore means to consult with and utilize the relevant expertise and skills of the Pakistani-American community.

Approved October 15, 2009.

4.12.1   Legislative History

- S. 1707, (H.R. 3642)

  - SENATE REPORTS:
    - No. 111-33 (Comm. on Foreign Relations)
  - CONGRESSIONAL RECORD, Vol. 155 (2009):
    - Sept. 24, considered and passed Senate.
    - Sept. 30, considered and passed House.

4.13   Title V

TITLE V — GENERAL PROVISIONS

Sec. 501.

(Including Rescissions of Funds)
No part of any appropriation contained in this Act shall remain available for obligation beyond the current fiscal year unless expressly so provided herein.

Sec. 502.

Subject to the requirements of section 503 of this Act, the unexpended balances of prior appropriations provided for activities in this Act may be transferred to appropriation accounts for such activities established pursuant to this Act, may be merged with funds in the applicable established accounts, and thereafter may be accounted for as one fund for the same time period as originally enacted.

Sec. 503.

(a) None of the funds provided by this Act, provided by previous appropriations Acts to the agencies in or transferred to the Department of Homeland Security that remain available for obligation or expenditure in fiscal year 2010, or provided from any accounts in the Treasury of the United States derived by the collection of fees available to the agencies funded by this Act, shall be available for obligation or expenditure through a reprogramming of funds that:

(1) creates a new program, project, or activity;

(2) eliminates a program, project, office, or activity;

(3) increases funds for any program, project, or activity for which funds have been denied or restricted by the Congress;

(4) proposes to use funds directed for a specific activity by either of the Committees on Appropriations of the Senate or the House of Representatives for a different purpose; or

(5) contracts out any function or activity for which funding levels were requested for Federal full-time equivalents in the object classification tables contained in the fiscal year 2010 Budget Appendix for the Department of Homeland Security, as modified by the joint explanatory statement accompanying this Act, unless the Committees on Appropriations of the Senate and the House of Representatives are notified 15 days in advance of such reprogramming of funds.

(b) None of the funds provided by this Act, provided by previous appropriations Acts to the agencies in or transferred to the Department of Homeland Security that remain available for obligation or expenditure in fiscal year 2010, or provided from any accounts in the Treasury of the United States derived by the collection of fees or proceeds available to the agencies funded by this Act, shall be available for obligation or expenditure for programs, projects, or activities through a reprogramming of funds in excess of $5,000,000 or 10 percent, whichever is less, that:

(1) augments existing programs, projects, or activities;

(2) reduces by 10 percent funding for any existing program, project, or activity, or numbers of personnel by 10 percent as approved by the Congress; or

(3) results from any general savings from a reduction in personnel that would result in a change in existing programs, projects, or activities as approved by the Congress, unless the Committees on Appropriations of the Senate and the House of Representatives are notified 15 days in advance of such reprogramming of funds.

(c) Not to exceed 5 percent of any appropriation made available for the current fiscal year for the Department of Homeland Security by this Act or provided by previous appropriations Acts may be transferred between such appropriations, but no such appropriation, except as otherwise specifically provided, shall be increased by more than 10 percent by such transfers:

Provided, That any transfer under this section shall be treated as a reprogramming of funds under subsection (b) and shall not be available for obligation unless the Committees on Appropriations of the Senate and the House of Representatives are notified 15 days in advance of such transfer.

(d) Notwithstanding subsections (a), (b), and (c) of this section, no funds shall be reprogrammed within or transferred between appropriations after June 30, except in extraordinary circumstances that imminently threaten the safety of human life or the protection of property.

Sec. 504.

The Department of Homeland Security Working Capital Fund, established pursuant to section 403 of Public Law 103-356 (31 U.S.C. 501 note), shall continue operations as a permanent working capital fund for fiscal year 2010:

Provided, That none of the funds appropriated or otherwise made available to the Department of Homeland Security may be used to make payments to the Working Capital Fund, except for the activities and amounts allowed in the President's fiscal year 2010 budget:

Provided further, That funds provided to the Working Capital Fund shall be available for obligation until expended to carry out the purposes of the Working Capital Fund:

Provided further, That all departmental components shall be charged only for direct usage of each Working Capital Fund service:

Provided further, That funds provided to the Working Capital Fund shall be used only for purposes consistent with the contributing component:

Provided further, That such fund shall be paid in advance or reimbursed at rates which will return the full cost of each service:

Provided further, That the Working Capital Fund shall be subject to the requirements of section 503 of this Act.

Sec. 505.

Except as otherwise specifically provided by law, not to exceed 50 percent of unobligated balances remaining available at the end of fiscal year 2010 from appropriations for salaries and expenses for fiscal year 2010 in this Act shall remain available through September 30, 2011, in the account and for the purposes for which the appropriations were provided:

> *Provided*, That prior to the obligation of such funds, a request shall be submitted to the Committees on Appropriations of the Senate and the House of Representatives for approval in accordance with section 503 of this Act.

Sec. 506.

Funds made available by this Act for intelligence activities are deemed to be specifically authorized by the Congress for purposes of section 504 of the National Security Act of 1947 (50 U.S.C. 414) during fiscal year 2010 until the enactment of an Act authorizing intelligence activities for fiscal year 2010.

Sec. 507.

None of the funds made available by this Act may be used to make a grant allocation, grant award, contract award, Other Transaction Agreement, a task or delivery order on a Department of Homeland Security multiple award contract, or to issue a letter of intent totaling in excess of $1,000,000, or to announce publicly the intention to make such an award, including a contract covered by the Federal Acquisition Regulation, unless the Secretary of Homeland Security notifies the Committees on Appropriations of the Senate and the House of Representatives at least 3 full business days in advance of making such an award or issuing such a letter:

> *Provided*, That if the Secretary of Homeland Security determines that compliance with this section would pose a substantial risk to human life, health, or safety, an award may be made without notification and the Committees on Appropriations of the Senate and the House of Representatives shall be notified not later than 5 full business days after such an award is made or letter issued:

Provided further, That no notification shall involve funds that are not available for obligation:

Provided further, That the notification shall include the amount of the award, the fiscal year for which the funds for the award were appropriated, and the account from which the funds are being drawn:

Provided further, That the Federal Emergency Management Agency shall brief the Committees on Appropriations of the Senate and the House of Representatives 5 full business days in advance of announcing publicly the intention of making an award under "State and Local Programs".

Sec. 508.

Notwithstanding any other provision of law, no agency shall purchase, construct, or lease any additional facilities, except within or contiguous to existing locations, to be used for the purpose of conducting Federal law enforcement training without the advance approval of the Committees on Appropriations of the Senate and the House of Representatives, except that the Federal Law Enforcement Training Center is authorized to obtain the temporary use of additional facilities by lease, contract, or other agreement for training which cannot be accommodated in existing Center facilities.

Sec. 509.

None of the funds appropriated or otherwise made available by this Act may be used for expenses for any construction, repair, alteration, or acquisition project for which a prospectus otherwise required under chapter 33 of title 40, United States Code, has not been approved, except that necessary funds may be expended for each project for required expenses for the development of a proposed prospectus.

Sec. 510.

Sections 519, 520, 522, 528, 530, and 531 of the Department of Homeland Security Appropriations Act, 2008 (division E of Public Law 110-161; 121 Stat. 2072, 2073, 2074, 2082) shall apply with respect to funds made available in this Act in the same manner as such sections applied to funds made available in that Act.

Sec. 511.

None of the funds made available in this Act may be used in contravention of the applicable provisions of the Buy American Act (41 U.S.C. 10a et seq.).

Sec. 512.

None of the funds made available in this Act may be used to amend the oath of allegiance required by section 337 of the Immigration and Nationality Act (8 U.S.C. 1448).

Sec. 513.

None of the funds appropriated by this Act may be used to process or approve a competition under Office of Management and Budget Circular A–76 for services provided as of June 1, 2004, by employees (including employees serving on a temporary or term basis) of United States Citizenship and Immigration Services of the Department of Homeland Security who are known as of that date as Immigration Information Officers, Contact Representatives, or Investigative Assistants.

Sec. 514.

(a) The Assistant Secretary of Homeland Security (Transportation Security Administration) shall work with air carriers and airports to ensure that the screening of cargo carried on passenger aircraft, as defined in section 44901(g)(5) of title 49, United States Code, increases incrementally each quarter until the requirement of section 44901(g)(2)(B) of title 49 is met.

(b) Not later than 45 days after the end of each quarter, the Assistant Secretary shall submit to the Committees on Appropriations of the Senate and the House of Representatives a report on air cargo inspection statistics by airport and air carrier detailing the incremental progress being made to meet the requirement of section 44901(g)(2)(B) of title 49, United States Code.

(c) Not later than 180 days after the date of the enactment of this Act, the Assistant Secretary shall submit to the Committees on Appropriations of the Senate and the House of Representatives, a report on how the Transportation Security Administration plans to meet the requirement for screening all air cargo on passenger aircraft by the deadline under section 44901(g) of title 49, United States Code. The report shall identify the elements of the system to screen 100 percent of cargo transported between domestic airports at a level of security commensurate with the level of security for the screening of passenger checked baggage.

Sec. 515.

Within 45 days after the end of each month, the Chief Financial Officer of the Department of Homeland Security shall submit to the Committees on Appropriations of the Senate and the House of Representatives a monthly budget and staffing report for that month that includes total obligations, on-board versus funded full-time equivalent staffing levels, and the number of contract employees for each office of the Department.

Sec. 516.

Except as provided in section 44945 of title 49, United States Code, funds appropriated or transferred to Transportation Security Administration "Aviation Security", "Administration" and "Transportation Security Support" for fiscal years 2004, 2005, 2006, 2007, and 2008 that are recovered or deobligated shall be available only for the procurement or installation of explosives detection systems, air cargo, baggage, and checkpoint screening systems, subject to notification:

> *Provided*, That quarterly reports shall be submitted to the Committees on Appropriations of the Senate and the House of Representatives on any funds that are recovered or deobligated.

Sec. 517.

Any funds appropriated to Coast Guard "Acquisition, Construction, and Improvements" for fiscal years 2002, 2003, 2004, 2005, and 2006 for the 110–123 foot patrol boat conversion that are recovered, collected, or otherwise received as the result of negotiation, mediation, or litigation, shall be available until expended for the Replacement Patrol Boat (FRC–B) program.

Sec. 518.

(a) None of the funds provided by this or any other Act may be obligated for the development, testing, deployment, or operation of any portion of a human resources management system authorized by section 9701(a) of title 5, United States Code, or by regulations prescribed pursuant to such section, for an employee, as that term is defined in section 7103(a)(2) of such title.

(b) The Secretary of Homeland Security shall collaborate with employee representatives in the manner prescribed in section 9701(e) of title 5, United States Code, in the planning, testing, and development of any portion of a human resources management system that is developed, tested, or deployed for persons excluded from the definition of employee as that term is defined in section 7103(a)(2) of such title.

Sec. 519.

Section 532(a) of Public Law 109-295 (120 Stat. 1384) is amended by striking "2009" and inserting "2010".

Sec. 520.

The functions of the Federal Law Enforcement Training Center instructor staff shall be classified as inherently governmental for the purpose of the Federal Activities Inventory Reform Act of 1998 (31 U.S.C. 501 note).

Sec. 521.

(a) Except as provided in subsection (b), none of the funds appropriated in this or any other Act to the Office of the Secretary and Executive Management, the Office of the Under Secretary for Management, or the Office of the Chief Financial Officer, may be obligated for a grant or contract funded under such headings by any means other than full and open competition.

(b) Subsection (a) does not apply to obligation of funds for a contract awarded—

> (1) by a means that is required by a Federal statute, including obligation for a purchase made under a mandated preferential program, including the AbilityOne Program, that is authorized under the Javits-Wagner-O'Day Act (41 U.S.C. 46 et seq.);

> (2) pursuant to the Small Business Act (15 U.S.C. 631 et seq.);

> (3) in an amount less than the simplified acquisition threshold described under section 302A(a) of the Federal Property and Administrative Services Act of 1949 (41 U.S.C. 252a(a)); or

> (4) by another Federal agency using funds provided through an interagency agreement.

(c)

> (1) Subject to paragraph (2), the Secretary of Homeland Security may waive the application of this section for the award of a contract in the interest of national security or if failure to do so would pose a substantial risk to human health or welfare.

> (2) Not later than 5 days after the date on which the Secretary of Homeland Security issues a waiver under this subsection, the Secretary shall submit notification of that waiver to the Committees on Appropriations of the Senate and the House of Representatives, including a description of the applicable contract and an explanation of why the waiver authority was used. The Secretary may not delegate the authority to grant such a waiver.

(d) In addition to the requirements established by subsections (a), (b), and (c) of this section, the Inspector General of the Department of Homeland Security shall review departmental contracts awarded through means other than a full and open competition to assess departmental compliance with applicable laws and regulations:

Provided, That the Inspector General shall review selected contracts awarded in the previous fiscal year through means other than a full and open competition:

Provided further, That in selecting which contracts to review, the Inspector General shall consider the cost and complexity of the goods and services to be provided under the contract, the criticality of the contract to fulfilling Department missions, past performance problems on similar contracts or by the selected vendor, complaints received about the award process or contractor performance, and such other factors as the Inspector General deems relevant:

Provided further, That the Inspector General shall report the results of the reviews to the Committees on Appropriations of the Senate and the House of Representatives no later than February 5, 2010.

Sec. 522.

Except as provided in paragraphs (1) and (2) of this section, none of the funds provided by this or previous appropriations Acts shall be used to fund any position designated as a Principal Federal Official, or any successor position, for any Robert T. Stafford Disaster Relief and Emergency Assistance Act (42 U.S.C. 5121 et seq.) declared disasters or emergencies—

(1) The Secretary of Homeland Security may waive the application of this section provided that any field position appointed pursuant to this waiver shall not hold the title of Principal Federal Official, shall functionally report through the Federal Coordinating Officer appointed under section 302 of the Robert T. Stafford Disaster Relief and Emergency Assistance Act (42 U.S.C. 5143), and shall be subject to the provisions of subsection (c) of section 319 of title 6, United States Code. The Secretary may not delegate the authority to grant such a waiver.

(2) Not later than 10 business days after the date on which the Secretary of Homeland Security issues a waiver under this section, the Secretary shall submit notification of that waiver to the Committees on Appropriations of the Senate and the House of Representatives, the Transportation and Infrastructure Committee of the House of Representatives, and the Homeland Security and Governmental Affairs Committee of the Senate explaining the circumstances necessitating the waiver, describing the specific role of any officials appointed pursuant to the waiver, and outlining measures taken to ensure compliance with subsection (c) of section 319 and subsections (c)(3) and (c)(4)(A) of section 313 of title 6, United States Code.

Sec. 523.

None of the funds made available in this or any other Act may be used to enforce section 4025(1) of Public Law 108-458 unless the Assistant Secretary of Homeland Security (Transportation Security Administration) reverses the determination of July 19, 2007, that butane lighters are not a significant threat to civil aviation security.

Sec. 524.

Funds made available in this Act may be used to alter operations within the Civil Engineering Program of the Coast Guard nationwide, including civil engineering units, facilities design and construction centers, maintenance and logistics commands, and the Coast Guard Academy, except that none of the funds provided in this Act may be used to reduce operations within any Civil Engineering Unit unless specifically authorized by a statute enacted after the date of the enactment of this Act.

Sec. 525.

None of the funds provided in this Act shall be available to carry out section 872 of the Homeland Security Act of 2002 (6 U.S.C. 452).

Sec. 526.

None of the funds made available in this Act may be used by United States Citizenship and Immigration Services to grant an immigration benefit unless the results of background checks required by law to be completed prior to the granting of the benefit have been received by United States Citizenship and Immigration Services, and the results do not preclude the granting of the benefit.

Sec. 527.

None of the funds made available in this Act may be used to destroy or put out to pasture any horse or other equine belonging to the Federal Government that has become unfit for service, unless the trainer or handler is first given the option to take possession of the equine through an adoption program that has safeguards against slaughter and inhumane treatment.

Sec. 528.

None of the funds provided in this Act under the heading "Office of the Chief Information Officer" shall be used for data center development other than for Data Center One (National Center for Critical Information Processing and Storage) until the Chief Information Officer certifies that Data Center One is fully utilized as the Department's primary data storage center at the highest capacity throughout the fiscal year.

Sec. 529.

None of the funds in this Act shall be used to reduce the United States Coast Guard's Operations Systems Center mission or its government-employed or contract staff levels.

Sec. 530.

None of the funds appropriated by this Act may be used to conduct, or to implement the results of, a competition under Office of Management and Budget Circular A–76 for activities performed with respect to the Coast Guard National Vessel Documentation Center.

Sec. 531.

Section 831 of the Homeland Security Act of 2002 (6 U.S.C. 391) is amended—

(1) in subsection (a), by striking "Until September 30, 2009" and inserting "Until September 30, 2010,"; and

(2) in subsection (d)(1), by striking "September 30, 2009," and inserting "September 30, 2010,".

Sec. 532.

The Secretary of Homeland Security shall require that all contracts of the Department of Homeland Security that provide award fees link such fees to successful acquisition outcomes (which outcomes shall be specified in terms of cost, schedule, and performance).

Sec. 533.

None of the funds made available to the Office of the Secretary and Executive Management under this Act may be expended for any new hires by the Department of Homeland Security that are not verified through the basic pilot program (E-Verify Program) under section 401 of the Illegal Immigration Reform and Immigrant Responsibility Act of 1996 (8 U.S.C. 1324a note).

Sec. 534.

None of the funds made available in this Act for U.S. Customs and Border Protection may be used to prevent an individual not in the business of importing a prescription drug (within the meaning of section 801(g) of the Federal Food, Drug, and Cosmetic Act) from importing a prescription drug from Canada that complies with the Federal Food, Drug, and Cosmetic Act:

> *Provided*, That this section shall apply only to individuals transporting on their person a personal-use quantity of the prescription drug, not to exceed a 90-day supply:

> *Provided further*, That the prescription drug may not be—

> > (1) a controlled substance, as defined in section 102 of the Controlled Substances Act (21 U.S.C. 802); or

> > (2) a biological product, as defined in section 351 of the Public Health Service Act (42 U.S.C. 262).

Sec. 535.

None of the funds made available in this Act may be used by the Secretary of Homeland Security or any delegate of the Secretary to issue any rule or regulation which implements the Notice of Proposed Rulemaking related to Petitions for Aliens To Perform Temporary Nonagricultural Services or Labor (H–2B) set out beginning on 70 FR 3984 (January 27, 2005).

Sec. 536.

The Secretary of Homeland Security, in consultation with the Secretary of the Treasury, shall notify the Committees on Appropriations of the Senate and the House of Representatives of any proposed transfers of funds available under subsection (g)(4)(B) of title 31, Unites States Code (as added by Public Law 102-393) from the Department of the Treasury Forfeiture Fund to any agency within the Department of Homeland Security:

> *Provided*, That none of the funds identified for such a transfer may be obligated until the Committees on Appropriations of the Senate and the House of Representatives approve the proposed transfers.

Sec. 537.

None of the funds made available in this Act may be used for planning, testing, piloting, or developing a national identification card.

Sec. 538.

If the Assistant Secretary of Homeland Security (Transportation Security Administration) determines that an airport does not need to participate in the basic pilot program (E-Verify Program) under section 402 of the Illegal Immigration Reform and Immigrant Responsibility Act of 1996 (8 U.S.C. 1324a note), the Assistant Secretary shall certify to the Committees on Appropriations of the Senate and the House of Representatives that no security risks will result from such non-participation.

Sec. 539.

(a) Notwithstanding any other provision of this Act, except as provided in subsection (b), and 30 days after the date that the President determines whether to declare a major disaster because of an event and any appeal is completed, the Administrator shall submit to the Committee on Homeland Security and Governmental Affairs of the Senate, the Committee on Homeland Security of the House of Representatives, the Committee on Transportation and Infrastructure of the House of Representatives, the Committees on Appropriations of the Senate and the House of Representatives, and publish on the website of the Federal Emergency Management Agency, a report regarding that decision, which shall summarize damage assessment information used to determine whether to declare a major disaster.

(b) The Administrator may redact from a report under subsection (a) any data that the Administrator determines would compromise national security.

(c) In this section—

> (1) the term "Administrator" means the Administrator of the Federal Emergency Management Agency; and

> (2) the term "major disaster" has the meaning given that term in section 102 of the Robert T. Stafford Disaster Relief and Emergency Assistance Act (42 U.S.C. 5122).

Sec. 540.

Notwithstanding any other provision of law, should the Secretary of Homeland Security determine that the National Bio- and Agro-defense Facility be located at a site other than Plum Island, New York, the Secretary shall have the Administrator of General Services sell through public sale all real and related personal property and transportation assets which support Plum Island operations, subject to such terms and conditions as necessary to protect government interests and meet program requirements:

> *Provided*, That the gross proceeds of such sale shall be deposited as offsetting collections into the Department of Homeland Security Science and Technology "Research, Development, Acquisition, and Operations" account and, subject to appropriation, shall be available until expended, for site acquisition, construction, and costs related to the construction of the National Bio- and Agro-defense Facility, including the costs associated with the sale, including due diligence requirements, necessary environmental remediation at Plum Island, and reimbursement of expenses incurred by the General Services Administration which shall not exceed 1 percent of the sale price or $5,000,000, whichever is greater:

> *Provided further*, That after the completion of construction and environmental remediation, the unexpended balances of funds appropriated for costs in the preceding proviso shall be available for transfer to the appropriate account for design and construction of a consolidated Department of Homeland Security Headquarters project, excluding

daily operations and maintenance costs, notwithstanding section 503 of this Act, and the Committees on Appropriations of the Senate and the House of Representatives shall be notified 15 days prior to such transfer.

Sec. 541.

The explanatory statement referenced in section 4 of Public Law 110-161 for "National Predisaster Mitigation Fund" under Federal Emergency Management Agency is deemed to be amended—

(1) by striking "Dalton Fire District" and all that follows through "750,000" and inserting the following:

(2) by striking "Santee and";

(3) by striking "3,000,000" and inserting "1,500,000";

(4) by inserting after the item relating to Adjutant General's Office of Emergency Preparedness the following:

and

(5) by striking "Public Works Department of the City of Santa Cruz, CA" and inserting "Monterey County Water Resources Agency, CA".

Sec. 542.

Sec. 543.

Sec. 544.

Sec. 545.

Sec. 546.

Sec. 547.

Sec. 548.

Sec. 549.

Sec. 550.

Sec. 551.

Sec. 552.

Sec. 553.

Sec. 554.

Sec. 555.

Sec. 556.

Sec. 557.

Sec. 558.

Sec. 559.

Sec. 560.

Sec. 561.

(a) Short Title.—

This section may be cited as the ``**American Communities' Right to Public Information Act**''.

(b) In General.—

Section 70103(d) of title 46, United States Code, is amended to read as follows:

``(d) Nondisclosure of Information.—

``(1) IN GENERAL.—Information developed under this section or sections 70102, 70104, and 70108 is not required to be disclosed to the public, including—

``(A) facility security plans, vessel security plans, and port vulnerability assessments; and

``(B) other information related to security plans, procedures, or programs for vessels or facilities authorized under this section or sections 70102, 70104, and 70108.

``(2) LIMITATIONS.—Nothing in paragraph (1) shall be construed to authorize the designation of information as sensitive security information (as defined in section 1520.5 of title 49, Code of Federal Regulations)—

``(A) to conceal a violation of law, inefficiency, or administrative error;

``(B) to prevent embarrassment to a person, organization, or agency;

``(C) to restrain competition; or

``(D) to prevent or delay the release of information that does not require protection in the interest of transportation security, including basic scientific research information not clearly related to transportation security.''.

(c) Conforming Amendments.—

(1) Section 114(r) of title 49, United States Code, is amended by adding at the end thereof the following:

``(4) LIMITATIONS.—Nothing in this subsection, or any other provision of law, shall be construed to authorize the designation of information as sensitive security information (as defined in section 1520.5 of title 49, Code of Federal Regulations)—

    ``(A) to conceal a violation of law, inefficiency, or administrative error;

    ``(B) to prevent embarrassment to a person, organization, or agency;

    ``(C) to restrain competition; or

    ``(D) to prevent or delay the release of information that does not require protection in the interest of transportation security, including basic scientific research information not clearly related to transportation security.''.

(2) Section 40119(b) of title 49, United States Code, is amended by adding at the end thereof the following:

``(3) Nothing in paragraph (1) shall be construed to authorize the designation of information as sensitive security information (as defined in section 15.5 of title 49, Code of Federal Regulations)—

    ``(A) to conceal a violation of law, inefficiency, or administrative error;

    ``(B) to prevent embarrassment to a person, organization, or agency;

    ``(C) to restrain competition; or

    ``(D) to prevent or delay the release of information that does not require protection in the interest of transportation security, including basic scientific research information not clearly related to transportation security.''.

Sec. 562.

Sec. 563.

Sec. 564.

(a) Short Title.—

This section may be cited as the ``**OPEN FOIA Act of 2009**''.

(b) Specific Citations in Statutory Exemptions.—

Section 552(b) of title 5, United States Code, is amended by striking paragraph (3) and inserting the following:

``(3) specifically exempted from disclosure by statute (other than section 552b of this title), if that statute—

    ``(A)(i) requires that the matters be withheld from the public in such a manner as to leave no discretion on the issue; or

        ``(ii) establishes particular criteria for withholding or refers to particular types of matters to be withheld; and

    ``(B) if enacted after the date of enactment of the OPEN FOIA Act of 2009, specifically cites to this paragraph.''.

Sec. 565.

(a) Short Title.—

This section may be cited as the ``**Protected National Security Documents Act of 2009**´´.

(b) Notwithstanding any other provision of the law to the contrary, no protected document, as defined in subsection (c), shall be subject to disclosure under section 552 of title 5, United States Code or any proceeding under that section.

(c) Definitions.—

In this section:

(1) PROTECTED DOCUMENT.—

The term ``protected document´´ means any record—

(A) for which the Secretary of Defense has issued a certification, as described in subsection (d), stating that disclosure of that record would endanger citizens of the United States, members of the United States Armed Forces, or employees of the United States Government deployed outside the United States; and

(B) that is a photograph that—

(i) was taken during the period beginning on September 11, 2001, through January 22, 2009; and

(ii) relates to the treatment of individuals engaged, captured, or detained after September 11, 2001, by the Armed Forces of the United States in operations outside of the United States.

(2) PHOTOGRAPH.—

The term ``photograph´´ encompasses all photographic images, whether originals or copies, including still photographs, negatives, digital images, films, video tapes, and motion pictures.

(d) Certification.—

(1) IN GENERAL.—

For any photograph described under subsection (c)(1), the Secretary of Defense shall issue a certification if the Secretary of Defense determines that disclosure of that photograph would endanger citizens of the United States, members of the United States Armed Forces, or employees of the United States Government deployed outside the United States.

(2) CERTIFICATION EXPIRATION.—

A certification and a renewal of a certification issued pursuant to subsection (d)(3) shall expire 3 years after the date on which the certification or renewal, is issued by the Secretary of Defense.

(3) CERTIFICATION RENEWAL.—

The Secretary of Defense may issue—

(A) a renewal of a certification at any time; and

(B) more than 1 renewal of a certification.

(4) NOTICE TO CONGRESS.—

The Secretary of Defense shall provide Congress a timely notice of the Secretary's issuance of a certification and of a renewal of a certification.

(e) Rule of Construction.—

Nothing in this section shall be construed to preclude the voluntary disclosure of a protected document.

(f) Effective Date.—

This section shall take effect on the date of enactment of this Act and apply to any protected document.

Sec. 566.

Sec. 567.

Sec. 568.

Sec. 569.

Sec. 570.

Sec. 571.

Sec. 572.

Sec. 573.

Sec. 574.

Sec. 575.

Sec. 576.

Sec. 577.

Sec. 578.

Sec. 579.

Sec. 580.

Of the amounts available under the heading "Counterterrorism Fund", $5,600,000 are rescinded.

4.14   Title XVIII

== TITLE XVIII — MILITARY COMMISSIONS ==

Sec. 1801. Short title.

This title may be cited as the ``**Military Commissions Act of 2009**´´.

Sec. 1802. Military commissions.

Chapter 47A of title 10, United States Code, is amended to read as follows:

``**Sec. 948a. Definitions**

``In this chapter:

``(1) ALIEN.— The term "alien" means an individual who is not a citizen of the United States.

``(2) CLASSIFIED INFORMATION.— The term "classified information" means the following:

``(A) Any information or material that has been determined by the United States Government pursuant to statute, Executive order, or regulation to require protection against unauthorized disclosure for reasons of national security.

``(B) Any restricted data, as that term is defined in section 11 y. of the Atomic Energy Act of 1954 (42 U.S.C. 2014(y)).

``(3) COALITION PARTNER.— The term "coalition partner" , with respect to hostilities engaged in by the United States, means any State or armed force directly engaged along with the United States in such hostilities or providing direct operational support to the United States in connection with such hostilities.

``(4) GENEVA CONVENTION RELATIVE TO THE TREATMENT OF PRISONERS OF WAR.— The term "Geneva Convention Relative to the Treatment of Prisoners of War" means the Convention Relative to the Treatment of Prisoners of War, done at Geneva August 12, 1949 (6 UST 3316).

``(5) GENEVA CONVENTIONS.— The term "Geneva Conventions" means the international conventions signed at Geneva on August 12, 1949.

``(6) PRIVILEGED BELLIGERENT.— The term "privileged belligerent" means an individual belonging to one of the eight categories enumerated in Article 4 of the Geneva Convention Relative to the Treatment of Prisoners of War.

``(7) UNPRIVILEGED ENEMY BELLIGERENT.— The term "unprivileged enemy belligerent" means an individual (other than a privileged belligerent) who—

``(A) has engaged in hostilities against the United States or its coalition partners;

``(B) has purposefully and materially supported hostilities against the United States or its coalition partners; or

``(C) was a part of al Qaeda at the time of the alleged offense under this chapter.

``(8) NATIONAL SECURITY.— The term "national security" means the national defense and foreign relations of the United States.

``(9) HOSTILITIES.— The term "hostilities" means any conflict subject to the laws of war.

``Sec. 948b. Military commissions generally

``(a) Purpose.— This chapter establishes procedures governing the use of military commissions to try alien unprivileged enemy belligerents for violations of the law of war and other offenses triable by military commission.

``(b) Authority for Military Commissions Under This Chapter.— The President is authorized to establish military commissions under this chapter for offenses triable by military commission as provided in this chapter.

``(c) Construction of Provisions.— The procedures for military commissions set forth in this chapter are based upon the procedures for trial by general courts-martial under chapter 47 of this title (the Uniform Code of Military Justice). Chapter 47 of this title does not, by its terms, apply to trial by military commission except as specifically provided therein or in this chapter, and many of the provisions of chapter 47 of this title are by their terms inapplicable to military commissions. The judicial construction and application of chapter 47 of this title, while instructive, is therefore not of its own force binding on military commissions established under this chapter.

``(d) Inapplicability of Certain Provisions.—

``(1) The following provisions of this title shall not apply to trial by military commission under this chapter:

``(A) Section 810 (article 10 of the Uniform Code of Military Justice), relating to speedy trial, including any rule of courts-martial relating to speedy trial.

``(B) Sections 831(a), (b), and (d) (articles 31(a), (b), and (d) of the Uniform Code of Military Justice), relating to compulsory self-incrimination.

``(C) Section 832 (article 32 of the Uniform Code of Military Justice), relating to pretrial investigation.

``(2) Other provisions of chapter 47 of this title shall apply to trial by military commission under this chapter only to the extent provided by the terms of such provisions or by this chapter.

``(e) Geneva Conventions Not Establishing Private Right of Action.— No alien unprivileged enemy belligerent subject to trial by military commission under this chapter may invoke the Geneva Conventions as a basis for a private right of action.

``Sec. 948c. Persons subject to military commissions

``Any alien unprivileged enemy belligerent is subject to trial by military commission as set forth in this chapter.

``Sec. 948d. Jurisdiction of military commissions

``A military commission under this chapter shall have jurisdiction to try persons subject to this chapter for any offense made punishable by this chapter, sections 904 and 906 of this title (articles 104 and 106 of the Uniform Code of Military Justice), or the law of war, whether such offense was committed before, on, or after September 11, 2001, and may, under such limitations as the President may prescribe, adjudge any punishment not forbidden by this chapter, including the penalty of death when specifically authorized under this chapter. A military commission is a competent tribunal to make a finding sufficient for jurisdiction.

``Sec. 948h. Who may convene military commissions

``Military commissions under this chapter may be convened by the Secretary of Defense or by any officer or official of the United States designated by the Secretary for that purpose.

``Sec. 948i. Who may serve on military commissions

``(a) In General.— Any commissioned officer of the armed forces on active duty is eligible to serve on a military commission under this chapter, including commissioned officers of the reserve components of the armed forces on active duty, commissioned officers of the National Guard on active duty in Federal service, or retired commissioned officers recalled to active duty.

``(b) Detail of Members.— When convening a military commission under this chapter, the convening authority shall detail as members thereof such members of the armed forces eligible under subsection (a) who, in the opinion of the convening authority, are best qualified for the duty by reason of age, education, training, experience, length of service, and judicial temperament. No member of an armed force is eligible to serve as a member of a military commission when such member is the accuser or a witness for the prosecution or has acted as an investigator or counsel in the same case.

``(c) Excuse of Members.— Before a military commission under this chapter is assembled for the trial of a case, the convening authority may excuse a member from participating in the case.

``Sec. 948j. Military judge of a military commission

``(a) Detail of Military Judge.— A military judge shall be detailed to each military commission under this chapter. The Secretary of Defense shall prescribe regulations providing for the manner in which military judges are so detailed to military commissions. The military judge shall preside over each military commission to which such military judge has been detailed.

``(b) Eligibility.— A military judge shall be a commissioned officer of the armed forces who is a member of the bar of a Federal court, or a member of the bar of the highest court of a State, and who is certified to be qualified for duty under section 826 of this title (article 26 of the Uniform Code of Military Justice) as a military judge of general courts-martial by the Judge Advocate General of the armed force of which such military judge is a member.

``(c) Ineligibility of Certain Individuals.— No person is eligible to act as military judge in a case of a military commission under this chapter if such person is the accuser or a witness or has acted as investigator or a counsel in the same case.

``(d) Consultation With Members; Ineligibility to Vote.— A military judge detailed to a military commission under this chapter may not consult with the members except in the presence of the accused (except as otherwise provided in section 949d of this title), trial counsel, and defense counsel, nor may such military judge vote with the members.

``(e) Other Duties.— A commissioned officer who is certified to be qualified for duty as a military judge of a military commission under this chapter may perform such other duties as are assigned to such officer by or with the approval of the Judge Advocate General of the armed force of which such officer is a member or the designee of such Judge Advocate General.

``(f) Prohibition on Evaluation of Fitness by Convening Authority.— The convening authority of a military commission under this chapter may not prepare or review any report concerning the effectiveness, fitness, or efficiency of a military judge detailed to the military commission which relates to such judge's performance of duty as a military judge on the military commission.

``Sec. 948k. Detail of trial counsel and defense counsel

``(a) Detail of Counsel Generally.—

``(1) Trial counsel and military defense counsel shall be detailed for each military commission under this chapter.

``(2) Assistant trial counsel and assistant and associate defense counsel may be detailed for a military commission under this chapter.

``(3) Military defense counsel for a military commission under this chapter shall be detailed as soon as practicable.

``(4) The Secretary of Defense shall prescribe regulations providing for the manner in which trial counsel and military defense counsel are detailed for military commissions under this chapter and for the persons who are authorized to detail such counsel for such military commissions.

``(b) Trial Counsel.— Subject to subsection (e), a trial counsel detailed for a military commission under this chapter shall be—

``(1) a judge advocate (as that term is defined in section 801 of this title (article 1 of the Uniform Code of Military Justice)) who is—

``(A) a graduate of an accredited law school or a member of the bar of a Federal court or of the highest court of a State; and

``(B) certified as competent to perform duties as trial counsel before general courts-martial by the Judge Advocate General of the armed force of which such judge advocate is a member; or

``(2) a civilian who is—

``(A) a member of the bar of a Federal court or of the highest court of a State; and

``(B) otherwise qualified to practice before the military commission pursuant to regulations prescribed by the Secretary of Defense.

``(c) Defense Counsel.—

``(1) Subject to subsection (e), a military defense counsel detailed for a military commission under this chapter shall be a judge advocate (as so defined) who is—

``(A) a graduate of an accredited law school or a member of the bar of a Federal court or of the highest court of a State; and

``(B) certified as competent to perform duties as defense counsel before general courts-martial by the Judge Advocate General of the armed force of which such judge advocate is a member.

``(2) The Secretary of Defense shall prescribe regulations for the appointment and performance of defense counsel in capital cases under this chapter.

``(d) Chief Prosecutor; Chief Defense Counsel.—

``(1) The Chief Prosecutor in a military commission under this chapter shall meet the requirements set forth in subsection (b)(1).

``(2) The Chief Defense Counsel in a military commission under this chapter shall meet the requirements set forth in subsection (c)(1).

``(e) Ineligibility of Certain Individuals.— No person who has acted as an investigator, military judge, or member of a military commission under this chapter in any case may act later as trial counsel or military defense counsel in the same case. No person who has acted for the prosecution before a military commission under this chapter may act later in the same case for the defense, nor may any person who has acted for the defense before a military commission under this chapter may act later in the same case for the defense, nor may any person who has acted for the defense before a military commission under this chapter act later in the same case for the prosecution.

``Sec. 948l. Detail or employment of reporters and interpreters

``(a) Court Reporters.— Under such regulations as the Secretary of Defense may prescribe, the convening authority of a military commission under this chapter shall detail to or employ for the military commission qualified court reporters, who shall prepare a verbatim record of the proceedings of and testimony taken before the military commission.

``(b) Interpreters.— Under such regulations as the Secretary of Defense may prescribe, the convening authority of a military commission under this chapter may detail to or employ for the military commission interpreters who shall interpret for the military commission, and, as necessary, for trial counsel and defense counsel for the military commission, and for the accused.

``(c) Transcript; Record.— The transcript of a military commission under this chapter shall be under the control of the convening authority of the military commission, who shall also be responsible for preparing the record of the proceedings of the military commission.

``Sec. 948m. Number of members; excuse of members; absent and additional members

``(a) Number of Members.—

   ``(1) Except as provided in paragraph (2), a military commission under this chapter shall have at least five members.

   ``(2) In a case in which the accused before a military commission under this chapter may be sentenced to a penalty of death, the military commission shall have the number of members prescribed by section 949m(c) of this title.

``(b) Excuse of Members.— No member of a military commission under this chapter may be absent or excused after the military commission has been assembled for the trial of a case unless excused—

   ``(1) as a result of challenge;

   ``(2) by the military judge for physical disability or other good cause; or

   ``(3) by order of the convening authority for good cause.

``(c) Absent and Additional Members.— Whenever a military commission under this chapter is reduced below the number of members required by subsection (a), the trial may not proceed unless the convening authority details new members sufficient to provide not less than such number. The trial may proceed with the new members present after the recorded evidence previously introduced before the members has been read to the military commission in the presence of the military judge, the accused (except as provided in section 949d of this title), and counsel for both sides.

``Sec. 948q. Charges and specifications

``(a) Charges and Specifications.— Charges and specifications against an accused in a military commission under this chapter shall be signed by a person subject to chapter 47 of this title under oath before a commissioned officer of the armed forces authorized to administer oaths and shall state—

   ``(1) that the signer has personal knowledge of, or reason to believe, the matters set forth therein; and

   ``(2) that such matters are true in fact to the best of the signer's knowledge and belief.

``(b) Notice to Accused.— Upon the swearing of the charges and specifications in accordance with subsection (a), the accused shall be informed of the charges and specifications against the accused as soon as practicable.

``Sec. 948r. Exclusion of statements obtained by torture or cruel, inhuman, or degrading treatment; prohibition of self-incrimination; admission of other statements of the accused

``(a) Exclusion of Statements Obtain by Torture or Cruel, Inhuman, or Degrading Treatment.— No statement obtained by the use of torture or by cruel, inhuman, or degrading treatment (as defined by section 1003 of the Detainee Treatment Act of 2005 (42 U.S.C. 2000dd)), whether or not under color of law, shall be admissible in a military commission under this chapter, except against a person accused of torture or such treatment as evidence that the statement was made.

``(b) Self-incrimination Prohibited.— No person shall be required to testify against himself or herself at a proceeding of a military commission under this chapter.

``(c) Other Statements of the Accused.— A statement of the accused may be admitted in evidence in a military commission under this chapter only if the military judge finds—

``(1) that the totality of the circumstances renders the statement reliable and possessing sufficient probative value; and

``(2) that—

``(A) the statement was made incident to lawful conduct during military operations at the point of capture or during closely related active combat engagement, and the interests of justice would best be served by admission of the statement into evidence; or

``(B) the statement was voluntarily given.

``(d) Determination of Voluntariness.— In determining for purposes of subsection (c)(2)(B) whether a statement was voluntarily given, the military judge shall consider the totality of the circumstances, including, as appropriate, the following:

``(1) The details of the taking of the statement, accounting for the circumstances of the conduct of military and intelligence operations during hostilities.

``(2) The characteristics of the accused, such as military training, age, and education level.

``(3) The lapse of time, change of place, or change in identity of the questioners between the statement sought to be admitted and any prior questioning of the accused.

``**Sec. 948s. Service of charges**

``The trial counsel assigned to a case before a military commission under this chapter shall cause to be served upon the accused and military defense counsel a copy of the charges upon which trial is to be had in English and, if appropriate, in another language that the accused understands, sufficiently in advance of trial to prepare a defense.

``**Sec. 949a. Rules**

``(a) Procedures and Rules of Evidence.— Pretrial, trial, and post-trial procedures, including elements and modes of proof, for cases triable by military commission under this chapter may be prescribed by the Secretary of Defense. Such procedures may not be contrary to or inconsistent with this chapter. Except as otherwise provided in this chapter or chapter 47 of this title, the procedures and rules of evidence applicable in trials by general courts-martial of the United States shall apply in trials by military commission under this chapter.

``(b) Exceptions.—

``(1) In trials by military commission under this chapter, the Secretary of Defense, in consultation with the Attorney General, may make such exceptions in the applicability of the procedures and rules of evidence otherwise applicable in general courts-martial as may be required by the unique circumstances of the conduct of military and intelligence operations during hostilities or by other practical need consistent with this chapter.

``(2) Notwithstanding any exceptions authorized by paragraph (1), the procedures and rules of evidence in trials by military commission under this chapter shall include, at a minimum, the following rights of the accused:

``(A) To present evidence in the accused's defense, to cross-examine the witnesses who testify against the accused, and to examine and respond to all evidence admitted against the accused on the issue of guilt or innocence and for sentencing, as provided for by this chapter.

``(B) To be present at all sessions of the military commission (other than those for deliberations or voting), except when excluded under section 949d of this title.

``(C)

``(i) When none of the charges preferred against the accused are capital, to be represented before a military commission by civilian counsel if provided at no expense to the Government, and by either the defense counsel detailed or the military counsel of the accused's own selection, if reasonably available.

``(ii) When any of the charges preferred against the accused are capital, to be represented before a military commission in accordance with clause (i) and, to the greatest extent practicable, by at least one additional counsel who is learned in applicable law relating to capital cases and who, if necessary, may be a civilian and compensated in accordance with regulations prescribed by the Secretary of Defense.

``(D) To self-representation, if the accused knowingly and competently waives the assistance of counsel, subject to the provisions of paragraph (4).

``(E) To the suppression of evidence that is not reliable or probative.

``(F) To the suppression of evidence the probative value of which is substantially outweighed by—

``(i) the danger of unfair prejudice, confusion of the issues, or misleading the members; or

``(ii) considerations of undue delay, waste of time, or needless presentation of cumulative evidence.

``(3) In making exceptions in the applicability in trials by military commission under this chapter from the procedures and rules otherwise applicable in general courts-martial, the Secretary of Defense may provide the following:

``(A) Evidence seized outside the United States shall not be excluded from trial by military commission on the grounds that the evidence was not seized pursuant to a search warrant or authorization.

``(B) A statement of the accused that is otherwise admissible shall not be excluded from trial by military commission on grounds of alleged coercion or compulsory self-incrimination so long as the evidence complies with the provisions of section 948r of this title.

``(C) Evidence shall be admitted as authentic so long as—

``(i) the military judge of the military commission determines that there is sufficient evidence that the evidence is what it is claimed to be; and

``(ii) the military judge instructs the members that they may consider any issue as to authentication or identification of evidence in determining the weight, if any, to be given to the evidence.

``(D) Hearsay evidence not otherwise admissible under the rules of evidence applicable in trial by general courts-martial may be admitted in a trial by military commission only if—

``(i) the proponent of the evidence makes known to the adverse party, sufficiently in advance to provide the adverse party with a fair opportunity to meet the evidence, the proponent's intention to offer the evidence, and the particulars of the evidence (including information on the circumstances under which the evidence was obtained); and

``(ii) the military judge, after taking into account all of the circumstances surrounding the taking of the statement, including the degree to which the statement is corroborated, the indicia of reliability within the statement itself, and whether the will of the declarant was overborne, determines that—

``(I) the statement is offered as evidence of a material fact;

``(II) the statement is probative on the point for which it is offered;

``(III) direct testimony from the witness is not available as a practical matter, taking into consideration the physical location of the witness, the unique circumstances of military and intelligence operations during hostilities, and the adverse impacts on military or intelligence operations that would likely result from the production of the witness; and

``(IV) the general purposes of the rules of evidence and the interests of justice will best be served by admission of the statement into evidence.

``(4)

``(A) The accused in a military commission under this chapter who exercises the right to self-representation under paragraph (2)(D) shall conform the accused's deportment and the conduct of the defense to the rules of evidence, procedure, and decorum applicable to trials by military commission.

``(B) Failure of the accused to conform to the rules described in subparagraph (A) may result in a partial or total revocation by the military judge of the right of self-representation under paragraph (2)(D). In such case, the military counsel of the accused or an appropriately authorized civilian counsel shall perform the functions necessary for the defense.

``(c) Delegation of Authority To Prescribe Regulations.— The Secretary of Defense may delegate the authority of the Secretary to prescribe regulations under this chapter.

``(d) Notice to Congress of Modification of Rules.— Not later than 60 days before the date on which any proposed modification of the rules in effect for military commissions under this chapter goes into effect, the Secretary of Defense shall submit to the Committee on Armed Services of the Senate and the Committee on Armed Services of the House of Representatives a report describing the proposed modification.

``Sec. 949b. Unlawfully influencing action of military commission and United States Court of Military Commission Review

``(a) Military Commissions.—

``(1) No authority convening a military commission under this chapter may censure, reprimand, or admonish the military commission, or any member, military judge, or counsel thereof, with respect to the findings or sentence adjudged by the military commission, or with respect to any other exercises of its or their functions in the conduct of the proceedings.

``(2) No person may attempt to coerce or, by any unauthorized means, influence—

``(A) the action of a military commission under this chapter, or any member thereof, in reaching the findings or sentence in any case;

``(B) the action of any convening, approving, or reviewing authority with respect to their judicial acts; or

``(C) the exercise of professional judgment by trial counsel or defense counsel.

``(3) The provisions of this subsection shall not apply with respect to—

``(A) general instructional or informational courses in military justice if such courses are designed solely for the purpose of instructing members of a command in the substantive and procedural aspects of military commissions; or

``(B) statements and instructions given in open proceedings by a military judge or counsel.

``(b) United States Court of Military Commission Review.—

``(1) No person may attempt to coerce or, by any unauthorized means, influence—

``(A) the action of a military appellate judge or other duly appointed judge under this chapter on the United States Court of Military Commissions Review in reaching a decision on the findings or sentence on appeal in any case; or

``(B) the exercise of professional judgment by trial counsel or defense counsel appearing before the United States Court of Military Commission Review.

``(2) No person may censure, reprimand, or admonish a military appellate judge on the United States Court of Military Commission Review, or counsel thereof, with respect to any exercise of their functions in the conduct of proceedings under this chapter.

``(3) The provisions of this subsection shall not apply with respect to—

``(A) general instructional or informational courses in military justice if such courses are designed solely for the purpose of instructing members of a command in the substantive and procedural aspects of military commissions; or

``(B) statements and instructions given in open proceedings by an appellate military judge or a duly appointed appellate judge on the United States Court of Military Commission Review, or counsel.

``(4) No appellate military judge on the United States Court of Military Commission Review may be reassigned to other duties, except under circumstances as follows:

``(A) The appellate military judge voluntarily requests to be reassigned to other duties and the Secretary of Defense, or the designee of the Secretary, in consultation with the Judge Advocate General of the armed force of which the appellate military judge is a member, approves such reassignment.

``(B) The appellate military judge retires or otherwise separates from the armed forces.

``(C) The appellate military judge is reassigned to other duties by the Secretary of Defense, or the designee of the Secretary, in consultation with the Judge Advocate General of the armed force of which the appellate military judge is a member, based on military necessity and such reassignment is consistent with service rotation regulations (to the extent such regulations are applicable).

``(D) The appellate military judge is withdrawn by the Secretary of Defense, or the designee of the Secretary, in consultation with the Judge Advocate General of the armed force of which the appellate military judge is a member, for good cause consistent with applicable procedures under chapter 47 of this title (the Uniform Code of Military Justice).

``(c) Prohibition on Consideration of Actions on Commission in Evaluation of Fitness.— In the preparation of an effectiveness, fitness, or efficiency report or any other report or document used in whole or in part for the purpose of determining whether a commissioned officer of the armed forces is qualified to be advanced in grade, or in determining the assignment or transfer of any such officer or whether any such officer should be retained on active duty, no person may—

``(1) consider or evaluate the performance of duty of any member of a military commission under this chapter; or

``(2) give a less favorable rating or evaluation to any commissioned officer because of the zeal with which such officer, in acting as counsel, represented any accused before a military commission under this chapter.

``Sec. 949c. Duties of trial counsel and defense counsel

``(a) Trial Counsel.— The trial counsel of a military commission under this chapter shall prosecute in the name of the United States.

``(b) Defense Counsel.—

``(1) The accused shall be represented in the accused's defense before a military commission under this chapter as provided in this subsection.

``(2) The accused may be represented by military counsel detailed under section 948k of this title or by military counsel of the accused's own selection, if reasonably available.

``(3) The accused may be represented by civilian counsel if retained by the accused, provided that such civilian counsel—

``(A) is a United States citizen;

``(B) is admitted to the practice of law in a State, district, or possession of the United States, or before a Federal court;

``(C) has not been the subject of any sanction of disciplinary action by any court, bar, or other competent governmental authority for relevant misconduct;

``(D) has been determined to be eligible for access to information classified at the level Secret or higher; and

``(E) has signed a written agreement to comply with all applicable regulations or instructions for counsel, including any rules of court for conduct during the proceedings.

``(4) If the accused is represented by civilian counsel, military counsel shall act as associate counsel.

``(5) The accused is not entitled to be represented by more than one military counsel. However, the person authorized under regulations prescribed under section 948k of this title to detail counsel, in such person's sole discretion, may detail additional military counsel to represent the accused.

``(6) Defense counsel may cross-examine each witness for the prosecution who testifies before a military commission under this chapter.

``(7) Civilian defense counsel shall protect any classified information received during the course of representation of the accused in accordance with all applicable law governing the protection of classified information, and may not divulge such information to any person not authorized to receive it.

``Sec. 949d. Sessions

``(a) Sessions Without Presence of Members.—

``(1) At any time after the service of charges which have been referred for trial by military commission under this chapter, the military judge may call the military commission into session without the presence of the members for the purpose of—

``(A) hearing and determining motions raising defenses or objections which are capable of determination without trial of the issues raised by a plea of not guilty;

``(B) hearing and ruling upon any matter which may be ruled upon by the military judge under this chapter, whether or not the matter is appropriate for later consideration or decision by the members;

``(C) if permitted by regulations prescribed by the Secretary of Defense, receiving the pleas of the accused; and

``(D) performing any other procedural function which may be performed by the military judge under this chapter or under rules prescribed pursuant to section 949a of this title and which does not require the presence of the members.

``(2) Except as provided in subsections (b), (c), and (d), any proceedings under paragraph (1) shall be conducted in the presence of the accused, defense counsel, and trial counsel, and shall be made part of the record.

``(b) Deliberation or Vote of Members.— When the members of a military commission under this chapter deliberate or vote, only the members may be present.

``(c) Closure of Proceedings.—

``(1) The military judge may close to the public all or part of the proceedings of a military commission under this chapter.

``(2) The military judge may close to the public all or a portion of the proceedings under paragraph (1) only upon making a specific finding that such closure is necessary to—

``(A) protect information the disclosure of which could reasonably be expected to cause damage to the national security, including intelligence or law enforcement sources, methods, or activities; or

``(B) ensure the physical safety of individuals.

``(3) A finding under paragraph (2) may be based upon a presentation, including a presentation ex parte or in camera, by either trial counsel or defense counsel.

``(d) Exclusion of Accused From Certain Proceedings.— The military judge may exclude the accused from any portion of a proceeding upon a determination that, after being warned by the military judge, the accused persists in conduct that justifies exclusion from the courtroom—

``(1) to ensure the physical safety of individuals; or

``(2) to prevent disruption of the proceedings by the accused.

``Sec. 949e. Continuances

``The military judge in a military commission under this chapter may, for reasonable cause, grant a continuance to any party for such time, and as often, as may appear to be just.

``Sec. 949f. Challenges

``(a) Challenges Authorized.— The military judge and members of a military commission under this chapter may be challenged by the accused or trial counsel for cause stated to the military commission. The military judge shall determine the relevance and validity of challenges for cause, and may not receive a challenge to more than one person at a time. Challenges by trial counsel shall ordinarily be presented and decided before those by the accused are offered.

``(b) Peremptory Challenges.— The accused and trial counsel are each entitled to one peremptory challenge, but the military judge may not be challenged except for cause.

``(c) Challenges Against Additional Members.— Whenever additional members are detailed to a military commission under this chapter, and after any challenges for cause against such additional members are presented and decided, the accused and trial counsel are each entitled to one peremptory challenge against members not previously subject to peremptory challenge.

``Sec. 949g. Oaths

``(a) In General.—

``(1) Before performing their respective duties in a military commission under this chapter, military judges, members, trial counsel, defense counsel, reporters, and interpreters shall take an oath to perform their duties faithfully.

``(2) The form of the oath required by paragraph (1), the time and place of the taking thereof, the manner of recording thereof, and whether the oath shall be taken for all cases in which duties are to be performed or for a particular case, shall be as provided in regulations prescribed by the Secretary of Defense. The regulations may provide that—

``(A) an oath to perform faithfully duties as a military judge, trial counsel, or defense counsel may be taken at any time by any judge advocate or other person certified to be qualified or competent for the duty; and

``(B) if such an oath is taken, such oath need not again be taken at the time the judge advocate or other person is detailed to that duty.

``(b) Witnesses.— Each witness before a military commission under this chapter shall be examined on oath.

``(c) Oath Defined.— In this section, the term "oath" includes an affirmation.

``Sec. 949h. Former jeopardy

``(a) In General.— No person may, without the person's consent, be tried by a military commission under this chapter a second time for the same offense.

``(b) Scope of Trial.— No proceeding in which the accused has been found guilty by military commission under this chapter upon any charge or specification is a trial in the sense of this section until the finding of guilty has become final after review of the case has been fully completed.

``Sec. 949i. Pleas of the accused

``(a) Plea of Not Guilty.— If an accused in a military commission under this chapter after a plea of guilty sets up matter inconsistent with the plea, or if it appears that the accused has entered the plea of guilty through lack of understanding of its meaning and effect, or if the accused fails or refuses to plead, a plea of not guilty shall be entered in the record, and the military commission shall proceed as though the accused had pleaded not guilty.

``(b) Finding of Guilt After Guilty Plea.— With respect to any charge or specification to which a plea of guilty has been made by the accused in a military commission under this chapter and accepted by the military judge, a finding of guilty of the charge or specification may be entered immediately without a vote. The finding shall constitute the finding of the military commission unless the plea of guilty is withdrawn prior to announcement of the sentence, in which event the proceedings shall continue as though the accused had pleaded not guilty.

``Sec. 949j. Opportunity to obtain witnesses and other evidence

``(a) In General.—

``(1) Defense counsel in a military commission under this chapter shall have a reasonable opportunity to obtain witnesses and other evidence as provided in regulations prescribed by the Secretary of Defense. The opportunity to obtain witnesses and evidence shall be comparable to the opportunity available to a criminal defendant in a court of the United States under article III of the Constitution.

``(2) Process issued in military commissions under this chapter to compel witnesses to appear and testify and to compel the production of other evidence—

``(A) shall be similar to that which courts of the United States having criminal jurisdiction may lawfully issue; and

``(B) shall run to any place where the United States shall have jurisdiction thereof.

``(b) Disclosure of Exculpatory Evidence.—

``(1) As soon as practicable, trial counsel in a military commission under this chapter shall disclose to the defense the existence of any evidence that reasonably tends to—

``(A) negate the guilt of the accused of an offense charged; or

``(B) reduce the degree of guilt of the accused with respect to an offense charged.

``(2) The trial counsel shall, as soon as practicable, disclose to the defense the existence of evidence that reasonably tends to impeach the credibility of a witness whom the government intends to call at trial.

``(3) The trial counsel shall, as soon as practicable upon a finding of guilt, disclose to the defense the existence of evidence that is not subject to paragraph (1) or paragraph (2) but that reasonably may be viewed as mitigation evidence at sentencing.

``(4) The disclosure obligations under this subsection encompass evidence that is known or reasonably should be known to any government officials who participated in the investigation and prosecution of the case against the defendant.

``Sec. 949k. Defense of lack of mental responsibility

``(a) Affirmative Defense.— It is an affirmative defense in a trial by military commission under this chapter that, at the time of the commission of the acts constituting the offense, the accused, as a result of a severe mental disease or defect, was unable to appreciate the nature and quality or the wrongfulness of the acts. Mental disease or defect does not otherwise constitute a defense.

``(b) Burden of Proof.— The accused in a military commission under this chapter has the burden of proving the defense of lack of mental responsibility by clear and convincing evidence.

``(c) Findings Following Assertion of Defense.— Whenever lack of mental responsibility of the accused with respect to an offense is properly at issue in a military commission under this chapter, the military judge shall instruct the members as to the defense of lack of mental responsibility under this section and shall charge the members to find the accused—

``(1) guilty;

``(2) not guilty; or

``(3) subject to subsection (d), not guilty by reason of lack of mental responsibility.

``(d) Majority Vote Required for Finding.— The accused shall be found not guilty by reason of lack of mental responsibility under subsection (c)(3) only if a majority of the members present at the time the vote is taken determines that the defense of lack of mental responsibility has been established.

``Sec. 949l. Voting and rulings

``(a) Vote by Secret Written Ballot.— Voting by members of a military commission under this chapter on the findings and on the sentence shall be by secret written ballot.

``(b) Rulings.—

``(1) The military judge in a military commission under this chapter shall rule upon all questions of law, including the admissibility of evidence and all interlocutory questions arising during the proceedings.

``(2) Any ruling made by the military judge upon a question of law or an interlocutory question (other than the factual issue of mental responsibility of the accused) is conclusive and constitutes the ruling of the military commission. However, a military judge may change such a ruling at any time during the trial.

``(c) Instructions Prior to Vote.— Before a vote is taken of the findings of a military commission under this chapter, the military judge shall, in the presence of the accused and counsel, instruct the members as to the elements of the offense and charge the members—

> ``(1) that the accused must be presumed to be innocent until the accused's guilt is established by legal and competent evidence beyond a reasonable doubt;

> ``(2) that in the case being considered, if there is a reasonable doubt as to the guilt of the accused, the doubt must be resolved in favor of the accused and the accused must be acquitted;

> ``(3) that, if there is reasonable doubt as to the degree of guilt, the finding must be in a lower degree as to which there is no reasonable doubt; and

> ``(4) that the burden of proof to establish the guilt of the accused beyond a reasonable doubt is upon the United States.

``Sec. 949m. Number of votes required

``(a) Conviction.— No person may be convicted by a military commission under this chapter of any offense, except as provided in section 949i(b) of this title or by concurrence of two-thirds of the members present at the time the vote is taken.

``(b) Sentences.—

> ``(1) Except as provided in paragraphs (2) and (3), sentences shall be determined by a military commission by the concurrence of two-thirds of the members present at the time the vote is taken.

> ``(2) No person may be sentenced to death by a military commission, except insofar as—

>> ``(A) the penalty of death has been expressly authorized under this chapter, chapter 47 of this title, or the law of war for an offense of which the accused has been found guilty;

>> ``(B) trial counsel expressly sought the penalty of death by filing an appropriate notice in advance of trial;

>> ``(C) the accused was convicted of the offense by the concurrence of all the members present at the time the vote is taken; and

>> ``(D) all members present at the time the vote was taken concurred in the sentence of death.

> ``(3) No person may be sentenced to life imprisonment, or to confinement for more than 10 years, by a military commission under this chapter except by the concurrence of three-fourths of the members present at the time the vote is taken.

``(c) Number of Members Required for Penalty of Death.—

``(1) Except as provided in paragraph (2), in a case in which the penalty of death is sought, the number of members of the military commission under this chapter shall be not less than 12 members.

``(2) In any case described in paragraph (1) in which 12 members are not reasonably available for a military commission because of physical conditions or military exigencies, the convening authority shall specify a lesser number of members for the military commission (but not fewer than 9 members), and the military commission may be assembled, and the trial held, with not less than the number of members so specified. In any such case, the convening authority shall make a detailed written statement, to be appended to the record, stating why a greater number of members were not reasonably available.

``Sec. 949n. Military commission to announce action

``A military commission under this chapter shall announce its findings and sentence to the parties as soon as determined.

``Sec. 949o. Record of trial

``(a) Record; Authentication.— Each military commission under this chapter shall keep a separate, verbatim, record of the proceedings in each case brought before it, and the record shall be authenticated by the signature of the military judge. If the record cannot be authenticated by the military judge by reason of death, disability, or absence, it shall be authenticated by the signature of the trial counsel or by a member of the commission if the trial counsel is unable to authenticate it by reason of death, disability, or absence. Where appropriate, and as provided in regulations prescribed by the Secretary of Defense, the record of a military commission under this chapter may contain a classified annex.

``(b) Complete Record Required.— A complete record of the proceedings and testimony shall be prepared in every military commission under this chapter.

``(c) Provision of Copy to Accused.— A copy of the record of the proceedings of the military commission under this chapter shall be given the accused as soon as it is authenticated. If the record contains classified information, or a classified annex, the accused shall receive a redacted version of the record consistent with the requirements of subchapter V of this chapter. Defense counsel shall have access to the unredacted record, as provided in regulations prescribed by the Secretary of Defense.

``Sec. 949p-1. Protection of classified information: applicability of subchapter

``(a) Protection of Classified Information.— Classified information shall be protected and is privileged from disclosure if disclosure would be detrimental to the national security. Under no circumstances may a military judge order the release of classified information to any person not authorized to receive such information.

``(b) Access to Evidence.— Any information admitted into evidence pursuant to any rule, procedure, or order by the military judge shall be provided to the accused.

``(c) Declassification.— Trial counsel shall work with the original classification authorities for evidence that may be used at trial to ensure that such evidence is declassified to the maximum extent possible, consistent with the requirements of national security. A decision not to declassify evidence under this section shall not be subject to review by a military commission or upon appeal.

``(d) Construction of Provisions.— The judicial construction of the Classified Information Procedures Act (18 U.S.C. App.) shall be authoritative in the interpretation of this subchapter, except to the extent that such construction is inconsistent with the specific requirements of this chapter.

``Sec. 949p-2. Pretrial conference

``(a) Motion.— At any time after service of charges, any party may move for a pretrial conference to consider matters relating to classified information that may arise in connection with the prosecution.

``(b) Conference.— Following a motion under subsection (a), or sua sponte, the military judge shall promptly hold a pretrial conference. Upon request by either party, the court shall hold such conference ex parte to the extent necessary to protect classified information from disclosure, in accordance with the practice of the Federal courts under the Classified Information Procedures Act (18 U.S.C. App.).

``(c) Matters To Be Established at Pretrial Conference.—

``(1) TIMING OF SUBSEQUENT ACTIONS.— At the pretrial conference, the military judge shall establish the timing of—

``(A) requests for discovery;

``(B) the provision of notice required by section 949p-5 of this title; and

``(C) the initiation of the procedure established by section 949p-6 of this title.

``(2) OTHER MATTERS.— At the pretrial conference, the military judge may also consider any matter—

``(A) which relates to classified information; or

``(B) which may promote a fair and expeditious trial.

``(d) Effect of Admissions by Accused at Pretrial Conference.— No admission made by the accused or by any counsel for the accused at a pretrial conference under this section may be used against the accused unless the admission is in writing and is signed by the accused and by the counsel for the accused.

``Sec. 949p-3. Protective orders

``Upon motion of the trial counsel, the military judge shall issue an order to protect against the disclosure of any classified information that has been disclosed by the United States to any accused in any military commission under this chapter or that has otherwise been provided to, or obtained by, any such accused in any such military commission.

``Sec. 949p-4. Discovery of, and access to, classified information by the accused

``(a) Limitations on Discovery or Access by the Accused.—

``(1) DECLARATIONS BY THE UNITED STATES OF DAMAGE TO NATIONAL SECURITY.— In any case before a military commission in which the United States seeks to delete, withhold, or otherwise obtain other relief with respect to the discovery of or access to any classified information, the trial counsel shall submit a declaration invoking the United States' classified information privilege and setting forth the damage to the national security that the discovery of or access to such information reasonably could be expected to cause. The declaration shall be signed by a knowledgeable United States official possessing authority to classify information.

``(2) STANDARD FOR AUTHORIZATION OF DISCOVERY OR ACCESS.— Upon the submission of a declaration under paragraph (1), the military judge may not authorize the discovery of or access to such classified information unless the military judge determines that such classified information would be noncumulative, relevant, and helpful to a legally cognizable defense, rebuttal of the prosecution's case, or to sentencing, in accordance with standards generally applicable to discovery of or access to classified information in Federal criminal cases. If the discovery of or access to such classified information is authorized, it shall be addressed in accordance with the requirements of subsection (b).

``(b) Discovery of Classified Information.—

``(1) SUBSTITUTIONS AND OTHER RELIEF.— The military judge, in assessing the accused's discovery of or access to classified information under this section, may authorize the United States—

``(A) to delete or withhold specified items of classified information;

``(B) to substitute a summary for classified information; or

``(C) to substitute a statement admitting relevant facts that the classified information or material would tend to prove.

``(2) EX PARTE PRESENTATIONS.— The military judge shall permit the trial counsel to make a request for an authorization under paragraph (1) in the form of an ex parte presentation to the extent necessary to protect classified information, in accordance with the practice of the Federal courts under the Classified Information Procedures Act (18 U.S.C. App.). If the military judge enters an order granting relief following such an ex parte showing, the entire presentation (including the text of any written submission, verbatim transcript of the ex parte oral conference or hearing, and any exhibits received by the court as part of the ex parte presentation) shall be sealed and preserved in the records of the military commission to be made available to the appellate court in the event of an appeal.

``(3) ACTION BY MILITARY JUDGE.— The military judge shall grant the request of the trial counsel to substitute a summary or to substitute a statement admitting relevant facts, or to provide other relief in accordance with paragraph (1), if the military judge finds that the summary, statement, or other relief would provide the accused with substantially the same ability to make a defense as would discovery of or access to the specific classified information.

``(c) Reconsideration.— An order of a military judge authorizing a request of the trial counsel to substitute, summarize, withhold, or prevent access to classified information under this section is not subject to a motion for reconsideration by the accused, if such order was entered pursuant to an ex parte showing under this section.

``Sec. 949p-5. Notice by accused of intention to disclose classified information

``(a) Notice by Accused.—

    ``(1) NOTIFICATION OF TRIAL COUNSEL AND MILITARY JUDGE.— If an accused reasonably expects to disclose, or to cause the disclosure of, classified information in any manner in connection with any trial or pretrial proceeding involving the prosecution of such accused, the accused shall, within the time specified by the military judge or, where no time is specified, within 30 days before trial, notify the trial counsel and the military judge in writing. Such notice shall include a brief description of the classified information. Whenever the accused learns of additional classified information the accused reasonably expects to disclose, or to cause the disclosure of, at any such proceeding, the accused shall notify trial counsel and the military judge in writing as soon as possible thereafter and shall include a brief description of the classified information.

    ``(2) LIMITATION ON DISCLOSURE BY ACCUSED.— No accused shall disclose, or cause the disclosure of, any information known or believed to be classified in connection with a trial or pretrial proceeding until—

        ``(A) notice has been given under paragraph (1); and

        ``(B) the United States has been afforded a reasonable opportunity to seek a determination pursuant to the procedure set forth in section 949p-6 of this title and the time for the United States to appeal such determination under section 950d of this title has expired or any appeal under that section by the United States is decided.

``(b) Failure To Comply.— If the accused fails to comply with the requirements of subsection (a), the military judge—

    ``(1) may preclude disclosure of any classified information not made the subject of notification; and

    ``(2) may prohibit the examination by the accused of any witness with respect to any such information.

``Sec. 949p-6. Procedure for cases involving classified information

``(a) Motion for Hearing.—

    ``(1) REQUEST FOR HEARING.— Within the time specified by the military judge for the filing of a motion under this section, either party may request the military judge to conduct a hearing to make all determinations concerning the use, relevance, or admissibility of classified information that would otherwise be made during the trial or pretrial proceeding.

    ``(2) CONDUCT OF HEARING.— Upon a request by either party under paragraph (1), the military judge shall conduct such a hearing and shall rule prior to conducting any further proceedings.

    ``(3) IN CAMERA HEARING UPON DECLARATION TO COURT BY APPROPRIATE OFFICIAL OF RISK OF DISCLOSURE OF CLASSIFIED INFORMATION.— Any hearing held pursuant to this subsection (or any portion of such hearing specified in the request of a knowledgeable United States official) shall be held in camera if a knowledgeable United States official possessing authority to classify information submits to the military judge a declaration that a public proceeding may result in the disclosure of classified information. Classified information is not subject to disclosure under this section unless the information is relevant and necessary to an element of the offense or a legally cognizable defense and is otherwise admissible in evidence.

``(4) MILITARY JUDGE TO MAKE DETERMINATIONS IN WRITING.— As to each item of classified information, the military judge shall set forth in writing the basis for the determination.

``(b) Notice and Use of Classified Information by the Government.—

``(1) NOTICE TO ACCUSED.— Before any hearing is conducted pursuant to a request by the trial counsel under subsection (a), trial counsel shall provide the accused with notice of the classified information that is at issue. Such notice shall identify the specific classified information at issue whenever that information previously has been made available to the accused by the United States. When the United States has not previously made the information available to the accused in connection with the case the information may be described by generic category, in such forms as the military judge may approve, rather than by identification of the specific information of concern to the United States.

``(2) ORDER BY MILITARY JUDGE UPON REQUEST OF ACCUSED.— Whenever the trial counsel requests a hearing under subsection (a), the military judge, upon request of the accused, may order the trial counsel to provide the accused, prior to trial, such details as to the portion of the charge or specification at issue in the hearing as are needed to give the accused fair notice to prepare for the hearing.

``(c) Substitutions.—

``(1) IN CAMERA PRETRIAL HEARING.— Upon request of the trial counsel pursuant to the Military Commission Rules of Evidence, and in accordance with the security procedures established by the military judge, the military judge shall conduct a classified in camera pretrial hearing concerning the admissibility of classified information.

``(2) PROTECTION OF SOURCES, METHODS, AND ACTIVITIES BY WHICH EVIDENCE ACQUIRED.— When trial counsel seeks to introduce evidence before a military commission under this chapter and the Executive branch has classified the sources, methods, or activities by which the United States acquired the evidence, the military judge shall permit trial counsel to introduce the evidence, including a substituted evidentiary foundation pursuant to the procedures described in subsection (d), while protecting from disclosure information identifying those sources, methods, or activities, if—

``(A) the evidence is otherwise admissible; and

``(B) the military judge finds that—

``(i) the evidence is reliable; and

``(ii) the redaction is consistent with affording the accused a fair trial.

``(d) Alternative Procedure for Disclosure of Classified Information.—

``(1) MOTION BY THE UNITED STATES.— Upon any determination by the military judge authorizing the disclosure of specific classified information under the procedures established by this section, the trial counsel may move that, in lieu of the disclosure of such specific classified information, the military judge order—

``(A) the substitution for such classified information of a statement admitting relevant facts that the specific classified information would tend to prove;

``(B) the substitution for such classified information of a summary of the specific classified information; or

``(C) any other procedure or redaction limiting the disclosure of specific classified information.

``(2) ACTION ON MOTION.— The military judge shall grant such a motion of the trial counsel if the military judge finds that the statement, summary, or other procedure or redaction will provide the defendant with substantially the same ability to make his defense as would disclosure of the specific classified information.

``(3) HEARING ON MOTION.— The military judge shall hold a hearing on any motion under this subsection. Any such hearing shall be held in camera at the request of a knowledgeable United States official possessing authority to classify information.

``(4) SUBMISSION OF STATEMENT OF DAMAGE TO NATIONAL SECURITY IF DISCLOSURE ORDERED.— The trial counsel may, in connection with a motion under paragraph (1), submit to the military judge a declaration signed by a knowledgeable United States official possessing authority to classify information certifying that disclosure of classified information would cause identifiable damage to the national security of the United States and explaining the basis for the classification of such information. If so requested by the trial counsel, the military judge shall examine such declaration during an ex parte presentation.

``(e) Sealing of Records of in Camera Hearings.— If at the close of an in camera hearing under this section (or any portion of a hearing under this section that is held in camera), the military judge determines that the classified information at issue may not be disclosed or elicited at the trial or pretrial proceeding, the record of such in camera hearing shall be sealed and preserved for use in the event of an appeal. The accused may seek reconsideration of the military judge's determination prior to or during trial.

``(f) Prohibition on Disclosure of Classified Information by the Accused; Relief for Accused When the United States Opposes Disclosure.—

``(1) ORDER TO PREVENT DISCLOSURE BY ACCUSED.— Whenever the military judge denies a motion by the trial counsel that the judge issue an order under subsection (a), (c), or (d) and the trial counsel files with the military judge a declaration signed by a knowledgeable United States official possessing authority to classify information objecting to disclosure of the classified information at issue, the military judge shall order that the accused not disclose or cause the disclosure of such information.

``(2) RESULT OF ORDER UNDER PARAGRAPH (1).— Whenever an accused is prevented by an order under paragraph (1) from disclosing or causing the disclosure of classified information, the military judge shall dismiss the case, except that, when the military judge determines that the interests of justice would not be served by dismissal of the case, the military judge shall order such other action, in lieu of dismissing the charge or specification, as the military judge determines is appropriate. Such action may include, but need not be limited to, the following:

``(A) Dismissing specified charges or specifications.

``(B) Finding against the United States on any issue as to which the excluded classified information relates.

``(C) Striking or precluding all or part of the testimony of a witness.

``(3) TIME FOR THE UNITED STATES TO SEEK INTERLOCUTORY APPEAL.— An order under paragraph (2) shall not take effect until the military judge has afforded the United States—

``(A) an opportunity to appeal such order under section 950d of this title; and

``(B) an opportunity thereafter to withdraw its objection to the disclosure of the classified information at issue.

``(g) Reciprocity.—

``(1) DISCLOSURE OF REBUTTAL INFORMATION.— Whenever the military judge determines that classified information may be disclosed in connection with a trial or pretrial proceeding, the military judge shall, unless the interests of fairness do not so require, order the United States to provide the accused with the information it expects to use to rebut the classified information. The military judge may place the United States under a continuing duty to disclose such rebuttal information.

``(2) SANCTION FOR FAILURE TO COMPLY.— If the United States fails to comply with its obligation under this subsection, the military judge—

``(A) may exclude any evidence not made the subject of a required disclosure; and

``(B) may prohibit the examination by the United States of any witness with respect to such information.

``Sec. 949p-7. Introduction of classified information into evidence

``(a) Preservation of Classification Status.— Writings, recordings, and photographs containing classified information may be admitted into evidence in proceedings of military commissions under this chapter without change in their classification status.

``(b) Precautions by Military Judges.—

``(1) PRECAUTIONS IN ADMITTING CLASSIFIED INFORMATION INTO EVIDENCE.— The military judge in a trial by military commission, in order to prevent unnecessary disclosure of classified information, may order admission into evidence of only part of a writing, recording, or photograph, or may order admission into evidence of the whole writing, recording, or photograph with excision of some or all of the classified information contained therein, unless the whole ought in fairness be considered.

``(2) CLASSIFIED INFORMATION KEPT UNDER SEAL.— The military judge shall allow classified information offered or accepted into evidence to remain under seal during the trial, even if such evidence is disclosed in the military commission, and may, upon motion by the United States, seal exhibits containing classified information for any period after trial as necessary to prevent a disclosure of classified information when a knowledgeable United States official possessing authority to classify information submits to the military judge a declaration setting forth the damage to the national security that the disclosure of such information reasonably could be expected to cause.

``(c) Taking of Testimony.—

``(1) OBJECTION BY TRIAL COUNSEL.— During the examination of a witness, trial counsel may object to any question or line of inquiry that may require the witness to disclose classified information not previously found to be admissible.

``(2) ACTION BY MILITARY JUDGE.— Following an objection under paragraph (1), the military judge shall take such suitable action to determine whether the response is admissible as will safeguard against the compromise of any classified information. Such action may include requiring trial counsel to provide the military judge with a proffer of the witness' response to the question or line of inquiry and requiring the accused to provide the military judge with a proffer of the nature of the information sought to be elicited by the accused. Upon request, the military judge may accept an ex parte proffer by trial counsel to the extent necessary to protect classified information from disclosure, in accordance with the practice of the Federal courts under the Classified Information Procedures Act (18 U.S.C. App.).

``(d) Disclosure at Trial of Certain Statements Previously Made by a Witness.—

``(1) MOTION FOR PRODUCTION OF STATEMENTS IN POSSESSION OF THE UNITED STATES.— After a witness called by the trial counsel has testified on direct examination, the military judge, on motion of the accused, may order production of statements of the witness in the possession of the United States which relate to the subject matter as to which the witness has testified. This paragraph does not preclude discovery or assertion of a privilege otherwise authorized.

``(2) INVOCATION OF PRIVILEGE BY THE UNITED STATES.— If the United States invokes a privilege, the trial counsel may provide the prior statements of the witness to the military judge during an ex parte presentation to the extent necessary to protect classified information from disclosure, in accordance with the practice of the Federal courts under the Classified Information Procedures Act (18 U.S.C. App.).

``(3) ACTION BY MILITARY JUDGE ON MOTION.— If the military judge finds that disclosure of any portion of the statement identified by the United States as classified would be detrimental to the national security in the degree to warrant classification under the applicable Executive Order, statute, or regulation, that such portion of the statement is consistent with the testimony of the witness, and that the disclosure of such portion is not necessary to afford the accused a fair trial, the military judge shall excise that portion from the statement. If the military judge finds that such portion of the statement is inconsistent with the testimony of the witness or that its disclosure is necessary to afford the accused a fair trial, the military judge, shall, upon the request of the trial counsel, review alternatives to disclosure in accordance with section 949p-6(d) of this title.

``Sec. 949s. Cruel or unusual punishments prohibited

``Punishment by flogging, or by branding, marking, or tattooing on the body, or any other cruel or unusual punishment, may not be adjudged by a military commission under this chapter or inflicted under this chapter upon any person subject to this chapter. The use of irons, single or double, except for the purpose of safe custody, is prohibited under this chapter.

``Sec. 949t. Maximum limits

``The punishment which a military commission under this chapter may direct for an offense may not exceed such limits as the President or Secretary of Defense may prescribe for that offense.

``Sec. 949u. Execution of confinement

``(a) In General.— Under such regulations as the Secretary of Defense may prescribe, a sentence of confinement adjudged by a military commission under this chapter may be carried into execution by confinement—

    ``(1) in any place of confinement under the control of any of the armed forces; or

    ``(2) in any penal or correctional institution under the control of the United States or its allies, or which the United States may be allowed to use.

``(b) Treatment During Confinement by Other Than the Armed Forces.— Persons confined under subsection (a)(2) in a penal or correctional institution not under the control of an armed force are subject to the same discipline and treatment as persons confined or committed by the courts of the United States or of the State, District of Columbia, or place in which the institution is situated.

``Sec. 950a. Error of law; lesser included offense

``(a) Error of Law.— A finding or sentence of a military commission under this chapter may not be held incorrect on the ground of an error of law unless the error materially prejudices the substantial rights of the accused.

``(b) Lesser Included Offense.— Any reviewing authority with the power to approve or affirm a finding of guilty by a military commission under this chapter may approve or affirm, instead, so much of the finding as includes a lesser included offense.

``Sec. 950b. Review by the convening authority

``(a) Notice to Convening Authority of Findings and Sentence.— The findings and sentence of a military commission under this chapter shall be reported in writing promptly to the convening authority after the announcement of the sentence.

``(b) Submittal of Matters by Accused to Convening Authority.—

``(1) The accused may submit to the convening authority matters for consideration by the convening authority with respect to the findings and the sentence of the military commission under this chapter.

``(2)

> ``(A) Except as provided in subparagraph (B), a submittal under paragraph (1) shall be made in writing within 20 days after the accused has been give an authenticated record of trial under section 949o(c) of this title.

> ``(B) If the accused shows that additional time is required for the accused to make a submittal under paragraph (1), the convening authority may, for good cause, extend the applicable period under subparagraph (A) for not more than an additional 20 days.

``(3) The accused may waive the accused's right to make a submittal to the convening authority under paragraph (1). Such a waiver shall be made in writing, and may not be revoked. For the purposes of subsection (c)(2), the time within which the accused may make a submittal under this subsection shall be deemed to have expired upon the submittal of a waiver under this paragraph to the convening authority.

``(c) Action by Convening Authority.—

``(1) The authority under this subsection to modify the findings and sentence of a military commission under this chapter is a matter of the sole discretion and prerogative of the convening authority.

``(2) The convening authority is not required to take action on the findings of a military commission under this chapter. If the convening authority takes action on the findings, the convening authority may, in the sole discretion of the convening authority, only—

> ``(A) dismiss any charge or specification by setting aside a finding of guilty thereto; or

> ``(B) change a finding of guilty to a charge to a finding of guilty to an offense that is a lesser included offense of the offense stated in the charge.

``(3)

> ``(A) The convening authority shall take action on the sentence of a military commission under this chapter.

> ``(B) Subject to regulations prescribed by the Secretary of Defense, action under this paragraph may be taken only after consideration of any matters submitted by the accused under subsection (b) or after the time for submitting such matters expires, whichever is earlier.

> ``(C) In taking action under this paragraph, the convening authority may, in the sole discretion of the convening authority, approve, disapprove, commute, or suspend the sentence in whole or in part. The convening authority may not increase a sentence beyond that which is found by the military commission.

``(4) The convening authority shall serve on the accused or on defense counsel notice of any action taken by the convening authority under this subsection.

``(d) Order of Revision or Rehearing.—

``(1) Subject to paragraphs (2) and (3), the convening authority of a military commission under this chapter may, in the sole discretion of the convening authority, order a proceeding in revision or a rehearing.

``(2)

``(A) Except as provided in subparagraph (B), a proceeding in revision may be ordered by the convening authority if—

``(i) there is an apparent error or omission in the record; or

``(ii) the record shows improper or inconsistent action by the military commission with respect to the findings or sentence that can be rectified without material prejudice to the substantial rights of the accused.

``(B) In no case may a proceeding in revision—

``(i) reconsider a finding of not guilty of a specification or a ruling which amounts to a finding of not guilty;

``(ii) reconsider a finding of not guilty of any charge, unless there has been a finding of guilty under a specification laid under that charge, which sufficiently alleges a violation; or

``(iii) increase the severity of the sentence unless the sentence prescribed for the offense is mandatory.

``(3) A rehearing may be ordered by the convening authority if the convening authority disapproves the findings and sentence and states the reasons for disapproval of the findings. If the convening authority disapproves the finding and sentence and does not order a rehearing, the convening authority shall dismiss the charges. A rehearing as to the findings may not be ordered by the convening authority when there is a lack of sufficient evidence in the record to support the findings. A rehearing as to the sentence may be ordered by the convening authority if the convening authority disapproves the sentence.

``Sec. 950c. Appellate referral; waiver or withdrawal of appeal

``(a) Automatic Referral for Appellate Review.— Except as provided in subsection (b), in each case in which the final decision of a military commission under this chapter (as approved by the convening authority) includes a finding of guilty, the convening authority shall refer the case to the United States Court of Military Commission Review. Any such referral shall be made in accordance with procedures prescribed under regulations of the Secretary.

``(b) Waiver of Right of Review.—

``(1) Except in a case in which the sentence as approved under section 950b of this title extends to death, an accused may file with the convening authority a statement expressly waiving the right of the accused to appellate review by the United States Court of Military Commission Review under section 950f of this title of the final decision of the military commission under this chapter.

``(2) A waiver under paragraph (1) shall be signed by both the accused and a defense counsel.

``(3) A waiver under paragraph (1) must be filed, if at all, within 10 days after notice of the action is served on the accused or on defense counsel under section 950b(c)(4) of this title. The convening authority, for good cause, may extend the period for such filing by not more than 30 days.

``(c) Withdrawal of Appeal.— Except in a case in which the sentence as approved under section 950b of this title extends to death, the accused may withdraw an appeal at any time.

``(d) Effect of Waiver or Withdrawal.— A waiver of the right to appellate review or the withdrawal of an appeal under this section bars review under section 950f of this title.

``Sec. 950d. Interlocutory appeals by the United States

``(a) Interlocutory Appeal.— Except as provided in subsection (b), in a trial by military commission under this chapter, the United States may take an interlocutory appeal to the United States Court of Military Commission Review of any order or ruling of the military judge—

``(1) that terminates proceedings of the military commission with respect to a charge or specification;

``(2) that excludes evidence that is substantial proof of a fact material in the proceeding;

``(3) that relates to a matter under subsection (c) or (d) of section 949d of this title; or

``(4) that, with respect to classified information—

``(A) authorizes the disclosure of such information;

``(B) imposes sanctions for nondisclosure of such information; or

``(C) refuses a protective order sought by the United States to prevent the disclosure of such information.

``(b) Limitation.— The United States may not appeal under subsection (a) an order or ruling that is, or amounts to, a finding of not guilty by the military commission with respect to a charge or specification.

``(c) Scope of Appeal Right With Respect to Classified Information.— The United States has the right to appeal under paragraph (4) of subsection (a) whenever the military judge enters an order or ruling that would require the disclosure of classified information, without regard to whether the order or ruling appealed from was entered under this chapter, another provision of law, a rule, or otherwise. Any such appeal may embrace any preceding order, ruling, or reasoning constituting the basis of the order or ruling that would authorize such disclosure.

``(d) Timing and Action on Interlocutory Appeals Relating to Classified Information.—

 ``(1) APPEAL TO BE EXPEDITED.— An appeal taken pursuant to paragraph (4) of subsection (a) shall be expedited by the United States Court of Military Commission Review.

 ``(2) APPEALS BEFORE TRIAL.— If such an appeal is taken before trial, the appeal shall be taken within 10 days after the order or ruling from which the appeal is made and the trial shall not commence until the appeal is decided.

 ``(3) APPEALS DURING TRIAL.— If such an appeal is taken during trial, the military judge shall adjourn the trial until the appeal is decided, and the court of appeals—

  ``(A) shall hear argument on such appeal within 4 days of the adjournment of the trial (excluding weekends and holidays);

  ``(B) may dispense with written briefs other than the supporting materials previously submitted to the military judge;

  ``(C) shall render its decision within four days of argument on appeal (excluding weekends and holidays); and

  ``(D) may dispense with the issuance of a written opinion in rendering its decision.

``(e) Notice and Timing of Other Appeals.— The United States shall take an appeal of an order or ruling under subsection (a), other than an appeal under paragraph (4) of that subsection, by filing a notice of appeal with the military judge within 5 days after the date of the order or ruling.

``(f) Method of Appeal.— An appeal under this section shall be forwarded, by means specified in regulations prescribed by the Secretary of Defense, directly to the United States Court of Military Commission Review.

``(g) Appeals Court To Act Only With Respect to Matter of Law.— In ruling on an appeal under paragraph (1), (2), or (3) of subsection (a), the appeals court may act only with respect to matters of law.

``(h) Subsequent Appeal Rights of Accused Not Affected.— An appeal under paragraph (4) of subsection (a), and a decision on such appeal, shall not affect the right of the accused, in a subsequent appeal from a judgment of conviction, to claim as error reversal by the military judge on remand of a ruling appealed from during trial.

``Sec. 950e. Rehearings

``(a) Composition of Military Commission for Rehearing.— Each rehearing under this chapter shall take place before a military commission under this chapter composed of members who were not members of the military commission which first heard the case.

``(b) Scope of Rehearing.—

 ``(1) Upon a rehearing—

  ``(A) the accused may not be tried for any offense of which the accused was found not guilty by the first military commission; and

``(B) no sentence in excess of or more than the original sentence may be imposed unless—

``(i) the sentence is based upon a finding of guilty of an offense not considered upon the merits in the original proceedings; or

``(ii) the sentence prescribed for the offense is mandatory.

``(2) Upon a rehearing, if the sentence approved after the first military commission was in accordance with a pretrial agreement and the accused at the rehearing changes his plea with respect to the charges or specifications upon which the pretrial agreement was based, or otherwise does not comply with pretrial agreement, the sentence as to those charges or specifications may include any punishment not in excess of that lawfully adjudged at the first military commission.

``Sec. 950f. Review by United States Court of Military Commission Review

``(a) Establishment.— There is a court of record to be known as the "United States Court of Military Commission Review" (in this section referred to as the "Court"). The Court shall consist of one or more panels, each composed of not less than three appellate military judges. For the purpose of reviewing decisions of military commissions under this chapter, the Court may sit in panels or as a whole, in accordance with rules prescribed by the Secretary of Defense.

``(b) Judges.—

``(1) Judges on the Court shall be assigned or appointed in a manner consistent with the provisions of this subsection.

``(2) The Secretary of Defense may assign persons who are appellate military judges to be judges on the Court. Any judge so assigned shall be a commissioned officer of the armed forces, and shall meet the qualifications for military judges prescribed by section 948j(b) of this title.

``(3) The President may appoint, by and with the advice and consent of the Senate, additional judges to the United States Court of Military Commission Review.

``(4) No person may serve as a judge on the Court in any case in which that person acted as a military judge, counsel, or reviewing official.

``(c) Cases To Be Reviewed.— The Court shall, in accordance with procedures prescribed under regulations of the Secretary, review the record in each case that is referred to the Court by the convening authority under section 950c of this title with respect to any matter properly raised by the accused.

``(d) Standard and Scope of Review.— In a case reviewed by the Court under this section, the Court may act only with respect to the findings and sentence as approved by the convening authority. The Court may affirm only such findings of guilty, and the sentence or such part or amount of the sentence, as the Court finds correct in law and fact and determines, on the basis of the entire record, should be approved. In considering the record, the Court may weigh the evidence, judge the credibility of witnesses, and determine controverted questions of fact, recognizing that the military commission saw and heard the witnesses.

``(e) Rehearings.— If the Court sets aside the findings or sentence, the Court may, except where the setting aside is based on lack of sufficient evidence in the record to support the findings, order a rehearing. If the Court sets aside the findings or sentence and does not order a rehearing, the Court shall order that the charges be dismissed.

``Sec. 950g. Review by United States Court of Appeals for the District of Columbia Circuit; writ of certiorari to Supreme Court

``(a) Exclusive Appellate Jurisdiction.— Except as provided in subsection (b), the United States Court of Appeals for the District of Columbia Circuit shall have exclusive jurisdiction to determine the validity of a final judgment rendered by a military commission (as approved by the convening authority and, where applicable, the United States Court of Military Commission Review) under this chapter.

``(b) Exhaustion of Other Appeals.— The United States Court of Appeals for the District of Columbia Circuit may not review a final judgment described in subsection (a) until all other appeals under this chapter have been waived or exhausted.

``(c) Time for Seeking Review.— A petition for review by the United States Court of Appeals for the District of Columbia Circuit must be filed by the accused in the Court of Appeals not later than 20 days after the date on which—

> ``(1) written notice of the final decision of the United States Court of Military Commission Review is served on the accused or on defense counsel; or

> ``(2) the accused submits, in the form prescribed by section 950c of this title, a written notice waiving the right of the accused to review by the United States Court of Military Commission Review.

``(d) Scope and Nature of Review.— The United States Court of Appeals for the District of Columbia Circuit may act under this section only with respect to the findings and sentence as approved by the convening authority and as affirmed or set aside as incorrect in law by the United States Court of Military Commission Review, and shall take action only with respect to matters of law, including the sufficiency of the evidence to support the verdict.

``(e) Review by Supreme Court.— The Supreme Court may review by writ of certiorari pursuant to section 1254 of title 28 the final judgment of the United States Court of Appeals for the District of Columbia Circuit under this section.

``Sec. 950h. Appellate counsel

``(a) Appointment.— The Secretary of Defense shall, by regulation, establish procedures for the appointment of appellate counsel for the United States and for the accused in military commissions under this chapter. Appellate counsel shall meet the qualifications of counsel for appearing before military commissions under this chapter.

``(b) Representation of United States.— Appellate counsel appointed under subsection (a)—

> ``(1) shall represent the United States in any appeal or review proceeding under this chapter before the United States Court of Military Commission Review; and

> ``(2) may, when requested to do so by the Attorney General in a case arising under this chapter, represent the United States before the United States Court of Appeals for the District of Columbia Circuit or the Supreme Court.

``(c) Representation of Accused.— The accused shall be represented by appellate counsel appointed under subsection (a) before the United States Court of Military Commission Review, the United States Court of Appeals for the District of Columbia Circuit, and the Supreme Court, and by civilian counsel if retained by the accused. Any such civilian counsel shall meet the qualifications under paragraph (3) of section 949c(b) of this title for civilian counsel appearing before military commissions under this chapter and shall be subject to the requirements of paragraph (7) of that section.

``Sec. 950i. Execution of sentence; suspension of sentence

``(a) In General.— The Secretary of Defense is authorized to carry out a sentence imposed by a military commission under this chapter in accordance with such procedures as the Secretary may prescribe.

``(b) Execution of Sentence of Death Only Upon Approval by the President.— If the sentence of a military commission under this chapter extends to death, that part of the sentence providing for death may not be executed until approved by the President. In such a case, the President may commute, remit, or suspend the sentence, or any part thereof, as he sees fit.

``(c) Execution of Sentence of Death Only Upon Final Judgment of Legality of Proceedings.—

``(1) If the sentence of a military commission under this chapter extends to death, the sentence may not be executed until there is a final judgment as to the legality of the proceedings (and with respect to death, approval under subsection (b)).

``(2) A judgment as to legality of proceedings is final for purposes of paragraph (1) when review is completed in accordance with the judgment of the United States Court of Military Commission Review and—

``(A) the time for the accused to file a petition for review by the United States Court of Appeals for the District of Columbia Circuit has expired, the accused has not filed a timely petition for such review, and the case is not otherwise under review by the Court of Appeals; or

``(B) review is completed in accordance with the judgment of the United States Court of Appeals for the District of Columbia Circuit and—

``(i) a petition for a writ of certiorari is not timely filed;

``(ii) such a petition is denied by the Supreme Court; or

``(iii) review is otherwise completed in accordance with the judgment of the Supreme Court.

``(d) Suspension of Sentence.— The Secretary of the Defense, or the convening authority acting on the case (if other than the Secretary), may suspend the execution of any sentence or part thereof in the case, except a sentence of death.

``Sec. 950j. Finality of proceedings, findings, and sentences

``The appellate review of records of trial provided by this chapter, and the proceedings, findings, and sentences of military commissions as approved, reviewed, or affirmed as required by this chapter, are final and conclusive. Orders publishing the proceedings of military commissions under this chapter are binding upon all departments, courts, agencies, and officers of the United States, subject only to action by the Secretary or the convening authority as provided in section 950i(c) of this title and the authority of the President.

``Sec. 950p. Definitions; construction of certain offenses; common circumstances

``(a) Definitions.— In this subchapter:

``(1) The term "military objective" means combatants and those objects during hostilities which, by their nature, location, purpose, or use, effectively contribute to the war-fighting or war-sustaining capability of an opposing force and whose total or partial destruction, capture, or neutralization would constitute a definite military advantage to the attacker under the circumstances at the time of an attack.

``(2) The term "protected person" means any person entitled to protection under one or more of the Geneva Conventions, including civilians not taking an active part in hostilities, military personnel placed out of combat by sickness, wounds, or detention, and military medical or religious personnel.

``(3) The term "protected property" means any property specifically protected by the law of war, including buildings dedicated to religion, education, art, science, or charitable purposes, historic monuments, hospitals, and places where the sick and wounded are collected, but only if and to the extent such property is not being used for military purposes or is not otherwise a military objective. The term includes objects properly identified by one of the distinctive emblems of the Geneva Conventions, but does not include civilian property that is a military objective.

``(b) Construction of Certain Offenses.— The intent required for offenses under paragraphs (1), (2), (3), (4), and (12) of section 950t of this title precludes the applicability of such offenses with regard to collateral damage or to death, damage, or injury incident to a lawful attack.

``(c) Common Circumstances.— An offense specified in this subchapter is triable by military commission under this chapter only if the offense is committed in the context of and associated with hostilities.

``(d) Effect.— The provisions of this subchapter codify offenses that have traditionally been triable by military commission. This chapter does not establish new crimes that did not exist before the date of the enactment of this subchapter, as amended by the National Defense Authorization Act for Fiscal Year 2010, but rather codifies those crimes for trial by military commission. Because the provisions of this subchapter codify offenses that have traditionally been triable under the law of war or otherwise triable by military commission, this subchapter does not preclude trial for offenses that occurred before the date of the enactment of this subchapter, as so amended.

``Sec. 950q. Principals

``Any person punishable under this chapter who—

``(1) commits an offense punishable by this chapter, or aids, abets, counsels, commands, or procures its commission;

``(2) causes an act to be done which if directly performed by him would be punishable by this chapter; or

``(3) is a superior commander who, with regard to acts punishable by this chapter, knew, had reason to know, or should have known, that a subordinate was about to commit such acts or had done so and who failed to take the necessary and reasonable measures to prevent such acts or to punish the perpetrators thereof,

``is a principal.

``Sec. 950r. Accessory after the fact

``Any person subject to this chapter who, knowing that an offense punishable by this chapter has been committed, receives, comforts, or assists the offender in order to hinder or prevent his apprehension, trial, or punishment shall be punished as a military commission under this chapter may direct.

``**Sec. 950s. Conviction of lesser offenses**

``An accused may be found guilty of an offense necessarily included in the offense charged or of an attempt to commit either the offense charged or an attempt to commit either the offense charged or an offense necessarily included therein.

``**Sec. 950t. Crimes triable by military commission**

``The following offenses shall be triable by military commission under this chapter at any time without limitation:

``(1) MURDER OF PROTECTED PERSONS.— Any person subject to this chapter who intentionally kills one or more protected persons shall be punished by death or such other punishment as a military commission under this chapter may direct.

``(2) ATTACKING CIVILIANS.— Any person subject to this chapter who intentionally engages in an attack upon a civilian population as such, or individual civilians not taking active part in hostilities, shall be punished, if death results to one or more of the victims, by death or such other punishment as a military commission under this chapter may direct, and, if death does not result to any of the victims, by such punishment, other than death, as a military commission under this chapter may direct.

``(3) ATTACKING CIVILIAN OBJECTS.— Any person subject to this chapter who intentionally engages in an attack upon a civilian object that is not a military objective shall be punished as a military commission under this chapter may direct.

``(4) ATTACKING PROTECTED PROPERTY.— Any person subject to this chapter who intentionally engages in an attack upon protected property shall be punished as a military commission under this chapter may direct.

``(5) PILLAGING.— Any person subject to this chapter who intentionally and in the absence of military necessity appropriates or seizes property for private or personal use, without the consent of a person with authority to permit such appropriation or seizure, shall be punished as a military commission under this chapter may direct.

``(6) DENYING QUARTER.— Any person subject to this chapter who, with effective command or control over subordinate groups, declares, orders, or otherwise indicates to those groups that there shall be no survivors or surrender accepted, with the intent to threaten an adversary or to conduct hostilities such that there would be no survivors or surrender accepted, shall be punished as a military commission under this chapter may direct.

``(7) TAKING HOSTAGES.— Any person subject to this chapter who, having knowingly seized or detained one or more persons, threatens to kill, injure, or continue to detain such person or persons with the intent of compelling any nation, person other than the hostage, or group of persons to act or refrain from acting as an explicit or implicit condition for the safety or release of such person or persons, shall be punished, if death results to one or more of the victims, by death or such other punishment as a military commission under this chapter may direct, and, if death does not result to any of the victims, by such punishment, other than death, as a military commission under this chapter may direct.

``(8) EMPLOYING POISON OR SIMILAR WEAPONS.— Any person subject to this chapter who intentionally, as a method of warfare, employs a substance or weapon that releases a substance that causes death or serious and lasting damage to health in the ordinary course of events, through its asphyxiating, bacteriological, or toxic properties, shall be punished, if death results to one or more of the victims, by death or such other punishment as a military commission under this chapter may direct, and, if death does not result to any of the victims, by such punishment, other than death, as a military commission under this chapter may direct.

``(9) USING PROTECTED PERSONS AS A SHIELD.— Any person subject to this chapter who positions, or otherwise takes advantage of, a protected person with the intent to shield a military objective from attack, or to shield, favor, or impede military operations, shall be punished, if death results to one or more of the victims, by death or such other punishment as a military commission under this chapter may direct, and, if death does not result to any of the victims, by such punishment, other than death, as a military commission under this chapter may direct.

``(10) USING PROTECTED PROPERTY AS A SHIELD.— Any person subject to this chapter who positions, or otherwise takes advantage of the location of, protected property with the intent to shield a military objective from attack, or to shield, favor, or impede military operations, shall be punished as a military commission under this chapter may direct.

``(11) TORTURE.—

> ``(A) OFFENSE.— Any person subject to this chapter who commits an act specifically intended to inflict severe physical or mental pain or suffering (other than pain or suffering incidental to lawful sanctions) upon another person within his custody or physical control for the purpose of obtaining information or a confession, punishment, intimidation, coercion, or any reason based on discrimination of any kind, shall be punished, if death results to one or more of the victims, by death or such other punishment as a military commission under this chapter may direct, and, if death does not result to any of the victims, by such punishment, other than death, as a military commission under this chapter may direct.

> ``(B) SEVERE MENTAL PAIN OR SUFFERING DEFINED.— In this paragraph, the term "severe mental pain or suffering" has the meaning given that term in section 2340(2) of title 18.

``(12) CRUEL OR INHUMAN TREATMENT.— Any person subject to this chapter who subjects another person in their custody or under their physical control, regardless of nationality or physical location, to cruel or inhuman treatment that constitutes a grave breach of common Article 3 of the Geneva Conventions shall be punished, if death results to the victim, by death or such other punishment as a military commission under this chapter may direct, and, if death does not result to the victim, by such punishment, other than death, as a military commission under this chapter may direct.

``(13) INTENTIONALLY CAUSING SERIOUS BODILY INJURY.—

> ``(A) OFFENSE.— Any person subject to this chapter who intentionally causes serious bodily injury to one or more persons, including privileged belligerents, in violation of the law of war shall be punished, if death

results to one or more of the victims, by death or such other punishment as a military commission under this chapter may direct, and, if death does not result to any of the victims, by such punishment, other than death, as a military commission under this chapter may direct.

``(B) SERIOUS BODILY INJURY DEFINED.— In this paragraph, the term "serious bodily injury" means bodily injury which involves—

``(i) a substantial risk of death;

``(ii) extreme physical pain;

``(iii) protracted and obvious disfigurement; or

``(iv) protracted loss or impairment of the function of a bodily member, organ, or mental faculty.

``(14) MUTILATING OR MAIMING.— Any person subject to this chapter who intentionally injures one or more protected persons by disfiguring the person or persons by any mutilation of the person or persons, or by permanently disabling any member, limb, or organ of the body of the person or persons, without any legitimate medical or dental purpose, shall be punished, if death results to one or more of the victims, by death or such other punishment as a military commission under this chapter may direct, and, if death does not result to any of the victims, by such punishment, other than death, as a military commission under this chapter may direct.

``(15) MURDER IN VIOLATION OF THE LAW OF WAR.— Any person subject to this chapter who intentionally kills one or more persons, including privileged belligerents, in violation of the law of war shall be punished by death or such other punishment as a military commission under this chapter may direct.

``(16) DESTRUCTION OF PROPERTY IN VIOLATION OF THE LAW OF WAR.— Any person subject to this chapter who intentionally destroys property belonging to another person in violation of the law of war shall punished as a military commission under this chapter may direct.

``(17) USING TREACHERY OR PERFIDY.— Any person subject to this chapter who, after inviting the confidence or belief of one or more persons that they were entitled to, or obliged to accord, protection under the law of war, intentionally makes use of that confidence or belief in killing, injuring, or capturing such person or persons shall be punished, if death results to one or more of the victims, by death or such other punishment as a military commission under this chapter may direct, and, if death does not result to any of the victims, by such punishment, other than death, as a military commission under this chapter may direct.

``(18) IMPROPERLY USING A FLAG OF TRUCE.— Any person subject to this chapter who uses a flag of truce to feign an intention to negotiate, surrender, or otherwise suspend hostilities when there is no such intention shall be punished as a military commission under this chapter may direct.

``(19) IMPROPERLY USING A DISTINCTIVE EMBLEM.— Any person subject to this chapter who intentionally uses a distinctive emblem recognized by the law of war for combatant purposes in a manner prohibited by the law of war shall be punished as a military commission under this chapter may direct.

``(20) INTENTIONALLY MISTREATING A DEAD BODY.— Any person subject to this chapter who intentionally mistreats the body of a dead person, without justification by legitimate military necessary, shall be punished as a military commission under this chapter may direct.

``(21) RAPE.— Any person subject to this chapter who forcibly or with coercion or threat of force wrongfully invades the body of a person by penetrating, however slightly, the anal or genital opening of the victim with any part of the body of the accused, or with any foreign object, shall be punished as a military commission under this chapter may direct.

``(22) SEXUAL ASSAULT OR ABUSE.— Any person subject to this chapter who forcibly or with coercion or threat of force engages in sexual contact with one or more persons, or causes one or more persons to engage in sexual contact, shall be punished as a military commission under this chapter may direct.

``(23) HIJACKING OR HAZARDING A VESSEL OR AIRCRAFT.— Any person subject to this chapter who intentionally seizes, exercises unauthorized control over, or endangers the safe navigation of a vessel or aircraft that is not a legitimate military objective shall be punished, if death results to one or more of the victims, by death or such other punishment as a military commission under this chapter may direct, and, if death does not result to any of the victims, by such punishment, other than death, as a military commission under this chapter may direct.

``(24) TERRORISM.— Any person subject to this chapter who intentionally kills or inflicts great bodily harm on one or more protected persons, or intentionally engages in an act that evinces a wanton disregard for human life, in a manner calculated to influence or affect the conduct of government or civilian population by intimidation or coercion, or to retaliate against government conduct, shall be punished, if death results to one or more of the victims, by death or such other punishment as a military commission under this chapter may direct, and, if death does not result to any of the victims, by such punishment, other than death, as a military commission under this chapter may direct.

``(25) PROVIDING MATERIAL SUPPORT FOR TERRORISM.—

    ``(A) OFFENSE.— Any person subject to this chapter who provides material support or resources, knowing or intending that they are to be used in preparation for, or in carrying out, an act of terrorism (as set forth in paragraph (24) of this section), or who intentionally provides material support or resources to an international terrorist organization engaged in hostilities against the United States, knowing that such organization has engaged or engages in terrorism (as so set forth), shall be punished as a military commission under this chapter may direct.

    ``(B) MATERIAL SUPPORT OR RESOURCES DEFINED.— In this paragraph, the term "material support or resources" has the meaning given that term in section 2339A(b) of title 18.

``(26) WRONGFULLY AIDING THE ENEMY.— Any person subject to this chapter who, in breach of an allegiance or duty to the United States, knowingly and intentionally aids an enemy of the United States, or one of the co-belligerents of the enemy, shall be punished as a military commission under this chapter may direct.

``(27) SPYING.— Any person subject to this chapter who, in violation of the law of war and with intent or reason to believe that it is to be used to the injury of the United States or to the advantage of a foreign power, collects or attempts to collect information by clandestine means or while acting under false pretenses, for the purpose of conveying such information to an enemy of the United States, or one of the co-belligerents of the enemy, shall be punished by death or such other punishment as a military commission under this chapter may direct.

``(28) ATTEMPTS.—

> ``(A) IN GENERAL.— Any person subject to this chapter who attempts to commit any offense punishable by this chapter shall be punished as a military commission under this chapter may direct.

> ``(B) SCOPE OF OFFENSE.— An act, done with specific intent to commit an offense under this chapter, amounting to more than mere preparation and tending, even though failing, to effect its commission, is an attempt to commit that offense.

> ``(C) EFFECT OF CONSUMMATION.— Any person subject to this chapter may be convicted of an attempt to commit an offense although it appears on the trial that the offense was consummated.

``(29) CONSPIRACY.— Any person subject to this chapter who conspires to commit one or more substantive offenses triable by military commission under this subchapter, and who knowingly does any overt act to effect the object of the conspiracy, shall be punished, if death results to one or more of the victims, by death or such other punishment as a military commission under this chapter may direct, and, if death does not result to any of the victims, by such punishment, other than death, as a military commission under this chapter may direct.

``(30) SOLICITATION.— Any person subject to this chapter who solicits or advises another or others to commit one or more substantive offenses triable by military commission under this chapter shall, if the offense solicited or advised is attempted or committed, be punished with the punishment provided for the commission of the offense, but, if the offense solicited or advised is not committed or attempted, shall be punished as a military commission under this chapter may direct.

``(31) CONTEMPT.— A military commission under this chapter may punish for contempt any person who uses any menacing word, sign, or gesture in its presence, or who disturbs its proceedings by any riot or disorder.

``(32) PERJURY AND OBSTRUCTION OF JUSTICE.— A military commission under this chapter may try offenses and impose such punishment as the military commission may direct for perjury, false testimony, or obstruction of justice related to the military commission.´´.

Sec. 1803. Conforming amendments.

(a) Uniform Code of Military Justice.—

(1) PERSONS SUBJECT TO UCMJ.—

Paragraph (13) of section 802(a) of title 10, United States Code (article 2(a) of the Uniform Code of Military Justice), is amended to read as follows:

``(13) Individuals belonging to one of the eight categories enumerated in Article 4 of the Convention Relative to the Treatment of Prisoners of War, done at Geneva August 12, 1949 (6 UST 3316), who violate the law of war.''.

(2) CONSTRUCTION OF MILITARY COMMISSIONS WITH COURTS-MARTIAL.—

Section 839 of such title (article 39 of the Uniform Code of Military Justice) is amended by adding at the end the following new subsection:

``(d) The findings, holdings, interpretations, and other precedents of military commissions under chapter 47A of this title—

``(1) may not be introduced or considered in any hearing, trial, or other proceeding of a court-martial under this chapter; and

``(2) may not form the basis of any holding, decision, or other determination of a court-martial.''.

(b) Appellate Review Under Detainee Treatment Act of 2005.—

Section 1005(e) of the Detainee Treatment Act of 2005 (title X of Public Law 109-359 [1]; 10 U.S.C. 801 note) is amended by striking paragraph (3).

Sec. 1804. Proceedings under prior statute.

(a) Prior Convictions.—

The amendment made by section 1802 shall have no effect on the validity of any conviction pursuant to chapter 47A of title 10, United States Code (as such chapter was in effect on the day before the date of the enactment of this Act).

(b) Composition of Military Commissions.—

Notwithstanding the amendment made by section 1802—

(1) any commission convened pursuant to chapter 47A of title 10, United States Code (as such chapter was in effect on the day before the date of the enactment of this Act), shall be deemed to have been convened pursuant to chapter 47A of title 10, United States Code (as amended by section 1802);

(2) any member of the Armed Forces detailed to serve on a commission pursuant to chapter 47A of title 10, United States Code (as in effect on the day before the date of the enactment of this Act), shall be deemed to have been detailed pursuant to chapter 47A of title 10, United States Code (as so amended);

(3) any military judge detailed to a commission pursuant to chapter 47A of title 10, United States Code (as in effect on the day before the date of the enactment of this Act), shall be deemed to have been detailed pursuant to chapter 47A of title 10, United States Code (as so amended);

(4) any trial counsel or defense counsel detailed for a commission pursuant to chapter 47A of title 10, United States Code (as in effect on the day before the date of the enactment of this Act), shall be deemed to have been detailed pursuant to chapter 47A of title 10, United States Code (as so amended);

(5) any court reporters detailed to or employed by a commission pursuant to chapter 47A of title 10, United States Code (as in effect on the day before the date of the enactment of this Act), shall be deemed to have been detailed or employed pursuant to chapter 47A of title 10, United States Code (as so amended); and

(6) any appellate military judge or other duly appointed appellate judge on the Court of Military Commission Review pursuant to chapter 47A of title 10, United States Code (as in effect on the day before the date of the enactment of this Act), shall be deemed to have been detailed or appointed to the United States Court of Military Commission Review pursuant to chapter 47A of title 10, United States Code (as so amended).

(c) Charges and Specifications.—

Notwithstanding the amendment made by section 1802—

(1) any charges or specifications sworn or referred pursuant to chapter 47A of title 10, United States Code (as such chapter was in effect on the day before the date of the enactment of this Act), shall be deemed to have been sworn or referred pursuant to chapter 47A of title 10, United States Code (as amended by section 1802); and

(2) any charges or specifications described in paragraph (1) may be amended, without prejudice, as needed to properly allege jurisdiction under chapter 47A of title 10, United States Code (as so amended), and crimes triable under such chapter.

(d) Procedures and Requirements.—

(1) IN GENERAL.—
Except as provided in subsections (a) through (c) and subject to paragraph (2), any commission convened pursuant to chapter 47A of title 10, United States Code (as such chapter was in effect on the day before the date of the enactment of this Act), shall be conducted after the date of the enactment of this Act in accordance with the procedures and requirements of chapter 47A of title 10, United States Code (as amended by section 1802).

(2) TEMPORARY CONTINUATION OF PRIOR PROCEDURES AND REQUIREMENTS.—

Any military commission described in paragraph (1) may be conducted in accordance with any procedures and requirements of chapter 47A of title 10, United States Code (as in effect on the day before the date of the enactment of this Act), that are not inconsistent with the provisions of chapter 47A of title 10, United States Code, (as so amended), until the earlier of—

(A) the date of the submittal to Congress under section 1805 of the revised rules for military commissions under chapter 47A of title 10, United States Code (as so amended); or

(B) the date that is 90 days after the date of the enactment of this Act.

Sec. 1805. Submittal to Congress of revised rules for military commissions.

(a) Deadline for Submittal.—

Not later than 90 days after the date of the enactment of this Act, the Secretary of Defense shall submit to the Committees on Armed Services of the Senate and the House of Representatives the revised rules for military commissions prescribed by the Secretary for purposes of chapter 47A of title 10, United States Code (as amended by section 1802).

(b) Treatment of Revised Rules Under Requirement for Notice and Wait Regarding Modification of Rules.—

The revised rules submitted to Congress under subsection (a) shall not be treated as a modification of the rules in effect for military commissions for purposes of section 949a(d) of title 10, United States Code (as so amended).

Sec. 1806. Annual reports to Congress on trials by military commission.

(a) Annual Reports Required.—

Not later than January 31 of each year, the Secretary of Defense shall submit to the Committees on Armed Services of the Senate and the House of Representatives a report on any trials conducted by military commissions under chapter 47A of title 10, United States Code (as amended by section 1802), during the preceding year.

(b) Form.—

Each report under this section shall be submitted in unclassified form, but may include a classified annex.

Sec. 1807. Sense of Congress on military commission system.

It is the sense of Congress that—

(1) the fairness and effectiveness of the military commissions system under chapter 47A of title 10, United States Code (as amended by section 1802), will depend to a significant degree on the adequacy of defense counsel and associated resources for individuals accused, particularly in the case of capital cases, under such chapter 47A; and

(2) defense counsel in military commission cases, particularly in capital cases, under such chapter 47A of title 10, United States Code (as so amended), should be fully resourced as provided in such chapter 47A.

4.14.1 Notes

[1] So in original, probably should be Title X of Public Law 109-148

4.15 Division E

4.15.1 DIVISION E — MATTHEW SHEPARD AND JAMES BYRD, JR. HATE CRIMES PREVENTION ACT

Sec. 4701. Short Title.

This division may be cited as the ``**Matthew Shepard and James Byrd, Jr. Hate Crimes Prevention Act**''.

Sec. 4702. Findings.

Congress makes the following findings:

(1) The incidence of violence motivated by the actual or perceived race, color, religion, national origin, gender, sexual orientation, gender identity, or disability of the victim poses a serious national problem.

(2) Such violence disrupts the tranquility and safety of communities and is deeply divisive.

(3) State and local authorities are now and will continue to be responsible for prosecuting the overwhelming majority of violent crimes in the United States, including violent crimes motivated by bias. These authorities can carry out their responsibilities more effectively with greater Federal assistance.

(4) Existing Federal law is inadequate to address this problem.

(5) A prominent characteristic of a violent crime motivated by bias is that it devastates not just the actual victim and the family and friends of the victim, but frequently savages the community sharing the traits that caused the victim to be selected.

(6) Such violence substantially affects interstate commerce in many ways, including the following:

(A) The movement of members of targeted groups is impeded, and members of such groups are forced to move across State lines to escape the incidence or risk of such violence.

(B) Members of targeted groups are prevented from purchasing goods and services, obtaining or sustaining employment, or participating in other commercial activity.

(C) Perpetrators cross State lines to commit such violence.

(D) Channels, facilities, and instrumentalities of interstate commerce are used to facilitate the commission of such violence.

(E) Such violence is committed using articles that have traveled in interstate commerce.

(7) For generations, the institutions of slavery and involuntary servitude were defined by the race, color, and ancestry of those held in bondage. Slavery and involuntary servitude were enforced, both prior to and after the adoption of the 13th amendment to the Constitution of the United States, through widespread public and private violence directed at persons because of their race, color, or ancestry, or perceived race, color, or ancestry. Accordingly, eliminating racially motivated violence is an important means of eliminating, to the extent possible, the badges, incidents, and relics of slavery and involuntary servitude.

(8) Both at the time when the 13th, 14th, and 15th amendments to the Constitution of the United States were adopted, and continuing to date, members of certain religious and national origin groups were and are perceived to be distinct "races". Thus, in order to eliminate, to the extent possible, the badges, incidents, and relics of slavery, it is necessary to prohibit assaults on the basis of real or perceived religions or national origins, at least to the extent such religions or national origins were regarded as races at the time of the adoption of the 13th, 14th, and 15th amendments to the Constitution of the United States.

(9) Federal jurisdiction over certain violent crimes motivated by bias enables Federal, State, and local authorities to work together as partners in the investigation and prosecution of such crimes.

(10) The problem of crimes motivated by bias is sufficiently serious, widespread, and interstate in nature as to warrant Federal assistance to States, local jurisdictions, and Indian tribes.

Sec. 4703. Definitions.

(a) Amendment.—

Section 280003(a) of the Violent Crime Control and Law Enforcement Act of 1994 (Public Law 103-322; 108 Stat. 2096) is amended by inserting "gender identity," after "gender,".

(b) This Division.—

In this division—

(1) the term "crime of violence" has the meaning given that term in section 16 of title 18, United States Code;

(2) the term "hate crime" has the meaning given that term in section 280003(a) [1] of the Violent Crime Control and Law Enforcement Act of 1994 (Public Law 103-322; 108 Stat. 2096), as amended by this Act;

(3) the term "local" means a county, city, town, township, parish, village, or other general purpose political subdivision of a State; and

(4) the term "State" includes the District of Columbia, Puerto Rico, and any other territory or possession of the United States.

Sec. 4704. Support for Criminal Investigations and Prosecutions by State, Local, and Tribal Law Enforcement Officials.

(a) Assistance Other Than Financial Assistance.—

    (1) IN GENERAL.—

        At the request of a State, local, or tribal law enforcement agency, the Attorney General may provide technical, forensic, prosecutorial, or any other form of assistance in the criminal investigation or prosecution of any crime that—

        (A) constitutes a crime of violence;

        (B) constitutes a felony under the State, local, or tribal laws; and

        (C) is motivated by prejudice based on the actual or perceived race, color, religion, national origin, gender, sexual orientation, gender identity, or disability of the victim, or is a violation of the State, local, or tribal hate crime laws.

    (2) PRIORITY.—

        In providing assistance under paragraph (1), the Attorney General shall give priority to crimes committed by offenders who have committed crimes in more than one State and to rural jurisdictions that have difficulty covering the extraordinary expenses relating to the investigation or prosecution of the crime.

(b) Grants.—

    (1) IN GENERAL.—

        The Attorney General may award grants to State, local, and tribal law enforcement agencies for extraordinary expenses associated with the investigation and prosecution of hate crimes.

    (2) OFFICE OF JUSTICE PROGRAMS.—

        In implementing the grant program under this subsection, the Office of Justice Programs shall work closely with grantees to ensure that the concerns and needs of all affected parties, including community groups and schools, colleges, and universities, are addressed through the local infrastructure developed under the grants.

    (3) APPLICATION.—

        (A) IN GENERAL.—

        Each State, local, and tribal law enforcement agency that desires a grant under this subsection shall submit an application to the Attorney General at such time, in such manner, and accompanied by or containing such information as the Attorney General shall reasonably require.

        (B) DATE FOR SUBMISSION.—

        Applications submitted pursuant to subparagraph (A) shall be submitted during the 60-day period beginning on a date that the Attorney General shall prescribe.

(C) REQUIREMENTS.—

A State, local, and tribal law enforcement agency applying for a grant under this subsection shall—

(i) describe the extraordinary purposes for which the grant is needed;

(ii) certify that the State, local government, or Indian tribe lacks the resources necessary to investigate or prosecute the hate crime;

(iii) demonstrate that, in developing a plan to implement the grant, the State, local, and tribal law enforcement agency has consulted and coordinated with nonprofit, nongovernmental victim services programs that have experience in providing services to victims of hate crimes; and

(iv) certify that any Federal funds received under this subsection will be used to supplement, not supplant, non-Federal funds that would otherwise be available for activities funded under this subsection.

(4) DEADLINE.—

An application for a grant under this subsection shall be approved or denied by the Attorney General not later than 180 business days after the date on which the Attorney General receives the application.

(5) GRANT AMOUNT.—

A grant under this subsection shall not exceed $100,000 for any single jurisdiction in any 1-year period.

(6) REPORT.—

Not later than December 31, 2011, the Attorney General shall submit to Congress a report describing the applications submitted for grants under this subsection, the award of such grants, and the purposes for which the grant amounts were expended.

(7) AUTHORIZATION OF APPROPRIATIONS.—

There is authorized to be appropriated to carry out this subsection $5,000,000 for each of fiscal years 2010, 2011, and 2012.

Sec. 4705. Grant Program.

(a) Authority to Award Grants.—

The Office of Justice Programs of the Department of Justice may award grants, in accordance with such regulations as the Attorney General may prescribe, to State, local, or tribal programs designed to combat hate crimes committed by juveniles, including programs to train local law enforcement officers in identifying, investigating, prosecuting, and preventing hate crimes.

(b) Authorization of Appropriations.—

There are authorized to be appropriated such sums as may be necessary to carry out this section.

Sec. 4706. Authorization for Additional Personnel to Assist State, Local, and Tribal Law Enforcement.

There are authorized to be appropriated to the Department of Justice, including the Community Relations Service, for fiscal years 2010, 2011, and 2012 such sums as are necessary to increase the number of personnel to prevent and respond to alleged violations of section 249 of title 18, United States Code, as added by section 4707 of this division.

Sec. 4707. Prohibition of Certain Hate Crime Acts.

(a) In General.-

Chapter 13 of title 18, United States Code, is amended by adding at the end the following:

``**Sec. 249. Hate Crime Acts**

``(a) In General.—

``(1) OFFENSES INVOLVING ACTUAL OR PERCEIVED RACE, COLOR, RELIGION, OR NATIONAL ORIGIN.— Whoever, whether or not acting under color of law, willfully causes bodily injury to any person or, through the use of fire, a firearm, a dangerous weapon, or an explosive or incendiary device, attempts to cause bodily injury to any person, because of the actual or perceived race, color, religion, or national origin of any person—

``(A) shall be imprisoned not more than 10 years, fined in accordance with this title, or both; and

``(B) shall be imprisoned for any term of years or for life, fined in accordance with this title, or both, if—

``(i) death results from the offense; or

``(ii) the offense includes kidnapping or an attempt to kidnap, aggravated sexual abuse or an attempt to commit aggravated sexual abuse, or an attempt to kill.

``(2) OFFENSES INVOLVING ACTUAL OR PERCEIVED RELIGION, NATIONAL ORIGIN, GENDER, SEXUAL ORIENTATION, GENDER IDENTITY, OR DISABILITY.—

``(A) IN GENERAL.— Whoever, whether or not acting under color of law, in any circumstance described in subparagraph (B) or paragraph (3), willfully causes bodily injury to any person or, through the use of fire, a firearm, a dangerous weapon, or an explosive or incendiary device, attempts to cause bodily injury to any person, because of the actual or perceived religion, national origin, gender, sexual orientation, gender identity, or disability of any person—

``(i) shall be imprisoned not more than 10 years, fined in accordance with this title, or both; and

``(ii) shall be imprisoned for any term of years or for life, fined in accordance with this title, or both, if—

``(I) death results from the offense; or

``(II) the offense includes kidnapping or an attempt to kidnap, aggravated sexual abuse or an attempt to commit aggravated sexual abuse, or an attempt to kill.

``(B) CIRCUMSTANCES DESCRIBED.— For purposes of subparagraph (A), the circumstances described in this subparagraph are that—

``(i) the conduct described in subparagraph (A) occurs during the course of, or as the result of, the travel of the defendant or the victim—

``(I) across a State line or national border; or

``(II) using a channel, facility, or instrumentality of interstate or foreign commerce;

``(ii) the defendant uses a channel, facility, or instrumentality of interstate or foreign commerce in connection with the conduct described in subparagraph (A);

``(iii) in connection with the conduct described in subparagraph (A), the defendant employs a firearm, dangerous weapon, explosive or incendiary device, or other weapon that has traveled in interstate or foreign commerce; or

``(iv) the conduct described in subparagraph (A)—

``(I) interferes with commercial or other economic activity in which the victim is engaged at the time of the conduct; or

``(II) otherwise affects interstate or foreign commerce.

``(3) OFFENSES OCCURRING IN THE SPECIAL MARITIME OR TERRITORIAL JURISDICTION OF THE UNITED STATES.— Whoever, within the special maritime or territorial jurisdiction of the United States, engages in conduct described in paragraph (1) or in paragraph (2)(A) (without regard to whether that conduct occurred in a circumstance described in paragraph (2)(B)) shall be subject to the same penalties as prescribed in those paragraphs.

``(b) Certification Requirement.—

``(1) IN GENERAL.— No prosecution of any offense described in this subsection may be undertaken by the United States, except under the certification in writing of the Attorney General, or a designee, that—

``(A) the State does not have jurisdiction;

``(B) the State has requested that the Federal Government assume jurisdiction;

``(C) the verdict or sentence obtained pursuant to State charges left demonstratively unvindicated the Federal interest in eradicating bias-motivated violence; or

``(D) a prosecution by the United States is in the public interest and necessary to secure substantial justice.

``(2) RULE OF CONSTRUCTION.— Nothing in this subsection shall be construed to limit the authority of Federal officers, or a Federal grand jury, to investigate possible violations of this section.

``(c) Definitions.— In this section—

``(1) the term "bodily injury" has the meaning given such term in section 1365(h)(4) of this title, but does not include solely emotional or psychological harm to the victim;

``(2) the term "explosive or incendiary device" has the meaning given such term in section 232 of this title;

``(3) the term "firearm" has the meaning given such term in section 921(a) of this title;

``(4) the term "gender identity" means actual or perceived gender-related characteristics; and

``(5) the term "State" includes the District of Columbia, Puerto Rico, and any other territory or possession of the United States.

``(d) Statute of Limitations.—

``(1) OFFENSES NOT RESULTING IN DEATH.— Except as provided in paragraph (2), no person shall be prosecuted, tried, or punished for any offense under this section unless the indictment for such offense is found, or the information for such offense is instituted, not later than 7 years after the date on which the offense was committed.

``(2) DEATH RESULTING OFFENSES.— An indictment or information alleging that an offense under this section resulted in death may be found or instituted at any time without limitation.``.

(b) Technical and Conforming Amendment.—

The table of sections for chapter 13 of title 18, United States Code, is amended by adding at the end the following:

``**§ 249. Hate crime acts.**``.

Sec. 4708. Statistics.

(a) In General.—

Subsection (b)(1) of the first section of the Hate Crime Statistics Act (28 U.S.C. 534 note) is amended by inserting "gender and gender identity," after "race,".

(b) Data.—

Subsection (b)(5) of the first section of the Hate Crime Statistics Act (28 U.S.C. 534 note) is amended by inserting ", including data about crimes committed by, and crimes directed against, juveniles" after "data acquired under this section".

Sec. 4709. Severability.

If any provision of this division, an amendment made by this division, or the application of such provision or amendment to any person or circumstance is held to be unconstitutional, the remainder of this division, the amendments made by this division, and the application of the provisions of such to any person or circumstance shall not be affected thereby.

Sec. 4710. Rule of Construction.

For purposes of construing this division and the amendments made by this division the following shall apply:

(1) IN GENERAL.—
Nothing in this division shall be construed to allow a court, in any criminal trial for an offense described under this division or an amendment made by this division, in the absence of a stipulation by the parties, to admit evidence of speech, beliefs, association, group membership, or expressive conduct unless that evidence is relevant and admissible under the Federal Rules of Evidence. Nothing in this division is intended to affect the existing rules of evidence.

(2) VIOLENT ACTS.—
This division applies to violent acts motivated by actual or perceived race, color, religion, national origin, gender, sexual orientation, gender identity, or disability of a victim.

(3) CONSTRUCTION AND APPLICATION.—
Nothing in this division, or an amendment made by this division, shall be construed or applied in a manner that infringes any rights under the first amendment to the Constitution of the United States. Nor shall anything in this division, or an amendment made by this division, be construed or applied in a manner that substantially burdens a person's exercise of religion (regardless of whether compelled by, or central to, a system of religious belief), speech, expression, or association, unless the Government demonstrates that application of the burden to the person is in furtherance of a compelling governmental interest and is the least restrictive means of furthering that compelling governmental interest, if such exercise of religion, speech, expression, or association was not intended to—

(A) plan or prepare for an act of physical violence; or

(B) incite an imminent act of physical violence against another.

(4) FREE EXPRESSION.—

Nothing in this division shall be construed to allow prosecution based solely upon an individual's expression of racial, religious, political, or other beliefs or solely upon an individual's membership in a group advocating or espousing such beliefs.

(5) FIRST AMENDMENT.—

Nothing in this division, or an amendment made by this division, shall be construed to diminish any rights under the first amendment to the Constitution of the United States.

(6) CONSTITUTIONAL PROTECTIONS.—

Nothing in this division shall be construed to prohibit any constitutionally protected speech, expressive conduct or activities (regardless of whether compelled by, or central to, a system of religious belief), including the exercise of religion protected by the first amendment to the Constitution of the United States and peaceful picketing or demonstration. The Constitution of the United States does not protect speech, conduct or activities consisting of planning for, conspiring to commit, or committing an act of violence.

Sec. 4711. Guidelines for Hate-Crimes Offenses.

Section 249(a) of title 18, United States Code, as added by section 4707 of this Act, is amended by adding at the end the following:

``(4) GUIDELINES.— All prosecutions conducted by the United States under this section shall be undertaken pursuant to guidelines issued by the Attorney General, or the designee of the Attorney General, to be included in the United States Attorneys' Manual that shall establish neutral and objective criteria for determining whether a crime was committed because of the actual or perceived status of any person.´´.

Sec. 4712. Attacks on United States Servicemen.

(a) In General.—

Chapter 67 of title 18, United States Code, is amended by adding at the end the following:

``Sec. 1389. Prohibition on attacks on United States servicemen on account of service

``(a) In General.— Whoever knowingly assaults or batters a United States serviceman or an immediate family member of a United States serviceman, or who knowingly destroys or injures the property of such serviceman or immediate family member, on account of the military service of that serviceman or status of that individual as a United States serviceman, or who attempts or conspires to do so, shall—

``(1) in the case of a simple assault, or destruction or injury to property in which the damage or attempted damage to such property is not more than $500, be fined under this title in an amount not less than $500 nor more than $10,000 and imprisoned not more than 2 years;

``(2) in the case of destruction or injury to property in which the damage or attempted damage to such property is more than $500, be fined under this title in an amount not less than $1000 nor more than $100,000 and imprisoned not more than 5 years; and

``(3) in the case of a battery, or an assault resulting in bodily injury, be fined under this title in an amount not less than $2500 and imprisoned not less than 6 months nor more than 10 years.

``(b) Exception.— This section shall not apply to conduct by a person who is subject to the Uniform Code of Military Justice.

``(c) Definitions.— In this section—

    ``(1) the term "Armed Forces" has the meaning given that term in section 1388;

    ``(2) the term "immediate family member" has the meaning given that term in section 115; and

    ``(3) the term "United States serviceman"—

        ``(A) means a member of the Armed Forces; and

        ``(B) includes a former member of the Armed Forces during the 5-year period beginning on the date of the discharge from the Armed Forces of that member of the Armed Forces.``.

(b) Technical and Conforming Amendment.—

The table of sections for chapter 67 of title 18, United States Code, is amended by adding at the end the following:

    ``§ 1389. Prohibition on attacks on United States servicemen on account of service.``.

Sec. 4713. Report on Mandatory Minimum Sentencing Provisions.

(a) Report.—

Not later than 1 year after the date of enactment of this Act, the United States Sentencing Commission shall submit to the Committee on the Judiciary of the Senate and the Committee on the Judiciary of the House of Representatives a report on mandatory minimum sentencing provisions under Federal law.

(b) Contents of Report.—

The report submitted under subsection (a) shall include—

    (1) a compilation of all mandatory minimum sentencing provisions under Federal law;

    (2) an assessment of the effect of mandatory minimum sentencing provisions under Federal law on the goal of eliminating unwarranted sentencing disparity and other goals of sentencing;

    (3) an assessment of the impact of mandatory minimum sentencing provisions on the Federal prison population;

(4) an assessment of the compatibility of mandatory minimum sentencing provisions under Federal law and the sentencing guidelines system established under the Sentencing Reform Act of 1984 (Public Law 98-473; 98 Stat. 1987) and the sentencing guidelines system in place after *Booker v. United States*, 543 U.S. 220 (2005);

(5) a description of the interaction between mandatory minimum sentencing provisions under Federal law and plea agreements;

(6) a detailed empirical research study of the effect of mandatory minimum penalties under Federal law;

(7) a discussion of mechanisms other than mandatory minimum sentencing laws by which Congress can take action with respect to sentencing policy; and

(8) any other information that the Commission determines would contribute to a thorough assessment of mandatory minimum sentencing provisions under Federal law.

4.15.2   Notes

[1] Set out as Sentencing Guideline under *Notes* of 28 U.S.C. 994

(Pub. L. 103–322, title XXVIII, § 280003(a), Sept. 13, 1994, 108 Stat. 2096.)

— The sub-section read exactly as follows:

(a) Definition.—

In this section, "hate crime" means a crime in which the defendant intentionally selects a victim, or in the case of a property crime, the property that is the object of the crime, because of the actual or perceived race, color, religion, national origin, ethnicity, gender, disability, or sexual orientation of any person.

4.16   Worker, Homeownership, and Business Assistance Act of 2009

111TH UNITED STATES CONGRESS
1ST SESSION

An Act
To amend the Supplemental Appropriations Act, 2008 to provide for the temporary availability of certain additional emergency unemployment compensation, and for other purposes.

Be it enacted by the Senate and House of Representatives of the United States of America in Congress assembled,

Section 1.   Short Title.

This Act may be cited as the ``**Worker, Homeownership, and Business Assistance Act of 2009**´´.

Sec. 2. Revisions to Second–Tier Benefits.

(a) In General.—

Section 4002(c) of the Supplemental Appropriations Act, 2008 (Public Law 110-252; 26 U.S.C. 3304 note) is amended—

(1) in paragraph (1)—

(A) in the matter preceding subparagraph (A), by striking "If" and all that follows through "paragraph (2))" and inserting "At the time that the amount established in an individual's account under subsection (b)(1) is exhausted";

(B) in subparagraph (A), by striking "50 percent" and inserting "54 percent"; and

(C) in subparagraph (B), by striking "13" and inserting "14";

(2) by striking paragraph (2); and

(3) by redesignating paragraph (3) as paragraph (2).

(b) Effective Date.—

The amendments made by this section shall apply as if included in the enactment of the Supplemental Appropriations Act, 2008, except that no amount shall be payable by virtue of such amendments with respect to any week of unemployment commencing before the date of the enactment of this Act.

Sec. 3. Third–Tier Emergency Unemployment Compensation.

(a) In General.—

Section 4002 of the Supplemental Appropriations Act, 2008 (Public Law 110-252; 26 U.S.C. 3304 note) is amended by adding at the end the following new subsection:

``(d) Third–Tier Emergency Unemployment Compensation.—

``(1) IN GENERAL.—If, at the time that the amount added to an individual's account under subsection (c)(1) (hereinafter 'second-tier emergency unemployment compensation') is exhausted or at any time thereafter, such individual's State is in an extended benefit period (as determined under paragraph (2)), such account shall be further augmented by an amount (hereinafter 'third-tier emergency unemployment compensation') equal to the lesser of—

``(A) 50 percent of the total amount of regular compensation (including dependents' allowances) payable to the individual during the individual's benefit year under the State law; or

``(B) 13 times the individual's average weekly benefit amount (as determined under subsection (b)(2)) for the benefit year.

``(2) EXTENDED BENEFIT PERIOD.—For purposes of paragraph (1), a State shall be considered to be in an extended benefit period, as of any given time, if—

    ``(A) such a period would then be in effect for such State under such Act if section 203(d) of such Act—

        ``(i) were applied by substituting '4' for '5' each place it appears; and

        ``(ii) did not include the requirement under paragraph (1)(A) thereof; or

    ``(B) such a period would then be in effect for such State under such Act if—

        ``(i) section 203(f) of such Act were applied to such State (regardless of whether the State by law had provided for such application); and

        ``(ii) such section 203(f)—

            ``(I) were applied by substituting '6.0' for '6.5' in paragraph (1)(A)(i) thereof; and

            ``(II) did not include the requirement under paragraph (1)(A)(ii) thereof.

    ``(3) LIMITATION.—The account of an individual may be augmented not more than once under this subsection.``.

(b) Conforming Amendment to Non-Augmentation Rule.—

    Section 4007(b)(2) of the Supplemental Appropriations Act, 2008 (Public Law 110-252; 26 U.S.C. 3304 note) is amended—

    (1) by striking "then section 4002(c)" and inserting "then subsections (c) and (d) of section 4002"; and

    (2) by striking "paragraph (2) of such section)" and inserting "paragraph (2) of such subsection (c) or (d) (as the case may be))".

(c) Effective Date.—

    The amendments made by this section shall apply as if included in the enactment of the Supplemental Appropriations Act, 2008, except that no amount shall be payable by virtue of such amendments with respect to any week of unemployment commencing before the date of the enactment of this Act.

Sec. 4. Fourth–Tier Emergency Unemployment Compensation.

(a) In General.—

Section 4002 of the Supplemental Appropriations Act, 2008 (Public Law 110-252; 26 U.S.C. 3304 note), as amended by section 3(a), is amended by adding at the end the following new subsection:

``(e) Fourth–Tier Emergency Unemployment Compensation.—

``(1) IN GENERAL.—If, at the time that the amount added to an individual's account under subsection (d)(1) (third-tier emergency unemployment compensation) is exhausted or at any time thereafter, such individual's State is in an extended benefit period (as determined under paragraph (2)), such account shall be further augmented by an amount (hereinafter 'fourth-tier emergency unemployment compensation') equal to the lesser of—

``(A) 24 percent of the total amount of regular compensation (including dependents' allowances) payable to the individual during the individual's benefit year under the State law; or

``(B) 6 times the individual's average weekly benefit amount (as determined under subsection (b)(2)) for the benefit year.

``(2) EXTENDED BENEFIT PERIOD.—For purposes of paragraph (1), a State shall be considered to be in an extended benefit period, as of any given time, if—

``(A) such a period would then be in effect for such State under such Act if section 203(d) of such Act—

``(i) were applied by substituting '6' for '5' each place it appears; and

``(ii) did not include the requirement under paragraph (1)(A) thereof; or

``(B) such a period would then be in effect for such State under such Act if—

``(i) section 203(f) of such Act were applied to such State (regardless of whether the State by law had provided for such application); and

``(ii) such section 203(f)—

``(I) were applied by substituting '8.5' for '6.5' in paragraph (1)(A)(i) thereof; and

``(II) did not include the requirement under paragraph (1)(A)(ii) thereof.

``(3) LIMITATION.—The account of an individual may be augmented not more than once under this subsection.´´.

(b) Conforming Amendment to Non-Augmentation Rule.—

Section 4007(b)(2) of the Supplemental Appropriations Act, 2008 (Public Law 110-252; 26 U.S.C. 3304 note), as amended by section 3(b), is amended—

(1) by striking "and (d)" and inserting ", (d), and (e) of section 4002"; and

(2) by striking "or (d)" and inserting ", (d), or (e) (as the case may be))".

(c) Effective Date.—

The amendments made by this section shall apply as if included in the enactment of the Supplemental Appropriations Act, 2008, except that no amount shall be payable by virtue of such amendments with respect to any week of unemployment commencing before the date of the enactment of this Act.

Sec. 5. Coordination.

Section 4002 of the Supplemental Appropriations Act, 2008 (Public Law 110-252; 26 U.S.C. 3304 note), as amended by section 4, is amended by adding at the end the following new subsection:

``(f) Coordination Rules.—

``(1) COORDINATION WITH EXTENDED COMPENSATION.—Notwithstanding an election under section 4001(e) by a State to provide for the payment of emergency unemployment compensation prior to extended compensation, such State may pay extended compensation to an otherwise eligible individual prior to any emergency unemployment compensation under subsection (c), (d), or (e) (by reason of the amendments made by sections 2, 3, and 4 of the Worker, Homeownership, and Business Assistance Act of 2009), if such individual claimed extended compensation for at least 1 week of unemployment after the exhaustion of emergency unemployment compensation under subsection (b) (as such subsection was in effect on the day before the date of the enactment of this subsection).

``(2) COORDINATION WITH TIERS II, III, AND IV.—If a State determines that implementation of the increased entitlement to second-tier emergency unemployment compensation by reason of the amendments made by section 2 of the Worker, Homeownership, and Business Assistance Act of 2009 would unduly delay the prompt payment of emergency unemployment compensation under this title by reason of the amendments made by such Act, such State may elect to pay third-tier emergency unemployment compensation prior to the payment of such increased second-tier emergency unemployment compensation until such time as such State determines that such increased second-tier emergency unemployment compensation may be paid without such undue delay. If a State makes the election under the preceding sentence, then, for purposes of determining whether an account may be augmented for fourth-tier emergency unemployment compensation under subsection (e), such State shall treat the date of exhaustion of such increased second-tier emergency unemployment compensation as the date of exhaustion of third-tier emergency unemployment compensation, if such date is later than the date of exhaustion of the third-tier emergency unemployment compensation.´´.

Sec. 6. Transfer of Funds.

Section 4004(e)(1) of the Supplemental Appropriations Act, 2008 (Public Law 110-252; 26 U.S.C. 3304 note) is amended by striking "Act;" and inserting "Act and sections 2, 3, and 4 of the Worker, Homeownership, and Business Assistance Act of 2009;".

Sec. 7. Expansion of Modernization Grants for Unemployment Resulting from Compelling Family Reason.

(a) In General.—

Clause (i) of section 903(f)(3)(B) of the Social Security Act (42 U.S.C. 1103(f)(3)(B)) is amended to read as follows:

``(i) One or both of the following offenses as selected by the State, but in making such selection, the resulting change in the State law shall not supercede any other provision of law relating to unemployment insurance to the extent that such other provision provides broader access to unemployment benefits for victims of such selected offense or offenses:

``(I) Domestic violence, verified by such reasonable and confidential documentation as the State law may require, which causes the individual reasonably to believe that such individual's continued employment would jeopardize the safety of the individual or of any member of the individual's immediate family (as defined by the Secretary of Labor); and

``(II) Sexual assault, verified by such reasonable and confidential documentation as the State law may require, which causes the individual reasonably to believe that such individual's continued employment would jeopardize the safety of the individual or of any member of the individual's immediate family (as defined by the Secretary of Labor).´´.

(b) Effective Date.—

The amendment made by this section shall apply with respect to State applications submitted on and after January 1, 2010.

Sec. 8. Treatment of Additional Regular Compensation.

The monthly equivalent of any additional compensation paid by reason of section 2002 of the Assistance for Unemployed Workers and Struggling Families Act, as contained in Public Law 111-5 (26 U.S.C. 3304 note; 123 Stat. 438) shall be disregarded after the date of the enactment of this Act in considering the amount of income and assets of an individual for purposes of determining such individual's eligibility for, or amount of, benefits under the Supplemental Nutrition Assistance Program (SNAP).

Sec. 9. Additional Extended Unemployment Benefits Under the Railroad Unemployment Insurance Act.

(a) Benefits.—

Section 2(c)(2)(D) of the Railroad Unemployment Insurance Act, as added by section 2006 of the American Recovery and Reinvestment Act of 2009 (Public Law 111-5), is amended—

(1) in clause (iii)—

(A) by striking "June 30, 2009" and inserting "June 30, 2010"; and

(B) by striking "December 31, 2009" and inserting "December 31, 2010"; and

(2) by adding at the end of clause (iv) the following: "In addition to the amount appropriated by the preceding sentence, out of any funds in the Treasury not otherwise appropriated, there are appropriated $175,000,000 to cover the cost of additional extended unemployment benefits provided under this subparagraph, to remain available until expended.".

(b) Administrative Expenses.—

Section 2006 of division B of the American Recovery and Reinvestment Act of 2009 (Public Law 111-5; 123 Stat. 445) is amended by adding at the end of subsection (b) the following: "In addition to funds appropriated by the preceding sentence, out of any funds in the Treasury not otherwise appropriated, there are appropriated to the Railroad Retirement Board $807,000 to cover the administrative expenses associated with the payment of additional extended unemployment benefits under section 2(c)(2)(D) of the Railroad Unemployment Insurance Act, to remain available until expended.".

Sec. 10. 0.2 Percent FUTA Surtax.

(a) In General.—

Section 3301 of the Internal Revenue Code of 1986 (relating to rate of tax) is amended—

(1) by striking "through 2009" in paragraph (1) and inserting "through 2010 and the first 6 months of calendar year 2011",

(2) by striking "calendar year 2010" in paragraph (2) and inserting "the remainder of calendar year 2011", and

(3) by inserting "(or portion of the calendar year)" after "during the calendar year".

(b) Effective Date.—

The amendments made by this section shall apply to wages paid after December 31, 2009.

Sec. 11. Extension and Modification of First-Time Homebuyer Tax Credit.

(a) Extension of Application Period.—

(1) IN GENERAL.—

Subsection (h) of section 36 of the Internal Revenue Code of 1986 is amended—

(A) by striking "December 1, 2009" and inserting "May 1, 2010",

(B) by striking "Section.—This section" and inserting "Section.—

``(1) IN GENERAL.—This section", and

(C) by adding at the end the following new paragraph:

``(2) EXCEPTION IN CASE OF BINDING CONTRACT.—In the case of any taxpayer who enters into a written binding contract before May 1, 2010, to close on the purchase of a principal residence before July 1, 2010, paragraph (1) shall be applied by substituting 'July 1, 2010' for 'May 1, 2010'.''.

(2) WAIVER OF RECAPTURE.—

(A) IN GENERAL.—

Subparagraph (D) of section 36(f)(4) of such Code is amended by striking ", and before December 1, 2009".

(B) CONFORMING AMENDMENT.—

The heading of such subparagraph (D) is amended by inserting "and 2010" after "2009".

(3) ELECTION TO TREAT PURCHASE IN PRIOR YEAR.—

Subsection (g) of section 36 of such Code is amended to read as follows:

``(g) Election to Treat Purchase in Prior Year.—In the case of a purchase of a principal residence after December 31, 2008, a taxpayer may elect to treat such purchase as made on December 31 of the calendar year preceding such purchase for purposes of this section (other than subsections (c), (f)(4)(D), and (h)).''.

(b) Special Rule for Long-time Residents of Same Principal Residence.—

Subsection (c) of section 36 of the Internal Revenue Code of 1986 is amended by adding at the end the following new paragraph:

``(6) EXCEPTION FOR LONG-TIME RESIDENTS OF SAME PRINCIPAL RESIDENCE.— In the case of an individual (and, if married, such individual's spouse) who has owned and used the same residence as such individual's principal residence for any 5-consecutive-year period during the 8-year period ending on the date of the purchase of a subsequent principal residence, such individual shall be treated as a first-time homebuyer for purposes of this section with respect to the purchase of such subsequent residence.''.

(c) Modification of Dollar and Income Limitations.—

(1) DOLLAR LIMITATION.—

Subsection (b)(1) of section 36 of the Internal Revenue Code of 1986 is amended by adding at the end the following new subparagraph:

``(D) SPECIAL RULE FOR LONG-TIME RESIDENTS OF SAME PRIN-CIPAL RESIDENCE.—In the case of a taxpayer to whom a credit under subsection (a) is allowed by reason of subsection (c)(6), subparagraphs (A), (B), and (C) shall be applied by substituting '$6,500' for '$8,000' and '$3,250' for '$4,000'.''.

(2) INCOME LIMITATION.—

Subsection (b)(2)(A)(i)(II) of section 36 of such Code is amended by striking "$75,000 ($150,000" and inserting "$125,000 ($225,000".

(d) Limitation on Purchase Price of Residence.—

Subsection (b) of section 36 of the Internal Revenue Code of 1986 is amended by adding at the end the following new paragraph:

``(3) LIMITATION BASED ON PURCHASE PRICE.—No credit shall be allowed under subsection (a) for the purchase of any residence if the purchase price of such residence exceeds $800,000.''.

(e) Waiver of Recapture of First-time Homebuyer Credit for Individuals on Qualified Official Extended Duty.—

Paragraph (4) of section 36(f) of the Internal Revenue Code of 1986 is amended by adding at the end the following new subparagraph:

``(E) SPECIAL RULE FOR MEMBERS OF THE ARMED FORCES, ETC.—

``(i) IN GENERAL.—In the case of the disposition of a principal residence by an individual (or a cessation referred to in paragraph (2)) after December 31, 2008, in connection with Government orders received by such individual, or such individual's spouse, for qualified official extended duty service—

``(I) paragraph (2) and subsection (d)(2) shall not apply to such disposition (or cessation), and

``(II) if such residence was acquired before January 1, 2009, paragraph (1) shall not apply to the taxable year in which such disposition (or cessation) occurs or any subsequent taxable year.

``(ii) QUALIFIED OFFICIAL EXTENDED DUTY SERVICE.—For purposes of this section, the term 'qualified official extended duty service' means service on qualified official extended duty as—

``(I) a member of the uniformed services,

``(II) a member of the Foreign Service of the United States, or

``(III) an employee of the intelligence community.

"(iii) DEFINITIONS.—Any term used in this subparagraph which is also used in paragraph (9) of section 121(d) shall have the same meaning as when used in such paragraph.".

(f) Extension of First-time Homebuyer Credit for Individuals on Qualified Official Extended Duty Outside the United States.—

(1) IN GENERAL.—

Subsection (h) of section 36 of the Internal Revenue Code of 1986, as amended by subsection (a), is amended by adding at the end the following:

"(3) SPECIAL RULE FOR INDIVIDUALS ON QUALIFIED OFFICIAL EXTENDED DUTY OUTSIDE THE UNITED STATES.—In the case of any individual who serves on qualified official extended duty service (as defined in section 121(d)(9)(C)(i)) outside the United States for at least 90 days during the period beginning after December 31, 2008, and ending before May 1, 2010, and, if married, such individual's spouse—

"(A) paragraphs (1) and (2) shall each be applied by substituting 'May 1, 2011' for 'May 1, 2010', and

"(B) paragraph (2) shall be applied by substituting 'July 1, 2011' for 'July 1, 2010'.".

(g) Dependents Ineligible for Credit.—

Subsection (d) of section 36 of the Internal Revenue Code of 1986 is amended by striking "or" at the end of paragraph (1), by striking the period at the end of paragraph (2) and inserting ", or", and by adding at the end the following new paragraph:

"(3) a deduction under section 151 with respect to such taxpayer is allowable to another taxpayer for such taxable year.".

(h) IRS Mathematical Error Authority.—

Paragraph (2) of section 6213(g) of the Internal Revenue Code of 1986 is amended—

(1) by striking "and" at the end of subparagraph (M),

(2) by striking the period at the end of subparagraph (N) and inserting ", and", and

(3) by inserting after subparagraph (N) the following new subparagraph:

"(O) an omission of any increase required under section 36(f) with respect to the recapture of a credit allowed under section 36.".

(i) Coordination with First-Time Homebuyer Credit for District of Columbia.—

Paragraph (4) of section 1400C(e) of the Internal Revenue Code of 1986 is amended by striking "and before December 1, 2009,".

(j) Effective Dates.—

> (1) IN GENERAL.—
>
>> The amendments made by subsections (b), (c), (d), and (g) shall apply to residences purchased after the date of the enactment of this Act.
>
> (2) EXTENSIONS.—
>
>> The amendments made by subsections (a), (f), and (i) shall apply to residences purchased after November 30, 2009.
>
> (3) WAIVER OF RECAPTURE.—
>
>> The amendment made by subsection (e) shall apply to dispositions and cessations after December 31, 2008.
>
> (4) MATHEMATICAL ERROR AUTHORITY.—
>
>> The amendments made by subsection (h) shall apply to returns for taxable years ending on or after April 9, 2008.

Sec. 12. Provisions to Enhance the Administration of the First-Time Homebuyer Tax Credit.

(a) Age Limitation.—

> (1) IN GENERAL.—
>
>> Subsection (b) of section 36 of the Internal Revenue Code of 1986, as amended by this Act, is amended by adding at the end the following new paragraph:
>
>> ``(4) AGE LIMITATION.—No credit shall be allowed under subsection (a) with respect to the purchase of any residence unless the taxpayer has attained age 18 as of the date of such purchase. In the case of any taxpayer who is married (within the meaning of section 7703), the taxpayer shall be treated as meeting the age requirement of the preceding sentence if the taxpayer or the taxpayer's spouse meets such age requirement.''.
>
> (2) CONFORMING AMENDMENT.—
>
>> Subsection (g) of section 36 of such Code, as amended by this Act, is amended by inserting "(b)(4)," before "(c)".

(b) Documentation Requirement.—

> Subsection (d) of section 36 of the Internal Revenue Code of 1986, as amended by this Act, is amended by striking "or" at the end of paragraph (2), by striking the period at the end of paragraph (3) and inserting ", or", and by adding at the end the following new paragraph:
>
>> ``(4) the taxpayer fails to attach to the return of tax for such taxable year a properly executed copy of the settlement statement used to complete such purchase.''.

(c) Restriction on Married Individual Acquiring Residence from Family of Spouse.—

Clause (i) of section 36(c)(3)(A) of the Internal Revenue Code of 1986 is amended by inserting "(or, if married, such individual's spouse)" after "person acquiring such property".

(d) Certain Errors with Respect to the First-time Homebuyer Tax Credit Treated as Mathematical or Clerical Errors.—

Paragraph (2) of section 6213(g) the Internal Revenue Code of 1986, as amended by this Act, is amended by striking "and" at the end of subparagraph (N), by striking the period at the end of subparagraph (O) and inserting ", and", and by inserting after subparagraph (O) the following new subparagraph:

``(P) an entry on a return claiming the credit under section 36 if—

``(i) the Secretary obtains information from the person issuing the TIN of the taxpayer that indicates that the taxpayer does not meet the age requirement of section 36(b)(4),

``(ii) information provided to the Secretary by the taxpayer on an income tax return for at least one of the 2 preceding taxable years is inconsistent with eligibility for such credit, or

``(iii) the taxpayer fails to attach to the return the form described in section 36(d)(4).``.

(e) Effective Date.—

(1) IN GENERAL.—

Except as otherwise provided in this subsection, the amendments made by this section shall apply to purchases after the date of the enactment of this Act.

(2) DOCUMENTATION REQUIREMENT.—

The amendments made by subsection (b) shall apply to returns for taxable years ending after the date of the enactment of this Act.

(3) TREATMENT AS MATHEMATICAL AND CLERICAL ERRORS.—

The amendments made by subsection (d) shall apply to returns for taxable years ending on or after April 9, 2008.

Sec. 13. 5-Year Carryback of Operating Losses.

(a) In General.—

Subparagraph (H) of section 172(b)(1) of the Internal Revenue Code of 1986 is amended to read as follows:

``(H) CARRYBACK FOR 2008 OR 2009 NET OPERATING LOSSES.—

``(i) IN GENERAL.—In the case of an applicable net operating loss with respect to which the taxpayer has elected the application of this subparagraph—

    ``(I) subparagraph (A)(i) shall be applied by substituting any whole number elected by the taxpayer which is more than 2 and less than 6 for '2',

    ``(II) subparagraph (E)(ii) shall be applied by substituting the whole number which is one less than the whole number substituted under subclause (I) for '2', and

    ``(III) subparagraph (F) shall not apply.

``(ii) APPLICABLE NET OPERATING LOSS.—For purposes of this subparagraph, the term 'applicable net operating loss' means the taxpayer's net operating loss for a taxable year ending after December 31, 2007, and beginning before January 1, 2010.

``(iii) ELECTION.—

    ``(I) IN GENERAL.—Any election under this subparagraph may be made only with respect to 1 taxable year.

    ``(II) PROCEDURE.—Any election under this subparagraph shall be made in such manner as may be prescribed by the Secretary, and shall be made by the due date (including extension of time) for filing the return for the taxpayer's last taxable year beginning in 2009. Any such election, once made, shall be irrevocable.

``(iv) LIMITATION ON AMOUNT OF LOSS CARRYBACK TO 5TH PRECEDING TAXABLE YEAR.—

    ``(I) IN GENERAL.—The amount of any net operating loss which may be carried back to the 5th taxable year preceding the taxable year of such loss under clause (i) shall not exceed 50 percent of the taxpayer's taxable income (computed without regard to the net operating loss for the loss year or any taxable year thereafter) for such preceding taxable year.

    ``(II) CARRYBACKS AND CARRYOVERS TO OTHER TAXABLE YEARS.—Appropriate adjustments in the application of the second sentence of paragraph (2) shall be made to take into account the limitation of subclause (I).

    ``(III) EXCEPTION FOR 2008 ELECTIONS BY SMALL BUSINESSES.—Subclause (I) shall not apply to any loss of an eligible small business with respect to any election made under this subparagraph as in effect on the day before the date of the enactment of the Worker, Homeownership, and Business Assistance Act of 2009.

``(v) SPECIAL RULES FOR SMALL BUSINESS.—

    ``(I) IN GENERAL.—In the case of an eligible small business which made or makes an election under this subparagraph as in effect on the day before the date of the enactment of the Worker, Homeownership, and Business Assistance Act of 2009, clause (iii)(I) shall be applied by substituting '2 taxable years' for '1 taxable year'.

``(II) ELIGIBLE SMALL BUSINESS.—For purposes of this subparagraph, the term 'eligible small business' has the meaning given such term by subparagraph (F)(iii), except that in applying such subparagraph, section 448(c) shall be applied by substituting '$15,000,000' for '$5,000,000' each place it appears.''.

(b) Alternative Tax Net Operating Loss Deduction.—

Subclause (I) of section 56(d)(1)(A)(ii) of the Internal Revenue Code of 1986 is amended to read as follows:

``(I) the amount of such deduction attributable to an applicable net operating loss with respect to which an election is made under section 172(b)(1)(H), or''.

(c) Loss from Operations of Life Insurance Companies.—

Subsection (b) of section 810 of the Internal Revenue Code of 1986 is amended by adding at the end the following new paragraph:

``(4) CARRYBACK FOR 2008 OR 2009 LOSSES.—

``(A) IN GENERAL.—In the case of an applicable loss from operations with respect to which the taxpayer has elected the application of this paragraph, paragraph (1)(A) shall be applied by substituting any whole number elected by the taxpayer which is more than 3 and less than 6 for '3'.

``(B) APPLICABLE LOSS FROM OPERATIONS.—For purposes of this paragraph, the term 'applicable loss from operations' means the taxpayer's loss from operations for a taxable year ending after December 31, 2007, and beginning before January 1, 2010.

``(C) ELECTION.—

``(i) IN GENERAL.—Any election under this paragraph may be made only with respect to 1 taxable year.

``(ii) PROCEDURE.—Any election under this paragraph shall be made in such manner as may be prescribed by the Secretary, and shall be made by the due date (including extension of time) for filing the return for the taxpayer's last taxable year beginning in 2009. Any such election, once made, shall be irrevocable.

``(D) LIMITATION ON AMOUNT OF LOSS CARRYBACK TO 5TH PRECEDING TAXABLE YEAR.—

``(i) IN GENERAL.—The amount of any loss from operations which may be carried back to the 5th taxable year preceding the taxable year of such loss under subparagraph (A) shall not exceed 50 percent of the taxpayer's taxable income (computed without regard to the loss from operations for the loss year or any taxable year thereafter) for such preceding taxable year.

``(ii) CARRYBACKS AND CARRYOVERS TO OTHER TAX-ABLE YEARS.—Appropriate adjustments in the application of the second sentence of paragraph (2) shall be made to take into account the limitation of clause (i).''.

(d) Anti-Abuse Rules.—

The Secretary of Treasury or the Secretary's designee shall prescribe such rules as are necessary to prevent the abuse of the purposes of the amendments made by this section, including anti-stuffing rules, anti-churning rules (including rules relating to sale-leasebacks), and rules similar to the rules under section 1091 of the Internal Revenue Code of 1986 relating to losses from wash sales.

(e) Effective Dates.—

(1) IN GENERAL.—

Except as otherwise provided in this subsection, the amendments made by this section shall apply to net operating losses arising in taxable years ending after December 31, 2007.

(2) ALTERNATIVE TAX NET OPERATING LOSS DEDUCTION.—

The amendment made by subsection (b) shall apply to taxable years ending after December 31, 2002.

(3) LOSS FROM OPERATIONS OF LIFE INSURANCE COMPANIES.—

The amendment made by subsection (d) shall apply to losses from operations arising in taxable years ending after December 31, 2007.

(4) TRANSITIONAL RULE.—

In the case of any net operating loss (or, in the case of a life insurance company, any loss from operations) for a taxable year ending before the date of the enactment of this Act—

(A) any election made under section 172(b)(3) or 810(b)(3) of the Internal Revenue Code of 1986 with respect to such loss may (notwithstanding such section) be revoked before the due date (including extension of time) for filing the return for the taxpayer's last taxable year beginning in 2009, and

(B) any application under section 6411(a) of such Code with respect to such loss shall be treated as timely filed if filed before such due date.

(f) Exception for TARP Recipients.—

The amendments made by this section shall not apply to—

(1) any taxpayer if—

(A) the Federal Government acquired before the date of the enactment of this Act an equity interest in the taxpayer pursuant to the Emergency Economic Stabilization Act of 2008,

(B) the Federal Government acquired before such date of enactment any warrant (or other right) to acquire any equity interest with respect to the taxpayer pursuant to the Emergency Economic Stabilization Act of 2008, or

(C) such taxpayer receives after such date of enactment funds from the Federal Government in exchange for an interest described in subparagraph (A) or (B) pursuant to a program established under title I of division A of the Emergency Economic Stabilization Act of 2008 (unless such taxpayer is a financial institution (as defined in section 3 of such Act) and the funds are received pursuant to a program established by the Secretary of the Treasury for the stated purpose of increasing the availability of credit to small businesses using funding made available under such Act), or

(2) the Federal National Mortgage Association and the Federal Home Loan Mortgage Corporation, and

(3) any taxpayer which at any time in 2008 or 2009 was or is a member of the same affiliated group (as defined in section 1504 of the Internal Revenue Code of 1986, determined without regard to subsection (b) thereof) as a taxpayer described in paragraph (1) or (2).

Sec. 14. Exclusion from Gross Income of Qualified Military Base Realignment and Closure Fringe.

(a) In General.—

Subsection (n) of section 132 of the Internal Revenue Code of 1986 is amended—

(1) in subparagraph (1) by striking "this subsection) to offset the adverse effects on housing values as a result of a military base realignment or closure" and inserting "the American Recovery and Reinvestment Tax Act of 2009)", and

(2) in subparagraph (2) by striking "clause (1) of".

(b) Effective Date.—

The amendments made by this act shall apply to payments made after February 17, 2009.

Sec. 15. Delay in Application of Worldwide Allocation of Interest.

(a) In General.—

Paragraphs (5)(D) and (6) of section 864(f) of the Internal Revenue Code of 1986 are each amended by striking "December 31, 2010" and inserting "December 31, 2017".

(b) Conforming Amendment.—

Section 864(f) of the Internal Revenue Code of 1986 is amended by striking paragraph (7).

(c) Effective Dates.—

The amendments made by this section shall apply to taxable years beginning after December 31, 2010.

Sec. 16. Increase in Penalty for Failure to File a Partnership or S Corporation Return.

(a) In General.—

Sections 6698(b)(1) and 6699(b)(1) of the Internal Revenue Code of 1986 are each amended by striking "$89" and inserting "$195".

(b) Effective Date.—

The amendments made by this section shall apply to returns for taxable years beginning after December 31, 2009.

Sec. 17. Certain Tax Return Preparers Required to File Returns Electronically.

(a) In General.—

Subsection (e) of section 6011 of the Internal Revenue Code of 1986 is amended by adding at the end the following new paragraph:

``(3) SPECIAL RULE FOR TAX RETURN PREPARERS.—

``(A) IN GENERAL.—The Secretary shall require than any individual income tax return prepared by a tax return preparer be filed on magnetic media if—

``(i) such return is filed by such tax return preparer, and

``(ii) such tax return preparer is a specified tax return preparer for the calendar year during which such return is filed.

``(B) SPECIFIED TAX RETURN PREPARER.—For purposes of this paragraph, the term 'specified tax return preparer' means, with respect to any calendar year, any tax return preparer unless such preparer reasonably expects to file 10 or fewer individual income tax returns during such calendar year.

``(C) INDIVIDUAL INCOME TAX RETURN.—For purposes of this paragraph, the term 'individual income tax return' means any return of the tax imposed by subtitle A on individuals, estates, or trusts.``.

(b) Conforming Amendment.—

Paragraph (1) of section 6011(e) of the Internal Revenue Code of 1986 is amended by striking "The Secretary may not" and inserting "Except as provided in paragraph (3), the Secretary may not".

(c) Effective Date.—

The amendments made by this section shall apply to returns filed after December 31, 2010.

Sec. 18. Time for Payment of Corporate Estimated Taxes.

The percentage under paragraph (1) of section 202(b) of the Corporate Estimated Tax Shift Act of 2009 in effect on the date of the enactment of this Act is increased by 33.0 percentage points.

Approved November 6, 2009.

4.16.1   Legislative History

- H.R. 3548, (H.R. 3404, S. 1647)

    - CONGRESSIONAL RECORD, Vol. 155 (2009):
        - Sept. 22, considered and passed House.
        - Nov. 4, considered and passed Senate, amended.
        - Nov. 5, House concurred in Senate amendement.

Chapter 5

Text and image sources, contributors, and licenses

5.1 Text

- **Barack Obama's First State of the Union Address** *Source:* https://en.wikisource.org/wiki/Barack_Obama'{}s_First_State_of_the_Union_Address?oldid=3606287 *Contributors:* Markles, Lombroso, Billinghurst, Jatkins, Tonyfuchs1019, SDrewthbot, Toliar, Jan1nad, CandalBot and Anonymous: 3

- **Barack Obama speech to joint session of Congress, September 2009** *Source:* https://en.wikisource.org/wiki/Barack_Obama_speech_to_joint_session_of_Congress%2C_September_2009?oldid=4273433 *Contributors:* John Vandenberg, King of Hearts, Cirt, Billinghurst, KeithTyler, Tonyfuchs1019 and George Orwell III

- **Barack Obama's Second State of the Union Address** *Source:* https://en.wikisource.org/wiki/Barack_Obama'{}s_Second_State_of_the_Union_Address?oldid=3602998 *Contributors:* Neo-Jay, Lombroso, Billinghurst, Jatkins, Tonyfuchs1019, SDrewthbot, Stevenliuyi and Anonymous: 2

- **Barack Obama's Third State of the Union Address** *Source:* https://en.wikisource.org/wiki/Barack_Obama'{}s_Third_State_of_the_Union_Address?oldid=3602999 *Contributors:* Pmsyyz, Lombroso, Tonyfuchs1019, SDrewthbot, Sotuu and Anonymous: 1

- **Barack Obama's Fourth State of the Union Address** *Source:* https://en.wikisource.org/wiki/Barack_Obama'{}s_Fourth_State_of_the_Union_Address?oldid=4233441 *Contributors:* Jerome Charles Potts, Tonyfuchs1019, CandalBot and Anonymous: 1

- **Barack Obama's Fifth State of the Union Address** *Source:* https://en.wikisource.org/wiki/Barack_Obama'{}s_Fifth_State_of_the_Union_Address?oldid=5767685 *Contributors:* Cirt, Tonyfuchs1019, Odder, P3Y229, Spydyspydy, Stewi101015 and Anonymous: 1

- **Barack Obama's Sixth State of the Union Address** *Source:* https://en.wikisource.org/wiki/Barack_Obama'{}s_Sixth_State_of_the_Union_Address?oldid=5209292 *Contributors:* Ezhiki, Illegitimate Barrister and Anonymous: 2

- **Barack Obama's Seventh State of the Union Address** *Source:* https://en.wikisource.org/wiki/Barack_Obama'{}s_Seventh_State_of_the_Union_Address?oldid=5565583 *Contributors:* Neo-Jay, Prosfilaes, Tonyfuchs1019, Tktru, George Orwell III, Illegitimate Barrister and Anonymous: 2

- **Barack Obama's First Inaugural Address** *Source:* https://en.wikisource.org/wiki/Barack_Obama'{}s_First_Inaugural_Address?oldid=5220722 *Contributors:* Yann, Zntrip, Sherurcij, Shii, John Vandenberg, King of Hearts, Sanbeg, Psychless, AdamBMorgan, Bibliomaniac15, Prosfilaes, Cirt, Iago4096, Billinghurst, Jatkins, 神樂坂秀吉, Jimmy Xu, Game-M, Goodtimber, הולב, Dromioofephesus, Tonyfuchs1019, Caytruc, Alexius08, SDrewthbot, Mickster810, Tjmj, Petersam, RG72, Beeswaxcandle, TVT-bot, Atkinson 291, Frglz, CandalBot, Gregory Heffley and Anonymous: 18

- **Barack Obama's Second Inaugural Address** *Source:* https://en.wikisource.org/wiki/Barack_Obama'{}s_Second_Inaugural_Address?oldid=4271900 *Contributors:* Lombroso, Billinghurst, Odder, Beeswaxcandle, Tranminh360 and Anonymous: 4

- **Statement by the President on the Passing of Leonard Nimoy** *Source:* https://en.wikisource.org/wiki/Statement_by_the_President_on_the_Passing_of_Leonard_Nimoy?oldid=5273941 *Contributors:* Cirt

- **Statement by the President on the Murder of Boris Nemtsov** *Source:* https://en.wikisource.org/wiki/Statement_by_the_President_on_the_Murder_of_Boris_Nemtsov?oldid=5266586 *Contributors:* Tar-ba-gan and Library Guy

- **President Obama Delivers Remarks on the 50th Anniversary of the Selma Marches** *Source:* https://en.wikisource.org/wiki/President_Obama_Delivers_Remarks_on_the_50th_Anniversary_of_the_Selma_Marches?oldid=5632551 *Contributors:* Green Giant, Cirt, Fæ, Nonexyst and Library Guy

- **Remarks by the President at the 2015 Gridiron Dinner** *Source:* https://en.wikisource.org/wiki/Remarks_by_the_President_at_the_2015_Gridiron_Dinner?oldid=5293471 *Contributors:* Cirt

- **President Obama Delivers Eulogy for the Honorable Reverend Clementa Pinckney** *Source:* https://en.wikisource.org/wiki/President_ Obama_Delivers_Eulogy_for_the_Honorable_Reverend_Clementa_Pinckney?oldid=5779021 *Contributors:* Rock drum

- **Cool clock, Ahmed. Want to bring it to the White House?** *Source:* https://en.wikisource.org/wiki/Cool_clock%2C_Ahmed._Want_to_ bring_it_to_the_White_House%3F?oldid=5752695 *Contributors:* Cirt

- **Statement by the President on the Shootings at Umpqua Community College, Roseburg, Oregon** *Source:* https://en.wikisource.org/wiki/ Statement_by_the_President_on_the_Shootings_at_Umpqua_Community_College%2C_Roseburg%2C_Oregon?oldid=5736659 *Contributors:* Cirt

- **Remarks by the President at the 2015 White House Astronomy Night** *Source:* https://en.wikisource.org/wiki/Remarks_by_the_President_ at_the_2015_White_House_Astronomy_Night?oldid=5775579 *Contributors:* Cirt and Library Guy

- **Remarks by Barack Obama in Address to the People of India** *Source:* https://en.wikisource.org/wiki/Remarks_by_Barack_Obama_in_ Address_to_the_People_of_India?oldid=5649449 *Contributors:* Green Giant and Illegitimate Barrister

- **President Obama's Statement on Keeping the Internet Open and Free** *Source:* https://en.wikisource.org/wiki/President_Obama'{}s_ Statement_on_Keeping_the_Internet_Open_and_Free?oldid=5117977 *Contributors:* Cirt

- **Lilly Ledbetter Fair Pay Act of 2009** *Source:* https://en.wikisource.org/wiki/Lilly_Ledbetter_Fair_Pay_Act_of_2009?oldid=2049181 *Contributors:* Markles, Maximillion Pegasus, Tonyfuchs1019, George Orwell III and Anonymous: 3

- **Children's Health Insurance Program Reauthorization Act of 2009** *Source:* https://en.wikisource.org/wiki/Children'{}s_Health_Insurance_ Program_Reauthorization_Act_of_2009?oldid=1191939 *Contributors:* Markles, Tarmstro99, Tonyfuchs1019, George Orwell III and Anonymous: 3

- **DTV Delay Act** *Source:* https://en.wikisource.org/wiki/DTV_Delay_Act?oldid=4340612 *Contributors:* Markles, Rrius, Tonyfuchs1019, George Orwell III, Robbie the Robot and Anonymous: 2

- **American Recovery and Reinvestment Act of 2009** *Source:* https://en.wikisource.org/wiki/American_Recovery_and_Reinvestment_Act_ of_2009?oldid=4427265 *Contributors:* Markles, Maximillion Pegasus, Tonyfuchs1019, SDrewthbot, George Orwell III, Robbie the Robot and Anonymous: 3

- **Omnibus Public Land Management Act of 2009** *Source:* https://en.wikisource.org/wiki/Omnibus_Public_Land_Management_Act_of_ 2009?oldid=1192294 *Contributors:* Markles, George Orwell III and Anonymous: 1

- **Edward M. Kennedy Serve America Act** *Source:* https://en.wikisource.org/wiki/Edward_M._Kennedy_Serve_America_Act?oldid=1189150 *Contributors:* Zntrip, Markles, Billinghurst, George Orwell III and Anonymous: 1

- **Fraud Enforcement and Recovery Act of 2009** *Source:* https://en.wikisource.org/wiki/Fraud_Enforcement_and_Recovery_Act_of_2009? oldid=1459423 *Contributors:* Markles, George Orwell III and Anonymous: 1

- **Public Law 111-22/Division A** *Source:* https://en.wikisource.org/wiki/Public_Law_111-22/Division_A?oldid=1240099 *Contributors:* Markles, George Orwell III and Anonymous: 1

- **Weapon Systems Acquisition Reform Act of 2009** *Source:* https://en.wikisource.org/wiki/Weapon_Systems_Acquisition_Reform_Act_of_ 2009?oldid=1166431 *Contributors:* Markles, Bsimmons666 and George Orwell III

- **Credit Card Accountability Responsibility and Disclosure Act of 2009** *Source:* https://en.wikisource.org/wiki/Credit_Card_Accountability_ Responsibility_and_Disclosure_Act_of_2009?oldid=3641523 *Contributors:* Markles, George Orwell III and Anonymous: 2

- **Public Law 111-31/Division A** *Source:* https://en.wikisource.org/wiki/Public_Law_111-31/Division_A?oldid=4426864 *Contributors:* SDrewth bot and George Orwell III

- **Enhanced Partnership with Pakistan Act of 2009** *Source:* https://en.wikisource.org/wiki/Enhanced_Partnership_with_Pakistan_Act_of_ 2009?oldid=1395412 *Contributors:* George Orwell III

- **Department of Homeland Security Appropriations Act, 2010/Title V** *Source:* https://en.wikisource.org/wiki/Department_of_Homeland_ Security_Appropriations_Act%2C_2010/Title_V?oldid=2309473 *Contributors:* George Orwell III and Anonymous: 1

- **National Defense Authorization Act for Fiscal Year 2010/Division A/Title XVIII** *Source:* https://en.wikisource.org/wiki/National_Defense_ Authorization_Act_for_Fiscal_Year_2010/Division_A/Title_XVIII?oldid=1457619 *Contributors:* George Orwell III

- **National Defense Authorization Act for Fiscal Year 2010/Division E** *Source:* https://en.wikisource.org/wiki/National_Defense_Authorization_ Act_for_Fiscal_Year_2010/Division_E?oldid=4729431 *Contributors:* Eliyak, Beeswaxcandle, George Orwell III and Anonymous: 1

- **Worker, Homeownership, and Business Assistance Act of 2009** *Source:* https://en.wikisource.org/wiki/Worker%2C_Homeownership% 2C_and_Business_Assistance_Act_of_2009?oldid=1532493 *Contributors:* George Orwell III

5.2 Images

- **File:111014_NetNeutrality_Final.ogv** *Source:* https://upload.wikimedia.org/wikipedia/commons/b/b2/111014_NetNeutrality_Final.ogv *License:* Public domain *Contributors:* http://www.whitehouse.gov/net-neutrality#section-watch-the-video *Original artist:* Barack Obama

- **File:2015_President_Obama_Hosts_Astronomy_Night_at_the_White_House.ogv** *Source:* https://upload.wikimedia.org/wikipedia/commons/ c/c1/2015_President_Obama_Hosts_Astronomy_Night_at_the_White_House.ogv *License:* Public domain *Contributors:* The White House *Original artist:* The White House

- **File:44_CongInvitation.jpg** *Source:* https://upload.wikimedia.org/wikipedia/commons/b/b2/44_CongInvitation.jpg *License:* Public domain *Contributors:* United States Congress Joint Committee on Inaugural Ceremonies *Original artist:* Lwalt (file); United States Congress Joint Committee on Inaugural Ceremonies (original)

- **File:50th_Anniversary_of_the_Selma_Marches_-_Former_President_George_W_Bush_listens_as_President_Obama_delivers_remarks_ at_the_foot_of_the_Edmund_Pettus_Bridge.jpg** *Source:* https://upload.wikimedia.org/wikipedia/commons/6/6d/50th_Anniversary_of_ the_Selma_Marches_-_Former_President_George_W_Bush_listens_as_President_Obama_delivers_remarks_at_the_foot_of_the_Edmund_ Pettus_Bridge.jpg *License:* Public domain *Contributors:* http://www.whitehouse.gov/blog/2015/03/08/behind-lens-selma-50-years-later also archived by the Internet Archive at https://web.archive.org/web/20150310072208/http://www.whitehouse.gov/blog/2015/03/08/behind-lens-selma-50-years-later *Original artist:* Official White House Photo by Lawrence Jackson

- **File:Barack_Obama_delivers_the_eulogy_at_the_funeral_of_Reverend_Clementa_Pinckney_2015-06-26.jpg** *Source:* https://upload. wikimedia.org/wikipedia/commons/8/88/Barack_Obama_delivers_the_eulogy_at_the_funeral_of_Reverend_Clementa_Pinckney_2015-06-26. jpg *License:* Public domain *Contributors:* Official White House Photo by Lawrence Jackson (WhiteHouse.gov *Original artist:* Lawrence Jackson

- **File:Barack_Obama_inaugural_address.ogv** *Source:* https://upload.wikimedia.org/wikipedia/commons/8/8b/Barack_Obama_inaugural_ address.ogv *License:* Public domain *Contributors:* [1] *Original artist:* Speech by Barack Obama. Recorded by White House staff. Converted by King of Hearts using SUPER.

- **File:Incomplete-document.svg** *Source:* https://upload.wikimedia.org/wikipedia/commons/1/13/Incomplete-document.svg *License:* Public domain *Contributors:*

- Based on File:Text-x-generic.svg *Original artist:* Inductiveload

- **File:Joe_Wilson'{}s_You_Lie_interruption.theora.ogv** *Source:* https://upload.wikimedia.org/wikipedia/commons/2/2a/Joe_Wilson%27s_ You_Lie_interruption.theora.ogv *License:* Public domain *Contributors:* http://www.whitehouse.gov/video/President-Obama-Address-to-Congress-on-Health-Insura http://www.whitehouse.gov/videos/2009/September/090909_JointSession.mp4 *Original artist:* Barack Obama White House

- **File:Joint_blog_close_PS-0774.jpg** *Source:* https://upload.wikimedia.org/wikipedia/commons/c/cf/Joint_blog_close_PS-0774.jpg *License:* Public domain *Contributors:* The White House - Blog Post -The President's Remarks, and a Letter from Ted *Original artist:* White House (Pete Souza)

- **File:Official_portrait_of_Barack_Obama.jpg** *Source:* https://upload.wikimedia.org/wikipedia/commons/e/e9/Official_portrait_of_Barack_ Obama.jpg *License:* CC BY 3.0 *Contributors:* http://change.gov/newsroom/entry/new_official_portrait_released/ *Original artist:* Pete Souza, The Obama-Biden Transition Project

- **File:PD-icon.svg** *Source:* https://upload.wikimedia.org/wikipedia/commons/6/62/PD-icon.svg *License:* Public domain *Contributors:* Created by uploader. Based on similar symbols. *Original artist:* Various. See log. (Original SVG was based on File:PD-icon.png by Duesentrieb, which was based on Image:Red copyright.png by Rfl.)

- **File:President_Obama_Delivers_Remarks_on_the_50th_Anniversary_of_the_Selma_Marches.webm** *Source:* https://upload.wikimedia. org/wikipedia/commons/1/1a/President_Obama_Delivers_Remarks_on_the_50th_Anniversary_of_the_Selma_Marches.webm *License:* Public domain *Contributors:* WhiteHouse.gov *Original artist:* The White House

- **File:President_Obama_tweet_to_student_Ahmed_Mohamed.jpg** *Source:* https://upload.wikimedia.org/wikipedia/commons/3/3d/President_ Obama_tweet_to_student_Ahmed_Mohamed.jpg *License:* Public domain *Contributors:* Screenshot from link, see also detailed link, and archived link. Text of tweet may also be seen at WhiteHouse.gov, archived. *Original artist:* Barack Obama

- **File:Statement_by_the_President_on_the_Passing_of_Leonard_Nimoy.jpg** *Source:* https://upload.wikimedia.org/wikipedia/commons/ a/aa/Statement_by_the_President_on_the_Passing_of_Leonard_Nimoy.jpg *License:* Public domain *Contributors:* http://www.whitehouse.gov/ the-press-office/2015/02/27/statement-president-passing-leonard-nimoy *Original artist:* The White House

- **File:Statement_on_the_Death_of_Leonard_S_Nimoy.pdf** *Source:* https://upload.wikimedia.org/wikipedia/commons/8/8c/Statement_on_ the_Death_of_Leonard_S_Nimoy.pdf *License:* Public domain *Contributors:* http://www.gpo.gov/fdsys/pkg/DCPD-201500133/pdf/DCPD-201500133. pdf *Original artist:* United States President Barack Obama

- **File:The_President_Delivers_a_Statement_on_the_Shooting_in_Oregon.webm** *Source:* https://upload.wikimedia.org/wikipedia/commons/ b/b3/The_President_Delivers_a_Statement_on_the_Shooting_in_Oregon.webm *License:* Public domain *Contributors:* The White House *Original artist:* White House

- **File:US-GreatSeal-Obverse.svg** *Source:* https://upload.wikimedia.org/wikipedia/commons/5/5c/Great_Seal_of_the_United_States_%28obverse% 29.svg *License:* Public domain *Contributors:* Extracted from PDF version of *Our Flag*, available here (direct PDF URL here.) *Original artist:* U.S. Government

- **File:US_President_Barack_Obama_taking_his_Oath_of_Office_-_2009Jan20.jpg** *Source:* https://upload.wikimedia.org/wikipedia/commons/ d/d7/US_President_Barack_Obama_taking_his_Oath_of_Office_-_2009Jan20.jpg *License:* Public domain *Contributors:* http://www.defenseimagery. mil/imagery.html#guid=4de8e17b0fbfafb8edfb0fa6cec854eaecfc1d42 *Original artist:* Master Sgt. Cecilio Ricardo, U.S. Air Force

5.3 Content license